Paul G.H. Engel

The social organization of innovation

A focus on stakeholder interaction

Royal Tropical Institute
The Netherlands

To Gerda, Henk, María, Laura and Karen

Acknowledgements

A study based on participatory action-research and case studies makes it difficult to do justice to all those who have, wittingly or unwittingly, contributed to its development. Of course, where possible I have cited each contribution specifically in the text. However, some people have made such an impact that even numerous references are not sufficient recognition. Niels Röling, the great facilitator, makes it all happen without anyone even noticing. Without his support this book would probably not have materialized. Joe Ascroft taught me that in development it is not only science that matters but art and craft as well. Anne van den Ban showed me intervention could be studied scientifically; Norman Long had his doubts, yet encouraged me to go on. John Simons' strong logic and precision were extremely stimulating. Most of all, my Chilean friends and colleagues taught me the real meaning and the strength of a 'soft system'.

Of those involved in the design and development of RAAKS, I can name only a few here: Stephan Seegers, Ab de Groot, Johan den Bakker, Emilia Solis, Monique Salomon, Luc Adolfse, Willem van Weperen and Annemarie Groot formed part of our team in various stages, also during the difficult times. Peter van Beek (Queensland DPI), Augusto Moreno (CIRAD), Niels Röling, Louk Box, Maria Koelen, André Boon, Lenneke Vaandrager and Willie van Wijde (WAU), Janice Jiggins (Andelst), Maria Fernandez (ICRE/IAC), Bertus Haverkort (ETC/ILEIA) and Jules Pretty (IIED) all made significant contributions. David Kaimowitz (ISNAR/IICA), Albert Meijering and Eelke Wielinga (Ministry of Agriculture, Nature and Fisheries), Jord Neuteboom (NOVEM), Kees Pette, Leen de Nie, Bouwe Oosten (OBL), Dominique Hounkonnou (CTA), Francisco Gonzalez, Daniel Rey and Jorge Echenique (AGRARIA), Fred van Sluis, Antonio Silva and Porfirio Masaya (PRIAG), Sergio Gomez (FLACSO), Nour-Eddine Sellamna, Yanick Lasica (ICRA/CIRAD), Henk de Zeeuw, Henk Kieft and Ann Waters-Bayer (ETC/ILEIA), John Grondel and Michael Velders (Global Village) found ways to invest in the idea and to actively support RAAKS' development.

There is simply no space here to list all of the researchers and students who brought their energy and enthusiasm to the cause of further developing knowledge systems thinking and RAAKS. In addition to the references in the text to those I am aware of, the appendix lists contributions made by graduate and post graduate students. Lastly, none of this would have ever been possible without the strong support I have received from my family and close friends. María, Laura and Karen have demonstrated what care and mutual support can accomplish. Of course, despite the many valuable contributions, any misrepresentations or skewed interpretations remain my own responsibility entirely.

Paul G.H. Engel

Royal Tropical Institute
KIT Press
P.O. Box 95001
1090 HA Amsterdam
The Netherlands
Telephone: +31 (0)20-5688272
Telefax: +31 (0)20-5688286
e-mail: kitpress@kit.nl

ACP-EU Technical Centre for Agricultural and
Technical Cooperation (CTA)
Postbus 380
6700 AJ Wageningen
The Netherlands
Telephone: +31 (0)317-467100
Telefax: +31 (0)317-460067
e-mail: cta@cta.nl

Stoas
P.O. Box 78
6700 AB Wageningen
The Netherlands
Telephone: +31 (0)317-472711
Telefax: +31 (0)317-424770
e-mail: LaV@stoas.nl

Table of contents

Figures, tables and boxes

Introduction: problem, purpose and design

A global challenge: organizing innovation

One intriguing issue of rural and agricultural development is why certain technological
innovations spread like wildfire, while others do not spread at all, even when pushed very *emergence*
hard. In addition, certain situations or combinations of events seem to invite the stakeholders in rural development to actively search for change and to implement new ideas
very quickly; yet other situations appear to stimulate defensive attitudes and the creation
of barriers to the implementation of new ideas. What makes it so difficult to get organized
and effectively promote desired developments?

A new era has begun in which ecological sustainability, alongside productivity and
social justice, has been recognized as a requirement for agricultural development. The result
is a world-wide debate on the type of technology needed to face this new challenge. One
thing we know for sure: the technologies we have at our disposal right now are not enough
to sustain agricultural development into the next century. We will have to improve the
performance of agricultural research and development if we are to meet the challenges
ahead.

A central aspect in this debate is that of 'manageability': can we actually 'steer' technology development in a specific direction, even if we knew which direction this should
be? Over the past forty years, the industrialization of agricultural production has reached
unprecedented levels. Its impact is increasingly global, with respect to both positive and
negative consequences. The negative consequences, however, are the ones that oblige us
to think more thoroughly about the manageability of technology development and
innovation. The irreversible deterioration of ecosystems in many parts of the world, the
unsolved social disruptions associated with agricultural rationalization, and the resource
limitations of our planet earth all force us to reflect upon the adequacy of current technological developments for achieving long term political and social objectives.

This book contends that one of the main problems standing in the way of developing sustainable solutions is the one-sidedness of our social and institutional learning processes. In
spite of our attempts to understand innovation processes in agriculture, our theories and *The Problem*
practices promote linear and exclusive ways of thinking and unidimensional 'rationalization', rather than empowering us to apply multiple rationalities – looking at things from
the standpoint of a farmer, as well as a researcher or a policymaker, for example – so that *The Need*
we can learn to adapt ourselves effectively to rapidly changing circumstances. I will argue
that the need for such empowerment can be seen and dealt with as a 'management
problem'. Social and institutional learning processes can be understood and managed in a
way that enhances rather than frustrates innovative thinking and multi-facetted develop- *Assumption*
ment. To achieve this, we have to recognize knowledge as a vital resource and begin to
actively manage it.

The context: current institutional arrangements under siege

Over the last two centuries, the agricultural innovation process has been progressively
institutionalized. Government, semi-government and private institutions have been created:
agricultural ministries, universities, research stations, extension agencies, industrial

research and development (R&D) departments and the like. All in all, societies have invested considerably in the creation of complex institutional arrangements, all for the sake of advancing technological innovation in agriculture. Over the last twenty years, however, degradation of natural resources and adverse social, economic and environmental effects have become increasingly associated with 'modern' agricultural development. This has brought the very nature of the institutions into question: can we expect those same institutions that contributed to the current problems to continue to play a decisive role, when our emphasis has so fundamentally changed? Can we expect government institutions to effectively reach the poor, if they have not yet been able to do so?

To make an effective contribution, not only to maintaining food security but to a variety of other national and international interests as well, alternative strategies are called for. 'Sustainable' is often used to refer to forms of agriculture that strike a delicate balance between the optimum use of available resources, ecological, social and economic demands and contemporary political objectives. Jan Pronk, the Netherlands' Minister of Development Cooperation, has summed this up: 'Achieving and maintaining sustainable agriculture has become one of the focal points, not only within Dutch agricultural and environmental policies, but also within those of the international development community. Until now, agricultural policies – whether oriented toward export production or local food production – have focused too narrowly on maximizing short-term profits rather than on long-term sustainable management of local resources by farmers.' (Reijntjes et al., 1992: xiii)

As a result, new institutions, both private and non-governmental, and new institutional arrangements, such as farming systems research/extension teams and networks, have evolved, while traditional institutions have been required to adjust or risk sinking into oblivion. In most European countries, extension services have been privatized. In many developing countries, non-governmental and private organizations effectively provide alternative services. Privatization, cost effectiveness, internationalization, user and market orientation are just a few of the challenges agricultural institutions face today.

This trend has put the *social organization of innovation* in agriculture on the agenda of policymakers and politicians. New institutional designs, new ways of organizing and financing agencies, hands-off policies, contract management and market control are some of the 'buzz words'. Non-agricultural actors seek to participate in the debate as well: environmentalists, consumer groups, animal health activists and nature and wildlife lobbyists are interested – not only as taxpayers, but also because of the evident effects of agricultural development upon society as a whole. In such debates, different actors use different models to contemplate the creation and use of knowledge in society, and hence to create the institutions to support it. These models, as we will see, are of great consequence to the way innovation processes are organized and managed and, eventually, to the direction innovation takes.

Managing innovation for sustainability?

In many countries, the degradation of natural resources and the environmental problems associated with 'modern' agriculture have helped to put sustainability firmly on the political agenda. However, we cannot point to technology as the sole culprit in what is wrong with agriculture today. Sustainable technologies are a necessary but not sufficient condition for sustainable agricultural development. As is painfully evident from the various war-ridden territories in the world today, sustainable development can only be achieved where and when people have worked out a way to live with each other. Adequate social organization is a prerequisite for sustainable development.

Sustainability requires patterns of social relationships adequate to the needs of the individuals and communities concerned. In this respect, Jan Pronk warns that '...sustainable agriculture can be realized only through the individual and collective activities of farmers and communities pursuing their own strategies to secure their livelihoods' (Reijntjes et al., 1992: xiii). Such patterns of social relationships must include adequate institutional arrangements. We cannot look at farmers alone – or, for that matter, policy-makers or researchers or development workers or even moneylenders – to re-orient and reorganize innovation in agriculture. Sustainable solutions will have to involve all of them. To achieve sustainable agriculture, not only must the social organization of agricultural innovation be adequate; it must also be sustainable.

Still subject the external & internal power plays that frustrate the process

This brings us to the question of intervention. Can the 'social organization of agricultural innovation' be subjected to purposive intervention with any hope of achieving social and ecological sustainability? Or is what we perceive as innovation merely the accidental outcome of an uncontrolled and uncontrollable series of events? Clearly, in this book innovation is taken to refer to *'change-on-purpose'*, propelled by individual and collective intentions. However, no straightforward relationship between intentions and effects can be postulated. To assume a simple causal relationship between what actors *intend* and what they *do* is problematic, let alone between what they intend to do and what the eventual results might be. However, it may be possible to find patterns: once an act of organization for innovation – such as establishing a farmer study group, an experiment station or an extension service – has been successful, the probability of its repetition increases; if there is no success, repetition is less likely. Thus an inquiry into patterns of organization that have evolved over the years may teach us something about how useful interventions can be designed and implemented.

innovation' is catalytic (see Capt. 26)

As we will see, however, we should entertain no illusions whatsoever with respect to the possibilities for 'control'. The social organization of innovation for agricultural production is 'social' in the sense that it emerges from diffuse social interactions among many different actors. The results may largely be due to the unintended consequences of such interactions. Seeking to manage agricultural innovation processes, therefore, means not to control but to *facilitate*, mostly by creating favourable conditions for innovation to occur. In this sense, our study is very much in line with conclusions drawn for example by Moss Kanter (1983, 1989) with respect to the management of innovation processes in large industrial companies.

focus on an "enabling environment"

Research

Purpose and design

The first purpose of this study is to try to improve our understanding of the social organization of innovation. How do different actors, or parties involved, organize themselves to achieve agricultural innovation? What do they actually do? And to what extent can we attribute what actually happens to the way actors organized themselves and to their individual or collective actions? Which actions were the most relevant to achieving the observed changes? The quest for answers to these and similar questions will be labelled the *exploratory path*: its aim is to draw conclusions from more than 25 relevant case studies done on four continents.

Such an exploratory effort seems very necessary. Although the study of the social organization of innovation in agriculture is relatively new, important progress has been made since Lionberger and Chang postulated the 'science–practice continuum' in 1970. However, since that period very little has changed fundamentally. As Röling (1993) observes, most authors remain within the narrow limits of 'linear thinking' with regard to the role of science and technology in society. Meanwhile, the emphasis of the public and policy debate has shifted considerably: the role of science in development is increasingly questioned, technological solutions are no longer seen as the only possible cures, and social problem solving has become an important issue. From such a perspective, we must recognize that what applied science can offer with respect to understanding the social organization of innovation, and intervening in it, is rather limited.

Another reason exploration of case study material is useful has to do with my intention to provide conceptual tools and methods to practitioners. Just as Checkland and Scholes (1990) concluded for industrial organizations, the ill-defined problem situations we are dealing with in theatres of agricultural innovation do not seem to permit us to search for straightforward explanations. We are far from being able to concern ourselves with ontology, or the 'essence of things or being in the abstract' (Concise Oxford Dictionary; Fowler et al., 1964). And I am not sure it is a good idea even to try. What we, as practitioners of agricultural innovation, need is '... a coherent intellectual framework ..., as *an epistemology* which can be used to try to understand and intervene usefully in the rich and surprising flux of everyday situations' (Checkland and Scholes, 1990: 24). Following the exploratory path should help us to formulate such a coherent conceptual framework for the social organization of innovation.

The second purpose of the study is to contribute to solving social organizational problems with respect to innovation. Our explorations should make it possible to suggest criteria and to develop a practical approach towards enhancing the effectiveness of innovation processes in practical situations. This is our *design path*: action research used to design a methodology to support intervention. Toward this end, an intensive networking effort has been carried out, involving researchers in seven different countries. This has yielded a methodological design and 15 experimental applications, in the Netherlands and six countries of Central America. The beneficiaries of the design path should be those who are engaged in managing and facilitating agricultural development: theirs is one of the most fascinating tasks there is.

Research questions and expected results

It would be preposterous to state that a consistent set of research questions has guided this research over the years. Rather, many questions surged up during my quest for understanding. While most were abandoned further along the line, some survived. This book focuses on the latter (Box 1). The exploratory path concerns mostly questions Q1 and Q2; the design path is directed towards questions Q3 to Q5. The questions are formulated in an open-ended, comprehensive sense. As the inquiry was an exploratory one, I began with an open mind. The inquiry was progressively delimited, as the possible answers became clearer. The book reflects this: Chapter 1 provides a general perspective, while the case studies in Chapters 2 to 5 spread out in a number of directions. In Chapter 6, most of the strings are pulled together again conceptually, and I attempt to bring my exploratory path to a close by answering research questions Q1 and Q2. Then, in Chapters 7 and 9 the discussion of designing takes up from the point where Chapter 1 ended. To answer questions Q4 and Q5, I attempted to propose a methodology along the lines discussed, and see if it works. The answer to research question Q3 at the beginning of Chapter 7 can be seen as the linking pin between the exploratory and the design path: it specifies the criteria a methodology should meet, on the basis of the preceding empirical research.

Clearly, my intention is to study innovation as a *process*, emerging from and at the same time helping to shape social action and interaction. Thus I take innovation to be a historical phenomenon. Innovation in agriculture is socially constructed among a variety of actors who are, one way or the other, *stakeholders* in the process. Also, admittedly these five questions are too broad to handle exhaustively in one study. The search will not be for definite answers, but I will try to formulate specific, relevant and useful ones. The intended 'end products' are specified in Box 2.

Nevertheless I am fully aware that, given the complexities of agricultural innovation as a historical process, any such study will inevitably generate more questions than answers. Therefore, the theoretical framework and methodological approach will remain 'unfinished'. To me, this is a virtue. It corresponds to trying to come to grips with the complexities of daily practice, without pretending to ever fully achieve it. In this respect, the study is a typical example of action research or, if you prefer, 'R&D'.

Research approach and methodology

The intended result of this study is the design of a conceptual framework that enables us to perceive and contemplate events and ideas in a coherent manner; it is not to formulate an 'objective' account of the essence of innovation in agriculture. It aims at providing *perspectives* that will be useful in trying to understand complex theatres (Box 3) of agricultural innovation, and will help in the design of effective interventions or management practices. Since this means the methodology should allow for the highest possible integration of theory and practice, the research has been empirically anchored in two different ways.

Box 3
Theatres of innovation

If we recognize, as Winograd and Flores (1986: 73) put it, that we are situated in a world that is not of our own making, and yet we reject the rationalistic notion of the existence of 'things' that are bearers of properties independent of interpretation, we cannot define our 'object of study' in the traditional sense. The domain of our studies may only 'arise in our concernful activities.' In other words, we ourselves create our object of study by applying distinctions to the events and ideas we perceive. Yet even if there is no object in the traditional objective sense, we still focus our studies upon certain events and ideas, and not others. Our choices and distinctions are motivated by our notions of what is relevant and what is interesting about the situations we study. Therefore, I have chosen 'theatres' of innovation as a metaphor to refer to the object of my studies.

This metaphor accommodates concepts such as individual agency, growth and sense-making, as well as diversity, multiplicity and interdependency. Theatres are places where partly premeditated, partly improvised actions are performed. Directors, managers, designers, stage builders, actors and audience interact intensively to produce both structure and serendipity. This metaphor also emphasizes the socially constructed context of human behaviour. Actions are not only discursive, yet discourse plays a very important role. Many actions are 'dramatized' to increase impact. Such dramatization by the actors of course requires considerable skill. Therefore, theatres are places where people face personal and collective challenges; they try to cope with these, initially without knowing whether or not their efforts may eventually be 'successful' in the eyes of their audiences and critics.

Theatres are also learning environments, which through acting, looking, listening, feeling and reflection on what has happened may stimulate personal growth for both actors and audience. Moreover, introducing the concept of a theatre instead of arena or system attempts to avoid – at least initially – an explicit *a priori* reference to either struggle or harmony. A theatre student may take up a position in the back row, quietly observing what is going on or may fully engage in the play, either as an active member of the public or even as an actor on stage.

First, it is grounded in my own practical experience as a professional. At every step of the way, I couldn't help asking myself what I would have done differently, had I known then what I think I know now. This aspect is less specifically addressed in the book; not only would such an account be rather boring to read, but also I am sure most readers will continually ask themselves the same question – and your answer, I believe, is what counts in practice. Second, the research has benefitted from the applied scientific inquiries which have increasingly become part of my professional career. Particularly after having joined the Communication and Innovation Studies Department of Wageningen University, I have been able to take an active part in a number of research projects which have provided me with opportunities to develop my ideas more systematically and to put them into practice, both as a researcher and as a consultant. The empirical materials for this book originate from these inquiries; the publication represents an effort to document and integrate these diverse experiences.

To enable the reader to assess the methods I have used to generate, organize and interpret the information presented, and hence to judge the trustworthiness of my arguments, the main methodological issues involved in both the exploratory and the design path will be addressed below.

The exploratory path

In travelling this path, my intentions were to identify and/or develop and probe perspectives different from the ones known to me in advance. Qualitative research methods, and first of all case studies (see Box 4) were used as the basis for my inquiries. Semi-structured interviews with key informants, secondary (published and unpublished) sources and group interviews helped to generate and organize relevant information. Also, I was careful to systematically cross-check information between sources. Interpretations were systematically fed back to those interviewed, so they could enrich the analysis with their observations and comment upon my interpretations. These comments often provided a stimulus to have another look at the way I had weighed salient issues, but seldom forced a fundamental recasting of interpretations. End results were presented (by means of a written research report) to those involved for a final check on details and a chance to comment upon and discuss our interpretations of the ideas and events studied. As can be seen in Box 4, Chapters 2, 3 and parts of 4 and 8 are based upon case study materials.

Second, I synthesized available case studies in search of regularities relevant to my inquiry. Each of these studies consisted of a review of relevant literature and a thorough analysis of the available case study materials. The first review focused on the effect of improved inter-institutional linkages on innovative impact. My own case study materials were analysed from this point of view (synthesis study 1). The results were again cross-checked with key informants in the area, who provided additional comments and insights. The preliminary report was also presented to an international workshop organized by ISNAR (November 1989; see Merrill-Sands and Kaimowitz, 1989), before the conclusions were finalized (Engel, 1990a). The results are presented in Chapter 3. The second synthesis study was done with Stephan Seegers. We screened all 20 case studies done for the ISNAR RTT/L study on patterns of interaction, leadership and coordination. Here too, preliminary results were cross-checked with the leaders of the research teams who had done the case studies. Our final results were presented to and accepted by ISNAR (Engel and Seegers, 1992). Versions of this paper have been presented and discussed with colleagues during scientific workshops at Hohenheim, Germany, and Wageningen, the Netherlands (Engel and Seegers, 1991; Engel, 1993c). Chapter 4 is based upon the final results of this study.

The third and final synthesis study in this book concerns networking among non-governmental development organizations. I was commissioned to carry out this study by ILEIA, the Centre for Information on Low External Input and Sustainable Agriculture,

Box 4
Empirical materials used

Title	Author(s)	Countries	Year	Chapter(s)
Case studies				
Peasant technology development	Engel	Colombia	1989	3, 4
Knowledge and information used by farm advisers	Engel	Netherlands	1989	2
AGROCOM study of farmers' information use	van Dijk, Engel, Leeuwis	Netherlands	1990	2
Knowledge and information system, horse sector	Engel, de Groot, Meijering, Eleveld	Netherlands	1990	8
Synthesis studies				
Impact of interinstitutional coordination	Engel	Colombia	1990	3
Towards effective linkage strategies	Engel, Seegers	Colombia, Philippines, Nigeria, Ivory Coast, Tanzania, Dominican Republic, Costa Rica	1992	4
Networking among NGDOs	Engel	Peru, West Africa, India	1993	5
Action research evaluation study				
RAAKS in Central America	Engel, Solis, Moreno and national research teams	Guatamala, El Salvador, Panama Costa Rica Nicaragua Honduras	1992/ 1993	8

Leusden, the Netherlands. They requested a review and synthesis of the lessons from self-evaluative case studies done by five different NGDO networks. Using a suggested format outlining the main questions to be answered, local researchers collected materials and discussed their preliminary documents during a workshop in Sri Lanka, in which all researchers and a number of outside specialists participated. To synthesize their experiences, I studied the final documents and invited comments upon my interpretations from selected specialists who had participated in the workshop. The results were published together with the individual case studies (Engel, 1993b). They were also presented and discussed with the working group on agricultural extension at the 1993 European Rural Sociology Conference (Engel, 1993c). Chapter 5 of this book is based upon the final results of this study. The eventual organization, interpretation and integration of the results of the case and synthesis studies required additional literature review. This is reflected in Chapter 6, where I propose answers to the research questions that guided my exploratory path.

The design path

The design path of the methodology to guide participatory inquiry mentioned in Box 2, now called RAAKS (rapid or relaxed appraisal of agricultural knowledge systems), can best be described as an intensive networking process that has taken place across many years and among many researchers and practitioners. It will be described in detail in Chapter 7. At this point it is useful to know that, to give this path an empirical 'anchor', three distinct steps have been included: first, a field test of the first RAAKS design, involving a *case study* within the horse sector in the Netherlands, presented in Chapter 8. The results obtained through semi-structured interviews with relevant stakeholders were discussed, consolidated and cross-checked with them during two consecutive workshops (Engel et al., 1990). The next step was an *expert consultation* on methodology in 1991. During this meeting, four specialists were asked to relate their experiences with RAAKS or approaches similar to RAAKS, while another 15 were asked to contribute to the discussion of these and other relevant experiences that were brought forward. The consultation brought out a very rich picture of salient issues to be considered in the design and further development of RAAKS. Some are presented and discussed in Chapter 7. The third step was a full-fledged *experimental application* of RAAKS in six countries in Central America. This led to a total of 14 different case studies, done by national research teams trained and guided by regional specialists. My involvement in this effort was limited to training the teams and specialists and contributing to the synthesis of results by directing a workshop. During this latter workshop, a day was spent evaluating RAAKS on the basis of the experiences gathered by national teams. The experiences with RAAKS in Central America (listed in Box 4 under action research) and their evaluation on the part of the researchers who did the studies are presented and discussed in detail in Chapter 8 (see 'Agricultural institutions in Central America'). Over the years a large number of case studies by graduate and post graduate students of the Department of Communication and Innovation Studies have added to the material available to support both the design and the exploratory path (see the Appendix).

Predispositions that have withstood the years

Notwithstanding the conceptual turmoil and methodological labyrinths that have pushed me on, eventually I also identified a number of constants in my reflections, which I consider relevant here. These could be called 'biases'; I prefer to call them predispositions. They represent a number of points of departure or anchors, which in spite of heavy weather have not succumbed and drifted away. In the light of the exploratory and qualitative nature of this research, I consider it indispensable to make them as explicit as I can, before asking you to read any further. They are:

• Human ways are central to my interest. Why do people do the things they do the way they do them? This is always the first question that springs to my mind when studying a situation. In spite of my original training as an irrigation agronomist this makes me, I suppose, a social scientist. Both in professional and in academic terms, this is a very fundamental choice indeed, and maybe a 'species-centric' one (as in 'ethnocentric').

- As a student of development, I was lightning-struck early in my career by a remark from Solon Barraclough (1974): 'Development is not just economics or sociology or technology, but history'. And it is the way we humans act and relate to each other that creates this history.

- Ecological sustainability is not just a problem of natural resources. It is a human, or better, a social problem as well. Its achievement is intrinsically linked with the way we humans go about our daily lives. Our actions, and the type and level of social organization we achieve to coordinate these, fundamentally affect our chances of survival. Any concept of ecological sustainability therefore must include a systematic notion of human 'agency' – the ability of human beings to appraise a situation, to decide, and to act accordingly – and its role in conceptualizing, achieving, maintaining (or alternatively, eliminating) sustainable practices.

- Social and technological innovation go hand in hand. 'Technologies' stem from and also affect the way we act and think. Moreover, if we accept that humans have the ability to reflect upon and learn from their experiences, social development, technological development and learning are intrinsically related.

- Collective human action is more than, and fundamentally different from, the sum total of individual activities. However, one cannot be understood without the other.

- Understanding as a basis for *designing useful practices* is at the core of my commitment to research. Interesting ideas are important, but useful ideas are my preference.

Assessment of outcomes

Box 2 provides a framework for assessing this book. I seek to defend its contributions to a conceptual framework first and foremost by arguing their usefulness to development professionals and researchers who need to scout complex theatres of agricultural innovation and design worthwhile interventions. This is consistent with my intention to contribute to meaningful discourse and reflection, rather than to an ontological explanation of the social organization of innovation, and particularly technological innovation, in agriculture. Second, I will demonstrate the internal consistency of the approach proposed, substantiate it on the basis of my research and demonstrate its foundation in current scientific thought. Necessarily, my arguments will be built up throughout the book, but Chapters 1, 6 and 9 contain the main issues.

The analytical perspectives (or windows, as they are called in RAAKS) I develop should be judged on the basis of their use and applicability on the one hand, and their validity on the other. In line with Suchman (1967: 120–121) I take validity to mean '...the degree to which any measure or procedure succeeds in doing what it purports to do'. Because the perspectives, or windows, are theoretical constructs designed to help achieve an understanding of the social organization of innovation processes, their validity depends mainly upon their effectiveness in bringing out relevant issues. Therefore 'relevant issues' must be defined when studying the social organization of innovation. I intend to do this in Chapter 6, when concluding my exploratory path. After that, each of the windows proposed for RAAKS can be evaluated with respect to its contribution to highlighting these issues. My arguments with respect to the windows are summarized in Chapter 7 (see 'RAAKS: an approach...' and 'Preliminary conclusions').

The methodology will also be defended first by demonstrating its usefulness to development professionals and researchers. Second, I will explore whether RAAKS does what it is designed to do. Following Checkland and Scholes (1990), this will be referred to as the efficacy of RAAKS. I will draw from my explorations a number of specific criteria by which a methodology of this kind should be measured and will evaluate RAAKS accordingly. Lastly, I will make a preliminary assessment of the actual *use and applicability* of the methodology under varying circumstances. The main arguments can be found in Chapters 7 and 8. Finally, the most important argument in all of these areas will be the interest of the readers of this book, which as yet I have no way of knowing.

Organization of the book

In summary, this book covers two intellectual journeys: an exploratory path and a design path. The first is an attempt to achieve a fresh look at and a more comprehensive understanding of relevant phenomena; the second, to develop and test a methodology for diagnosing problematical situations and designing solutions together with relevant stakeholders. Chapter 1 lays out an initial conceptual framework for both routes, demonstrating how conceptual and methodological issues are intrinsically related.

Chapters 2 to 5 present the results of the case studies. Chapter 2 offers a detailed view of the ways farmers, extension workers and subject-matter specialists interact to achieve innovation, and the patterns that evolve as a result of their partly planned, partly spontaneous interaction. Chapter 3 draws attention to inter-institutional coordination and its broad impact on innovation in agricultural practices. Chapter 4 analyses why successful inter-organizational alliances emerge, and specifies the conditions that must be met. Chapter 5 focuses on the emergence of a particular type of alliance – networks of non-governmental development organizations – and highlights a number of management issues in such a process.

Chapter 6 draws lessons from the case studies. With the help of additional theoretical inputs, an outline is given for the foundation of an empirically based, conceptually coherent and at the same time practical approach to understanding the social organization of innovation in complex situations. Chapter 7 focuses on intervention: are useful interentions indeed conceivable? What criteria must a methodology meet to be seen as effective and useful? In the same chapter, RAAKS is introduced: a participatory action research methodology aimed at improving performance related to innovation. Chapter 8 reviews a number of initial field experiences with RAAKS, discussing its relevance and applicability to development practice. Lessons are drawn with regard to its use by different actors and under different circumstances.

Finally, Chapter 9 summarizes the results of the research and design processes and looks back upon the relevance of this study for understanding and managing knowledge and innovation processes in complex, ill-defined situations in which many different social actors are stakeholders.

In general, the book offers material that is intended to help readers understand and study the approach, or to design their own. The accompanying manual *Networking for innovation: a participatory actor-oriented methodology* (Salomon and Engel, 1997) is a guide to applying the RAAKS methodology. It introduces this methodology, explores each of the proposed windows in detail, and provides tools and other materials to use in implementing a RAAKS study.

A readers' guide

As outlined in Box 5, there are several ways to read this book. Depending on your intentions and interest, several worthwhile routes are available. The first option is of course to read through the chapters as they appear in the book. This is the 'endurance option' – a route that will provide you with everything the author is able to offer at this point. On the other hand, you might choose the 'executive option', and skip everything but Chapter 9. You will then gain a general idea of what has been done, and of the main results of the study. (Reading Chapter 9 is also a good way to get an overview, before beginning with any of the other options.) The only thing you can do in even less time is to read the 'Table of contents'. However, even though it might give you something to do while waiting in a traffic jam, this option does not appeal to me. For those who have little time but do have some previous knowledge of the subject, I would advise the 'professional option': glance through the Introduction and Chapter 1, skip 2 to 5, skim Chapters 6, 7 and 8, and read Chapter 9 thoroughly.

There are also options for those who want to study the book but would like to do so from a more empirical, or theoretical angle – or perhaps to the contrary you prefer a more practical approach. Any of these options should include a quick reading of the Introduction. The 'empiricist' might then concentrate on Chapters 2 to 5 plus Chapter 8, while the 'theorist' might focus on Chapters 1, 6, 7 and 9. After reading the Introduction, the more practically inclined 'activist' who wants to set to work immediately might decide to go directly to Chapters 7 and 8, depending on Chapter 9 for a taste of the general content. Readers who are specifically interested in the practical application of the RAAKS methodology will also want to explore *Networking for innovation,* the manual described above. Whatever choice you make, I definitely hope your initial selection will tempt you to go on to read the rest as well!

Box 5
Options for reading this book

Option	Read chapters
Endurance	Introduction, 1, 2, 3, 4, 5, 6, 7, 8, 9
Executive	9
Traffic jam	Table of contents
Professional	(Introduction, 1), 6, 7, 8, 9
Empiricist	Introduction, 2, 3, 4, 5, 8, 9
Theorist	Introduction, 1, 6, 7, (8), 9
Activist	Introduction, 7, 8, 9 + manual

1. Diving into the deep: choosing a soft knowledge systems perspective

Thinking of intervening in a complex social problem such as agricultural innovation creates a dilemma reminiscent of the centipede in a parable cited by Koestler (1968: 205): 'When the centipede was asked in which order he moved his hundred legs, he became paralysed and starved to death because he had never thought of it before and had left his legs to look after themselves.' Should we 'mess with' the way creative social processes such as innovation are organized? Some argue we should not; others rely on the 'invisible hand' of the market. Both are too easy. After all, we regularly allocate manpower and financial resources to innovation. On what do we base such decisions, if not on thorough reflection on what we are currently doing? My close exposure to and intense experiences among deprived, all too often misunderstood farm families in developing countries have kept me from giving up in looking for ways to facilitate innovation processes: time and again these families allowed me to participate in their search for relevant innovations in their farming and household practices. They never questioned the need for outside support; they did frequently question its quality. I learned that in their eyes the social organization of innovation is taken very seriously indeed.

To avoid starving to death, the centipede will have to go beyond just thinking, and assume an interventionist position. It will need to design and implement useful actions, taking a stance as to what the 'desired state of affairs' is. This requires two things: first, useful theoretical perspectives, making it possible to identify the various available options and help in making a choice between them; and second, a procedure for arriving at a strategy, articulating both ends and means in a specific enough manner to allow implementation. This chapter lays the foundation for such an effort. It defines a starting point for both the 'exploratory path' and the 'design path' we hope to travel in this book. It explains why a soft knowledge systems perspective was chosen to focus on understanding and intervening in complex innovation theatres. It also provides a brief introduction to the two main components of such a perspective, soft systems methodology (e.g. Checkland, 1988, 1989; Checkland and Scholes, 1990) and knowledge systems thinking (e.g. Röling, 1986, 1988; Röling and Engel, 1990, 1991). In conclusion, some of the implications of the choices made for the research presented in this book are drawn out.

Initial considerations in designing useful interventions

In the diffuse and often unintentional processes underlying innovation, what requirements must be met by an intervention if it is to be considered potentially useful? The following remarks must be taken as a first, intuitive approach to the problem. They stem from reflections on practice rather than from scientific inquiry.

- Any approach or methodology should aim more at facilitation than control. A focus on facilitation means accepting that full control of all relevant processes is impossible. It accepts that innovation-related processes are largely self-guiding, yet are affected by the opportunities and constraints inherent in the way relevant stakeholders interact. It also presumes that no single actor can develop a fully comprehensive view of all processes relevant to innovation. Hence, allowing for *partiality* is a necessary ingredient of facilitation. Moreover, facilitation emphasizes *process* rather than product. This suggests that in designing useful interventions, we will need to focus on the quality of the process rather than looking only at the outcomes of innovation-related processes.

- Given the many actors at many levels who take decisions affecting agricultural innovation, any practical approach should account for the diffuse, social and often epiphenomenal (cf. Lindblom, 1990) character of innovation processes. A centrally managed innovation process is not an option; instead, distributed responsibilities, differences of perceptions and/or interests must be incorporated. Interventions may seek to facilitate mutual adjustments between actors who seem to be committed to innovation in similar ways, but should not necessarily seek to mend actors' differences in perceptions and/or interests. However, in many theatres continuing power struggles among actors seem more predictive of the type of innovation that occurs and its success than are their accommodations to each other. Any methodology for intervention in complex innovation theatres should therefore allow for arbitrariness, facing the fact that those concerned will continue to make their own judgements in terms of means and ends, and creating space for adaptation to the context and for new perceptions, positions and relevant relationships.

- Interventions should anticipate considerable degrees of randomness in innovation processes. Unintended consequences of intentional as well as unintentional actions can be expected to affect innovation, whether positively or negatively. However, the famous remark of Gelia Castillo, 'waiting for perfection is a form of abdication' (cited by Röling, 1988) sums up the situation. In complex innovation theatres 'the best means to an end' does not exist. Numerous possible combinations of ends and means compete in the perceptions of those who will be involved in making a choice among possible actions. Innovation strategies therefore are not only highly judgmental; they also have to make do with large degrees of uncertainty about what stakeholders actually want, think and will require if they are to commit themselves. Intervention methodologies may seek to decrease such uncertainties, yet at the same time they will have to adjust to a considerable degree of persistent uncertainty and randomness.

- It also seems important to take into account the structural forms that emerge and evolve in complex innovation theatres when several actors articulate innovation strategies and succeed in moving towards a relatively well-defined set of objectives. An approach to intervention should take such forms and their influence on the process of agricultural innovation into account. It should therefore seek to define which forms to look at, and how to probe their influence. Intervention in the social organization of innovation requires an understanding of ways and means to strategize beyond the level of actions by individual actors; it also requires an ability to assess the consequences of such strategizing.

- Finally, I would propose that a methodology related to intervention in the social organization of innovation will have to remain *'manageable'* with regard both to time span and participants. Given the complex and appreciative character of such interventions, wide participation of relevant stakeholders seems to be indicated. But if an intervention is to be useful, tangible objectives and specific choices with respect to timing and participation will be needed. Therefore, the process, inputs, outputs and procedures of the approach itself must be defined.

A knowledge systems perspective

The knowledge systems perspective developed by Röling and others at Wageningen Agricultural University (cf. Röling 1986, 1988) provides a practical way of looking at the social organization of innovation. Initially, recognition of its practical value rather than a balanced scientific inquiry precipitated this choice. The holistic, inclusive character of the knowledge systems perspective has enormous potential for stimulating discussion and learning among practitioners. A number of additional reasons for choosing it to guide this inquiry can also be offered. The first is its potential for combining, and even integrating, macro and micro perspectives. As development professionals, we need to be able to look at human actions at different levels. Both personal and collective strategizing matter. I felt *systems* thinking could help me look at emergent qualities and their relevance to the innovation process.

The second reason is the focus the knowledge systems perspective provides on *sharing knowledge among relevant stakeholders,* rather than simply on extension efforts. We have learned the hard way that extension alone cannot be held responsible for the success or failure of innovation. What about research, education, mass communication and policymaking, to name a few? A knowledge systems perspective can take all of these aspects into account.

This perspective also resolves some practical questions that have been on our minds since the 1970s. Why must we content ourselves with seeing people only in their roles as innovators, adopters, laggards or worse? Can't we incorporate a more comprehensive view of 'human agency' in our thinking about innovation? Aren't what people know and what they do intrinsically related? The knowledge systems perspective recognizes these points (Röling, 1988). Finally, additional reasons to choose the knowledge systems perspective are its potential for looking at innovation in agriculture as a social effort, requiring joint competence of interrelated actors (rather than the sum of individual competencies), plus its focus on developing a diagnostic framework for analysis and design and management of interventions. Such a perspective suits the purposes of this study and coincides with my experience that in the field 'everybody depends on everybody else' to make innovation work.

A soft systems approach to facilitating innovation

The knowledge systems perspective did not, initially, provide a methodological approach to intervention. Checkland's *soft systems methodology* (e.g. Checkland 1989; Checkland and Scholes, 1990) however, did supply a basis for the development of such an approach. Developed and used widely for organizational problem solving in complex organizations, this methodology seemed extremely well-suited to situations in which stakeholders have radically different perceptions as to their problems, goals and possible options for achieving these goals. Soft systems methodology focuses on facilitating the design of useful interventions. It recognizes widely different yet equally relevant world-views of stakeholders. As a result, soft systems methodology suits the high degree of complexity as well as the appreciative and emergent character of the social organization of innovation. Moreover, its central concern is the improvement of human practices – not with a scientifically 'best' solution but by achieving one that is practical, and fits the views and interests of those involved as well as possible. This coincides with the purpose of our study. *tactical aims*

Another important consideration is that learning-in-practice and choice-making are central to soft systems methodologies. The attempt of this approach is to stimulate an interactive learning process among participants, facilitating the creation of new perspectives, different interpretations and hence new propositions and accommodations among stakeholders. Of course, care must be taken to specify the conditions under which people will work together for change, so that relevant actors will be able to participate effectively.

A third asset is the emphasis of soft systems methodologies on such active participation of stakeholders. Although this appears easier to achieve in the corporate environments where Checkland et al. developed their methods, wide participation is definitely an essential element of a methodology for probing the social organization of innovation. If any such process is to succeed, the perceptions, propositions and dispositions of relevant social actors will have to be taken into account. Nevertheless, a number of questions remain, such as who is to participate, and who decides and how, where the social organization of innovation is concerned? As the next sections show, this is where the combination of soft systems methodology with a knowledge systems perspective pays off. The first can be used to structure the process of inquiry, while the second suggests useful analytical perspectives that can support learning about the social organization of innovation in practice.

Systems thinking, systems practice[1]

Systems thinking is just that: *thinking*. It is an approach to studying the world and intervening in it, which has grown out of the efforts and experiences of many scientists and practitioners who found themselves wrestling with a situation like that of the centipede. Hence, systems thinking has been developed as an approach – not necessarily the only viable one – to probing and dealing with complex situations. It has been taken up by many disciplines in many situations. As a result, the 'systems approach' is an extremely diverse phenomenon. Below, those elements of systems thinking relevant to this research are briefly introduced. At the same time, I will take the opportunity to show the links between my approach and the work of scholars I have found particularly inspiring or helpful.

Creating and using systemic images

Although no agreed definition for the 'system' concept is found in the literature, it is generally taken to refer to an 'image or metaphor of the adaptive whole, which may be able to survive in a changing environment' (Checkland and Scholes, 1990: 19). This metaphor has spurred diverse people to look at a variety of natural or social phenomena from a 'systems perspective' – that is, *as if* the set of components they are studying were behaving like such an adaptive whole. To study such phenomena, system theorists create abstract constructs, often called 'systems' or 'system models'. To avoid confusion due to the many ways these same words are used, in this study we refer to such constructs as *systemic images*. This pays tribute to the fact that one of the main assets of systems thinking may be its capacity to stimulate our imagination.

Consequently, the term 'system' will be used only to refer to a way of thinking – as in 'systems thinking' – or in referring to procedures, mechanisms or sets of activities *designed* as wholes, such as a heating system or a car. To refer to something in the perceived world I want to consider as a whole, the word 'whole' will be used. If necessary each case will specify whether I refer to an *abstract* or a *tangible* whole. Liberally interpreting Checkland and Scholes (1990: 25), the following description of systems thinking can then be derived: systems thinking *establishes one or more constructed abstract wholes or 'systemic images', which can be set against the perceived world to help us study it*. The aim of such

1. *I owe this title to Peter Checkland (1981).*

study may be more adequate intervention, illumination of certain aspects, or generally learning more about this perceived world.

Systems learning: hard and soft systems thinking

The ongoing debate among systems scientists has led to two complementary traditions in systems thinking and systems practice: the 'hard systems' tradition, taking the world to be systemic; and the 'soft systems' tradition, which 'creates the process of inquiry as a system' (Checkland and Scholes, 1990). To characterize and clarify the soft systems thinking used in this book, a brief summary of the main differences between these two traditions follows (also see Table 1).

Hard systems thinkers take their systemic images to be models, simplified *representations* of real world wholes. 'The essence of the use of models is to create a material or formal representation of the system to be investigated which is easier to study than the system itself' (Kramer and de Smit, 1987: 117). Representation is central to hard systems thinking. The more closely the outcomes predicted by their models coincide with observed events the better, in terms of supplying knowledge. Another characteristic of hard systems thinking is its emphasis on processes of transformation. 'The way in which inputs are processed into outputs determines the *function* of a system' (Fresco, 1986: 41). Hard systems thinkers think of their systems as performing a function that can be described as transforming inputs into outputs. These transformations are captured in models, constructed with the help of so-called 'black boxes', systemic images which specify only incoming and outgoing relationships, setting aside what happens in between (Kramer and de Smit, 1987: 53). Röling (1994: 5) cites Rabbinge (1993) to point out the generic definition hard systems thinkers use in constructing systemic images: 'A system is a limited part of reality with well-defined boundaries.'

Soft systems thinkers do not take the world to be systemic; nor do they assume their systemic images can be developed into representations of wholes or parts of wholes in the 'real' world. Systemic images can instead be used to build instruments of inquiry. In soft systems thinking such images are constructed to develop different perspectives; these stimulate reflection and debate and an accommodation, even if partial, between social actors and practices. As a consequence, for soft or 'social constructivist' thinkers a system is a construct with *'arbitrary boundaries for discourse about complex phenomena to emphasize wholeness, interrelationships and emergent properties'* (Röling, 1994: 6). By emphasizing its arbitrary, or rather its *appreciative* nature – that is, people looking from different perspectives may construct different systemic images, even if they abide by the same general rules – Röling's definition sets the stage for deconstruction, debate and accommodation.

The explicit statement of a purpose is an important aspect of a 'soft' approach to defining systemic images. 'Systems' do not *have* a purpose, they are *assigned* one. Any description of a purposeful whole must be given from a declared perspective. Due to the appreciative character of such perspectives or world-views, multiple perspectives are always available; these can be used to construct different images of the same situation (Checkland and Scholes, 1990). Consequently, for soft systems thinkers systemic images are 'windows' on the world rather than representations of the world. Each image implies a way of looking at the world; thus images can be constructed to reflect different world-views or perspectives. They are '... a means to an end, which is to have a well-structured and coherent debate about a problematical situation in order to decide how to improve it. That debate is structured by using the models based on a range of world-views to question perceptions of

Table 1
Hard and soft systems thinking: a comparison

Hard systems thinking	Soft systems thinking
The world (W) is systemic... or can be taken as if...	W is not systemic... but sometimes it is useful to take it *as if*...
Images are to be systemic...	Systemic images are used when this is helpful
The methodology of inquiry (M) may be systemic ...	M is designed as a system, possibly a learning system...
Systems images are used to construct models to represent the world (or parts of it)...	Systems images are used to construct windows to study the world...
System images are concerned with processes, inputs and outputs...	System images concern social actors, their activities and relationships...
The aim of hard systems thinking is to improve one's knowledge about the world by improving one's models...	The aim of soft systems thinking is to improve human performance through debate and reflection...
Processes are functionally articulated into a goal-seeking whole... goals are inherent in the whole	Social actors may behave as a systemic whole – if they wish and know how to do this... boundaries and goals are permanently negotiated or renegotiated.

the situation' (Checkland and Scholes, 1990: 42). What is sought in the debate is an accommodation among varying interests, concerns and propositions. 'It is wrong to see SSM (soft systems methodology; PE) simply as consensus seeking. That is the occasional special case within the general case of seeking accommodations, in which the conflicts endemic in human affairs are still there, but are subsumed in an accommodation which different parties are prepared to "go along with" ' (Checkland and Scholes, 1990: 29).

In soft systems thinking, do images necessarily have to be systemic? Checkland and Scholes (1990: 23–25) emphasize the systemic nature of the inquiry, rather than that of the images (or 'systems models'): 'SSM is a systemic process of inquiry which also happens to make use of systems models. It thus subsumes the hard approach, which is a special case of it, one arising when there is local agreement on some system to be engineered.' The images Checkland proposes are constructed by connecting sets of activities to make a purposeful whole – a human activity system.[2] Particularly in view of the present weakness of soft systems methodology in addressing the cultural, social and political aspects of inquiry (discussed later), the possibility of constructing useful windows on the basis of disciplinary thinking cannot be ruled out.

One of the most important systemic images soft systems thinkers create and use is the one that guides their intervention. SSM is used as a learning system, leading to the creation of a cyclic learning process, engaged in by a team of researchers as they apply systems thinking to the real world (Checkland and Scholes, 1990: 27). A more sophisticated version distinguishes between two streams of inquiry – logic-based or cultural – and guides would-be 'improvers' into a learning process that leads to the implementation of changes

---

2. *For further discussion, see The systems thinkers' tool kit II, further on in this section.*

meant to improve a problematical situation (Checkland and Scholes, 1990: 28). During this process the methodology helps generate paradoxes: differences between systemic discourse and observed practice. These stimulate reflection and action (or modifications to action) in subsequent learning cycles. As a result, soft systems methodologies seem well suited to facilitating social learning processes among actors in theatres of agricultural innovation.

A much simplified summary of learning cycles in the soft and hard traditions of systems thinking: *hard* systems thinkers create systemic images to guide the construction of models to represent transformation processes. In subsequent learning cycles they perfect their images by comparing the outcomes predicted by their models to observations in the real world. The purpose of hard systems learning is to achieve useful simulations of real world processes, to help achieve an ontological understanding of the world, often to increase human abilities to predict events. *Soft* systems thinkers, on the contrary, construct images – not necessarily systemic ones – to derive heuristic windows; that is, windows that can help thinkers discover things for themselves. In subsequent learning cycles relevant windows are developed and used to study human practices. The aim of soft systems learning is to generate and achieve accommodations among relevant actors, to improve organized human performance.

Some criticisms of soft systems thinking

Soft systems approaches have been criticized severely for their emphasis on harmony and consensus seeking (Jackson, 1985). As has been noted, consensus is one special case among many types of accommodation in human organizations. However, those who have lived through the social impairments, power struggles, conflicts and (as I once heard Norman Long put it) 'battles over images' that play a role in the social organization of the searching and coordination related to innovation, may be inclined to shy away from using apparently naive attempts like soft systems approaches to address such topics. However, on the contrary, if as I have argued the roots of innovation lie in a continuous and inter-active probing among social actors – searching for divergence as well as accommodation – soft systems learning cycles will generally provide opportunities within which the conflicting parties find a way of addressing each other. Since this is true only if a number of conditions are fulfilled, soft systems methodologies are not always the best means to tackle problems. A second challenge is thus to *specify* the types of situations in which soft systems methodologies are most useful.

On the other hand, not all conflicts involving power must be dealt with immediately or at the same time. Innovation in agricultural practices, although sometimes seen as 'revolutionary', is generally a process of slow but insistent tinkering with underlying principles, conventions and rules. The chains of decisions that lead to particular innova-tions are often too long and diffuse to point a finger at the one who 'pulled the trigger'. To improve this process, the notion proposed by Lindblom (1990) of meticulously probing constraining influences that stand in the way of those searching for alternative developments seems a viable and useful contribution.

To make soft systems methodology into a tool for facilitating innovation in complex agricultural theatres, we will have to be very explicit about who is to participate, why and how. This will require the introduction of the notion of relevant diversity and the specification of minimum conditions and quality standards for communicative interaction among actors in the process. Which diversity is relevant will have to be discovered along the way, as will the necessary conditions and standards of communication. However, in view of the social character of innovation processes in complex theatres, the need to encourage a strong or even extreme 'competition of ideas' (Lindblom, 1990) seems obvious.

Another limitation of the soft systems tradition is a lack of adequate operational tools to use in exploring the relational dimensions of social interaction. As Checkland and Scholes (1990: 48) rightfully observe, the social science literature does not easily yield useful 'systemic images'. In the complex, multi-actor situations common in agricultural innovation theatres, this is especially true. Greater emphasis on probing and assessing the influence of social relationships was needed. To achieve this, we would have to zoom in on the selective perceptions, judgement-making and relationship-managing of social actors engaged in probing ends, means, opportunities and constraints with the intention of improving their practices or developing new ones. The range of issues to which soft systems thinking can be applied would need to be amplified by including an appreciative, social relationship-focused dimension. Only then would it be possible to pay explicit attention to the many issues of power and influence that play a role in enabling and/or impairing social interaction in complex innovation theatres.

Another critical issue is the emphasis on 'wholeness' in systems thinking: 'Holistic ambitions for social scientists and citizens alike often mark the scientific model of society...' (Lindblom, 1990: 226). Often, this is associated with the aspiration of eventually shaping a single, comprehensive theory, which will answer all questions from a distinct set of universally valid axioms. When we, including Röling (1993), emphasize 'wholeness' we definitely do not aspire to such a 'unified theory'. Rather, this refers to probing among the events and ideas that appear to be relevant to our inquiry, searching for coherence. We see a need to find not a unified scientific theory that produces understanding, but more comprehensive ways of *debating*: the ever growing degree of complexity of social and technological issues makes this essential.

In my view, however, Röling's definition must be amended. Two fundamental issues that systems thinkers should and often do emphasize must be built in: *randomness* and *choice*. Earlier, it was shown that innovation, as a social process, cannot be understood unless its epiphenomenal character is fully recognized. In complex innovation theatres, much 'just happens'. This means that systemic images of complex innovation theatres must allow for many degrees of randomness, to accommodate the unexpected, the irrational, the unknown. Moreover, the element of choice is fundamental. Innovation emerges from complex and diffuse processes of social inquiry and interaction, during which social actors continuously make choices. In constructing systemic images, soft systems thinkers too should therefore include the element of choice. Soft systems methodologies need to emphasize the ongoing construction and reconstruction of views, opinions, propositions, interpretations and commitments.

The systems thinkers' tool kit I: concepts

Address these debates

To study something as if it were a 'system', according to Kramer and de Smit (1987: 19), the following questions must be answered: which entities are part of this 'something'? which entities are not a part, but influence it? how do the entities within this 'something' relate to each other? (4) how do these entities within relate to those outside? These questions imply some *boundary* is to be drawn, distinguishing entities inside from those in the environment of the 'something'. At the same time a *level of analysis* is chosen, to reduce the complexity to manageable proportions. The result of such an inquiry is a systemic image (or 'system' in Kramer and de Smit's terms) composed of: a set of entities placed within a boundary, a set of entities placed in this environment, a set of relation-

NGOs
CB initiatives

villages
gov't
private sector

THE SOCIAL ORGANIZATION OF INNOVATION

ships between the entities within the boundary, and a set of relationships between those entities within the boundary and those in the environment. Of course, each entity within or outside the boundary can in itself be thought of as a system, while at the same time the systemic image can be looked at as one entity within a wider 'whole'. It follows that hierarchies in systems thinking, like boundaries, are tools for constructing images, not accounts of phenomena that can be observed in the world.

In systems thinking, the concept of *hierarchy* is often misunderstood. Hierarchy refers to the orders or levels of assembly at which systemic images, their relationships and their emergent properties can be constructed. Unlike its use with respect to bureaucracies, in systems thinking a hierarchy doesn't necessarily imply authority or direct control. The degrees of freedom entities have within a larger whole depend on the nature of the *relationships* assumed (or designed) to exist between them. If such relationships are understood as 'structural couplings', defined as 'a history of mutual concordant structural changes [which continue] as long as the units do not disintegrate' (Maturana and Varela, 1984: 50), the relationship can be understood as a mutual perturbing ('tickling') without a one-sided power to decide or instruct. If on the contrary these relationships are understood – or have been designed – such that one entity is to impose absolute authority over the others, a two-sided mutual 'tickling' reverts to one-sided 'hammering', with the unfortunate entity on the wrong end having no choice but to do as it is told.

According to Checkland and Scholes (1990: 19) hierarchy is closely tied to the systems thinking concept of *emergence*. Emergence refers to the idea that the whole has properties that cannot be fully understood in terms of the properties of its component parts. 'Emergent' properties may be associated with a systemic image created at a specific hierarchical level; however, these properties would not be apparent in studying each entity or component separately, nor by simply taking the sum total of their properties. The types of properties that can be expected to emerge depends upon the level of analysis or assembly of systemic images chosen. The properties a researcher will look for at each level depend upon his or her sense-making or theorizing with regard to the phenomena studied, and on the systemic images constructed in accord with these theories.

[handwritten margin note: Emergence: justification for my methodology Connects with Capra]

Probably one of the most hotly debated issues in systems thinking is *behaviour*. Most systems analysis is done in the hope of understanding, predicting, engineering or influencing the behaviour of 'something or somebody' considered to be one whole. Behaviour is generally defined as subsequent changes in the state of a whole over time (Kramer and de Smit, 1987: 50). However, the use made of this concept is far less 'objective' than it may appear. Determining the variables to be used in describing such changes of state introduces elements of human choice in the analysis. Further, with Maturana and Varela (1984: 111) I believe that to speak of 'behaviour' implies the existence of an external observer, who describes these changes and decides how to 'make sense' of them, perhaps by singling out 'relevant' or 'effective' actions. These choices – which govern the observers' observations – are *appreciative:* they mirror his or her own volitions, dispositions, preoccupations and concerns. In studying social organization, such appreciative choices need to be made explicit; they are closely tied to the way systems evolve and, for example, to the function or purpose attributed to the whole by the observer.

Another key notion in systems thinking is *communication*. While communication is often associated with control, in a soft systems perspective this is misleading. Communicative interaction is one very important way in which mutual adjustment takes place among social actors. Effective and sustained communication is fundamental to developing and maintaining standards of competent performance in and between human practices (Gremmen, 1993). Furthermore, communication processes play an important role in

[handwritten margin note: Rlsp > Communication]

creating and disseminating the results of other means of coordination, including central-ized decision making. Communication, taken as a process, is not the same as 'convergence', as Rogers and Kincaid (1981) suggest. Communicative interactions among social actors can lead to either convergence or divergence in understanding, beliefs and/or actions.

The systems thinkers' tool kit II: creating systemic images in practice

Not all systemic images are constructed in the same way. First, the entities described may differ. A choice of *systemic* components from all possible components is generally done on the basis of perceived relevance to the phenomena being studied and debated. Therefore social system thinkers may take people, organizations, political parties, societies and so forth as entities; agricultural scientists select crops, weeds, pathogens, insects or soil types when they study cropping systems. Boundaries are also defined on the basis of relevance: 'Within the boundaries all relevant interactions and feedback are included, so that all those components that are capable of reacting as a whole to external stimuli form a system' (Fresco, 1986: 41). Choices of entities and boundaries go hand in hand: when new relevant entities are identified, these are included and boundaries are shifted.

Just as choices of what will 'fill the boxes' differ, the way the systemic images them-selves are designed may differ as well. In hard systems thinking, most systemic images are *input/output arrangements*. In fact, naming inputs and outputs as entities is considered vital. Hence, the modelling language is based upon *nouns* (Checkland and Scholes, 1990). The structural arrangement of the image as well as an eventual model are based upon chains of input/output transformations. The transformation *process* is the central focus: 'a transformation or a series of transformations brought about the throughput of a system as a result of which the throughput is changed in position, shape, size, version or some other respect' (Miller and Rice, 1967; cited by Kramer and de Smit, 1987: 51). The function of the whole is to achieve the required transformations in accord with previously set specifications. The purpose of creating the images is to build a model that can be used to study the processes. Most farming systems and industrial processing models are examples of such systemic images and models. Some of the early knowledge systems approaches (see for example Beal et al., 1986; Swanson, 1986) reflect a similarly functional perspective.

Checkland has introduced a different type of systemic images: 'purposeful holons known as "human activity systems" ' (Checkland and Scholes, 1990: 36). Here the model-ling language is based on *verbs* (describing activities), and 'the modelling process consists of assembling and structuring the minimum necessary activities to carry out the transforma-tion process...' The structuring of systemic image follows logical contingencies, specifying the logical sequence in which activities are to be performed to achieve optimum perfor-mance. The function of the whole is seen as 'doing the job well'. Different specifications may also be possible, according to the perspective or 'world-view' of different actors. The purpose of creating the images is to facilitate an accommodation among the perspectives stakeholders and to improve their collective performance. I will refer to this type of systemic images as *activity arrangements*. They are developed not to achieve a representa-tion of the real world but to construct meaningful arrangements that can be used to evaluate human practices. Activity arrangements have been fundamental to the develop-ment of the soft tradition in systems thinking. A number of the early knowledge systems images resembled activity arrangements more than input/output arrangements (see for example: Havelock, 1969; Nagel, 1980; Röling, 1988; Haverkort and Engel, 1990).

For the sake of studying social relationships among actors, I propose to distinguish a third type of systemic images: *actor arrangements*. The modelling language in actor arrangements is based on names, referring to individuals and/or collectivities within a

given domain of human activity. The modelling process consists of assembling actors and
their relationships that are relevant to the mission(s) attributed to the whole. The function
of the whole is seen as joining together individual competent performances to achieve a
joint performance. The purpose of building such images is to study and if possible improve the interactions that support joint performance. The structuring of actor arrangements can be based on a variety of theoretical perspectives regarding the relevance of
social interaction to innovation. For example, assuming integration affects performance,
one could study the frequency and importance of contacts between actors (Chapter 3); if,
on the other hand, we see coordination of tasks as an important indicator of successful
innovation, we may look at ways configurations of power and influence emerge among
actors (Chapter 4); or if mutual adjustments among actors are considered central to the
study, one may look at communication networks (Chapter 2). As will become apparent in
this book, the use of different images of this type allows us to strengthen the appreciative,
social-relationship-focused character of soft systems methodologies.

The knowledge and information systems perspective[3]

The knowledge and information systems (KIS) perspective has been constructed as a
diagnostic framework: it can be used to unearth the organizational forms that enable
and/or constrain knowledge processes such as generation, transformation and use of
knowledge and information. It focuses on organizations and/or persons, and the links and
interactions among them (Röling and Engel, 1990). The definition has evolved over the
years; a recent one is given by Röling (1992b):

> *The articulated set of actors, networks and/or organizations expected or managed
> to work synergically to support knowledge processes which improve the
> correspondence between knowledge and environment, and/or the control provided
> through technology use in a given domain of human activity.*

Since they are framed in a soft systems perspective, the boundaries of a system are not
given, but tied into its objective or function. They depend upon the perspective of the
analyst and are therefore bound to vary with the function or purpose this analyst has in
mind for the system. And as both 'correspondence' and 'control' may mean something
entirely different to each actor involved, a struggle over purposes, perspectives and
boundaries is implicit in this definition. For soft systems analysts, therefore, system
boundaries are arbitrary; in any situation a large number of different wholes could be
named. As a result, the definition above should not be taken as an ontological description
of what *is*, but rather as a verbal 'rich picture' (Checkland and Scholes, 1990: 45) of what
could evolve, if and when the social actors involved were to construct it in such a manner.

The explicit purpose of developing knowledge systems thinking is to develop a
diagnostic framework for analysis, design and management (Röling, 1992b). The knowledge systems perspective provides stakeholders with a useful approach to reviewing their
interactions in the light of stated objectives, to design more effective forms of
communication and cooperation; the aim is to help develop proposals for action in
practical situations. A KIS has a potential for synergy – bringing together actors so that they
achieve results that exceed what could have been expected from the sum of their
individual efforts. This is to be taken not so much as an inherent property of a KIS but as a
property that may emerge when certain conditions prevail: for example, when relevant

3. *This section draws on the first part of Engel, 1991.*

actors *decide* to work together as if they were one 'system'. The KIS perspective, in other words, serves the purpose of stimulating joint reflection and design of intervention. Explanations are left to the stakeholders, but the perspective helps draw attention to a number of salient issues. 'Purpose' rather than 'explanation' is emphasized. This seemed to make the KIS an appropriate heuristic perspective to use for inquiry into the social organization of innovation.

'Purpose' needs to be more clearly articulated PR?

The knowledge systems perspective has emerged as a result of a large number of 'formative experiences' (Röling, 1992b) of applied social scientists who have tried to come to grips with the complex phenomenon of facilitating innovation, primarily in agriculture. To guide inquiry in the search for relevant issues and propositions, the KIS perspective makes a number of assumptions and offers a number of useful perspectives; each of these includes a number of lessons from experience. I will briefly review these contributions in the light of this study, along with a number of critical issues.

Assumptions

The most central proposition of knowledge systems thinking is that, in effect, knowledge processes are *socially constructed*; because of this, actors may seek to influence if not manage them. Röling points to the emergence of such thinking in several parts of the world as that of '...an idea whose time had come' (Röling, 1992b: 48). However, this may well be the only similarity among the various schools of thought. Scholars focus on a variety of issues. Some (Lionberger and Chang, 1970) emphasize the 'science–practice continuum' as a continuum of interrelated knowledge processes, some the 'diffusion of innovations' (Rogers, 1983, 1986), others the development and utilization of technology (Kaimowitz et al., 1990; Swanson, 1986), still others the interaction of different relevant communities or subsystems (Nagel, 1980; Havelock, 1986; Röling, 1988). As a consequence, the knowledge systems perspective has already yielded a number of tools, each based upon a different theoretical conceptualization of knowledge processes and their articulation in practice. Röling (1990) for example describes 'one-way models', in which knowledge or technology is supposed to flow from research to farmers and not the other way around, and 'two-way models', which use the concept of feedback on needs and problems from technology users to research and other actors who control resources relevant to innovation. As he points out the first set of models, in which scientists develop products which extension has to sell, are the most common and influential.

Knowledge is socially constructed

A second proposition underlying the knowledge systems perspective is the understanding of communication as a form of social interaction. Knowledge, communication and information are intrinsically related, yet are distinguished for analytical purposes. People actively make sense out of their experiences in the world. They build theories that attribute causes to effects, and apply these to control the socio-natural environment for their purposes (Röling and Engel, 1990). *Knowledge* is taken very broadly to mean the concepts, ideas, insights and routines (including mental routines) people use to impute meaning to events and ideas. Knowledge is implicit in individual and social actions. *Information*, on the contrary, is taken as explicit. It is defined as a pattern imposed on a carrier such as sound, radio waves, paper, diskettes, electronic cables and so forth. A given set of people intend that other people will understand these patterns and attribute meaning to them. This may require these recipients to use skills they have acquired, such as listening, reading, interpreting computer data, and/or their use of specific artefacts, perhaps reading glasses or computer terminals. This creates what is referred to as the 'information paradox'. Although social actors who produce information generally do so to express a particular meaning, they are never sure whether the intended beneficiaries will attach that same

Communication, knowledge + info are intrinsically related

significance. One farmer listening to a radio programme promoting the use of agro-chemicals may hear a recommendation from a world that is better off, not as something meant for a farmer with no money; another might interpret it as propaganda for substances that will destabilize the environment; yet another may rush to the shop to buy the product. Finally, within the knowledge systems tradition, *communication* is generally the production, exchange and processing of information (including symbolic information) between two or more social actors (cf. Oomkes, 1986). This may lead to a shared understanding, but not necessarily. Communicative interaction is not uncommitted; each participant brings in his or her own world-view, interests, concerns and objectives. Therefore, communication is an inherent part of social strategizing. Chapter 7 returns in detail to the role knowledge and communication play in innovative performance. This will also imply making amendments to the visions expressed above, in which knowledge is a relatively static 'asset' of people and communication is merely a relationship between individuals.

A third central assumption in the knowledge systems perspective is that *innovation* is the desired outcome of a knowledge system (Röling, 1992b: 52). The link between knowledge, technology and innovation is generally assumed to be a direct one, yet this link is rarely probed in depth. Widespread use of knowledge, information or technology is often equated with innovation, which is seen as the result of a process of discovery, development and spread. The common denominator of the various schools of thought is the view that studying the social organization of innovation is important. Further, all have an *organizational focus*. Each defines a number of tasks to be completed and coordinated to accomplish innovation. Each school however defines such tasks in a more or less different manner, depending upon whether technology, knowledge or information is taken as the main resource to be used in achieving innovation. From there, conceptualizations and inquiries move in entirely different directions. Given the intentions of each of the schools to contribute to the design of more adequate forms of organization for innovation, as I will demonstrate later, these differences have great consequences. For the moment it seems sufficient to point out that the major difference resides in the way 'knowledge processes' are defined. This will be further illustrated later, when I address the ways 'functional differentiation' can be viewed from a knowledge systems perspective. Since the late 1980s, what has set the 'Wageningen school' of knowledge systems thinking apart is first its emphasis on the soft, appreciative character of the social organization of innovation; second, its emphasis on qualitative research; and third, its commitment to social learning and social construction of new forms of organization for innovation among stakeholders. The first point leads to an inclusive and heuristic, rather than mutually exclusive, descriptive definition of tasks to be fulfilled by actors in a knowledge 'system': this leads to the definition of 'systemic images' and 'windows' rather than 'models'. The second point follows on from this; it favours the development of new, useful perspectives to generate reflection and debate, rather than a comprehensive explanatory theory growing out of scientific research. The third point results in systematic attention to actor participation in design and implementation, to anticipation and accommodation among social actors, and to innovation as a social process.

Theory base Wageni

Useful perspectives

Research on knowledge and information systems has incorporated and/or developed a number of analytical perspectives that are relevant to a study of the social organization of innovation.

Focusing on intentionality, context and performance

This perspective helps analysts to study the intentions upon which social actors' innovation strategies are based, or to explore a lack (or apparent lack) of such intentions. It assumes that, in general terms, the purpose of an agricultural KIS (AKIS) is to facilitate continuous innovation in agriculture-related practices. An effective AKIS therefore makes available all of the intermediate outputs – such as technologies, software, expert systems, trained professionals and information – necessary to develop the practices deemed relevant to agricultural development. Even when such broad intentionality is recognized, the specific *mission* of an AKIS will be a subject of ongoing debate among stakeholders. Each stakeholder or group of stakeholders may entertain a quite different view of the tasks to be accomplished. As a result, each may also have a different definition of intermediate outputs.

An example from the Dutch horse husbandry sector illustrates this point. Those engaged in exporting Dutch horses may breed for a fierce, independent character – an important criterion in top quality horses that compete in international races. Those who envisage the horse sector in the Netherlands as primarily an important recreational sector, serving hundreds of thousands of often inexperienced riders, may on the contrary seek a rather quiet, adaptable character. Consequently, each has a different preferred definition of what the 'state of the art' in Dutch horse breeding is all about (Engel et al., 1990).

The evaluation of AKIS *performance* must, therefore, take this diversity into account. A first question is how many fundamentally different views there are among stakeholders as to the mission of the whole, and what this means for a definition of the 'state of the art' with respect to intermediate or later outputs. The next questions are whether the AKIS effectively produces these outputs, yielding agricultural knowledge and information to support each of these views; whether it does so efficiently; and finally whether the type of agricultural innovation that emerges as a result is adequate with respect to each of the missions defined by the stakeholders.

As I have shown, the first and last questions are particularly complicated. A determination of the type of innovation desired and the direction of change it implies is generally the outcome of a political process: it is seldom the responsibility of the actors in the AKIS alone. Whereas formerly the yardstick was on-farm productivity alone, societal objectives – clean drinking water, food security, fresh air, healthy forests, rural employment – play increasingly important roles; the political, administrative, technical and economical context also plays an important role. The success of an AKIS is of course strongly mediated by the effects of international and national agricultural trade and price policies, rules and regulations, and environmental, communication, educational and research policies, available resources and so forth. All of these can represent incentives or, on the contrary, impediments to achieving the type of innovation required. As a result, *multi-intentionality*, different or even conflicting views on the type of development to be pursued, is common.

When more than one set of circumstances is included, multi-intentionality increases. For example, while Dutch vegetable farmers, due to environmental considerations, have come to use substrate as a substitute for soil in their greenhouses – and as a consequence see 'substrate use' as the state of the art in vegetable production – Israeli farmers feel no need to revert to 'artificial soil'; for them, competent performance dictates the use of relatively neutral desert soil types, with efficient irrigation systems (Ravensbergen, 1991). The animated discussions regarding sustainable agricultural development, and the many points of view as to what this term means, are another case in point.

Focusing on functional specialization

AKIS actors are many: farmers' organizations, cooperatives, specialized services, and groups or study clubs; agro-based industries; public and private research, extension, and training institutions; agricultural press and information services; agricultural policy units; and formal and informal networks of many kinds. More recently, environmental and consumer groups are claiming increasingly important roles. One way to investigate the social organization of innovation in agriculture is to look into the division of labour among its stakeholders. How are tasks defined? Who does what? Social actors, alone or together, occupy a 'niche' in the agricultural innovation theatre and develop their own comparative advantages. As a result, these performances evolve over time into practices in their own right, involved in particular socio-natural processes and adhering to formal and informal standards of competent performance.

The division of labour among social actors in complex innovation theatres cannot be studied in practice without further specifying what we mean by 'knowledge processes'. Many characterizations have been proposed. Some take knowledge, some innovation and some technology as the 'active ingredient'. Engel and Röling (1991) suggest looking at anticipation, generation, transformation, transmission, storage, retrieval, integration, diffusion and utilization of knowledge. Nagel (1980) distinguishes identification of needs, generation of innovations, operationalization for utilization, dissemination, utilization and evaluation of experiences, while Swanson (1986) mentions technology development, transfer and utilization (cited by Röling, 1988: 203). Havelock (1986) talks of generation, exchange and utilization; Kaimowitz et al. (1990) suggest technology production, delivery, monitoring and evaluation. At the same time the journal *Knowledge* sees the creation, diffusion and utilization of knowledge as the main functions. As a result, to define a perspective on the functional specialization among social actors in agricultural innovation theatres, the researcher will have to make a choice, aware that each choice reflects a *specific model* for thinking about the process of achieving innovation in agriculture, and as a result, has particular implications for the analysis to come.

Drawing attention to integration with resource linkages

Evidence suggests that an effective AKIS exhibits high levels of integration, with strong links among core actors (see also Chapter 4). For innovation in businesses Moss Kanter (1983) and Wissema and Euser (1988) stress the importance of cooperation and integration of efforts. Specific organizational procedures that establish, maintain or improve integration are called linkage mechanisms (Kaimowitz et al., 1990). In more complex wholes, linkage mechanisms become more sophisticated and diverse. Further, a degree of redundancy in both formal and informal linkage mechanisms is sometimes reported as having a positive impact on integration (Grooters, 1990).

An integration perspective is based on an assumption that, in particular situations, improving linkages among social actors relevant to particular types of innovation can lead to improved performance. For any particular situation, the types of resource linkages seen as most relevant to innovation must be defined; one could focus on communicative, collaborative, administrative and/or financial linkages, or instead on formal versus informal links (Kaimowitz et al., 1990).

However, this can also lead to hegomony. Must relate to poor.

Segmentation refers to a process by which certain categories of actors establish strong linkages due to common elements in their situations (such as being financed by the same agency), shared concerns (perhaps similar lines of products or services) or a common strategy (such as the promotion of ecological agriculture). Other actors may then target their services and support to a category, rather than to separate actors. Currently, 'product chain' integration is developing rapidly in the Netherlands; one may argue that these chains, rather than functional specialization among practitioners, will become the dominant pattern along which 'practices' will be organized in the near future. Chain linking emphasizes shared interests and concerns related to primary production and sales more than innovation. In a way, it reflects 'vertical integration' rather than the 'horizontal integration' found in knowledge networks. As the Dutch horse sector (Engel et al., 1990) study suggests, segmentation may be seen as positive by some social actors, while others experience it as a serious impairment to innovation and sector integration. Other types of segmentation may be present when social actors decide to link up their efforts related to a particularly vulnerable agroecological zone or culturally homogeneous group.

Zooming in on actors, strategies and constraints

The multiple character of an AKIS is invigorated by the relative autonomy that generally characterizes social actors in innovation theatres. Each acts according to an individual strategy and operational agenda. They use their own resources, intellectual and otherwise, to achieve their own long and short term objectives. AKIS performance, therefore, must be seen as an outcome based on the views and actions of many, not necessarily cooperating, social actors. *Agency* is therefore a centrally important notion. Actors in theatres of agricultural innovation '...are capable (even within severely restricted social space) of formulating decisions, acting upon them, and innovating or experimenting' (Long, 1992: 24–25, referring to Giddens). Actors may be individuals or collectivities organized in such a way as to be able to formulate and carry out decisions (Long, 1992: 23, citing Hindess, 1986: 115), or at the very least, able to effectively influence decisions made by other actors. Actors define their own groupings; social categories that have no visible structure except in the eyes of the researcher obviously cannot be taken as actors. The approach that characterizes this book is to attribute to social actors the capacity to strategize, recognizing at the same time that enabling and/or constraining conditions will arise, due to emergent social forms. Thus we postulate a degree of autonomy as well as certain limits on the free-dom of social actors. Koestler (1968) describes the tension between individual autonomy and the constraints imposed from a systems perspective: '... the canon represents the codes of conduct ... the "rules of the game".... But these constraints do not exhaust the system's degrees of freedom; they leave room for more or less *flexible strategies*...' Moreover, from our point of view such constraints are to a large degree appreciative. The actor actively participates in contextualizing, interpreting or even creating them.

Government, private or non-governmental organizations can, in our view, also be studied as social actors. Institutionalization provides stability to such social subassemblies. The same two-sidedness holds here: the idea that social actors actively abide by some rules while working to modify others seems a fruitful heuristic device to use in studying human and organizational behaviour. Koestler (1968) describes this as the polarity between a self-assertive and an integrative tendency in the behaviour of a 'system' component. Similarly, each actor can be thought of as trying to assert uniqueness, while maintaining a certain level of integration within the higher level whole. This is important because the actor generally derives at least part of its identity, power and 'room for manoeuvre' from the latter. Maturana and Varela (1986: 77) refer to the operational independence of a component within a *structural coupling*. This results in mutual interdependence among social actors in complex innovation theatres, a situation which is not always recognized by those involved (Kaimowitz et al., 1990; Woodhill and Röling, 1993). This has led research-ers to emphasize *perceived* interdependence in their inquiries.

Defining a perspective on actors and their strategies requires, first, the selection of relevant actors. Such a selection will necessarily be based on a partial view of the theatre. Therefore, those who have a different view – and, accordingly, define their boundaries

THE SOCIAL ORGANIZATION OF INNOVATION

differently – may dispute the selection. A partial view does not necessarily mean a partisan view, although some stakeholders might interpret it as such. Holding the selection up for discussion among stakeholders can help to produce an inclusive list of social actors which, in the view of the various parties involved, at least does not exclude crucial members of each of the relevant factions. Following this, both formal mandates and informal strategies can be studied. In addition, the views and interpretations of the actors themselves regarding their mutual interdependence (or alleged interdependence), and the opportunities and constraints they see with respect to innovation in their current practices, can provide extremely relevant insights that will stimulate reflection and debate.

Knowledge networks

To successfully make available 'state of the art' knowledge and information among its actors, a continuous circulation of intermediate outputs must occur within the AKIS. This 'alternating current' leads to chains of product transformations, in which each actor transforms what he/she receives into suitable new forms, anticipating the demands of his/her particular clientele. The circulation itself may be based on informal transactions, barter (such as trading industrial know-how – Carter, 1989), or sales (for example, software, patents, licensing, consultancy), or may involve the regulation of channelling (e.g. pre-competitive cooperation, project groups, meetings). An increasing amount of evidence suggests that networks of individuals play pivotal roles in maintaining the flow of finished or partially completed knowledge products and sustaining innovation (see for example Carter, 1989; Wissema and Euser, 1988). Field research in the Netherlands and Colombia corroborates the importance of both formal and informal networks (Grooters, 1990; Engel, 1993). The evidence shows that successful networks such as Dutch horticultural study clubs exhibit high degrees of member control.

I take knowledge networks to be the more or less formalized, relatively stable pattern of communication and interaction among social actors who share a common concern (cf. Box, 1989: 76). Such patterns emerge as a result of relation-building efforts among actors. Studies of knowledge networks focus on the generation, sharing and use of knowledge and information among network members. These networks may be found within organizations or across organizations and institutions. The rules governing knowledge sharing and information exchange in networks are only partially known, and the ways these rules differ from those of commodity barter have yet to be explored in depth. It is clear that trading informal know-how 'is a robust institution that is well adapted to the special requirements of informational exchange' (Carter, 1989). Reciprocity is often stressed as a critical success factor in information bartering. Rogers and Kincaid (1981) emphasize the 'strength of weak ties'. Most participants in effective knowledge networks share a common rationality, that is, their knowledge bases are similar enough that interpreting each others' information is easy and fast. In addition, informal networks are generally embedded in long-standing social relationships; mutual understanding and trust are essential, to facilitate sharing knowledge and information. Networks may be spontaneous and totally informal, or designed to serve a specific purpose.

Since all actors are active, knowing subjects with respect to their own practices, they are at the same time both sources and users of knowledge and information on agriculture. A basic assumption behind networking activities is that each participant holds certain clues to understanding and solving the 'farming puzzle'. Farmers no longer rely solely upon their own practical knowhow, experience and research-based technical knowledge. As practitioners, they actively engage in communication with others to acquire relevant knowledge and information. Marketing knowledge and information from cooperative auctions or advisory services play increasingly important roles. Also, policy-related

[handwritten margin notes: Importance of relation-building; Reciprocity; Long-standing social rlsps; Mutual undtg + trust; Common rationality; Assumption: each participant holds a piece of the puzzle]

knowledge and information produced by national or international policy bodies increasingly determines farm results. Similar comments can be made about researchers, extension workers and other actors in complex theatres of agricultural innovation. For example, research suggests that exposure to and integration of many different types of knowledge and information – through active involvement in a number of different networks, plus ample availability of information of all sorts – are crucial to an extension worker's effectiveness in modern agriculture (Engel, 1989).

The knowledge network perspective enables us to focus on specific concerns or types of knowledge (including marketing, farm management, bookkeeping, soil preparation, feeding, but also sustainability, soil erosion, cost reduction, automation, nutrient management and so forth), and to trace the way relevant actors acquire, share and use knowledge and information related to these concerns. Empirical research can be directed either at revealing the priority concerns of different sets of actors, or at tracing the communication practices they use to share knowledge, information, ideas and experiences.

Selah

Understanding the coordination of tasks among actors.

Agricultural innovation has come to depend increasingly upon the combined activities of multiple actors, such as farmers, farmer networks, governmental and non-governmental organizations, agro-based industries and formal and informal markets. As Mintzberg puts it,

> ... *every organized human activity – from making pots to the placing of a man on the moon – gives rise to two fundamental and opposing requirements: the division of labour into various tasks to be performed, and the coordination of these tasks to accomplish the activity (Mintzberg, 1983: 2).*

This perspective focuses on how such coordination is achieved, if at all, among actors in complex innovation theatres. But the social organization of innovation involves many actors, multiple interests and multi-faceted interactions. What seems right in the eyes of one may seem wrong to another. In fact, from an outsider's point of view, activities carried out by innovating actors often seem contradictory or even chaotic. Social actors pursue their own strategic objectives, with much autonomy. Each has a different knowledge base and responds to a distinct set of opportunities. Coordination in such theatres is not a simple question of imposing control in the traditional, top-down sense of the word. Recognizing the diffuse, mostly self-guiding nature of innovation processes, we should be particularly interested in the self-regulative capacities of social wholes. Coordination, therefore, refers to the occurrence – by either design or default – of sophisticated *coordinating mechanisms* that help enable or, on the contrary, impair the ability of social actors to adequately perform as parts of a whole. Just how much 'room for manoeuvre' each individual actor needs may be one of the most challenging questions for managers of innovation processes in complex agricultural theatres.

Mintzberg (1983) has developed an important line of thought related to coordination. He analyses the ways coordination of tasks can be achieved in organizations, and sums up (1983: 151–155) the possibilities. Depending on which components of the organization most effectively 'pull their own weight', and taking into account external factors, a particular coordinating mechanism can be expected to prevail. The first and most hierarchical (in a bureaucratic sense) of the coordinating mechanisms Mintzberg identifies is *direct supervision*. A boss supervises staff, instructs them and checks their output. This mechanism is found for example in an organization with short lines of command, in which top management is directly involved in all or most important decisions; all control rests directly with the top. Coordination can also be achieved through *standardization*, for

NDP can be seen as a coordinating mechanism

So can my systemic image?

which Mintzberg identifies three sorts: standardization of *outputs, skills and/or work processes*. Different types of actors value different types. Standardization of outputs is generally preferred by middle managers who want to run 'their own shop'. This leads to the formation of separate divisions within an organization, each responsible for developing and marketing specific products and/or services. When the operating core or 'field' staff of an organization are responsible for coordination, standardization of knowledge and skills is required. Each employee has learned how to do the job; no one needs to instruct them. Standardization of work processes on the other hand gives the responsibility for coordination to specialists, who design technical and administrative standards and procedures. Others must comply with the rules and regulations applicable to their role in the organization. The organization is designed to regulate work processes to the highest possible degree; this eliminates uncertainties so it can run smoothly, like a well-oiled machine. A fifth mechanism identified by Mintzberg is *mutual adjustment*. Administrative and other support staff often favour such arrangements; it gives them power to directly influence operations by making *ad hoc* decisions. Until recently, Mintzberg claims, such adjustments were largely left to chance. 'But in recent years, *organizations have developed a whole set of devices to encourage liaison contacts between individuals,* devices that can be incorporated into the formal structure. In fact, these *liaison devices* represent the most significant contemporary development in organization design – indeed, the only serious one since the establishment of planning and control systems a decade or two earlier' (Mintzberg, 1983: 82). At the end of his book, almost as an afterthought, Mintzberg (1983: 293) looks beyond the five mechanisms identified to standardization of *norms*: a sixth coordinating mechanism, leading to coordination by means of a shared ideology.

The predominant influence of one set of key actors within the organization, endorsing its own favourite prime coordinating mechanism, leads an organization to take on a particular structural shape; or, as Mintzberg puts it, a *basic configuration*. Each basic configuration is characterized by a particular type of actors who exert leadership, and by the key coordinating mechanisms they use to impose or facilitate coordination. Most organizations, however, experience different 'pulls' simultaneously. This is only natural, as most organizations include top managers, middle managers, specialists, support and operating staff. The configuration observed therefore reflects the degree to which each set of actors can assert its claims within the organization. Those who are successful may see their favourite coordination mechanisms gain momentum and contribute to shaping the organization.

   Another line of explanations to be included in my argument singles out incentives. Sims and Leonard (1989) suggest four possible parties who are capable of establishing positive incentives for competent performance in an AKIS: national policymakers, farmer organizations, agro-industry and financial donors. The strong influence of agricultural producers on the Dutch AKIS is well known. In Europe, there may be other parties who potentially influence the AKIS: the European Union (EU), environmentalist and consumer groups. In Chapter 4, I will combine the two lines of argument of Mintzberg and Sims and Leonard to explore how coordination is achieved in agricultural innovation. Hopefully, this will allow us to open a window on leadership and the use of power and influence in complex innovation theatres.

An eye on knowledge management[4]
Using the AKIS perspective to look systematically at the social organization of innovation may allow us to define a useful approach to knowledge management in complex theatres

4. *This section makes use of Engel, 1991.*

of agricultural innovation. I have identified the multiplicity of actors and perspectives, diversity in types of knowledge and information, and a considerable degree of randomness as inherent qualities of the diffuse and largely self-guiding social process called innovation. What is more, such complexity may be a prerequisite for the ability of a particular AKIS to quickly adapt to changing circumstances. Multiple wholes that are capable of handling knowledge and information of diverse types and sources are potentially well equipped to make rapid adjustments to unexpected changes in demands and circumstances. Further, they relate naturally to a multi-functional, sustainable agriculture that does not solely stress the value of productivity, but also societal values of a less quantifiable nature, such as those named earlier – clean drinking water, fresh air and so forth.

Under such circumstances, can anything be 'managed'? I have shown how views of what an AKIS is meant to accomplish and what type of agricultural development is desirable may differ greatly among social actors. Declared missions may be contradictory and sometimes lead to open conflict, as is the case at times for the objectives of the environmental vis-à-vis agricultural lobbies in the Netherlands. In such cases, each relevant actor has its managers and strategists. Certain segments or functional units may show some degree of unified management. But that does not, generally, hold true for the whole: there it is generally not possible to identify one single management unit, nor any central manager. The multiplicity of social actors in innovation theatres is reflected in the involvement of a large variety of managers and management styles, which affects probing for innovation. In such a situation, the task of the knowledge manager can never be straightforwardly oriented to objectives. Typically it is not only the means that are in dispute; it is the ends as well. And different lobbies defend different interests. Desirable long-term developments for the agricultural sector are decided politically. The contribution of managers at various levels may then be to facilitate the *process of inquiry* into relevant objectives, options and conditions; and to tend to the design and implementation of effective *cooperation and communication strategies* aimed at improving the quality of inquiry and the transparency of its outcomes. Wissema and Euser (1988) speak of creating 'win–win situations' as a condition for successful cooperation in industrial innovation. Moss Kanter (1983) argues that without specific incentives and management support, the organization is apt to leap into 'default', where ideas and initiatives are suffocated and innovativeness is stifled. I suggest there is a need for facilitation related to innovation and social learning, aimed at integrating individual efforts to achieve a joint innovative performance; such facilitation efforts will be labelled *knowledge management*.

Facilitating innovation at different levels of analysis

Knowledge management tasks will need to be performed by many different individuals at a number of levels. At least four can be distinguished: individual, network, organization and the theatre as a whole. First, at the level of the individual, farmers, extension workers and researchers can be considered knowledge managers avant la lettre. Farmers are not recipients and reproducers, but creative managers and integrators of knowledge and information from a large number of sources including practical experience – their own and that of friends and colleagues. Farm-related communication patterns reflect diversity (Schiefer, 1991), and in the process different groups of farmers develop significantly different management styles (Bolhuis and van der Ploeg, 1985). Extension staff create and work to maintain a surprising degree of autonomy in handling knowledge and information, standing firm against centralist tendencies to standardize their behaviour and messages (Wagemans, 1987; Engel, 1989). The use of knowledge and information by individual farmers and extension workers will be addressed with the help of two case studies in Chapter 2.

Second, one may look at knowledge management in networks of social actors, at how different types of knowledge are shared and integrated among practices (or fail to become connected) and how actors create joint performances. We can also look for ways that information is stored and retrieved among members of a network, and at other tangible activities of network members. We may ask ourselves when and why social actors decide to invest in networking, and look at the dynamics of networking or at its sustainability over time. A number of recent studies have pioneered this line of research. Box (1989, 1990) studied knowledge networks in the Atlantic Zone of Costa Rica; Plucknett et al. (1990), networking in international agricultural research; Nelson and Farrington (forthcoming) compiled experiences with respect to information exchange networking for agricultural development; and Alders et al. (1993) compiled worldwide experience in networking for low external input and sustainable agriculture. My contribution to this last book forms the basis for Chapter 5.

Third, one may focus on knowledge management within an organization or institution. This might include:
- monitoring and evaluation of the circulation of essential knowledge products or half products;
- development of shared language and culture used in probing for knowledge and information;
- appraisal and adjustment of internal communications and coordinating mechanisms related to probing innovations;
- mapping, organizing and management of organizational learning, including the development and use of a company thesaurus, reporting and debriefing procedures, in-service training programmes, study groups, expert consultations, information systems and other instruments;
- stimulating the formation of knowledge networks or task forces on strategic issues, filling expected or unexpected gaps in the organization knowledge base;
- appraisal and, if necessary, modification of incentive structures;
- allocation of resources to alleviate constraints on probing behaviour;
- externally, a knowledge manager is concerned with the management of interfaces between her/his own organization and the external sources and users of relevant knowledge and information.

The management of knowledge and information within organizations falls outside the scope of this book (in this area, see for example Jorna and Simons, 1992). 'Learning organizations' have received considerable attention; see e.g. Senge, 1990; Argyris, 1992; Swieringa and Wierdsma, 1992.

Finally, one may consider the orchestration of the AKIS as a whole. At this level facilitation would aim at strengthening overall AKIS performance. Unified management is usually impossible. Instead, the objective is to use cooperation, communication and networking efforts to create added value. From the literature, I can suggest that the following areas merit particular attention (see also Röling, 1989; Verkaik and Dijkveld Stol, 1989):
- developing a shared culture, policy and purpose;
- developing and maintaining a shared language and thesaurus, to facilitate exchanges of experiences and information;
- avoiding reverse incentives, such as unspannable social distances between actors, which would block both formal and informal communication;
- enhancing links and institutional articulations at strategic interfaces;
- enhancing the use of informal networks, for example with the support of electronic media;

- linking and/or integrating existing computer-based information systems within the AKIS;
- monitoring and enhancing strategic cooperation among key actors;
- segmenting the area of concern into useful knowledge domains, centred on traditional and non-traditional user groups;
- enhancing user control through political, market or technical coordinating mechanisms;
- strengthening the responsiveness of the whole to societal objectives, environmental influences and market opportunities;
- avoiding isolation of the collectivity from external sources of knowledge and information, or from non-traditional target groups;
- seeking strategic investments in physical infrastructure, human resources and programmes, and financial flexibility in funding;
- identifying key segments of the whole, and using this to balance resource allocations in accordance with performance requirements; and
- developing AKIS management information systems including consideration of their design, operation, potential and limitations.

Main criticisms

Criticisms of the KIS perspective have been sustained and frequent. The latest overview has been given by Leeuwis (1993). Earlier versions have been presented by Leeuwis, Long and Villareal (1991). The main points include:

- This perspective does not consider the role of human agency and power in forging innovations (Leeuwis, Villareal, Long, 1991; Leeuwis, 1993). This criticism has been taken very seriously. As a result, the KIS perspective has been enriched with specific conceptualizations that make it useful in studying issues of agency, power and influence. Nevertheless, handling power issues within a soft systems perspective can be problematical. Interventions are necessarily tied into power structures, which soft systems methodologies will have to find ways to deal with. In this study I will attempt to facilitate this by, first, developing some conceptual tools for studying leadership, power and influence in practical situations (Chapters 3, 4 and 6) and second, developing an approach to design that helps take power issues – insofar as these seem pertinent to designing adequate interventions in particular innovation theatres – into account, rather than obscuring them (Chapters 7, 8).

- The use of the KIS perspective as a 'practical tool' as opposed to its supposed aspiration to offer an explanatory theory creates tension (or confusion) (Leeuwis, 1993: 55). The KIS perspective provides no adequate theory to explain agricultural innovation (Leeuwis, Long and Villareal, 1991). In my view, this is not so much a criticism as a statement of fact. As a soft systems perspective, KIS 'theorizing' should have left behind long ago any pretension to offering general explanations of what is observed in practice. The much criticized 'KIS disorders' (Röling, 1989), 'common threats' (Blum, 1990) and supposedly 'normative statements' (Röling and Engel, 1990) are no more and no less than lessons from experience. They are articulated by practitioners, and are meant to be used to frame questions for discussion among stakeholders – not as explanations. In soft systems methodologies, the explaining is to be left to the social actors themselves; they are considered 'knowledgeable and capable' enough to generate explanations relevant to their own situation. The lessons of experience thus represent the contours of an 'epistemology'; they do not even come close to pretending to be an 'ontological' description of what happens in the social world. Instead of faulting KIS as a perspective,

(handwritten margin note:) for my R, power issues looked at by studying the M&E frameworks of CB initiatives & also the focus & application of 'emancipatory' activities

this particular criticism in fact points to the ever growing need to develop a more ontological understanding of the social organization of innovation.

- The KIS perspective overemphasizes formal institutions and relationships at the expense of informal ones (Grooters, 1990). In fact, early attempts to formulate the 'knowledge systems perspective' in particular suffered from a pro-institutional bias. 'Agricultural knowledge system' was defined as a broader term, yet empirical studies often focused primarily on institutional mandates, functions and interactions. Informal links were often subsumed within discussions of formal interactions. Research by Pijnenburg (1988), Box et al. (1989, 1990), Grooters (1990), van Dijk, Leeuwis and Engel (1991), Rap (1992), Stolzenbach (1992), Obate (1992) and Millar (1992), however, has contributed significantly to our ability to see formal links in perspective. Further, this study hopes to contribute to the creation of new and useful perspectives for analysing the role of informal links in innovation processes.

- The definitions of knowledge and information used in knowledge systems thinking are problematic. Leeuwis (1993) criticizes the ambiguity of the information concept used. While Röling and Engel (1990) accept the paradoxical nature of information – it is present in matter/energy, and yet different people may attribute different meanings to it – Leeuwis (1993: 56) seems to insist on solving this contradiction by denying the usefulness of distinguishing between knowledge, the 'real world' and information. Leeuwis' argument focuses on two key issues: does information as matter/energy have a meaningful existence of its own, and can we assign objective qualities to information? Second, can a sharp distinction be made between 'knowledge' and the 'real world'? From the point of view of a scientist looking for mutually exclusive categories on which to build an unambiguous theory about what happens in the world, of course not. Yet, from the point of view of one who intends to engage in meaningful discourse about what we *perceive* as happening in the world, a different question must be asked: is it useful to make a distinction between the three? Then the answer is – yes! It is useful to create a distinction between our perceptions of the world and the 'real stuff', implying we accept our own arbitrariness and partiality with respect to understanding what is going on. From a soft systems perspective, this distinction implies nothing more and nothing less than a creative paradox, which can stimulate discussion and debate. From this practical point of view, we agree with Leeuwis (1993: 56) that '...information has no meaning if it cannot be internalized, and by being internalized, it becomes part of a stock of knowledge'. But then our ways part: by attributing meaning to what I read in my newspaper and internalizing it, the paper does not cease to exist, even if only as a sorrowful remnant of an erstwhile proud pine forest.

- In his third and most important critique, Leeuwis (1993) puts his finger on an important weakness: in early versions of knowledge systems thinking the individual–cognitive dimensions of knowledge and communication were much emphasized, to the detriment of social, intersubjective and practical (i.e. practice-oriented) dimensions. Over-reliance on cognitive psychology and information theory led to conceptualizing human beings primarily as information processors. The following chapters demonstrate the possibility of developing a more sophisticated conceptualization, based on an understanding of 'knowing' rather than 'knowledge', 'competent performance' rather than 'the use of new technologies' and 'communicative interaction' rather than communication as the 'transfer of messages between senders and receivers'. This brings the social dimensions of the knowledge processes we study within reach. I am afraid, however, that it still may not eliminate all remnants of what Leeuwis (1993) calls the '...optimistic 'enlightenment' thinking that characterized the early days of extension and extension science'. Even the most relativist of facilitators, if they are to intervene, must feel that even if not perceivable at present, somewhere at the end of the tunnel some light must shine.

Developing a soft knowledge systems perspective

What I intend to do in this book is to develop the knowledge systems perspective further: to integrate this perspective with soft systems methodology, creating a soft knowledge systems approach that will enable stakeholders to diagnose and strengthen the ways they organize themselves for innovation. The *design path* is intended to yield this result. While travelling this path, we will not be primarily concerned with developing one particular explanation for everything we observe. Instead, we will focus on agriculture as a domain of inquiry and evaluate a variety of 'windows' that can facilitate a closer look at pertinent issues. The most important purpose is to suggest ways to improve innovation-related action among stakeholders in practical situations. The methodology sought is one that will encourage relevant social actors to consider working *together* rather than against each other, as one important way to increase the potential for sustainable development. Therefore, as Leeuwis et al. (1991: 24) have rightfully observed, we maintain that, in a process of designing interventions and assuring they will be worthwhile, it is useful to promote the idea of a shared mission or common purpose. What this mission is, to what degree it is shared by the relevant actors – and who these 'relevant' actors are – is to be determined along the way by those actors who consider themselves stakeholders.

Purpose

Further, the emphasis will be on individuals and/or organizations concerned with regional or sectoral agricultural development. I will not specifically address the facilitation of innovation processes within organizations, nor focus on the overall orchestration of nationwide or international AKISs. However, these chapters show that what makes a knowledge and information system successful as a whole are the patterns of relationships that result from individual and organizational interactions: these are the sustenance of the social organization of innovation. It follows that much of what may come out of this research may later be found to be relevant not only to the level of individual and organizational networking, but also within organizations or knowledge systems.

Finally, building blocks for an overall perspective on the social organization of innovation will also be sought and developed. This is the purpose of the *exploratory path*. A stroll along this path can help in achieving a more comprehensive understanding of the social organization of innovation and the issues involved in improving it. It has also helped the developers of the RAAKS methodology detailed in *Networking for innovation* in creating additional windows to support analysis and intervention.

2. Communication for innovation in Dutch agriculture

The case studies in this chapter focus on individual persons: natural actors who, as part of their daily activities, communicate with other actors to acquire new ideas and/or knowledge. We look at the practical use of knowledge and information in specific situations. The focus is on two categories of social actors who are relevant to most theatres of agricultural innovation: farmers and farm advisors. Their communication related to innovation takes place in the context of daily work. Therefore, in each case, their daily practice is the starting point for our research.

This chapter shows that – if our aim is to understand the processes involved in communication for innovation – we must look beyond the notion of 'transfer of knowledge'. Even when in the context of an extension service, this leads to gross oversimplification. Rather, communication takes place in multiple and diverse networks, in which all participants are both 'source' and 'user' of knowledge and information.[1] As the case studies show, communication networks are the more or less formalized, more or less stable patterns that emerge as a result of social actors' purposive efforts to communicate with each other in order to generate and share knowledge, ideas and experiences. Such networks are typically 'value-added' ones: each participant contributes his or her part to the process. In the cases, both farm advisers and farmers are found to behave as professional knowledge and information managers *avant-la-lettre*.

The chapter is organized as follows. First, we look at the use of knowledge and information by farm advisers (see 'Case A: the use of agricultural knowledge …'). Second, we take the farmers' perspective (see 'Case B: the agricultural communication network …'): how does the farmer go about gathering the knowledge and information he or she needs to take important decisions? This permits us to trace existing communication networks from two radically different perspectives. Both cases are situated in a mixed farming area in the province of North Brabant in the south of the Netherlands.

Case A: The use of agricultural knowledge and information by farm advisers

This example comes from what at the time was called the Government Extension Service, in Tilburg, North Brabant, in the south of the Netherlands. This is primarily a mixed farming area, with a strong dedication to intensive animal husbandry. To study the use of knowledge and information by farm advisers, in close consultation with key informants, I selected one topic, which is locally very important: the on-farm, outdoor storage of animal manure. That is, the temporary storage of animal manure in an outside tank or silo on the farm premises. Storage of manure is of great importance in the Netherlands because of its environmental implications. In the years 1986–1988 it was one of the main topics for the government advisory service. In 1988, though no longer the hottest topic of the day, it represented an issue of such importance that all extension advisers had to cope with it

---

1. Here we extend a line of argument laid out by Rogers and Kincaid (1981), who were among the first to address the issue of communication networks for agricultural innovation.

many times during their careers.

Information was collected through in-depth interviews with five randomly selected advisers, out of a total of 17 who covered the area. In addition, one extension unit head, himself a farm economics specialist, and the two relevant subject-matter specialists were interviewed. The interviews focused on the advisory cycle, starting with a request from the farmer and ending with an 'advice' from the adviser; they brought out the use of knowledge and information during this cycle. In the following paragraphs I will first look at the use of documentary information. After that, I will analyse the advisory cycle itself, including the types of knowledge and information used to complete it successfully.

Actual use of documentary information: the information portfolio

As part of their interview, I asked advisers to provide me with a set of the documents they wanted to have at hand when requested to advise a farmer on 'on-farm, outside storage of animal manure'. I was interested in what written documentary information the advisers actually carried with them when going to meet a farmer who wanted advice on this topic. From experience, I knew advisers were showered with documentary information of all kinds, much of which ended up on a shelf back home, if not in the wastebasket. Therefore I was not very interested in the total amount of information an adviser might have at his or her disposal. I wanted to focus on information that was *actively used*. I labelled this 'the information portfolio,' as advisers took it along on farm visits. The results are summarized in Figure 1 and Table 2.

In Table 2, the first thing that catches the eye is the diversity and broad coverage among the individual information portfolios. The figure illustrates this too. On this one topic alone, a total of 109 documents were collected from the five advisers. *No* documents were found which all of the advisers kept close at hand, and only two appeared in four of the five portfolios studied. Of the considerable amount of documentary information received from industry, farmer organizations, farm journals and newspapers that are represented in the individual portfolios, only very few are kept handy by more than one adviser in the sample. Another telling detail was the fact that, of all the official documents provided on the topic by the agency's subject-matter specialists, very few were actually carried along in the portfolio, even though a considerable number were explicitly intended to be taken along on farm visits. It appears that advisers search out and value such information in a very personal, individual way.

The availability in the portfolios of policy and technical information derived from the government or from specialists or research sources was more standardized – but not as much as one might have expected! Of the 13 documents kept at hand by at least three of the five advisers interviewed (see Table 2), 11 are from such sources. With little exaggeration, these 13 could be called the standard portfolio. However, these 13 represent only 12% of the total number of documentary pieces of information on this topic carried by these five advisers!

What provokes such diversity in the use of information? The study came up with at least three plausible lines of explanation. First, individual adaptation of the portfolio occurs as a result of an adviser's *own appreciation* and priorization of the problems that most affect producers in his or her district. Problems these farmers are currently wrestling with will be studied more carefully by the advisor in searching for and reviewing information, to develop a strong 'offering' for them.

Table 2
Documentary information on 'outside storage of animal manure' hand carried by advisers showing source and overlap among advisers

Type of source	Number of documents carried by >1 adviser [+]			
	Total	2	3	4
Government policy	38	15	4	0
Specialists/national research	18	8	3	1
Regional experimental stations	18	9	4	1
Service industries	9	3	2	0
Farmers' organizations	3	1	0	0
Dailies/journals	20	1	0	0
Total pieces documentary information	109	37	13	2
% total overlap	100	34	12	2

Source: Engel, 1989

Figure 1
Overlap and diversity in information portfolios of farm advisors

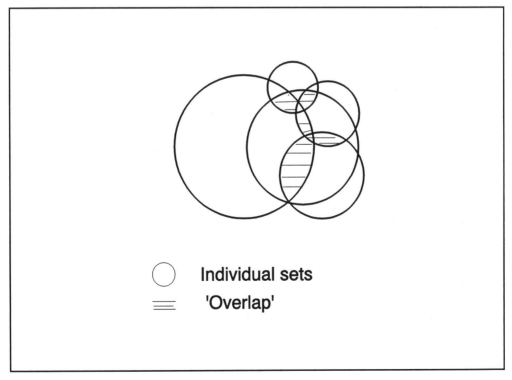

◯ Individual sets

≡ 'Overlap'

Source: Engel, 1989

Second, the personal interests and *specialization* of the adviser play an important role. If he or she is more interested in technical than in managerial matters, more technical and less managerial information will be selected. Pre-service and in-service training of the advisers of course plays an important part here as well, as do the relationships advisers develop with various subject-matter specialists. One interesting observation was that such tendencies seem to be reinforced by the relationships an adviser develops with his or her clients. The interests and strengths of a given adviser become known in the farm community, and increasingly he or she will be the one called upon in this area. This in turn further stimulates personal development along these lines, etc. In other words, a positive feedback loop develops, connecting expectations and specialization.

Third, advisers select their information with great care. Their criteria are related to the usefulness of each piece of information to their work:

- relevance: does the piece contribute specifically to the solution of the problems currently felt to be most relevant in the district covered?
- added value: does the use of a piece of information produce an immediate benefit to the completion of an advisory cycle?
- suitability: does the information fit nicely into the approach and logic the adviser uses in his or her work?
- appropriation: has the adviser, or close colleagues, been actively involved in developing the piece of information, so that they feel it is their own, to use as they see fit? (For example, they may have participated in gathering and evaluation the data used, or may have produced the piece themselves.)
- ease of use: is the piece of information concise, brief, and to the point, ready to be used?
- availability: can the piece be left with the farmer, if desired? Some were reluctant to take anything with them to the farm that could not be replaced if left behind.

The data show that 'relevance' and 'suitability' vary over time. Two pieces of documentary information found with two different advisers in essence contained the same message: sources where a farmer could obtain a subsidy for constructing new manure storage. Both were articles from agricultural journals, which advisers review regularly. The articles were published six months apart. One adviser picked out the first article while the other picked the second. Presumably each advisor choose the article that, at the time, was the most relevant and suitable for themselves.

Of course, it is not possible to generalize on the basis of this one study, and more research is definitely needed. A different topic could easily yield very different results. However, the data can't be disregarded as specific only to this group of advisers. For example, during an independent check I was able to confirm that, in the eyes of their supervisors, none of the advisers interviewed was anything less than good in his/her job. Second, when presented to the advisers the data didn't as much as raise an eyebrow. In fact, my description of the use of documentary information, its origin and consequences were considered 'normal practice'. Faced with a structural overload of documents coming at them from all sides, advisers learn to develop very selective strategies for choosing and using information.

In a discussion of these findings with the advisers and some of their superiors, we were able to put forward at least four important propositions:

- Quality in advisory work seems to depend not so much on standardization as on diversified access to information from a variety of sources. Managers of farm advisory services, however, often seem to believe the opposite.

- Advisers develop professional strategies for information acquisition and selection. They use clear criteria to make autonomous decisions on information: information that in their eyes is useless or vague is not kept. The quality of their work depends upon these strategies.

- The *degrees of freedom* advisers are allowed in developing and carrying out such strategies may be just as relevant to the quality of their advisory work as are the standardized information packages offered to them by specialists. A degree of *redundancy* or overlap in information offerings may well be functional. Both help advisers to construct effective portfolios that are timely and situation- and client-specific.

- This freedom and the *diversity* of goals, specializations, and niches recognizable in the work of agricultural advisers reflect a decentralized management of innovation processes, a feature well-known as important to successful innovation (Evenson et al., 1979; Moss Kanter, 1983).

Eliciting the structure underlying professional information use: the 'main menu'

During the interviews, advisers were asked to describe the events during an advisory cycle: from the moment a farmer makes the first contact, asking for advice on 'outside storage of manure' to the moment the cycle is completed and advice is given. They were asked to focus on the last time they completed such a cycle, to describe a real example, not a generalized account. The cycle normally included at least a few phone calls back and forth, and one or two farm visits by the adviser. Interviews suggested that the way extension workers analyse manure problems with farmers at farm level can be seen as 'variations on a theme'. Although each account was different, there were similarities in the issues that were the subsequent focus. This common ground can be made explicit by superimposing an analytical framework, which I labelled the adviser's 'main menu' (as in the 'main menu' of a software application). The *'main menu'* (Figure 2) suggests a way of grouping aspects that represent a part of the knowledge and skills of the farm adviser. When discussing a problem with a farmer, this enables him or her to focus on relevant issues, to ask the right questions at the right moment, to perform analyses and weigh different factors, and to provide specific pieces of factual information. All of this contributes to a successful completion of the advisory cycle.

Common items in the main menu became apparent in the practice of the Dutch advisers: problem reconnaissance, problem definition, comparison of alternative solutions, choice of a solution, implementation and followup. The resemblance to traditional problem-solving models is striking. However, these are not necessarily sequential steps in a process, but clusters of issues that may be addressed in any sequence. Also, all clusters are not always attended to, or some may be less intensely used. Rather, the clusters represent *fields of analysis* to be accessed as needed. 'The more experienced in manure storage farmers become, the more their need for information decreases' was a typical remark. He meant that more experienced farmers would not need his help in problem reconnaissance or definition; they would immediately ask for solutions, or simply ask the advisor for an opinion (sometimes a second opinion) as a followup. This, however, would not necessarily exclude the possibility of later returning to reconnaissance or definition, to clarify points or review the validity of the conclusions reached in view of new information.

In addition to suggesting fields of analysis, the main menu groups a variety of *types of knowledge* and enables the adviser to ask the right questions at the right time. On the one hand, it refers to knowledge *about* farming. Issues to be considered concern the current situation of the farm and its operations, as well as the strategy used by this particular farmer. On the other hand, it links to knowledge of opportunities and limitations faced by the farmer or by this type of farmer – the social, economic, technical, institutional and cultural context within which the farm must develop. Knowledge of the *context* of the farming operations includes knowledge and know-how about laws and regulations, subsidies and norms for the particular area and type of farm. Second, it includes knowledge about, in this case, technologies to store, process, and/or improve the quality of animal manure: the range of technical options available to the farmer to solve the problem. Finally, it includes knowledge of the opportunities and constraints of the market with respect to selling or transporting manure to areas of demand; quality norms for different types of manure; prices; and quality norms, prices and quantities required for different types of manure. All types of knowledge implicit in the 'main menu' should be understood to relate not only to existing opportunities and limitations, but also to any expected or unexpected future developments.

Figure 2 summarizes the main menu in two dimensions. The fields of analysis are indicated along the vertical axis, with types of knowledge relevant to 'outside storage of animal manure' and required for discussions about implementation on a particular farm on the horizontal axis. The sequence in which fields of analysis and knowledge types are presented is arbitrary. During an advisory cycle, each relevant[2] *knowledge field* – a cell in the matrix, i.e a cluster of issues corresponding to one field of analysis and one type of knowledge – can be accessed at any moment. This helps to generate the questions, information and/or answers needed at that point in the process of interaction between the adviser and his or her client. In every encounter between adviser and client, the path eventually chosen in moving from one knowledge field (cell) to another will be contingent upon the initial situation of the farmer, the approach both farmer and advisor chose in confronting the issues at stake, and the professional competence of the adviser. Each advisory cycle is unique: the outcome of a professional communicative interaction between two individuals. At the same time, the systematic approach of the professional adviser is apparent. As the concept of the 'main menu' suggests, the advisor supports his or her work with a 'basket' of issues, organized in such a way as to permit the successful completion of a great variety of advisory cycles on a topic of concern.

Like the information portfolio, the main menu evolves during interaction between farmers and advisers. However, even more than for the portfolio, previous education and in-service training seem to influence the methods advisers develop to approach their clients. Discussions with colleagues on priorities and priority issues play an important role as well. Subject-matter specialists, particularly during initial in-service training courses and when visiting farmers with the adviser, may influence decisively this learning process. It seems clear, however, that the 'main menu' does not simply reflect an approach chosen by an individual adviser. The 'problem-solving approach' has been a characteristic element in Dutch extension work in recent decades. One could hypothesize therefore that the main menu is also related to the agency's style. In fact, the main menu reflects both the considerable standardization of the extension approach used by the Dutch extension service, as well as the considerable 'degrees of freedom' an extension officer has in creating situation- and client-specific adaptations of the advisory process.

---

2. Not all fields are necessarily deemed relevant: for fields marked 'X' in Figure 2, interviews did not produce relevant issues or questions. This may in itself suggest interesting questions, which I will not further explore here.

Figure 2

The 'main menu' on manure storage: knowledge fields relevant to generating situation- and farm-specific advice on on-farm storage[a]

Fields of analysis \ Knowledge and information types	Farm I Current situation	Farm II Management strategy	Context I Technical developments	Context II Agricultural policies	Context III Market opportunities
Reconnaissance/ opinion formation	What is/has been done already?	What objectives? Continuity?	Alternatives?	Laws, regulations, norms, subsidies	Opportunities? Now? Future?
	#1		#2	#3	
Problem definition	Actual storage capacity and production	Solutions applied earlier?	Norms	X	Sales possible? Where?
	#1	#3	#1		
Comparison of alternative solution strategies	Costs/benefits	Closeness-of-fit	Alternatives?	Subsidy?	Timing, costs benefits
	#1			#2	#2
Comparison/choice of feasible solutions	Costs, purchase, maintenance	X	Guarantees supplier	X	X
			#2		
Follow up on implementation	Construction process	X	X	Correct application of rules?	X

[a] Boxes in the matrix represent knowledge fields (knowledge type x field of analysis); the number of pieces of documentary information relevant to a specific knowledge field found in the 'standard portfolio' is marked with an '#'; an 'X' marks those knowledge fields not discernable as separate issues during the interviews, although from a logical or technical point of view they might well be relevant.

Source: Engel, 1989a

The evidence presented regarding the main menu reinforces, in my view, some of the conclusions drawn earlier from the study of information portfolios. It confirms the *professionalism* of agricultural advisers and the way they organize their approach around clusters of relevant issues. The main menu also reflects the way advisers select documentary information to focus on particular clusters of issues and tasks. Finally, the main menu illustrates the wide scope of the knowledge and information advisers use to do their job. It demonstrates the comprehensive thinking required to adequately address common daily problems together with farmers. And it shows the flexibility advisers must master, if they are to address a variety of topics and keep up with farmers' interests as they evolve. All in all, it makes clear that advisers' activities go far beyond simply 'transferring' a particular technical option or message.

Looking at the number of documentary pieces of information supporting each of the knowledge fields in Figure 2, we see that some, like 'policy trends' and 'evaluation of the current farm management strategy', are strongly supported, with three documents each.

The reconnaissance of the farmers' management strategy is not supported by documents. Apparently, advisers expect, first, that some issues will merit more elaborate and technical treatment, and second, that some information must come from the farmer, with little input or structuring from the adviser. On the other hand, some issues are quite simple and clear-cut, such as the definition of the 'actual production and storage capacity'. Here one sheet giving the procedure for calculation of these values suffices. A spreadsheet could do the same job. Such findings confirm our earlier conclusion that advisers very carefully select the pieces of information they carry with them, keeping their immediate usefulness during all or a part of the advisory cycle in view.

A more general potential conclusion is that any farm adviser will use a 'basket of issues', well-organized to facilitate use, well-rooted in his or her understanding of farming and well-stocked with information of different types, to be able to complete the large number of advisory cycles he or she attends to annually. The 'basket' is problem-oriented and specifically designed to cope with the job. It provides some *flexibility*, enabling them to provide a tailor-made service to their individual clients; and at the same time, it provides a *structure*, focusing their attention on central issues. This makes it possible for them to work systematically and efficiently. It would be very difficult for any formal 'information planner' to come up with a better alternative.

The main menu also reflects a limitation inherent in focusing on the advisory cycle in a very particular case, and using this to trace the use of knowledge and information by farm advisers: the study did not specifically take into account the 'extra-advisory-cycle' activities of farm advisers, such as writing brochures, leaflets, reports, etc. Issues involved in drawing up policy documents, writing didactic materials, exchanging information with colleagues were touched upon only if directly relevant to the specific advisory cycle studied. This drawback had to be accepted, however, to benefit from the close relationship to actual practice that is one of the strong features of such a 'process approach'.

Knowledge transfer or networking?

During the case study, another issue came up that seemed of particular relevance to the social organization of innovation. As mentioned earlier, the use of the concept 'knowledge transfer' to describe the way knowledge about outside storage of animal manure is generated and exchanged among the relevant actors in northeastern Brabant results in a gross oversimplification of the activities of the extension service. Those activities, as identified from the interviews, can better be described as a continuous process of client and practice-oriented *integration* of knowledge and information from a variety of sources at all organizational levels. At each level, this process results in concrete products: advice, a letter, comments on a draft policy document, a technical note, a recommended scheme for spreading manure on farms in accordance with current regulations, an experiment in reducing the volume of manure production at the farm level, etc. Each of these products is directly relevant to the work of one or more participants in the processes at various levels. In each case, location-specific, regional and national policy-related knowledge are integrated routinely, as are technical and economic disciplinary and sector knowledge.

The interactive mechanisms by which such integration is achieved vary. Documentary information and telephone conversations play an important role at every level. At the level of communication between farmers, farm advisers and subject-matter specialists (those closest to agricultural practice), farm visits, individual coaching and service meetings are most frequently mentioned. At the level of interactions between heads of service, subject-matter specialists, researchers and policymakers, the mechanisms mentioned most often are project groups or other sorts of temporary task groups. To integrate these two levels, regional or national task groups are generally used. In such task groups, people from all levels in the organization are included. To the person looking in from outside, it is striking that the more closely one approaches the field level, the more the dominant role in integrating knowledge appears to be played by interpersonal communication mechanisms.

These mechanisms have in common their creation of joint learning opportunities among people who possess different types of knowledge relevant to the subject at stake. They are joined together in a task-oriented communication setting, where it is possible to take advantage of the qualities each of them has for designing whatever product is the objective. Clearly, in analysing such settings it is more appropriate to conceptualize them as a temporary intensification of communication network articulation around a specific issue, rather than a transfer of knowledge and information. Articulation is intentionally created between already existing networks, to make use of the various relevant insights that have been developed within each one. The reliance on person-to-person contacts, or even confrontations, seems another characteristic common to such integrative mechanisms.

What is commonly held to be a process of knowledge transfer can therefore better be understood as a step-wise integration of knowledge, information, ideas and experiences by means of temporary, task-oriented articulations of networks among relevant actors. Entering such settings, each participant brings along the relevant ideas and insights generated within his or her more permanent networks. From each such event, each takes away new building blocks to support his or her own work, as well as the specific product or service designed by the task group, which reflects the insights of all those involved. Not surprisingly, in the Dutch extension service the people who manage 'projects' like this, which bring networks together, often seem more powerful than those who simply manage the 'line'.

Case B: The agricultural communication network in Asten, North Brabant[3]

This second case addresses the use of information sources by agricultural producers. It reviews some of the results of a baseline survey done as part of the introduction of AGROCOM videotex services in the municipality of Asten, in the Province of North Brabant in the south of the Netherlands (see van Dijk, Leeuwis and Engel, 1990; Engel, 1993). This shows the diversity of sources farmers use to obtain their information, and the roles various parties play in satisfying farmers' diverse needs for information. Farmers are seen making use of a widespread, diverse network of sources to obtain the information needed to manage their farm. This network, however, is by no means amorphous. Different actors engage in different types of relationships, with farmers and among themselves, each offering distinct types of support, including information. Within the network, professional actors must find their own 'niche'.

The survey relied heavily on qualitative research methods, including open-ended questionnaires. Its design benefitted from a previous case study among farm advisers (Engel, 1989; see above). Two main types of information were distinguished: first, information directly applicable to decision making at farm level; this was in turn subdivided into strategic and operational farm management information. *Strategic* information has direct

---

3. Data presented were generated as a part of the baseline survey done for the AGROCOM Evaluation Study on the use of videotex in agriculture (van Dijk, Leeuwis and Engel, 1990); these paragraphs are adapted from Engel, 1993.

relevance to answering questions, and to addressing issues of a tactical and strategic nature in the future. *Operational* information includes information with immediate relevance to the daily management of the farm business. The second type of information considered was more general; it related to developments within the farm's socio-political and economic environment. This was grouped under three main subtypes: technical, concerning technical and scientific developments; political, concerning rules and regulations affecting farm operations; and market related, concerning the development of prices, consumer demands, national and international developments. Moreover, four different types of use of information were distinguished:[4]

- the use of information for opinion formation, to keep abreast with what others are doing;
- the use of information to help in defining current problems, or with respect to a specific needed farm management intervention;
- the use of information to compare alternative solutions or potential interventions; and
- the use of information in implementing a solution or intervention, after this had been selected as the most appropriate one.

During interviews, whenever possible specific examples of situations in which the use of information could be expected to play an important role were taken as a point of departure. Farmers were asked to name the sources of information they use regularly in such situations, the types of information they obtain from these sources and the way it is put to use. These data were subsequently organized to reflect the top five most important information sources, based on the number of times each source was mentioned by respondents. The results for each type of information and for each type of information use are presented in Tables 3 and 4. Sources are ranked according to the number of times each source was mentioned: '1' indicates the top-ranked information source.

Sources and types of information

Looking at Table 3, the diversity of farmers' information sources catches the eye, even when only the top five sources in each category are included. Apparently, farmers and horticulturalists in the region of Asten have developed over time a diverse, multi-facetted communication network to enable them to obtain the information they need. Farm journals stand out. According to farmers, they cover a broad spectrum of information needs very adequately. Though not too surprising in the Netherlands, where they have traditionally occupied a very important niche in the agricultural information market, this result suggests that farm journals are a 'carrier wave' of sorts, with a very basic role in facilitating the exchange of agricultural information. Farmers and horticulturalists feel that by regularly reading their journals they can keep ahead of relevant developments that will affect agriculture.

A second category, made up of what we will call *'farm visitors'* seems to stand out as well. They regularly visit the farm or have personal contacts with the farmers. First and fore-

---

4. *In retrospect, this reflects an interesting omission: the use of information as an input to production of new information was not included. Yet, the various record keeping activities, management software, etc. of Dutch farmers produce a great deal of information for further analysis. Clearly, our decision to closely follow the traditional phases of a problem-solving/decision making model affected our analysis. In later research, we corrected for this by using the more comprehensive 'experiential learning' model (Kolb, 1986).*

Table 3
Five most used information sources, by type of information

	Type of information				
Source	Strategic	Operational	Technical	Policy	Market
Farm journals	4	3	1	1	1
Product extension[a]	1	2			5
Independent extension[b]	5	5		5	
Colleagues[c]		4	5	5	
Accounting bureau	1			5	
Service extension[d]		1			
Agricultural bank	3				
Research institute			1		
Agricultural exposition			4		
Manufacturers[e]			3		
Government agencies				1	
Farmers' organizations				4	
Dailies				3	4
Buyers[f]					1
Teletext					3

[a] 'Product' extension is provided by the personnel of companies that sell inputs such as animal feed, chemicals etc. to farmers and at the same time provide technical advice

[b] 'Independent' extension comes from the recently privatized former government extension service

[c] Includes informal and formal contacts via study clubs

[d] 'Service' extension comes from people such as veterinary doctors, who provide a service as well as technical advice to farmers

[e] Includes manufacturers and sellers of equipment

[f] Includes auctions and others who buy agricultural outputs

Source: van Dijk, Engel and Leeuwis, 1991

most, they are connected to sales of inputs. Large animal feed cooperatives or companies in the Netherlands generally operate extension services of their own. Their philosophy: without correct management, our feeds will not generate the desired benefits. These extension workers apparently become trusted advisers on farm operations and strategies. The same seems to hold for veterinary doctors and others who deliver on-farm services, although according to our data they seem to focus primarily on operational matters. Farm advisers of the independent extension service (formerly a governmental body) and colleague farmers (through informal contacts and study clubs), play an important role as well.[5] For all of these farm visitors, frequent personal contacts facilitate the building of a strong relationship of mutual trust and shared interests. The importance of this to

5. Our sample reflects the importance of animal production – dairy, pigs and poultry – in the area. From these data, it is not possible to say whether the conclusions would hold true where field crops predominate. We feel quite confident, however, that they do hold for modern greenhouse horticultural areas.

Table 4
Five most important information sources, by type of information use

Source	Type of information use			
	Opinion formation	Determine needs	Compare alternatives	Implement solutions
Service extension[a]	2	1	3	1
Product extension[b]	5	2	2	2
Colleagues[c]	3		5	
Accounting bureau		3	4	
Independent extension[d]		4		4
Manufacturers[e]		4	1	
Farm journals	1			
Dailies/mass media	4			
Buyers[f]		4		
Government				3
Farmers' organizations				5

[a] 'Service' extension comes from people like veterinary doctors, who provide a service as well as technical advice to farmers

[b] 'Product' extension is provided by the personnel of companies that sell inputs such as animal feed, chemicals etc. to farmers and at the same time provide technical advice

[c] Includes informal and formal contacts via study clubs

[d] 'Independent' extension comes from the recently privatized former government extension service

[e] Includes auctions and others who buy agricultural outputs

[f] Includes manufacturers and sellers of equipment

Source: van Dijk, Engel and Leeuwis, 1991

information transfer is well established in extension literature (van den Ban and Hawkins, 1988; Fearne, 1991). At the same time, interpersonal communication facilitates *custom-made* advice that closely fits the situation of the farmer and of his/her farm at a particular moment in time.

A third category of information sources appears much more specialized. These sources are consulted by farmers when they need a specific type of information. Some are considered very important indeed, though not as important as other information categories. Farmers and horticulturalists who need market information go straight to the source, the buyers. The same applies for information on rules, regulations or policies; government agencies are consulted. For first-hand information on technical developments, they consult the experiment station. Here we also find the first 'electronic' means of communication: teletext. Its market information, mostly on prices, is valued.

Sources and type of information use

Table 4 relates sources of information to the type of use for which they are considered most relevant. Once again, diversity is a striking feature, as are the roles farmers assign to different sources. One notable feature is the broad influence of product- and service-related advice. Advisers in these areas seem to be tied into all major decision making processes at the farm level. Colleagues and independent extension advisers, as well as the accounting bureau and the manufacturers of farm technology are consulted in a more limited, more specific manner. Again, the role of the farm journals is evident. Although journals do not appear to play a role in other forms of information use, their role in general opinion formation, in maintaining a vision of what is going on is pivotal. Farmers rely upon the farm journals, with their broad coverage of issues, to stay current, to be 'on top' of developments that may affect their operations.

The agricultural communication network

The networks articulated by farmers and horticulturalists in Asten can be seen as complex, multiple networks of relationships that facilitate the exchange of knowledge and information of different types, for different purposes. Different subsets of actors – including farmers, as an important source – generate and exchange knowledge and information with regard to inputs and farm equipment, or farming operations, or strategic planning, or sales of farm produce. Farmers themselves, but also farm journals and to a lesser extent the various farm visitors, play an active role in articulating such sets into networks. Furthermore, each of the actors seeks access to specific sources of specific types of information to be used for specific purposes. Clearly, active communication by relevant social actors helps shape the networks.

We can visualize the agricultural communication network articulated by farmers in Asten, North Brabant as depicted in Figure 3. In the centre are the farmers, who maintain communication relationships with other actors in the process of managing and developing their farms. Their most noticeable characteristic is that they are always *learning*: managing, interpreting and incorporating knowledge and information from a large number of other actors into the way they go about their daily work. A first 'layer' of information sources (the most directly linked to farm operations and strategy) is made up of those who regularly visit the farm. I have called this the *advisory* line. The second layer includes information services that reach out to the farm, without actually sending people there. This may be called the *information* line. The third 'layer' are the information sources available to the farmer if and when he or she chooses to access them. Let's call this the *documentation* line.

Advisory line actors establish long-term personal relationships of mutual trust and shared interests with the farmers. Their information support is mainly geared towards farm operations and strategies (Table 3), and addresses several types of information use (Table 4). Their advice is directed at the specific situation of the farmer and his/her farm, at a given moment in time. Ideally, it is 'contextually sensitive'. To obtain a result that fits the context well, advisers target their information at individuals, not groups; at specific types of farms, not all farms; and, most probably, at specific types of individuals, not all individuals. Their information is custom made, very specific and to-the-point, and easily insertable into day-to-day farm practices. Every adviser therefore can serve only a limited number of farms and farmers; the time and energy expended per client is high.

Information line actors provide a broad offering of information, covering various aspects related to farm management, particularly the rapidly changing farm environment (Table 3). To be able to do this they make use of the mass communication media that are directed at specific audiences of farmers, horticulturalists, floriculturalists, dairy farmers and so forth. The information offered is oriented towards the needs of such an audience by

Figure 3

The agricultural communication network in Asten, the Netherlands

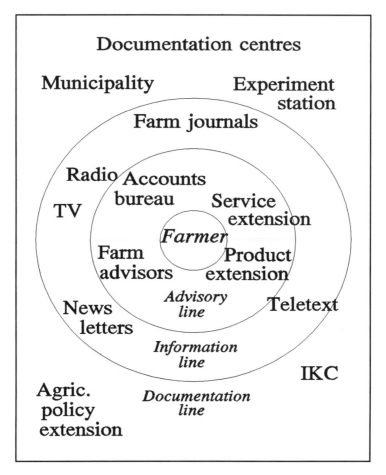

studying the target audience and following up to see the extent to which information is actually used. The information offered is client oriented, yet not custom made. The farmer him or herself must still make a considerable investment, processing the information, selecting the relevant pieces, and integrating these into his or her farm management and strategic thinking. Second line actors generally specialize in supporting one type of information use, particularly opinion formation, to help farmers stay on top of events (table 4). They often act in support of first line or third line actors, publishing their articles and advertising the benefits of their services or products. Many first or third line actors in Asten publish their own newsletters or weeklies, which may be a part of the second line of the agricultural communication network. Farmers, however, did not rate these among the first five in any of the categories.

Documentation line actors generally possess specialized knowledge or skill. They know all there is to know about one particular issue – technical innovations for a certain type of farm, arranging loans, financial advice, bookkeeping, farm machinery or installations; or they know the official rules and regulations or represent farmers before municipal or national bodies. Normally they do not visit the farm on a regular basis. Nevertheless, they provide information services to farmers, as well as first and second line actors. The type of information they provide depends upon their expertise, not necessarily on the needs of a specific target audience of farmers. They are part of the 'supply side' of the information market. As a result, they are specialized both in the type of information they provide, and in the type of information use they support. Their ability to provide contextually sensitive information is necessarily limited. That's why they often rely on first and second line actors to 'translate'. Third line actors generally use specialists, supported by large databases, and official publications in general mass media. Sometimes the databases can be accessed directly by second and first line actors or farmers, but generally an 'information specialist' or intermediary is required to provide access to the relevant 'available' databases, since these are often not compatible.

Communication networks as value-added networks

As I have shown, the agricultural communication network in Asten is a highly diversified universe: it displays a variety of social actors who specialize in distinct types of support. What is more, their support is targeted to quite specific individuals, groups or categories of farmers. In other words, none of the actors is 'just a pipeline', pushing through messages from one end to the other, without adding value along the way. Each party within the network adds a specific value to its contributions, to make these useful to its users. From the baseline survey, we can draw some preliminary insights into exactly what value is added by various actors. At the least, we can outline some of the factors critical to the success or failure of social actors who play a part in the *lines of action* distinguished within the network. To do this, I will reflect upon the expectations of the potential users of the services or information products actors contribute to network operations (Table 4).

What do users expect when they access a service that provides documentary information? Our baseline study suggests at least two crucial factors: they feel this particular service will provide them with as complete as possible a picture of what is available in a certain field and relevant to them; and they feel they can rely upon the source to provide them with information that will be accepted in negotiations with other parties or in case the use of the information has unexpected consequences. Take the case of a database on policy information related to manure storage. In accessing it, a farmer expects to find all the details on the laws and regulations related to his or her type of farm. The database would be of little use if some details were there and others not, in an unpredictable fashion; or if the figures provided were out of date, so that in negotiations with the municipality about building storage facilities for manure the figures used were not acceptable. At the same time, the farmer would not expect the database to contain items unrelated to manure storage. He or she will not be frustrated if it contains no information at all on tomorrow's weather. Also, this particular database would not be accessed very frequently, as plans for building manure storage facilities is not something one does every day. In fact, farmers would probably be happy to obtain this type of information through a third person, for example a farm adviser.

In the same way, one can ask what moves farmers to read farm journals, or, in more general terms, to access sources in the information line. Our data and additional views collected during the interviews suggest that what farmers most often want in information from these sources is (preferably guaranteed) coverage. Information line sources should cover a broad range of topics and provide enough information about them to keep a farmer up to date, including technical developments, policy changes and market trends. At the same time, as farmers are accustomed to using a variety of media for this purpose, they are very selective. Messages should therefore be easily recognizable and directly relevant to

Table 5

Critical issues for actors intervening in agricultural communication networks to consider

Position	Critical issues	
Advisory line	Situation specificity	Immediate applicability
Information line	Recognizability	Relevance
Documentation line	Completeness	Formality

their situation, as they perceive it themselves. The information produced by sources in the information line is of such a general nature, yet so important to keep track of, that farmers are apt to rely on 'scanning'. That is, they take only a quick look at most things, and read only a few articles, or parts of articles, with care. Farm journals, daily newspapers and so forth adjust their layouts to match this pattern, facilitating quick access to the main ideas or to those parts a particular farmer might think are relevant. In other words, farmers regularly invest in accessing information line sources. They spend only the time they think is needed to extract the relevant bits from each source. Frustration creeps in when, in spite of considerable time investment, one misses out on relevant new developments, or the source doesn't seem to provide the type of information you expect from it.

Actors in the *advisory line*, again, must reckon with a variety of expectations from their clients. For private or government agents alike, their communication relationship with farmers is based upon mutual trust among individuals. Such trust is based, on the part of the agent, on efficient service delivery, good products, relevant opinions and good advice, probably in combination with a warm personality, good communication skills and efficient backup from a company or organization, to name just a few factors. However, in the advisory line, no product or advice is 'good', nor is any delivery 'efficient', unless it is custom made: specifically tailored to the situation, the personality and the problems of one particular client. Moreover, it should be possible to integrate into his/her daily operations and farm management without running into any barriers.

Some preliminary conclusions from the case studies

Both case studies illustrate a number of basic characteristics of communication for innovation, as seen in practice. It is problem-oriented, situation-specific, and requires a high degree of processing and use of professional information. The information sources available to the farmers in these cases are diverse, rich, and cover a wide range of interests. Information is made available in a way that permits autonomous selection, interpretation and adaptation – in both form and content – to current local agendas. The mechanisms that support communication for innovation provide learning opportunities to those who participate. They are organized so as to stimulate associative, broadly inclusive thinking on relevant issues.   The interpretative or 'soft' nature of communication for innovation contrasts sharply with the normative or 'hard' character of communication used to achieve administrative control. The picture that emerges is, in fact, very similar to what has been written about the management of innovation in large companies (cf. Mintzberg, 1983; Moss Kanter, 1983). Communication for innovation is quite different from communication for control. The latter requires well spelled-out, formalized agreements and standard procedures, the former a flexible, sometimes redundant approach to information management. Some characteristics, such as a strong accent on hierarchy and compartment-alization, tend to prove fatal to innovation, but may be essential to effective and efficient administrative control. Another feature of communication for innovation is that it can be seen as a purposive activity. Social actors in agricultural innovation theatres develop professional strategies to generate and exchange knowledge and information. Such strategies are closely integrated in their daily practice, because communication for innovation is all or part of their job. At the same time, it is obvious that communication is embedded in more comprehensive social relationships among the actors involved. Communication can be understood only as one aspect of the relationships that develop between farmers, veterinary doctors, district extension managers, farm advisers, specialists and other social actors in innovation theatres.

In summary, on the basis of this evidence, it seems very difficult to uphold the notion of 'transfer of knowledge', even with respect to the activities of extension services. In the first place, all of the social actors in innovation theatres seem to be – at the same time – users as well as sources of knowledge and information. For studying innovation at the level of the individual actors, this argues strongly for using the concept of 'learning-in-practice' rather than 'knowledge utilization'. Second, evidence from the case studies strongly supports the idea that innovation in agriculture is not the work of individual actors; instead, it should be seen as a social process. Consciously or unconsciously, each participant contributes a specific piece to the jigsaw puzzle of agricultural innovation. In this process, multiple and diverse communication networks play a decisive role. Such communication networks may occur spontaneously among communities with related interests. However, the evidence underscores that it is also possible to intentionally design and strategically articulate networks in or between organizations – to create networks to encourage particular desired outputs; further, these networks can to some degree be managed or facilitated. Third, the notion of 'knowledge transfer' seems clearly at odds with our findings that agricultural communication networks are 'value-added networks', in which each social actor contributes his or her particular competence to the functioning of the network. The step-wise, task-oriented integration of different strands of knowledge and information generated among social actors in innovation theatres can be better understood as the result of networking efforts among sets of actors who share an interest in a common concern or issue.

3. Impact of inter-institutional coordination in Nariño

When institutional support for farmer innovation is poor, this is often attributed to weak inter-institutional coordination. The underlying assumption is that better linkages lead to improved impact (Kaimowitz et al., 1990). But is that always the case? This chapter presents empirical evidence suggesting that a direct relationship between inter-institutional coordination and innovative impact might exist. It will shed light on three central questions: 1) can we argue for a direct link between inter-institutional coordination and innovative impact? 2) what factors seem to play an important role in forging effective institutional performance? and 3) which contextual factors are relevant? In addition, a number of specific linkage mechanisms (see 'Drawing attention to integration' in Chapter 1) are identified that proved particularly effective in forging an alliance among relevant social actors in the Nariño Highlands.

To answer the questions listed, I will focus on 'agricultural innovation', 'system integration' and 'sustainability of institutional performance'. Productivity per unit of land will be the primary indicator of *agricultural innovation*. Considering the technological options open to peasants, this best reflects the use of improved technologies in agricultural production. *Integration* includes formal and informal, financial, administrative and informative links among institutions. It includes such mechanisms as coordinated plans of action, regular coordination meetings, collaborative task groups, and the regular exchange of information and materials. In this case, it also includes the provision of resources by the integrated rural development programme (DRI) for operational and staff costs, and by the Colombo-Dutch bilateral technical assistance project ICA-CCH (ICA Convenio Colombo-Holandés) for key activities, additional staff, transport and/or materials in priority areas. Informal links are broadly defined as personal contacts between colleagues and incidental exchanges of information; they are rarely concerned with staff or materials. To address *sustainability of institutional performance*, I will ask myself what chances the institutions will have to maintain their level of performance if conditions change.

We open this section with a sketch of agricultural performance in the Nariño Highlands from the 1970s to the mid 1980s (see 'Agricultural performance and innovation', below). I then review the core institutions involved in the development and transfer of agricultural technologies in the region (see 'Agricultural institutions ...'). Next, the level of coordination among these institutions, the role of institutional leadership, strategic consensus, particular linkage mechanisms and contextual factors (see 'Inter-institutional coordination) are examined. Finally, I look into the issue of sustainability of institutional performance in the post-1985 period (see 'Sustainability of institutional performance') and draw conclusions on the material presented.

Agricultural performance and innovation

Small, mixed farms, 85% of which cover less than 5 hectares, are the predominant source of agricultural production in the Nariño Highlands (URPA, 1987). There are a limited number of large, commercial farms in the region as well. The main crops grown by

Nariño's peasant farmers are potatoes, maize, beans, wheat and barley; the two other main agricultural activities are dairy farming and the production of the *curí*, a species of guinea pig. Because there are difficulties in interpreting production trends, particularly due to extreme market conditions, potatoes and barley are not considered in the analysis.

Until the mid 1970s, the role of the Nariño Highlands in the national economy, in terms of food crop production, was marginal. The crops produced in this region were not a part of the dynamic production increases recorded nationally. Yet over 50% of the region's population were dependent on agriculture for a livelihood, compared to 20% nationally, and agriculture accounted for about 30% of the output of the region. In all agricultural domains, apart from potatoes, yields were stagnant. Development of the predominantly peasant economy in the Nariño Highlands was hampered by lack of capital and expertise. Low levels of labour productivity, poor yields per hectare, and inadequate marketing facilities contributed to lack of growth and an economy geared towards satisfying local demand. There were few opportunities for peasant farmers to improve their situation.

Halfway through the 1970s, Colombia abandoned large-scale land reform as its main focus and developed a policy aimed at modernizing peasant agriculture via state intervention. Peasant farmers were defined as farmers who owned less than 20 hectares of land, did not have considerable capital resources and for whom agricultural production was the major source of income. The two main vehicles for implementing this policy were the Integrated Rural Development Programme (DRI) and the National Food and Nutrition Plan (PAN). The objectives of these programmes were to enhance the role of the peasant farming sector in the national economy and to improve the living standards of the rural population. Emphasis was placed on introducing new food production technologies, improving marketing facilities and providing basic rural infrastructure. The responsibility for developing and introducing new technologies was assigned to the Colombian Agricultural Institute (ICA). The DRI was initiated in 1974–1975. In Nariño, the ICA took up its task in cooperation with other government institutions, including the Agricultural Bank (Caja Agraria) and the Colombo-Dutch bilateral assistance project (Convenio Colombo-Holandés).

The level of agricultural production in Nariño during the ensuing decade can be taken as a measure of the effectiveness of agricultural institutions in bringing about technological change. All new agricultural technologies made available to Nariño's peasant farmers were developed and introduced by or in close cooperation with ICA and DRI, and most peasant farmers relied on DRI credit to incorporate new technologies into their farming operations. Moreover, DRI records suggest that government institutions indeed achieved considerable coverage of the total peasant population during this period. During the period, production and yield figures were compiled twice by the Regional Agricultural Planning Unit (URPA, 1983 and 1987). Although there may be some disagreement on the details of these studies, little doubt exists among experts as to their accurate reflection of the general trends for agricultural production in the Nariño Highlands (ICA-CCH, 1984). Without leaning too much on such figures, they will be used to illustrate, in a general sense, the development of agricultural production in the region. I will briefly outline the results per agricultural production domain relevant to this study.

Maize and beans

The acreage under maize decreased in the 1970s, stabilizing in the early 1980s. Acreage in beans increased significantly between 1980 and 1986. In both cases, however, the level of adoption of improved technologies was low and yields stagnated.

Wheat

Wheat yields declined in the 1970s. However, in the period 1980–1986 a 60% increase in yield, combined with a 45% increase in planted area, more than doubled output. A large part of the new area under wheat may have been a result of a substitution of wheat for barley (URPA, 1983).

Dairy

Milk production rose slowly in the 1970s and then increased considerably in the early 1980s. This trend can be attributed partly to an increase in the number of productive animals (about 30% between 1973 and 1983), and partly to increased production per head (about 60% over the same period). There were several reasons for this growth. Favourable government credit schemes made it attractive for peasants to enter dairy farming. Milk collection, transport and processing received a boost from the establishment of a regional dairy cooperative, COOPROLACTEOS, which increased its daily raw milk intake from about 10,000 litres in 1980 to 35,000 in 1986. The gate price for raw milk increased steadily between 1977 and 1984, making milk a stable source of family income. Finally, improved pasture seeds were introduced. Institutional sales of such seeds to peasant farmers alone accounted for some 800 newly established hectares of improved pastures among some 1,000 farmers (ICA-CCH Annual Reports).

Curies

The development of improved technology for curí breeding and husbandry had a significant impact on the region's curí producers, many of whom were women. In 1980, only a few producers used improved technologies. Between 1985 and 1987, however, according to the Financial Corporation in Support of Cooperatives (CORFAS) – a non-profit private organization – 236 peasant women obtained credit, enabling them to adopt improved technologies. In addition, 40 male farmers obtained credit through the DRI/Agricultural Bank programme for the same purpose.

Whereas the 1970s were characterized by stagnation, apart from potatoes, during the early 1980s a significant increase in agricultural production was achieved in three domains – wheat, dairy and curies – while in two domains – maize and beans – production remained stagnant. Given the close relationship that can be assumed under the conditions described between government intervention, the introduction of improved technologies and production increases, this would suggest that in the case of wheat, dairy and curí production, institutional support to smallholder innovation was effective; whereas in the case of maize and beans it was not. If integration among core institutions is to be considered a key to achieving an impact on agricultural innovation, during this period we would expect to see effective integration for wheat, dairy and curies; on the other hand, for maize and beans we would expect that there was no integration, or that it was ineffective.

Agricultural institutions and their activities

The actors in the agricultural innovation theatre in the Nariño Highlands were many. However, not all were equally relevant to developing and introducing improved technologies with peasant farmers. Several entities were involved in specific tasks, some of which have already been mentioned. COOPROLACTEOS for example was important, but its contribution was limited to a specific group of peasants (dairy producers). The cooperative, during the period studied, played no role in orienting institutional efforts. The contribution of the National Service for Vocational Training, SENA, was limited to training farmer

Table 6
Research programme at the ICA Regional Centre for Agricultural Research

Programme	1966	1982	1987
Cereals	+	+	+
Maize	+	+	+
Dairy production	+	+	+
Dairy production	+		+
Potatoes	+	+	+
Grain legumes		+	+
Intercropping		+	+
Horticulture		+	+
Fruticulture		+	+
Soils	+	+	+
Agricultural machinery	+	+	+
Entomology	+	+	+
Phytopathology	+	+	+
Agricultural economics			+

Sources: ICA, 1966; ICA/Extension reports, 1982 and 1987

leaders, farmers and operators, without much followup. The ICA-UNICEF programme collaborated with CORFAS in organizing curí breeding and production among peasant women. The Colombian Agrarian Reform Institute, INCORA, provided organizational and some technical support to a few farm cooperatives. The University of Nariño supported efforts in certain domains.

The institutional actors who played more general roles were ICA/Research, ICA/Extension, the Regional DRI Office, the Agricultural Bank and the Colombo-Dutch project, ICA-CCH. Their mandate concerned the introduction of improved technologies to peasant farming, thereby raising the living standards of the peasant population in the area. The *Regional Centre for Agricultural Research* was established in Obonuco in 1946 and since 1963 has been responsible for ICA research activities in Nariño. There were two *ICA District Extension Offices* in the Highland region: one in Ipiales, at the southernmost border of the province, and one in the provincial capital, Pasto. In addition, field offices were maintained in various municipalities in both districts. The *Regional DRI Office* located in Pasto was responsible for implementing the Integrated Rural Development Programme in Nariño. The *Caja Agraria*, through its main office in Pasto and its subsidiary offices in all the municipalities of the province, was the main supplier of agricultural credit; all DRI agricultural loans to peasant farmers were channelled through its system. The *Colombo-Dutch project ICA-CCH* was initially based with ICA/Research in Obonuco, but later with ICA/Extension in Pasto, and operated from 1974 to 1985. Below I will briefly review the main functions of these institutions with respect to innovations in peasant agricultural production in Nariño.

Research

The research programmes carried out by ICA/Research at the Obonuco station between 1966 and 1987 are indicated in Table 6. All programmes were associated with national ICA research programmes; some were replications of research carried out at ICA's National Research Centre at Tibaitatá (ICA, 1966). In an evaluation carried out by a visiting Dutch team in 1973, the dairy research programme scored high in terms of on-station performance but low on disseminating technology to peasant farmers (Oosterberg and van der Kuip, 1973). Although the station continued to conduct research on the problems faced by medium- and large-scale producers, as part of the national ICA dairy research programme, it started to place more emphasis on adapting research results to meet the needs of smallscale producers in Nariño. With the support of ICA-CCH, an intensive small dairy farming unit was established in 1975.

The efforts of ICA/Research in wheat, beans and maize focused mainly on breeding and selecting varieties. A large number of varieties were introduced after the 1960s, many of which have been accepted by Nariño's farmers. Research on potatoes had been conducted since 1966, and a number of more productive varieties were introduced. The ICA-Nariño variety developed at the regional station became one of the most widely used varieties in the Nariño Highlands. ICA/Research was also actively involved in producing seed potatoes, both on-station and with selected peasant producers. In response to both regional and national demands for new technologies, ICA/Research embarked upon several new programmes in the early 1980s, including grain legumes, intercropping, horticulture and fruticulture. The agricultural economics research programme was started in 1985, to enhance the practical applicability of research recommendations, working through farm budget evaluations. Programmes within particular disciplines, on soils, farm machinery, entomology and phytopathology, help in specific problem areas.

Table 7
Communication plans for technology transfer (PCTT) in Pasto District, 1983

PCTT subjects	Municipalities #	Villages #	Peasants[a] #	Publications[a] #
Dairy	7	18	190	820
Wheat	2	9	250	550
Curies	3	6	96	4700
Maize	5	8	235	0
Beans	4	7	270	120
Potatoes	3	12	280	720
Fruits	7	14	270	1550

[a] *Number of peasants refers to those directly involved in programme activities, while number of publications refers to all books and/or brochures produced; not all of these were necessarily used immediately or within the course of one PCTT.*

Source: Annual Report ICA-CCH, 1983

Extension

During the early 1970s, ICA/Extension operated as part of the Regional Rural Development
Project and focused on organizing and supporting farmers' groups. This approach was
abandoned in 1975. The extension service then reverted to carrying out individual farm
visits and providing credit assistance, backed by DRI; inevitably, this resulted in reduced
coverage. In 1981, the ICA Communication Department developed a methodology aimed
at improving the effectiveness and efficiency of advisory services to small farmers. Known
as the 'communication plans for technology transfer', or PCTT methodology, it focused on
adequate planning, preparation and implementation of multimedia extension programmes. Further, it provided a means to clearly define extension objectives, target groups,
activities and programme contents. Group events, meetings and demonstrations – in
which systematic planning of extension events with farmers in a village was a key element
– were added to individual visits. Individual technical assistance and credit services
continued to be of central importance.

Between 1981 and 1983, nine PCTT plans were prepared and implemented. Their
design was in the hands of the district staff and field workers supported regionally and
nationally by the ICA Communication Department. The main peasant agricultural activities
were covered. Improved planning and preparation, plus the systematic involvement of
subject-matter specialists, made it possible to back up plans with continuous production of
high-quality extension materials, such as slide shows, booklets, brochures, posters and an
ICA newsletter. And, since 1983, agricultural news programmes have been available on the
local radio. All didactic materials were produced professionally to ensure easy access by
peasant producers, women and school-age children.

By 1983, the ICA-DRI programme had reached about 4,250 peasant families in 12
municipalities in the Nariño Highlands, a significant increase over the previous coverage.
By 1987 the number reached had increased to around 8,000 in 16 municipalities (ICA-DRI
reports). This probably represents about 10–15% of the relevant smallholders in the
region:[1] a considerable institutional achievement, given the conditions in the area and the
resources available. Moreover, since its initiation, the programme appeared to have
achieved considerable coverage among the smallest peasant producers. For example,
within the municipality of Pasto in 1979, 80% of DRI credit users held less than 10
hectares, and over 60% held less than 5 (annual report ICA-CCH, 1979: 25).

On-farm research

In the late 1970s, ICA/Extension began to place far greater emphasis on using on-farm
trials to help adapt research recommendations to local conditions. A coordinator for on-
farm adaptive research was assigned to the district office to help the extension staff design
and manage trials and process results. The trials concentrated on varieties and fertilization.
Adaptive research for dairy, pastures and horticulture was implemented and evaluated
jointly by ICA/Research, ICA/Extension and subject-matter specialists from ICA-CCH. From
1978 onwards, extension staff maintained continuous on-farm trials on improved pastures,
fodder crops and wheat, using on average about 15 different locations; on-farm trials were
also conducted for several horticultural crops. Potato extension programmes widely used

---

1. *Due to the unreliability of the census data, this figure can only be taken as an educated guess, and used to give
an idea of the order of magnitude. It was therefore checked with several independent sources, who agreed it
probably does reflect the coverage of the programme at this stage.*

on-farm demonstrations. At the same time, linear programming studies, farm budget and other economic evaluations of pilot farm operations, carried out by the ICA-CCH provided valuable insights into alternative technical opportunities for peasant farmers. After the economics section of ICA-CCH was established in 1978, both research and extension incorporated a farm management perspective in developing and applying research recommendations. Adaptive research on commercial curí production was taken up by ICA/Extension and ICA-CCH in collaboration with the University of Nariño and the ICA Veterinary Centre in Pasto. In this research, a peasant cooperative – supported by INCORA – and individual peasant farmers played a leading role as innovators; they kept detailed records of their operations and participated in the interpretation and analysis of the results.

Resource provision

The Nariño Highlands was one of the first regions in Colombia in which DRI became operational. DRI quickly became the sole source of financing for ICA/Extension's personnel and operational costs and, through Caja Agraria, it funded most of the credit made available to peasant farmers. This gave DRI considerable influence. It used its pivotal position to formulate a strategy for developing Nariño's peasant sector, and actively reinforced this strategy by selectively allocating financial resources. Apart from its support for ICA/Extension's adaptive research programmes, however, DRI did not finance research. This was consistent with the trend in Colombian agricultural policy at the time, to place more emphasis on a 'go straight to the farmer' approach and concentrate less on research. National research expenditures dropped from 0.42% of the agricultural gross domestic product in 1970 to 0.18% in 1978; after 1985, with the help of external financing, this figure again approached the 1970 level (Montes Llamas, 1987). Because of the lack of financial support from DRI, the regional research centre faced serious financial constraints during the late 1970s and early 1980s.

Support from ICA-CCH, however, enabled the centre to set up collaborative programmes with ICA/Extension on potatoes, dairy, pastures, horticulture and fruticulture. Moreover, the ICA-CCH project provided for a number of key subject-matter specialists, both Colombian and Dutch, to be specifically assigned to developing extension packages in their fields of expertise. These subject-matter specialists played a vital role in the collaborative programmes: they collected and adapted research recommendations, implemented on-farm research projects, assisted in the development of technical extension materials and trained extension staff. The resources provided by ICA-CCH also had considerable impact on PCTT operations. ICA-CCH communication specialists assisted in strengthening the methodology and introduced a number of complementary elements. These included: participatory diagnosis, which increased farmer participation in extension decision making (Engel, 1984, 1990b; Lopera et al., 1985); a method for 'translating' technical terminology to peasant vocabulary in written materials, making these more effective for peasants with little formal education; and a five-minute radio news programme, broadcast twice daily, containing up-to-the-minute news on meetings, demonstrations and research recommendations as well as interviews with men and women farmers and other farm women. These radio programmes proved very successful among peasant farmers (Guerrón and Verbaken, 1985).

Inter-institutional coordination

In this section I will look at the degree of integration achieved between the core institutions and the programmes they introduced, as described above. The period of the early 1980s, when a take-off in production for dairy, curies and wheat was seen, is of particular interest. Can it be argued that a more significant degree of institutional integration was achieved among core institutions during that period? Can it be shown that such integration was not achieved for maize and beans, which remained stagnant? And if so, can specific linkage mechanisms be identified, which particularly facilitated integration in the three 'high impact domains'? I will attempt to answer these three questions and look into some influential external factors as well.

During the 1975–1978 period, there were strong links between DRI, ICA/Extension and Caja Agraria, on the one hand, and ICA/Research and ICA-CCH, on the other. The first three institutions had offices in the town of Pasto – indeed, ICA/Extension was in the same building as Caja Agraria; the latter two were located some miles away, at Obonuco. In 1978, however, ICA-CCH became a pilot programme within ICA/Extension, was provided with additional subject-matter specialists, and moved into the ICA/Extension offices in Pasto. Nonetheless, it maintained many of its ties with ICA/Research and continued its involvement in on-station research programmes at the Obonuco experimental station. This move proved crucial to elevating the level of integration between research and extension. Links were very weak during the early and mid 1970s, being limited to irregular informal contacts; but from 1978 links were systematically developed and strengthened. Within the domains relevant to ICA-CCH a high level of coordination of tasks was achieved. After a period of adjustment, ICA/Extension and ICA-CCH subject-matter staff played the role of 'integrators' within the system, facilitating coordination among all core institutions, including research. One example of such integrated efforts was the 'Unidad Minifundio', a mixed farm unit (1 ha) collectively designed and operated at the experimental station by an interdisciplinary group made up of ICA/Extension, ICA-CCH and ICA/Research specialists.

Institutional integration also had a considerable effect on the DRI credit programme. Before 1978, ICA/Extension had started to promote DRI credit to peasant farmers, but its impact was limited. The main reason was that its technical support, as well as credit, focused on individuals rather than groups; there was no backup from group or mass communication media. In addition, priorities were not clearly defined and, with the possible exception of the potato programme, technical messages were poorly articulated. Beginning in 1978, and particularly during the early 1980s (after the PCTT methodology was introduced), assistance from ICA-CCH subject-matter specialists in setting economic and technical priorities, formulating extension contents and developing extension materials became permanent elements in ICA/Extension's activities. Mass media backup – printed, audiovisual and radio – was provided. Technical issues were often discussed at regional and national ICA-CCH committee meetings. Further, beginning in 1982, DRI, along with ICA/Extension and ICA/Research representatives, formally took part in ICA-CCH national coordination meetings.

When I look in more detail at the way in which coordination was achieved during the early 1980s, two issues seem particularly relevant. In the first place, institutional leadership and a considerable degree of strategic consensus were achieved. In the second place, coordination of development and transfer tasks among institutions was quite effective. Paulino's story, in the example, illustrates both this success and a rather innovative way to avoid risk. The following section looks at the linkage mechanisms that underpinned these achievements.

Paulino's choice: The story of Paulino Jojoa, a peasant farmer in the Nariño Highlands in the southernmost part of Colombia, illustrates the mutual adjustment achieved among a number of core institutions, creating an unprecedented solution.

Around 1980, Paulino and his family owned a 1.4 hectare farm in a village close to Pasto, the regional capital. He had long had the idea of investing in improved curí raising, but so far the bank had not been keen on helping him. But now the ICA-CCH farm economists, using the evidence collected elsewhere and from adaptive trials at the Obonuco experimental station, had been able to convince the Caja Agraria of the profitability of curí breeding – when using improved technology for housing, feeding and breeding. The bank became willing to lend Paulino the money to build a permanent guinea pig shed.

However, Paulino's risk was considerable: he was the first peasant farmer to acquire such a loan; if, unexpectedly, the guinea pig adventure did not provide the expected benefits and the loan went sour, he would lose his smallholding to the bank. Who would give a dime for an empty guinea pig shed? His solution was proverbial: instead of building a shed, he asked for a bigger loan, to build a house. Since he was backed by ICA/Extension and ICA-CCH, Caja Agraria agreed. And a house he built: at least the walls, the roof, the windows and the design – including the exterior paint – were those of a fancy rural home. Then, instead of transferring his family to it (as everyone expected), they stayed were they were, in their own, old mud block house next to the new building. Meanwhile, Paulino arranged the inside of the new 'shed' to hold a large number of guinea pigs, exactly following the technical specifications of the specialists. Up until 1987, when I saw him last, he was continuing to produce high quality guinea pigs, providing himself and his family with a good, stable income. Because of this, he and his son had also acquired leadership roles in the village. On the other hand, if the loan had gone sour, he would have been able to sell the 'shed' to rich urbanites as a fancy rural home, thus avoiding the loss of his own house and farm!

Institutional leadership and strategic consensus

Technical leadership was and had been for a long time in the hands of ICA, the institution with the knowledge and experience in the region that would be necessary to successfully develop and introduce improved technologies to peasant producers. Since the mid 1970s, political leadership had been in the hands of DRI, the leading agency in the implementation of the Integrated Rural Development Programme. ICA/Research had been in Nariño since 1946, and had set up research programmes on most of the important crops and animal husbandry activities relevant to small farmers. The expertise within the ICA-CCH team complemented the technical capacity of ICA/Research in dairy, horticulture and fruticulture, and was instrumental in developing awareness about the technical possibilities of curí production. At the same time, ICA/Extension had long experience in the field with the highland peasants. Its most significant contribution was undoubtedly the introduction of the PCTT methodology – a 'flexible extension management system' that developed before the concept was introduced – which provided the tools for systematically planning and implementing multimedia extension campaigns directed at groups of peasant farmers at village level. ICA-CCH added subject-matter specialists, economists and communication specialists to the team.

After a slow start, DRI asserted its political leadership in Nariño in 1978; by then, DRI was financing all peasant-oriented operations of ICA/Extension and Caja Agraria. Before approving the national component of the budget for ICA-CCH operations, it insisted the project move to the ICA/Extension Office and integrate itself, becoming a pilot project

Table 8

Programme priorities among core institutions in the Nariño Highlands, 1982 to 1986[a]

Programme	1982			1984				1986		
	E	R	C	E	R	C	D	E	R	D
Dairy	+	+	+	+	+	+	+	+	+	+
Curies	+		+	+		+		+		
Pasture/fodder	+	+	+	+	+	+	+	+	+	+
Wheat/barley	+	+		+	+		+	+	+	+
Potatoes	+	+		+	+		+	+	+	+
Maize	+	+		+	+		+	+	+	+
Beans	+	+		+			+	+	+	+
Intercrop		+			+				+	
Vegetables	+	+	+	+	+				+	
Fruits	+		+	+	+			+	+	
Agricultural economics	+		+	+			+		+	
Communication	+		+	+			+	+		
Soils		+			+				+	
Agricultural machinery		+			+				+	
Entomology		+			+				+	
Phytopathology		+			+				+	
Veterinary service	+		+			+		+		

[a] E=ICA/Extension; R=ICA/Research; C=ICA-CCH; D=DRI

Sources: ICA, ICA-CCH and DRI Annual Reports

within DRI. By participating actively in the national coordinating committee and in ICA-CCH joint evaluation missions, DRI acquired considerable influence over the development of the bilateral technical assistance project. Yet, at the same time it permitted the project to play an innovative role: although DRI policy was *not* to finance subject-matter specialists, it did so in Nariño, to help fulfil bilateral counterpart requirements; and although DRI policy did not include financing for research, it did finance on-farm research in Nariño. DRI leadership was further strengthened in 1983 when district planning seminars organized by DRI formulated the priorities that were to guide the disbursement of loans to peasant farmers. These priorities were carefully chosen to reflect both the needs of the peasant producers and the ongoing programmes of ICA, to make the best use of the technical expertise already available in the region. The eventual result was a considerable strategic consensus among core institutions. During the 1978–1985 period they shared a common goal – to improve the well-being of peasants by introducing improved agricultural technologies – and directed their activities towards a specific, well-defined client group, as stipulated by the DRI programme. Table 8 shows the extent to which a strategic consensus on priorities was reached. Each of the institutions maintained certain programmes of their own, in accord with their individual mandate; however, programme priorities with respect to the peasant sector mostly coincided.

THE SOCIAL ORGANIZATION OF INNOVATION

A number of specific linkage mechanisms contributed to the development and reinforcement of leadership and strategic consensus:

- to carry out its tasks of planning, budgeting, financing and monitoring activities in the region, the DRI regional office established strong links with the national DRI office and with a number of organizations operating in Nariño. Regular meetings of this *DRI Departmental Committee* were attended by policymakers and representatives from extension, training, marketing, input distribution and, to some degree, farmers; it discussed credit targeting policies, staff and other allocation of resources.
- the *DRI Technical Committee* responsible for Nariño met monthly and involved the directors of all relevant agricultural institutions. These meetings were intended to boost coordination, rather than control; they reinforced targeting of resources towards institutional goals and strengthened the links, mostly informal, among technical institutions. Decisions concerning the allocation of resources were taken at higher levels.
- the quarterly *ICA-CCH national and regional coordinating committee meetings*, reinforced by bi-annual joint evaluation missions, strengthened international, national and regional coordination. They focused on agricultural development in Nariño, government policy and technical opportunities for peasant farmers and, in response to identified constraints and technical opportunities, re-allocated ICA-CCH project funds.

The DRI Departmental Committee generally assigned priorities on the basis of national policy and the current contribution of the planted area to regional and/or national agricultural output. ICA-CCH coordinating committees placed more emphasis on identifying and exploring future high-potential domains for peasant production, hence the priority attached to horticulture, curies and fruticulture. Both committees commanded considerable resources for their tasks. Therefore, in terms of targeting resources, DRI and ICA-CCH efforts complemented each other to a large degree (see Table 8). While a general coincidence between integration of efforts and joint targeting is apparent in the table, as yet it is not possible to know whether this was related to the impact achieved in dairy, curies and wheat, as opposed to maize and beans. DRI's leadership in targeting dairy and wheat most probably did contribute greatly to the success of the institutional interventions in these domains. The limited success in curies, on the other hand, suggests the importance of ICA-CCH's technical and financial leadership. But why didn't DRI achieve the same success with maize and beans? To address this question I must dive deeper into the linkage mechanisms that lay at the roots of institutional performance at farm level.

Performance of technology development and transfer tasks

A number of formal linkage mechanisms were established within the innovation theatre related to peasant agriculture in Nariño. The most frequently used ones, in brief, are:

- *Collaborative task groups* of technicians were regularly established at district level to carry out specific activities jointly, such as multidisciplinary survey reports, a multimedia extension campaign, design and implementation of an on-farm or on-station experimental programme, or production of a training manual or extension brochure. Some of these groups were temporary, meeting intensively over a period of some months. Others were rather permanent, meeting each month over a period of four years, as did the group that managed the intensive mixed farming unit at the regional research centre.

- *Subject-matter specialists* (technical, economic and communication) assumed responsibility for coordinating adaptive research, staff training, extension programmes and the

Table 9
Number of subject-matter specialists assigned to the Nariño Highlands, 1974 to 1984

Specialist field	1974-1976	1976-1978	1978-1980	1980-1982	1982-1984
Dairy production	4	4	3	2	2
Pastures/fodder	1	1	1	1	1
Curies	-	-	-	1	2
Milk processing	2	1	1	1	1
Horti/fruticulture	-	-	3	3	3
Socioeconomics	-	-	2	2	2
Extension/communication	-	-	-	2	3
Total	5	6	11	13	14

Source: ICA-CCH Final Report, 1985

production of extension materials. They needed both technical and communication skills, and maintained close links with farmers, extension workers and researchers. As shown in Table 9, the sharp increase in the number and coverage of subject-matter specialists in 1978–1980 coincided with the ICA-CCH move to ICA/Extension and with the subsequent shift of emphasis towards impact and dissemination.

• Systematic programmes of *on-farm trials* and experiments were performed by research or extension staff in collaboration with farmers, to adapt technologies to the specific conditions of a community or a zone. Generally, these trials involved formal agreements between the farmer and the implementing institution, including subsidized inputs and, in the case of high risk operations, compensation.

Table 10 shows the relationship between the use of certain task-related linkage mechanisms within specific agricultural production domains in Nariño in 1981 and the institutional impact. The table suggests clearly that in this case the use of collaborative task groups, subject-matter specialists and on-farm trials is associated with high impact. Training, measured by the existence of training manuals in 1981, cannot be said to make a clear contribution to impact on these domains. Apparently, although impact cannot be achieved *without* training field workers, if other linkages fail, training alone is not enough.

External factors

A number of external factors had a positive effect on system integration and performance as well. First, agricultural policy related to the peasant sector was relatively stable between 1975 and 1985, providing time for the institutions involved to organize their relationships. The experience in Nariño suggests that even when adequate formal and informal linkage mechanisms are in place, as was the case in 1978, impact will be noticeable only after a considerable time lag. It appears that institutions need time to work out their roles and reach a degree of consensus on priorities. Visible results at the farm level are also not reached overnight. Our data suggest this 'warming-up' period of mutual adjustment took about two years.

Table 10

Impact versus presence of specific task-related linkage mechanisms, 1981

Linkage mechanism	High impact domains			Low impact domains	
	Dairy[a]	Curies	Wheat	Maize	Beans
Collaborative task groups	yes	yes	yes	no	no
Subject-matter specialists	yes	yes	yes	no	no
On-farm trials	yes	yes	yes	no	yes[b]
Training manuals	yes	yes	yes	yes	yes

[a] 'Dairy' includes pasture management; the two cases are identical

[b] Demonstrations were held, but on-farm evaluations were not as widespread and systematic as for wheat

Sources: ICA-CCH Reports, ICA-DRI report, this research

Second, financial and human resources were available and adequate throughout the period 1978–1985. DRI financed field staff, operations and credit; ICA-CCH provided financing for additional specialist support, training, contingency funds and some operational costs. In addition, ICA-CCH funds proved particularly helpful in exploratory research, such as for curies, and in overcoming temporary budgetary constraints that could have hindered the smooth operation of already agreed field programmes.

Third, adequate marketing opportunities were available in most domains, particularly dairy farming. Rising farm gate prices and the establishment of new milk collection and processing industries made dairy farming attractive to many peasant farmers in Nariño.

One external factor that had a negative effect on the performance of all the core institutions was centralized decision making. ICA/Research programmes in Nariño, for example, tended to follow national priorities. Thus, although FAO had recommended as early as 1952 that the regional research station should initiate research on curí production (Muñoz, 1970), this was not done. These protein-rich animals are eaten only in certain parts of Colombia, and were therefore not regarded as a national priority. The decision to carry out adaptive research in curí husbandry was eventually taken at the district level by ICA-CCH, without the involvement of ICA/Research, and was later approved by regional and national ICA-CCH committees. The PCTT extension methodology provides another example. Although an effective extension planning and management instrument, it did not incorporate the use of farmer participation in setting extension priorities. Having identified this as a constraint, ICA-CCH, together with ICA/Extension, set out to fill this gap, introducing participatory diagnosis as an element of the methodology (Engel, 1984). However, although it proved efficient in the field, was tested by ICA field staff in another peasant region, was adopted nationwide by the ICA-UNICEF project and used by CORFAS in Nariño, it did not become a formal part of the national PCTT design.

A final example of the irrationalities stemming from centralized decision making concerns ICA's publications policy. During the period under study, ICA encouraged research and extension staff to write technical publications by offering salary incentives for publishing any materials officially. However, if *extension* publications were to be accepted for official publication, approval from the publications council at the national headquarters was necessary. This process involved a minimum of 47 actions, including decisions by people from eight different ICA units. Inevitably, many titles were either published too late for extension purposes or remained 'unofficial'. In 1981, only one title was published officially for Nariño. Over the following few years, publication procedures for this region were relaxed somewhat; local printing and audiovisual facilities were established under a Dutch grant, and local printing of provisional editions of all extension publications emanating from the Nariño districts was allowed before submission for official screening and approval. This resulted in a sharp increase in the regional production and use of didactic materials; 11 titles were published in 1984 alone.

Sustainability of institutional performance

A more general conclusion that flows from the discussion above is that to a certain degree institutional performance can be 'managed', i.e. that certain actions enhance it, whereas others work against it. This section will explore this line of reflection a little further by looking at the sustainability of institutional performance with respect to innovations in peasant agriculture. To do this I will take a close look at the situation in Nariño from 1985 to 1987. What are the prospects for the core institutions with respect to sustaining their impact? The argument will centre around three types of events: policy shifts, a decline in system integration, and the emergence of organized user control.

Policy shifts

Agricultural policies in Colombia have shifted rapidly since 1985: the focus, which was on the highland peasant-farming areas, is now centred on the development of the country's lowland agricultural frontier areas. As a result, the DRI budget has been cut considerably and the DRI has concentrated its efforts in Nariño on marketing and infrastructural projects. DRI funding for agricultural technology programmes has been reduced to a minimum and, although credit is still provided, little financing is available for extension services. ICA/Extension policy has also changed. By establishing District Information Centres, some efforts have been redirected into setting up a new information system for rural areas. One such centre was to be established in Pasto. However, the initiative has suffered from lack of funds and, by 1987, had added little to the already existing human resources, infrastructure and practices in Nariño. In 1987, ICA announced yet another extension policy, termed an 'integrated model for regional development' and imple-mented through regional training and technology diffusion centres (CRECEDs). CRECEDs are designed to integrate research and extension services within each agro-ecological zone and, through Advisory Boards, to plan the type and extent of producer participation in technology generation and diffusion (ICA, 1987). In 1987, it was unclear whether this initiative would have the resources required for successful implementation. Meanwhile, financial resources for extension have become even more limited.

The ICA-CCH bilateral project was terminated in June 1985. As a result, ICA/Extension lost most of its subject-matter specialists; some were rescued when ICA transferred them to the ICA/Research regional station in Obonuco. This was possible because in 1983 ICA succeeded in obtaining external funding for research. This went some way towards reducing the financial constraints on the Obonuco research station; it was formally designated as the national research station for peasant agriculture, and also became the headquarters for the national cereals research programme. By 1988, however, the financial situation had deteriorated considerably; the station was faced with budget cuts of up to 60% for some programmes, and operational expenses were stripped to a bare minimum.

At this point, operational expenses for on-farm research could be met only if external funds, either from the private sector or foreign donors, were available.

Decline in system integration

The decline in DRI's resources has been accompanied by a decline in the institutional leadership provided by DRI, particularly with regard to technology development. By 1987, in addition to their normal programming and administrative tasks, extension area managers were also expected to assume the tasks of subject-matter specialists. They have continued to organize adaptive trials, but have been able to devote very little time to adapting new technologies or developing new extension materials. Extension programming is illustrative: since 1985, very little time has been available to design new PCTT plans or even improve existing ones. Most PCTT plans in operation in 1987 were designed in 1983. In the period 1984–1987, emphasis was placed on increasing coverage by repeating past programmes; the number of farmers reached doubled. Meanwhile, however, the development of new subject-matter content stagnated, and production of written extension materials decreased from 15 titles in 1983 to 5 in 1987, of which two were reprints and two were one-page leaflets. The reduction in the number of subject-matter specialists also had a serious effect on research–extension integration, in that it led to the demise of collaborative task groups. As a result, inter-institutional coordination declined considerably between 1985 and 1987, with collaboration between research and extension reverting to predominantly informal relationships.

Organized user control

While the configuration of institutions that, beginning in the early 1980s, had successfully forged an impact on peasant agriculture came under extreme pressure, other organizations entered the agricultural scene in full force. In the future, cooperatives, non-government and user organizations may be able to address some of the problems outlined in previous paragraphs. The establishment of such organizations is a comparatively recent development and, at the end of the study in 1987, the degree to which they will be able to influence technology development and transfer in Nariño, and who their main beneficiaries among producers will be, remained unclear. The milk cooperative, COOPROLACTEOS, and the cereal growers' association, FENALCE, are both strong and articulate enough to take on a leadership role and demand services from the relevant institutions. Also, a regional beer brewery, Bavaria, has recently started to finance ICA's adaptive research on barley.

COOPROLACTEOS has already played a leading role in some areas. It is likely to strengthen its involvement in technology development for dairy producers. Established in 1977 with Dutch assistance, it has grown into a multi-million peso organization producing a wide range of dairy products for Nariño and other regions. Its membership consists mainly of small and medium producers, whose interests it represents at both regional and national levels. With respect to small producers, FENALCE may play a more influential role in setting technology development and transfer priorities, but is less firmly rooted in Nariño than COOPROLACTEOS. Further, DRI has established a national association for DRI users, ANDRI, with a regional chapter in Nariño. However, it is unlikely ANDRI will have much influence on institutional policies. The curí producers association, ASOCUY, has not yet established itself as a strong regional organization.

In 1986, ICA/Research established an advisory council for its regional research centre at Obonuco. Council meetings are attended by commercial farmers, agricultural professionals and a peasant farmer representative. Prior to this, there was no mechanism whereby peasant farmers could exert a direct influence on the research policy of the centre. However, strong limitations of a sociocultural nature do stand in the way of effective participation by the peasant farmer representative.

Tentative conclusions

Against the background of this review of agricultural performance in the peasant sector of Nariño, a number of tentative conclusions can be drawn. First, the period during which system integration was at its peak appears to coincide remarkably well with a period of increased impact on agricultural performance. Hypothesizing a direct link between improved inter-institutional coordination and successful agricultural innovation does not seem too farfetched. Second, strong institutional leadership and strategic consensus developed among core institutions during this same period. This was closely related to the effective allocation of financial resources, in line with well-defined institutional policies and priorities. Therefore, this case suggests that leadership, strategic consensus and resource linkages play an important role in forging inter-institutional coordination. Third, a number of task-related linkage mechanisms have been identified that can be directly associated with high institutional performance and impact. However effective general policies and leadership may be, apparently a number of explicit linkage mechanisms must be operative as well. In this case, collaborative task groups, subject-matter specialists and on-farm adaptive trials provided linkages.

The feature these linkage mechanisms have in common seems to be the creation of learning opportunities. Some, such as collaborative task groups, provide interdisciplinary and/or inter-institutional learning settings for professional staff who otherwise are engaged in developing their own areas of specialization. Others, like on-farm trials, help create opportunities to learn from and with farmers. For subject-matter specialists, for example, this puts professionals in a liaison position, which enables them to collect and integrate knowledge and information from a variety of relevant sources into practically tested packages of technical recommendations. This leads me to suggest that the existence of learning opportunities, as well as the integration of knowledge and information from various relevant sources, must be considered important elements in explaining the degree of effectiveness of interventions in agricultural innovation theatres.

As far as contextual factors are concerned, it seems clear that stable agricultural policies, adequate financial and human resources, and incentives for agricultural development at farm level are necessary conditions for effective performance of agricultural institutions. This is of course not new. It does however underline the importance of the particular conditions we found in the Nariño theatre at the time of the study. Additionally, a degree of decentralization in decision making is probably also associated with high performance; centralized decision making may effectively block institutional performance and integration at district and field level.

I conclude from this case study that although integration seems an important factor in explaining institutional impact with respect to smallholder innovation in agriculture, it is not enough. Strategic consensus, institutional leadership and adequate allocation of funds play an important role as well. In addition, what appears to give effective linkage mechanisms such a prominent role is their contribution to the creation of joint learning opportunities among the relevant social and institutional actors. Therefore, the case study suggests that innovative impact on smallholder agriculture requires relevant social actors to not only liaise effectively but also to find allies and develop shared competences for achieving innovation in agricultural practices. We will follow up this point in Chapter 4.

4. The emergence of innovation configurations

Chapter 3 argues that there is a positive relationship between inter-institutional coordination and innovative impact. Institutional leadership, strategic consensus and resource linkages seem important to accomplishing coordination. This chapter takes the issue a number of steps further: How do institutions actually achieve coordination? How do they nudge each other into making mutual adjustments? What role does institutional leadership actually play? Eventually, this process provides an instrument to study these and related questions in practical situations.

First, using the Nariño case study material, we look at how specific patterns of interactive relationships emerge. Generally this involves a limited set of core actors who, by virtue of the human, financial and other resources they command, are able to wield considerable influence upon others, and effectively direct the course of agricultural innovation (see 'Creating a successful ...', below). The pattern formed by such an alliance is labelled an *institutional configuration*.[1] Such a configuration is the result of accommodations made among core actors with respect to their views, procedures and resource allocations.

I then present preliminary conclusions on the social organization of agricultural innovation drawn from this chapter, and suggest that institutional configurations are part of a broader phenomenon: *innovation configurations.* These emergent structures help actors in complex innovation theatres to act jointly – they are the closest we come to a joint management structure for coordinating tasks in such theatres (see 'Configurations as emergent joint management structures').

This result is further evaluated with the help of the ISNAR RTTL case studies (Engel and Seegers, 1992). Effective institutional leadership appears to lead to the emergence of particular institutional configurations, bound together in a mesh made up of specific relationships and coordinating mechanisms and demonstrating characteristic strengths and weaknesses, as far as innovative performance is concerned (see 'Driving forces in agricultural ...', below). This makes it possible to propose the use of *basic* configurations – a way of characterizing patterns of inter-institutional relationships in practical situations (see 'Basic configurations: a conceptual tool ...', below). Our conclusion is that if we are to understand the social organization of innovation better, institutional leadership, power, coordination and linkages need to be studied as a whole, and within the context of the social relationship patterns of which they are a part. Analysing existing alliances by comparing and contrasting them to basic configurations provides a practical way to do this.

---

1. I use the term 'configuration' in the same sense as Mintzberg (1983), who uses it to refer to mental and spatial arrangements of organizational parts that help us to understand the behaviour of the whole. Here 'institutional' refers to governmental, non-governmental or privately owned organizations that perform a function relevant to agricultural innovation.

Creating a successful institutional alliance: Nariño

The last chapter shows differences in institutional impact before and after 1978, when the Dutch bilateral development project (ICA-CCH) was integrated with the Integrated Rural Development Programme (DRI) in Nariño. It appeared that the combination of institutions resulting from that move successfully achieved both coordination and impact. How this alliance was created, why, and how it operated is what I intend to explore further in this section.

One of the main objectives of DRI in Nariño was to increase small farmer family income by introducing improved technology at farm level. This was complementary to its other programmes, such as rural housing. Yet DRI designers knew improving on-farm agricultural practices was not something DRI could do all by itself. It depended heavily on the cooperation of ICA, one of the few institutions that combined long-standing experience working with peasant farmers in the field with the technical expertise needed to suggest on-farm improvements. It also needed the agricultural bank, Caja Agraria (CA), with its institutional presence in most of the municipalities, to provide facilities for handling credit. As a result, DRI's intention to encourage innovation in the agricultural practices of small farmers created a functional interdependence among these institutions – in the eyes of DRI planners. However, the Colombian government was foresighted; it created not only a wish to collaborate on the part of DRI, but also gave DRI the means to reinforce this and build a coalition of institutions to do the job. DRI was made the financing agency for ICA/Extension and provided the money for a new line of credit. In one single move this made the CA the most important source of credit for peasant farmers in Nariño. Earlier, CA had never been able to effectively attend to this target category, by far the largest segment of Nariño's rural population.

The lack of integration with ICA/Research during DRI's first years of existence demonstrates the importance such resource linkages have in forging institutional alliances. During the early DRI period, until 1978, there was well-organized coordination of tasks between CA and ICA/Extension, but no significant collaboration with ICA/Research existed. This was consistent with DRI policy: it insisted on using technologies 'available on the shelf' rather than spending time and money doing more research.

As Chapter 3 shows, integration with the Dutch project 'ICA Convenio Colombo-Holandés' (ICA-CCH) changed all this. There we see that ICA-CCH originally worked closely with ICA/Research. In 1978, however, under pressure from DRI, it was transferred, to be integrated with ICA/Extension. DRI still did not want to finance research, but in the negotiations preceding the redesign of the development cooperation project it had to accept financing for adaptive research and subject-matter specialists, who would play a role as counterparts to the Dutch experts and as liaisons between research and extension. In return, DRI reinforced its institutional coalition with specialists in dairy production, veterinary services, horti/fruticulture and socioeconomics, funded by the Dutch (see Table 9). Later on, other specialists were added in the same way. Typically, this was not a one-time negotiation. Every two years, when the bilateral cooperation project was evaluated, the same issue (a fundamental policy difference between DRI and ICA-CCH) had to be reviewed and renegotiated.

Negotiating institutional accommodations

In fact, adjustments among the institutions took place almost continuously at various levels. This can be seen, for example, in the changing composition of the two coordinating bodies that controlled the ICA-CCH project, the national coordinating committee (NCC) and the regional executive committee (REC). To give one example: DRI representatives had participated directly in the NCC since 1978. An ICA/Research representative who had been a committee member earlier was taken off just when the DRI representative came on. However, the ICA representative was reinstalled in 1982: at this time the balance had again shifted somewhat in favour of ICA. Readjustments in the role of the Dutch ICA-CCH project, an important actor since 1974 in the Nariño theatre, are also shown by its name and general objectives. Its name in the period 1974–1978 translates as 'improving the life standards of peasants in Nariño, with emphasis on the production and processing of milk'. After 1978, under the influence of DRI, the name became more integrated: 'agricultural development of smallholder producers'. While the main thrust of the project remained focused on the development of improved agricultural practices at farm level, this change in emphasis had specific results: a scope that went beyond dairy and milk, and a wider range of subject-matter specialists, including new emphasis on socioeconomics and communication. In fact, minor adjustments were implemented every two years, based on the periodic evaluations. These were jointly performed by ICA and Dutch experts and, after 1978, DRI representatives.

These examples suggest that inter-institutional relationships are the result of negotiations among institutions over objectives, tasks and resource allocations: they are never static. Their content and shape are continuously being readjusted in practice. Some readjustments are planned in advance and sealed in formal agreements; others may be *ad hoc*, remaining largely informal. The origin of accommodation is a wish and/or need to cooperate, perceived by a number of social actors. In the case of Nariño, DRI had an obvious need to link up with ICA and CA. DRI had no presence at all at farmer level in the region; smallholder agriculture was an unknown territory. Government institutions that did work with smallholders in Nariño included INCORA (involved in land reform) and CECORA (supporting formation of peasant cooperatives). However, political support for these institutions had diminished dramatically during the early seventies. Moreover, DRI was intended to intervene in agricultural production, not in organizing farmers: its main purpose was the modernization of peasant agriculture. Therefore, it focused on collaboration with ICA, with its long-standing institutional presence and experience both in working with smallholders in extension and in agricultural research in the Highlands; and CA, which as a bank had offices in most municipal capitals. Further, CA had considerable experience in extending credit to private farmers in Nariño, though not the smallest ones. ICA was very interested in having DRI take over financial support of its extension activities: the regional rural development project that had financed ICA/Extension had ended in 1975. Collaboration with DRI meant an opportunity to continue and even significantly increase ICA operations in Nariño. This was also true for CA, an institution that as yet had not been able to develop a line of credit that effectively served very small farmers.

Initially, DRI and the primarily technical ICA specialists gave very little attention to the role of on-farm adaptation, socioeconomic constraints, local agro-industries and social differentiation within the peasant population. The 1978 ICA-CCH evaluation and the changes it precipitated changed this. The conclusion was that if the improved technologies developed at the ICA Obonuco research station were to achieve widespread impact, there would have to be collaboration with ICA/Extension. ICA/Extension was 100% DRI financed, so this implied collaboration with DRI. In the negotiations that followed, DRI agreed to finance ICA-CCH counterpart staff and their operational costs. This meant a significant strengthening of ICA/Extension, particularly by adding subject-matter specialists and adaptive on-farm research in dairy, pastures, horti/fruticulture, socioeconomics and communication. This was a significant result: prior to the negotiations, DRI had not been willing to finance either such specialists or their activities. As I have argued in Chapter 3, the active participation of the ICA-CCH project had great relevance to other actors, for several reasons: it provided a link with ICA/Research and brought in external technical expertise; further, ICA-CCH devoted a considerable part of its resources to on-farm adaptation of improved agricultural practices. It also insisted on evaluating socioeconomic and communication parameters that affect the adaptation and adoption of improved technologies by smallholders. ICA/Extension, because of the restrictions imposed by DRI, did not have the means to do so. ICA/Research, left out for the same reason, had no funds and was unable to respond adequately. Other actors were either too weak or too insignificant. This 'flaw' in the original design of their programme was probably apparent to some of the managers responsible for the DRI programme.

This case illustrates how, to achieve their individual objectives – including survival as an institution! – institutions may have to rally behind one banner and coordinate their efforts. This is only possible when all relevant stakeholders recognize their mutual interdepend-ence, whether this is financial, technical, political or otherwise. The eventual result is a process of negotiation in which shared objectives are defined, tasks and responsibilities are assigned and resources are allocated. The banner eventually adopted in 1978 by DRI, CA, ICA and ICA-CCH as their own was formulated roughly as follows: *to improve the income of smallholder families in the Nariño Highlands by introducing improved technology at farm level.* We can call this their joint mission statement: it sums up intentions, strategy and intended beneficiaries. It reflects a 'theory of intervention,' agreed among the institutional actors involved. In this case, it projects the view that using improved agricultural technologies will cause farm family incomes to rise. This 'modernist' perception was grounded primarily in on-station experimental results, which showed productivity increases resulting from improved farming practices.

Multiple leadership

In the Nariño innovation theatre of smallholder agriculture, clearly several actors were able to command authority over the innovation process at the level of the small farm: DRI, through its selective allocation of budgets, financing only those institutional programs it perceived as necessary to achieve its ends; ICA, making use of its region-wide presence and technical expertise in smallholder agriculture; and ICA-CCH, by negotiating its technical and financial contribution. In a more subtle way, CA was also one of this group: it stuck to the national credit regulations even when lending to smallholder families, demanding for example that land or equipment be available as collateral.[2] This led Paulino to his proverbial design solution for the guinea pig 'shed' (Chapter 3). Its lending policy, therefore, had a distinct influence on the spread of technological innovations, particularly as the ones offered by ICA relied heavily on capital inputs. Eventually, after becoming firmly established as a regional milk processing cooperative, COOPROLACTEOS added a market orientation to the dairy alliance. The pattern of social relationships emerging from the respective efforts of these institutions is therefore multi-faceted, based on multiple

---

2. *This use of credit procedures compatible with the national standards the bank used in other situations was also the direct reason that credit for a rural women's programme implemented by ICA-UNICEF was not channelled through this bank, but through a private organization. The collateral that was routinely requested would have prevented CA from extending credit to women (let alone to groups, as was the intention of the project), except in rare cases.*

leadership. It reflects the objectives, strategies and resources of the various actors. Its impact must be understood as the result of their combined efforts.

If we look at various actors with respect to their degree of influence on technological developments in smallholder agriculture between 1978 and 1985, we see that some – notably DRI, ICA, ICA-CCH and, to a lesser extent, CA more than others (such as ICA/ Research, University of Nariño, SENA and ICA-UNICEF) can rightfully be referred to as core actors. They represented the main driving forces behind innovation in smallholder practices in Nariño during that period. This changed after 1985, when ICA-CCH was terminated and DRI withdrew its support, first for adaptive research and over a number of years for ICA/Extension as a whole. At first this was due to a shift in financing policies, which moved away from the relatively quiet rural areas of Nariño to areas of greater conflict. Later, the slow but steady growth of a policy of decentralization initiated by the central government, which gradually transferred control over agricultural extension from ICA to municipal authorities, was also influential. As a consequence, the combined influence of the national institutions that had spearheaded agricultural development among smallholders declined, while other actors, including private companies such as the local beer factory; a non-governmental agency, CORFAS; and the farmer cooperative, COOPROLACTEOS strengthened their grip. Characteristically, the latter two had been established with significant support from the Dutch Government, DRI and UNICEF.

Coordinating mechanisms

The Nariño case also serves to illustrate the mechanisms by which core institutions put their leadership into effect. We have seen how DRI implemented budget allocations and control to force ICA/Extension to spend DRI resources only on items consistent with the DRI programme. DRI effectively controlled the types of agricultural specialists ICA could allocate to the programme, the money it could spend on specific budget items (such as personnel, travel expenses, transport, didactic materials, equipment and so forth.) DRI also established a framework for extension activities: it specified which farmers were 'smallholder farmers' and could be supported, defined farmer-staff ratios, and decided which areas and which crops and animal husbandry activities could be included. Finally, DRI's instructions on monitoring, reporting and evaluation were very precise.

On the other hand, ICA/Extension struggled to impose its own approach to group extension (PCTT – see Chapter 3) and designed technical recommendations, staff qualifications, extension materials and visiting schedules according to its own standards. Also, its staff, together with staff of other core institutions, participated in setting regional DRI priorities. Its close association with the ICA-CCH project made it possible for ICA to readjust its recommendations to smallholder circumstances, and to significantly improve its analysis of small farm economics as well as the quality of its extension and training materials. It even became possible to assign a small number of specialists to themes (such as guinea pigs and fruit trees) that were *not* DRI priorities, but nevertheless, in the eyes of ICA and ICA-CCH, were promising possible future alternatives for smallholder agriculture. The ICA-CCH project played an important role in initiating and legitimizing such 'new' technical alternatives, defining technically and economically feasible packages of recommendation for farmers, and providing in-service training to ICA field staff. Moreover, as we have seen in Chapter 3, the project was instrumental in installing mechanisms for achieving mutual adjustment between the core institutions: there were coordinating committees, collaborative task groups, on-farm trials and liaison officers.

The sort of negotiation and mutual adjustment among institutional actors described above cannot take place without regular communication. Communication mechanisms and events were many. Representatives of DRI, ICA and CA met regularly with representatives of institutions that participated in other programmes sponsored by DRI during meetings of the DRI departmental committee. This committee discussed national and departmental policy issues, programme priorities and readjustments. For ICA, the monthly DRI technical committee meeting was more important. Directors of all institutions involved in the DRI programme were included. During the meetings, implementation of DRI national policies and the coordination of activities among institutions were the most important topics; the committee had an advisory capacity with respect to DRI programme decisions. DRI programme evaluations and budget talks were held separately, bilaterally between DRI and each institution, each year. Each quarter, national and regional coordinating committees of the ICA-CCH, made up of the core actors DRI, ICA-CCH and ICA/E, met with Colombian and Dutch policymakers. In addition to covering the affairs of the ICA-CCH project, these meetings served as a complement to the DRI meetings, particularly for technical matters. These meetings were also particularly relevant as gatherings where *ad hoc* solutions to immediate problems could be designed or complementary activities chosen to fill in blanks in already established DRI or ICA programmes.

Communication between extension workers, subject-matter specialists and researchers occurred during field visits and implementation and evaluation of on-farm trials and joint task groups. The latter were formed as interdisciplinary groups assigned to specific tasks – designing, monitoring and evaluating on-farm trials or designing and producing didactic materials for extension purposes. Such a group was also formed for the adaptive on-station research programme on intensive dairy production, sometimes meeting as often as once a week. Moreover, subject-matter specialists played an important role in extension itself; this guaranteed intensive exposure to farmers and their opinions. Researchers were sometimes invited to take part as well. Monthly staff meetings were held regularly to discuss matters of policy administration. Every three months, there were technical staff meetings to discuss progress with respect to stated goals of the ICA-CCH project. ICA-CCH technical programme evaluations took place biannually, internal evaluations and budget discussions annually.

Informal communication was encouraged by putting ICA/Extension and ICA-CCH in the same office space within the CA office building. Further, in the small professional community, informal contacts were always abundant. Social contacts among extension district managers, researchers, subject-matter specialists and other DRI related staff were frequent, as many lived in Pasto, the departmental capital; often they had attended the same university. A number of subject-matter specialists who had formerly worked as on-station researchers maintained strong links with the research station staff. The fact that ICA-CCH experts continued to carry out tasks at the experimental station also promoted further integration.

We may conclude that the effective institutional alliance created in Nariño was due to the combined leadership of a number of core institutions, each of which negotiated a space for itself within the common framework adhered to by all. This included an effective 'platform' (Röling, 1994a,b) for achieving mutual adjustments among institutional actors, consisting of a diverse array of both formal and informal communication links. The outline of the common framework was provided by the DRI programme. By means of its control of financial resources and programme priorities, it co-opted other institutional actors into joining in its approach to improving the fate of a significant part of the smallholders in Nariño. In effect, DRI can be said to have taken the overall leadership in the agricultural innovation process among smallholders. Yet in practice, in one way or the other, every one of the core institutions wielded considerable influence. Deftly using its expertise, ICA provided technical leadership, defining technically and economically viable options for the present and the future, and demonstrating practical results at farm level. ICA-CCH served as a connection between research and extension and as a source of external expertise and funding; this was used to increase awareness of socioeconomic contingencies and of different technical as well as methodological options among staff (including national staff) and policymakers. Paraphrasing Maturana and Varela (1984), the bond between the core actors might best be described as *operational independence within a situation of structural coupling*.

Resource linkages

The relevance of resource transfers in determining the outcome of innovation processes is underscored by the Nariño case study results. First, it is obvious that DRI could not have played its role without its control over financial resources. The influence of the ICA-CCH project also depended heavily on its resource contribution: expertise and financing for activities that were complementary to the DRI programme (socioeconomic studies, technical support for guinea pig husbandry, the establishment of a fruit tree collection and nursery, and the production of communication programs and materials). In addition, ICA-CCH funds enabled ICA/Extension to operate more flexibly within the framework set by DRI and ICA regulations and timing. For example, before DRI credit regulations were completely clear and officially decided, ICA-CCH provided credit to a small number of peasant farmers. They were later instrumental in its socioeconomic evaluation and demonstration programme, and valuable time was saved. The same was true for the publication of extension materials: although ICA officially had budgets to publish and print such materials, these were administered centrally at the national office and were generally insufficient to cover the demands of the regions. ICA-CCH funding enabled ICA-CCH and ICA/Extension teams in Nariño to produce and distribute their own materials. This both saved time and facilitated timely delivery. It also helped to assure participation of field staff in the development of materials.

ICA's leadership was contingent upon its command of experienced personnel from the entire region, and its long-standing technical expertise in Highland agriculture. Apparently, if a social actor is to be successful in becoming a 'driving force' in an agricultural innovation theatre, the actor must have 'something' to negotiate with. This cannot be simply financial resources. Effective institutional alliances, as we have seen, are not built on financial arrangements alone. The 'something' can be any resource, as long as other core actors perceive it as relevant and necessary for achieving the joint mission: money, technical expertise, connections, institutional presence in a region, relevant prior experiences, ideas, etc. On the other hand, the Nariño case suggests that the financial side of institutional alliances should not be underestimated: the withdrawal of core funding by the Dutch Government and DRI was an important factor, causing a deep crisis within the alliance of social actors who had effectively supported the technical improvement of smallholder agriculture in Nariño for a considerable period. Other actors/alliances were then needed, and for a number of activities such as dairy, barley and guinea pigs, others actually did take over (Engel, 1989b).
    Second, the inter-institutional relationships that govern resource transfers – and/or the influence of one institution on the performance of the whole – are not mere links. They are better understood as social relationships among institutional actors who, as part

of their strategies, create technical and organizational solutions and/or blockages that help them put their stamp on the course of agricultural innovation. In this sense, agricultural innovation can be understood as a continuing process of negotiation or renegotiation among social actors who to some extent perceive a common problem or concern regarding the use of relevant resources. Given the multiple interests involved in agricultural innovation, it can be expected that in any given theatre there will be a variety of interpretations of such 'common' concern, reflecting the world views, intentions and strategies of different actors.

Finally, it is apparent that over a given period of time there will be relatively stable patterns of institutional relationships, as a result of strategic consensus among core actors with respect to a shared mission; an agreed division of tasks and responsibilities; and mechanisms to achieve coordination and/or adjustment of tasks and resource allocations along the way. If the Nariño case is any indication, one would expect such patterns to include a number of closely integrated core institutions. They will have surrounded themselves with other social actors who share all or part of their concerns, and yet cannot do much about these concerns on their own. In this situation, the core institutions can rally these other actors and incorporate them; this allows the one or more core institutions, in effect, to direct the course of innovation. Once established, such *institutional configurations* may be expected to enable core actors to jointly recognize problems and/or opportunities, to formulate decisions and set priorities in a coordinated manner, and to act upon them, as well as to be able to experiment and make innovations in their joint behaviour or otherwise act as one whole. In accordance with the criteria set out by Long (Long, 1992: 24–25; referring to Giddens), I suggest we seriously study the possibility of understanding such configurations as emergent social forms, that enable organizations and institutions to exert some form of collective agency.

Configurations as emergent joint management structures

Above I argue that in complex innovation theatres relatively stable patterns of institutional relationships may emerge among social actors. I have labelled such patterns *institutional configurations*. What do these patterns entail? Can they be interpreted as forms of social organization? And next: do they matter? I will argue that they do. In my eyes, institutional configurations represent the closest we will find to an emerging *joint management structure* in complex innovations theatres. As a relatively stable pattern of relationships, such a configuration enables the institutions that are part of it to concentrate on what they do best, within an overall organizational framework that lays out tasks and responsibilities for each of them, specifies how coordination is to be achieved and which, hopefully, fits what each participant perceives as a joint mission. I will not pretend to extract a clear-cut theory from this analysis; however, a diagnostic framework, contributing to meaningful analysis and discourse on leadership and coordination in complex agricultural innovation theatres, may be possible.

The reason institutional configurations evolve in the first place has to do with perceived interdependence among core actors. This assertion is supported not only by the Nariño case study; it has also been proposed by a number of authors (see for example Kaimowitz et al., 1990). The emphasis on 'perception' underscores the *appreciative* dimension of social actors' behaviour in complex innovation theatres, DRI simply did not see ICA/ Research as relevant to achieving its aims; relevant technologies were available on the shelf, so why spend scarce resources on research? On the other hand, the Coffee Growers' Federation of Colombia decided to invest in breeding and research to develop a rust-resistant coffee variety some three decades before the disease even entered Colombian plantations. When they released the new Colombia variety in 1979, Federation officials initially avoided publicity. Information on the new variety was held among researchers and policymakers, not because they saw coffee growers as irrelevant, but because they feared they would be unable to meet the demand for seeds that would have been generated by publicity. When in 1983 rust was discovered in Colombia, the situation changed dramatically: the Federation's provincial committees requested local seed multi-plication sites and some took seed multiplication into their own hands (Kaimowitz, 1989).

In the same way, those responsible for the National Coconut Development Programme (NCDP) in Tanzania, designed to resuscitate its ailing coconut industry, used foreign funding and technical expertise in the development and delivery of improved coconut growing technology. However, initially they did not fully involve farmers in verifying the profitability and acceptability of the technologies under farm conditions. Also, the social actors engaged in marketing inputs and produce were not involved directly (Lupanga, 1990). On the contrary, Nigerian Government institutions responsible for improving the Cassava processing research and technology transfer clearly believed the private sector, particularly the industrial branch, would play a pivotal role in making improved processing technology available. Strong linkages with international and national private firms were therefore set up (Ekpere and Idowu, 1990a).

I conclude that social actors who are responsible for designing and implementing inter-ventions in agricultural innovation theatres differ in their appreciation of the relevance to innovation of particular social actors, including their functional interdependence. The ideas of core actors with respect to the need for institutional cooperation, that is what we might see as their 'institutional intervention model', play a role in the way configurations evolve. This becomes even clearer when we look at cases in which parallel sets of social actors emerge, who seem involved in similar tasks. Aroceno-Francisco (1989) illustrates the emergence of two parallel sets of institutions involved in potato technology development and delivery in the Philippines. They failed to integrate their efforts, as each felt nothing could be gained from working with the other. Both were independently financed and felt equally competent to carry out their assigned tasks. An unwillingness to follow through on agreements was the result. In another case, as we will see in Chapter 8, the social actors involved recognized three separate 'blood lines' in horse husbandry in the Netherlands: those involved in horse breeding and export; those involved in competitive horse riding and racing; and those involved in recreational horseback riding. Mutual interdependence was judged to be far greater among social actors belonging to the same 'blood line' than across 'blood lines'. The horse husbandry innovation theatre therefore had three segments and sets of social actors, and at least those who experienced no immediate problems were content with this (Engel et al., 1990).

Only those who, for one reason or another, think such institutions should cooperate more will find such a situation problematical. In the horse husbandry case, the recreational horseback riding segment protested because its actors felt excluded from relevant know-ledge and information other segments had at their disposal, and received a relatively small share of the government support given to the sector (Engel et al., 1990). The Philippines case shows how difficult it may be to change an established structural arrangement:

In the mid-1980s, the situation changed. The members of these core agencies in the seed potato subsystem expressed a desire to form closer relationships. This coincided with the imminent ... reduction of resources .... Meetings were held to discuss plans for collaboration .... However, no significant integration resulted.

Although those involved felt closer integration would maximize the use of limited resources, no one really wanted to make it happen. The intense feeling of competition among the researchers continued to persist (Arocena-Francisco, 1989: 6).

In the Nariño case as well, the relevance of *accommodation* among core actors with respect to views and interests is apparent: the factors mentioned earlier – strategic consensus on a declared mission; an agreed division of tasks and responsibilities; and agreed procedures for coordinating and, if needed, adjusting tasks and resource allocations – are all present. Apparently what is needed is a 'theory of intervention' that is at least partially shared, regarding what to achieve and how to achieve it. Moreover, this must be laid down in specific principles and procedures that will guide programme design and implementation. This requires an intensive process of *negotiation on the allocation and use of resources*, which must be ongoing; it cannot be completed and forgotten. The outcome of this process, the formal and informal mechanisms by which the use of resources to accomplish particular tasks is regulated, we have labelled coordinating mechanisms. The particular sets of mechanisms used may vary widely from one sector to another, or from one crop to another, and may have a decisive influence on performance with respect to innovation, as shown in the CIDT case.

> Compagnie Ivoirienne des Fibres Textiles (CIDT): CIDT is a mixed company in which the government of Ivory Coast holds the majority of shares. Until 1977, CIDT worked with cotton. In 1978 it became a regional development corporation for the savanna zone, responsible for all field crops. In addition to cotton, it is now responsible for the improvement of rice, maize, millet, sorghum, ground nuts and yam production.
>
> CIDT finances cotton research directly, and its budget is indexed to the price of cotton. One cotton researcher is a full-time liaison between CIDT and the research institute (IDESSA). Inputs for cotton production are delivered by CIDT directly to the farmers, generally free of charge; farmers have no choice but to use the recommended technologies, particularly since CIDT is the only cotton buyer. The use of contract farming means that the farmer's only risk factor in growing cotton is the value of labour used during the growing season.
>
> For other crops, CIDT finances research in a rather *ad hoc* fashion, based on the amount of external financing from the government or international donors; a single researcher serves as a liaison between the research institute and CIDT for all non-cotton crops. For these crops there is no contract farming.
>
> At village level, CIDT has constructed a storeroom and established a 'chief farmer' in each village. One CIDT extension agent works with approximately 100 peasant farmers; in total, CIDT covers about 124 000 farmers (85%) in the savanna zone.

The impact of this institution reflects its design. Cotton development is successful: a farmer who wants to plant cotton has easy (and free) access to the latest technologies; intensive research and marketing support is available. New varieties, inputs and information for maize and rice are available, but problems may arise due to late arrival of inputs or differences between farmers' demands and what they actually get. Locally very important crops like millet, sorghum and yam receive considerably less attention from both research and extension. Only one new variety of yam has been introduced, and that was five years prior to the study cited. (*Source:* Eponou, 1990a)

Another way to illustrate the importance of a well-developed assortment of coordination mechanisms is to look at what happens when the mission of a successful configuration of institutional actors is changed or modified. In the above case, stimulated by CIDT's success in cotton development, the Ivory Coast government modified its mandate so that the organization became a regional development corporation. When this happened, it did not lead to equally successful performance in food crops (Eponou, 1990a). Once established successfully, an institutional configuration seems to have a momentum of its own. It goes on doing what it was designed to do and can do best. But also, different crops, circumstances and objectives seem to require different configurations of actors and relationships, even if the actors themselves are roughly the same. This is underlined by the example from the Dominican Republic.

Rice in the Dominican Republic: The highly successful development of the rice sector during the 'Trujillo Era' (1929–1959) demonstrated the success of market-led innovation. Entrepreneurial farmers took advantage of the opportunities provided by large investments in the irrigation and industrial infrastructure and the national population's steadily increasing demand for rice. The land reform initiated in the 1960s caused a gradual differentiation in the hitherto rather homogeneous group of rice growers of all sizes: on the one hand there were 'private farmers' (holding up to 31 hectares planted in rice); on the other hand 'public farmers' emerged, who were beneficiaries of the land reform (each with three hectares at most). During the 1960s and 1970s several government services were created, resulting in a strengthening of policy-led influence on rice innovation, particularly with respect to the public sector farmers. During the 1980s, however, productivity among public farmers still lagged far behind the private sector (on average, 2.58 tons/ha, in comparison with 3.37). The government objective of self-sufficiency in rice had not been achieved.

Taking into account the long-standing technical support from the Chinese Mission and hence the technical strength of the actors in the rice innovation theatre, Perez (1990) offers various factors to explain this situation. The most important are frequent shifts in the philosophy, methodology, organization and operations of the extension service, including frequent changes of key personnel; continuous lack of resources, leading to extreme dependency on external financial donors, each of which in turn imposed their own view with respect to managing institutional relationships related to innovation, hereby aggravating already existing discontinuities. In addition, the technology offered by the extension agencies to the public sector did not fit their production systems and conditions well enough. Finally, in a situation where on-farm prices for rice were kept low while input costs rose continuously, public farmers could not earn a minimum income from their crop. (*Source*: Perez, 1990)

This example shows that an institutional alliance with success in developing and promoting improved technologies among commercial farmers will not necessary achieve the same degree of success with peasant farmers. The supportive mix of interventions and technical options they offer may not be compatible with the realities faced by peasant farmers. In this case, the large and entrepreneurial farmers are able to reap the benefits of the opportunities offered by the 'Trujillo Era' configuration; others, in this case the public farmers, are not. The haphazard attempts to complement the package with government services did not change that. Case studies in several Central American countries with respect to small grain producers (see Chapter 8) point in the same direction: a particular configuration of institutions serves a particular constituency well; constituencies with radically different needs and/or constraints need to go elsewhere to receive adequate support. They may have to fall back on informal networks or direct relationships with input suppliers to obtain technical information (Jaén and Palacios, 1993). We conclude that, in the process of becoming successful, institutional configurations are tailored to the needs and circumstances of a *particular constituency* of farmers. Once established, shifting their focus towards a significantly different constituency would require a major rethinking of their design and a restructuring of their operations. Institutional configurations develop routines, customary ways of thinking and doing things that correspond to the institutional design, the categories of beneficiaries, the technologies and the situations they know or have learned to deal with. Such routines are laid down in particular coordinating mechanisms such as contract farming, free or commercial distribution of inputs and services, research and extension financing, staff–farmer ratios, coordinating committees, informal information networks or liaison offices. Therefore, effecting a change of direction in the agricultural innovation process means achieving a renegotiation of the principles and customs that previously governed inter-institutional relationships. Without this, the principles and customs underlying collective institutional behaviour may limit performance, even if objectives and intentions have changed.

This means that institutional configurations which succeed in attending to the needs of a particular category of agricultural producers cannot be expected to automatically serve other constituencies in an equally competent manner. Configurations of social actors cannot simply begin to cope with new challenges, constraints and perhaps a different range of technical and organizational solutions. Institutional configurations are the result of negotiations among social actors: they represent particular accommodations based on a shared idea of what has to be done, who is to benefit, and why and how (a 'theory of intervention'). Success proves the goodness-of-fit of the configuration to a particular type of innovation in a particular situation, not necessarily its ability to deal with other objectives, other technological developments, beneficiaries and/or conditions.

A final relevant aspect of institutional configurations is their time and situation-specific nature. As we have seen in the Nariño case, one can speak of a configuration only as being stable within a given period of time. Since configurations are socially constructed, their stability depends upon continuing effective support from all involved actors. As soon as one core actor withdraws a significant part of its support, a new situation arises in which strategies and institutional relationships will be reviewed and possibly renegotiated; a realignment of actors may occur. Exactly how such re-configurations occur, and how these may affect agricultural development, seems to me an interesting field of empirical study.

Innovation configurations

From the above I conclude that institutional configurations can be seen as emerging forms of social organization, which result from lasting relationships among individual social actors who recognize their mutual interdependence with respect to some common objective or concern. A degree of appreciation of each others' competence must develop, to assure a minimum level of cooperation. A process of accommodation of views and interests among core actors leads to a shared 'theory of intervention', specifying individual tasks and responsibilities plus an array of coordinating mechanisms that establish coordination and mutual adjustments among the actors. Coordinating mechanisms will include a joint mission, priority setting and resource allocation procedures, as well as a meshwork of formal and informal communication relationships. Once consolidated, an institutional configuration demonstrates particular characteristics (such as a given leadership pattern and effectiveness in addressing the needs of specific farmer constituencies) and a momentum of its own (left to itself, in unchanged conditions, it is apt to go on doing what it can do best).

Institutional configurations can be seen as one form of *innovation* configuration, a more general concept that I believe can further contribute to the understanding, facilitation, and management of complex innovation theatres. An innovation configuration can be seen as the agreed management structure that is socially constructed by a set of social actors, enabling them to make decisions and act collectively. As such, it forms the basis for collective forms of agency in complex innovation theatres. Thus innovation configurations provide an organizational perspective that can be used in unravelling and discussing organized forms of interaction, and hopefully, in understanding their impact upon the direction taken by agricultural innovation. They do this in part by drawing attention to emergent forms of social organization.

Driving forces in agricultural innovation theatres: the role of institutional leadership

Several authors have discussed the predominant influence of certain types of actors upon agricultural innovation. Sims and Leonard (1990) describe a situation in which the absence of external pressure (for example, from donors and/or government) leads to research outputs that are not relevant to farmer's needs – particularly resource poor farmers. Here, I do not consider these pressures to be external. Rather, such actors exercise a very tangible influence upon the innovation process; therefore they should be included as actors in the theatre being studied. On the other hand, farmers are also actors. Röling (1990) emphasizes the need for farmer or user control, to ensure effectiveness and relevance in technology development. Kaimowitz (1991) has suggested four types of actors capable of exerting significant pressure upon innovation processes: national policymakers; foreign agencies, including donors; farmers and their organizations; and the private sector. The cases suggest a fifth 'driving force': research and development. The research community often seems to be the most important driving force behind technology development, exchange and implementation. In this case, technological development may respond more to 'what is technically possible' than to 'what is socially desirable or economically feasible'. Technology push can also come from a dominant presence of agricultural input suppliers. Röling (1990: 4–6) labels development situations 'technology-driven' when international, national, governmental or non-governmental research and development institutions are left considerable 'room of manoeuvre' in developing their policies and practice. A relatively recent development, which lies outside the scope of this book, is the considerable influence consumers, tourists, environmentalists and nature conservation groups may have on agricultural innovation.

Five types of institutional leadership in agricultural innovation theatres

I conclude that there are five or more types of social actors who have the potential power and means to exercise leadership and co-opt others into coordinated efforts: those who represent the market; those who formulate and implement government policies; farmers and their representatives; those who are involved in research and development; and donor agencies. Earlier paragraphs show how forms of social organization emerge among institutional actors in complex innovation theatres, coming to serve as something close to a joint management structure for generating coordinated behaviour: the institutional configurations. I pointed to the strong relationship between the emergence of a particular configuration of institutional actors and the capacity of core actors to exercise leadership, to accommodate each other's views and interests, and to direct or co-direct the innovation process. Here we explore whether particular types of leadership might be associated with particular coordination mechanisms, strengths and weaknesses in joint performances related to innovation. To answer this question we reviewed the case study materials and focused our attention on three issues (Engel and Seegers, 1992):[3]

- situations in agricultural innovation theatres where strong institutional leadership by a single core actor was evident.
- the core actors and principal coordinating mechanisms associated with such situations, and,
- the most common problems, strengths and weaknesses reported in such situations.

Strong institutional leadership by a single core actor does not mean other actors exercise no leadership at all. It means that, in the opinion of the researchers, and taking all factors into consideration, the over-all leadership of one actor was of predominant importance in achieving and maintaining the configuration as a whole. This is illustrated by the Nariño case: I have shown (Chapters 3 and 4) that several actors contribute crucial pieces to the 'leadership puzzle' for smallholder agricultural innovation in the Highlands. Yet it is evident that the rural development programme DRI 'pulled them together' in a relatively successful institutional configuration between 1978 and 1985. It did so precisely by allowing other core actors a degree of autonomy to design and direct the activities in which they are most competent: ICA assumed leadership over technical matters concerning smallholder agriculture, developing technical recommendations and extension programs according to its own standards; the ICA-CCH project too was allowed operational autonomy, within a common policy framework. I would classify the Nariño configuration during that period as 'policy led', as it was DRI, the institution representing general government policy, which laid out and reinforced the common framework that set the stage for successful accommodations among actors.

Market led innovation

Where the market is accepted as the place where the success or failure of agricultural innovation is eventually determined, those social actors who control the marketing and/or processing of agricultural products lead the pack: marketing boards; traders; trading companies or boards; agro-industries; and, increasingly, retail or fast-food chains. This is clearest for export crops: coffee and rice in Colombia (Kaimowitz, 1989; Agudelo, 1989); cotton and rice in Côte d'Ivoire (Eponou, 1990a); apples in Chile (Bemelmans, 1992; Chavez Tafur, 1994). Perhaps the strongest coordination mechanism in market led innovation is its focus on one or a number of 'commodities'. The 'theory of intervention' is geared towards producing a product that corresponds to national or international market standards. Research is organized in commodity research programmes. Extension approaches are likewise commodity oriented; specialists concentrate on developing

---

3. *A note on bias: in this chapter I concentrate on forms emerging from the interaction between institutional actors. Since our case study materials cover settings in which governmental, and some private, but hardly any non-governmental agencies play a role, this is a logical enough course of action. Also, it seems adequate to our present purpose of studying leadership, power and influence in agricultural innovation theatres. Eventually, it will have to be complemented by further research, part of which is presented in Chapter 5 where I study networking among non-governmental organizations for sustainable agricultural development.*

adequate 'technological packages'. In the workplace, coordination is achieved through cooperative agreements and/or commercial contracts among actors. Contract farming is widely adopted to guarantee the use of improved technologies by producers. Company field staff and technical advisers supervise the use of prescribed technological packages and report on bottlenecks in production (Eponou, 1990a; Chavez Tafur, 1994). When and where necessary, links with external research and extension agencies are activated. Engel (1990a), referring to the post-1985 period, provides an example of a local beer factory that finances the costs of barley research in South Colombia. Agudelo (1989) describes a cooperative agreement between the Rice Growers Association of Colombia, contracting research with CIAT and ICA. Eponou (1990a) provides examples for cotton, maize and rice.

In market led innovation theatres, there generally seem to be relatively efficient linkage arrangements. Orientation to the market obliges social actors to be aware of technological developments and opportunities, and to anticipate possible constraints. Kaimowitz (1989) describes the often informal mechanisms that over a period of more than 15 years led to the development and utilization of the rust-resistant coffee variety described earlier – a part of the successful rust prevention and control strategy of the Colombian Coffee Growers' Federation. Also, the funding of research and extension may simply be indexed to output figures (Eponou, 1990a). Where they are not, financing of research, development and extension still tends to follow market trends closely. In general, the private sector spends more money on linking these elements than does the public sector (Pray and Echeverría, 1990). Other problems such as lack of perceived interdependence and lack of leadership and focus do not appear in the case studies of market led innovation theatres.

Market led theatres do evidence some lack of sensitivity to social and environmental problems. Core commercial actors are interested in building effective relationships with a limited number of commercial farmers who can provide the products, quality and quantities they need. The number of farmers involved is dictated by the market shares the core actors command, and by the current level of on-farm productivity. Normally, their strategy is to increase this level rather than to increase the number of farmers they work with. Thus they work with a small proportion of the rural population. As a result, otherwise successful developments of commercial agriculture often report social differentiation as a side effect. An example from the apple export sector in Chili is given by Chavez-Tafur (1994). It is also apparent from Perez's (1990) observations of bias in favour of commercial farmers as opposed to 'public' farmers in the case of rice in the Dominican Republic, above. Nevertheless core actors in market led innovation may recognize the adverse social effects of market trends. Since 1968, the Colombian Coffee Growers' Federation has run the Coffee Zone Diversification and Development Program. It helps smaller peasant producers in particular to become less dependent upon coffee alone. It has not succeeded in replacing large areas of coffee with other crops, but has had some success in promoting the production and marketing of alternative crops like fruits. For smaller coffee producers in less competitive coffee areas this support has been especially important (Kaimowitz, 1989).

Another problem often associated with market led technological innovation is the deterioration of ecologically sensitive areas, such as the savannas of West Africa or the steep slopes of the Andes in Latin America, due to commercial mono-cropping systems. This, however is not limited to market led innovation. Whether core actors in market led innovation theatres are willing and able to direct technological developments towards more sustainable forms of agriculture, or whether such a change will require strong pressure from other actors such as government, non-government agencies or donors, is a matter of intense debate. Experience with integrated pest management in Indonesia (van de Fliert, 1993) seems to indicate that strong national policy pressure may indeed be necessary.

Policy led innovation

If the course of innovation is mainly directed by the government, we can speak of a policy led innovation theatre. In such cases, the government is normally the main source of finance for research and extension, and non-governmental and commercial actors are relatively weak with respect to research and development. The government imposes leadership by implementing agricultural policies, regulations and/or agricultural development programmes and projects. It may do this independently or with the help of donor agencies. As a result, core actors include government bodies such as the Ministry of Planning or Agriculture and its central or decentralized agencies. Coordinating mechanisms are rooted in the ways government policies are constructed: in planning (national or other levels) and project approval procedures, technology certification procedures, national development programmes, official mandates of governmental or semi-governmental institutions, and in bureaucratic procedures related to budget negotiations, allocation of resources, monitoring and control.

Policy led innovation theatres are often associated with large numbers of field staff, bureaucracy and a lack of operational flexibility. Frequent shifts in policies, organization and approaches (Palmieri, 1990a; Perez, 1990; Lupanga and Kasonta, 1990); inadequate resources (Perez, 1990; Eponou, 1990a); and a lack of integration with the private sector for marketing and input supplies (Lupanga, 1990) are commonly mentioned problems in policy driven configurations. Institutional instability also seems very characteristic. In addition, a degree of marginalization of research institutions is often mentioned. Government policies are frequently based on an assumption that technology and information is available 'on the shelf', and simply communicating it to farmers will be enough to assure application (Engel, 1990a). Lupanga (1990) shows how isolated research efforts may become when this happens, for a case related to cattle in central Tanzania. Palmieri (1990a) and Perez (1990) report on the limited value of technological recommendations to farmers in policy driven theatres, due to lack of cooperation between research and extension agencies. Status differences between researchers and extension workers are often reported, but the impact is not seen as very important. When research and extension are financed from different, independent sources (various donors, for example), a failure to recognize mutual interdependence may aggravate coordination problems.

Just as for market led innovation, policy led innovation may contribute to social differentiation. In addition, government programmes fit the intentions and conditions of some farmers better than others. As seen in Chapter 3, the delivery of improved technology to between 10–15% of peasant families in the Nariño Highlands was an impressive success for the ICA-DRI Programme between 1975 and 1987 (Engel, 1990a). Most of the technical improvements, however, required the smallholder to obtain credit. In this situation, it is not access to technology that limits technical innovation, but limited access to credit. As a result, only smallholders with such access could possibly benefit. Azucena cites a similar case for corn in the Philippines (1989). Moreover, in policy led innovation theatres, real influence by farmers on the course of agricultural innovation remains the exception. On the other hand, policy led innovation may be more sensitive to national priorities – perhaps social welfare and equity, ecological sustainability, or the production of staple food crops. A good example of policy led innovation that quickly accommodated new demands for ecological sustainability is described by van de Fliert (1993). Strong support from the central government allowed considerable progress in a relatively short time, replacing smallholder strategies based on pesticides with integrated pest management.

Farmer led innovation

Here, leadership is in the hands of farmers. Most case study evidence, however, from the ISNAR RTTL study in developing countries points to *lack* of influence, rather than effective leadership by farmers. Naturally, innovative farmers play a role as individuals. The obstacles impeding effective farmer participation in developing alternative technologies are many. This is not because farmers are not active innovators. Pijnenburg (1988) for example shows how colonists acquire new knowledge of farming areas that were previously completely unknown to them, without the intervention of a single institutional actor. Informal links among farmers, and when possible with institutions, are documented by Box (1990). Stolzenbach (1992) describes the way smallholders in Mali learn by continuously improvising and evaluating new options. Brouwers (1993) describes and analyses how small farmers in Benin learn and adapt their agricultural practices. Thus the reason for a lack of farmer leadership is most likely a lack of 'listening' skills and respect for farmer knowledge on the side of agricultural institutions and professionals (Engel, 1990b).

The coordinating mechanisms governing farmer led innovation have been given particular attention lately. Millar (1992) points up the role of indigenous knowledge and beliefs in decision making with respect to on-farm innovation. Ashby (1990) and Khan (1992), in reference to smallholders in Colombia and Pakistan respectively, cite the gap between farmers' and researchers' views on priorities for innovation in agricultural practices. Biggs (1989) describes various modes of research–farmer interaction, from contracting farmers' services to perform scientific experiments to strengthening farmers' informal research. Informal networks between researchers, extension workers and farmers play an important role (Box, 1990). Further, examples from the Netherlands and Chile show farmers forming study groups and maintaining frequent contacts with extension workers and researchers (Grooters, 1990; Altmann, 1989).

One can argue that innovation theatres led by farmers' associations and cooperatives, such as the Colombian Coffee Growers' Association, fall in the category of farmer led innovation. However, where such farmer organizations acquire strong influence on the basis of their economic power, as in an important export industry, farmer control often seems secondary to market control. To survive, such organizations must operate as agri-businesses, giving priority to market demands over those of, for example, small farmers. Moreover, in such businesses the influence of farmers is often limited to a small number of leaders, generally larger entrepreneurs or agricultural professionals. The case studies we reviewed (Engel and Seegers, 1992) include several in which a farmer driven theatre chose such a market orientation and, as a result, became industry driven. In the case of the coffee growers in Colombia, however, they did not forget to direct specific programmes at their 'roots' in the farming community: they attempted to counteract some of the adverse social consequences of economic decisions based on industrial priorities (Kaimowitz, 1989). In other cases, cooperatives may consider it in their interest to focus on particular groups of resource poor farmers, as for COOPROLACTEOS, the milk processing cooperative in the south of Colombia.

Often, the problems associated with farmer driven (or mostly farmer driven) theatres have to do with the quality of the farmer organizations themselves: their capacity for effective decision making regarding technology development, relationships with the rank-and-file membership and the degree to which they represent the variety of interests of farmers in the area. Village groups, farmers' associations and cooperatives often best reflect the interests of somewhat better-off farmers. Many members may fail to recognize their immediate concerns in the modernization policies of their organization. Such arguments are cited for non-governmental organizations as well. As a result, both farmer organizations and local NGOs may be under considerable pressure from members to achieve real improvements in farm level income in a brief period. Therefore, they may channel resources to projects that promise immediate results rather than those for the medium or long term. Experience suggests that farmer cooperatives must grow fairly large and market-oriented before they are able to allot much financing to research and development. Therefore, lack of resources is another prevalent issue when farmer led innovation is discussed. Unless research and development costs can be directly related to economic returns, farmers' associations generally will not fund them unless support is available from government or other intermediary agencies. After an extensive study of the rise and fall of local farmer cooperatives in Nariño, Moreno and Villota (1984) conclude that a main reasons that farmer organizations are slow to emerge and hard to maintain in resource poor farming communities is the discontinuity in the support from such agencies.

Research and development led innovation

Here, decisions about the course of innovation are mostly in the hands of researchers. Research institutions are given a relatively free hand to determine their priorities, research approach and ways of linking with other actors to disseminate their results. The influence research institutions can wield is rooted in the types of technologies and technical recommendations they are able to offer, and the value these add to the performance of various actors in the theatre. When they offer technologies that require considerable investments or expense to implement, their recommendations for improvements in farm practices will only be relevant to farmers with access to financial resources. If they concentrate on low-external-input-agriculture, they may loose the interest of the most commercially oriented farmers. Coordination of tasks in R&D led innovation theatres is rooted mainly in the definition of what a 'competent' researcher is and does: his or her prior qualifications, the accepted research approaches (such as on-station experimental research, farming systems research, on-farm research), accepted research protocols (e.g. plot designs, data collection methods, data processing routines) and the type of results expected (new varieties, fundamental or applied scientific publications, practical recommendations and so forth).

In R&D led innovation one may perhaps distinguish between two general trends, each with different ways of dividing and coordinating tasks: technology push and technology development. The difference lies in the type of interfaces built up among key actors. Technology push assumes that ready-to-disseminate technological packages are available or easy to put together. Dissemination strategies are designed using the 'linear model' (Röling, 1993): technologies are developed by research and transferred by extension to farmers, who adopt them. If necessary, feedback is given and passed back up the chain. Technology *development*, on the contrary, does not assume that technological packages are easily replicable; a need for local (re)design and (re)development is expected, to suit specific local conditions, available opportunities and skills. Strategies are based on sharing experiences, knowledge and information among relevant actors so that effective technological solutions to location-specific problems can emerge (Alders et al., 1993). The world-wide LEISA network is just one example of such an approach (Reijntjes et al., 1992). The difference is in the role played by farmers and other sources of indigenous knowledge. Researchers emphasize *participatory methods,* so that local actors can co-direct innovation. The development of such methods has received significant attention during the last decade. Examples include Biggs (1989); Haverkort et al. (1991); Jiggins and de Zeeuw (1992); Merrill-Sands and Kaimowitz (1989). In such settings, the effect of farmer influence can be increased when more attention is paid to creating adequate 'learning settings' (Rap, 1992).

A strong point often associated with R&D driven configurations based on a technology development model is their flexibility in dealing with complex and diverse agro-ecological and social environments. Their capacity to develop 'tailor-made' technology, fitting the needs and possibilities of specific groups of farmers, is largely unquestioned. However, their weakness seems to be in the replication of results. While appropriate technological solutions are developed on a small scale, their wider application lags behind. Building and maintaining links with extension workers and their agencies may be complicated (Lupanga and Kasonta, 1990). As a consequence, a very limited number of farmers actually reap the benefit of R&D led developments. The cost per farmer to replicate such efforts and serve a larger community is often inhibitory in terms of research and extension personnel and finances. Further, farmer control over research is generally limited to those innovative farmers who participate in on-farm research programmes.

Donor led innovation

In some situations, donors hold the key to innovation. Selective funding of particular research and development activities, combined with the recruitment and allocation of technical personnel, can allow donors to directly influence the course of innovation. More indirectly, donors bring in equipment and install infrastructure that facilitate particular types of research; they may pay extra allowances to field staff, or may recruit particular technical experts to evaluate project performance. Shetto (1992: 70) concludes that in Mbozi district, Mbeya region, Tanzania, 'Donor funding and policy orientations have a strong influence on the direction of performance of research and extension'. As a result among other things, very little research has been done on traditional crops like finger millet, sweet potatoes, cassava and sorghum; priority crops have been the object of most plant protection and soil research, and agro-engineering is seen as tractorization. Post-harvest techniques receive little attention.

A constraint often associated with donor led innovation is lack of institutional sustainability. Inter-institutional cooperation, even if successful, may collapse if the donor withdraws (Engel, 1990a). Perez (1990) mentions the lack of continuity in approach caused by dependence on ever varying sources of external financing. Shetto (pers. comm.) puts her finger on the same issue: each project evaluation, or a change in expatriate or other personnel, may cause a significant shift in focus. Important coordinating mechanisms, such as project committees, task forces, extension approaches or lending policies may change 'overnight'. As a result, donor driven theatres are praised for their flexibility and focus and yet, at the same time, loathed for their discontinuity and trendiness. Research efforts in donor driven theatres are mostly directed at applied and adaptive rather than fundamental research (cf. Lupanga and Kasonta, 1990). This accords with the assumption – often at the core of donor 'theories of intervention' – that the donor's objective is to develop effective ways of doing things in a relatively brief period of time, and then transfer responsibility for continuing the work to government agencies. In the context of such a short term target orientation, resource allocations are generally adequate. Lack of familiarity with local circumstances may hamper effective operations, particularly when project duration is too short.

Research and extension activities coordinated via donor projects generally use mechanisms such as project coordination committees, project allowances for field staff, better transportation and communication facilities, foreign advisers and superior equipment to direct and coordinate the planning and implementation of tasks. The mission to be accomplished, participating institutions, and coordinating mechanisms generally receive ample attention during project negotiations. User control in donor driven configurations is as variable as are the approaches to extension and research, and very sensitive to trends in the donor community. It is often difficult for donors to build up strong, independent user organizations that are able to survive their own withdrawal. Strategies that have been successful include the formation of organizations on a commercial basis and the transfer of all or some donor tasks and responsibilities, with the corresponding resources, to national non-governmental organizations. Both COOPROLACTEOS and CORFAS were established in Nariño with support from the Dutch Government, but, once established, succeeded in negotiating national support from DRI to significantly extend their operations (Engel, 1990a).

The role of leadership and coordination in complex innovation theatres

The discussion above leads me to conclude that institutional leadership does matter. Generally, various social actors are potentially in a position to influence the direction innovation processes take. Their ways of achieving such influence differ. *Farmers* depend upon their capacity to organize themselves into groups with enough clout to pressure other actors to take their views seriously; otherwise they require intermediaries, such as non-governmental development organizations, to articulate their views and bring them to the attention of other relevant actors. *Market actors* are actors who control the marketing or processing channels for agricultural produce. They influence innovation processes through the prices they pay, the technological packages they recommend and the quality standards they apply. Where necessary they use their financial resources to coordinate with or among other actors. National *policymakers* exercise leadership by formulating and implementing policies, allocating government budgets, setting priorities and otherwise laying down rules and regulations. *Research and development actors* affect the opportunities of other actors via the type of technologies they offer or, alternatively, are willing to study and develop. Depending upon specific circumstances, this set of actors might include commercial companies as well: input suppliers, seed multiplication companies, and so forth. *Donor agencies*, finally, use their financial resources and knowhow as leverage to impose coordination upon actors in the agricultural innovation theatre who are seen as relevant to their mission. Since in most theatres at least some of the social actors mentioned play significant roles simultaneously, it seems obvious that bringing about and maintaining coordination of tasks in complex agricultural innovation theatres is a complex social phenomenon.

Therefore it seems clear that the relevance of institutional leadership in complex innovation theatres lies in its power to influence the course of innovation. Leading social actors may use a number of mechanisms to influence decisions made by other actors with respect to innovation. Exercising such influence leads to the gradual development of a pattern of relationships among social actors who perceive each other as relevant to their shared cause. As a consequence, particular configurations evolve; these represent the way tasks are defined and coordinated among social actors. Such configurations are structural arrangements in which accommodations among actors are 'stored'. They reflect the accepted models and ground rules for collective behaviour with respect to agricultural innovation.

My arguments underline the role particular types of leadership play in creating such configurations. The evidence suggests that distinct core actors, specific coordinating mechanisms, and characteristic strengths and weaknesses of the innovative performance of the theatre as a whole are associated with particular types of leadership. I therefore propose the following hypothesis for use in the study of institutional configurations in complex innovation theatres: where one single type of social actor commands the social interaction related to innovation effectively, characteristic one-sided configurations emerge, which demonstrate particular strengths and weaknesses. The next section proposes an instrument designed along these lines for use in analysing configurations of actors and relationships with respect to innovation.

Basic configurations: a conceptual tool for studying leadership and coordination in complex innovation theatres

Using the above hypothesis, I propose to construct a number of ideal types: hypothetical descriptions of innovation configurations in which the balance of power is extremely skewed in favour of one single type of institutional actor. In line with Mintzberg's (1983) approach to organizational configurations, these ideal types will allow us to single out the intricate ways in which different types of actors impose their leadership in concrete situations, as well as the possible consequences for agricultural development. The purpose is first of all to debate the balance of power between relevant social actors with respect to innovative performance; and second, to explore its impact upon the course of agricultural innovation. These ideal types will be called *basic configurations*. For now, five types will be distinguished: industry driven, farmer driven, policy driven, research and development driven and donor driven. In line with my hypothesis, each of these theoretical constructs will specify coordinating mechanisms as well as the strengths and weaknesses related to innovative performance that can be expected to characterize a particular configuration. In the following paragraphs, I outline what such a definition would entail and briefly discuss the scope and possible uses of the basic configurations.

Five basic configurations

Industry[4] driven configurations

The social actors who control access to the markets for agricultural produce may be traders, retailers, marketing boards and/or agro-industries, and sometimes consumer organizations. These actors, working with entrepeneurial farmers, are the core of the industry driven configuration in agriculture. Their relationships dominate the theatre: innovations that increase the profit margins of the participants in the 'product chain' are promoted. This does not necessarily increase profitability at farm level: innovation may be implemented to improve the logistics involved in transporting the product (on-farm milk collection tanks, for example) or to comply with international product quality standards (perhaps *haricots verts*, green beans for the French market from small irrigation schemes in Africa, for example). Entrepreneurial farmers are not necessarily large-scale or rich farmers, but those with a more commercial outlook who see their farm as a way to earn a cash income; for them, profitability is a yardstick to measure their performance. They might even be contract farmers. Generally, agro-commercial or agro-industrial establishments take an active part in developing and transferring technologies. Research and extension are financed mostly from, and often even indexed to, market sales.

---

4. As not the 'market' itself but the social actors who control access to it are the ones in the driver's seat, I prefer the term 'industry', as a 'branch of trade or manufacture' (Fowler and Fowler, 1964).

As the quantity and quality of the produce that goes to market is what determines the returns of the sector, one would expect the *standardization of agricultural products and production technology* to be the primary coordination mechanisms. The aim of technological developments is generally to increase productivity and competitiveness. As a consequence, agriculture is split up into sectors and subsectors, each producing a narrow range of agricultural commodities: dairy, pigs, potato, grains, cotton, etc. An even more sophisticated pattern may evolve when interdependent actors articulate their efforts in production chains serving particular markets with products of a guaranteed quality. Market orientation is a strong point of these configurations; lack of sensitivity to social differentiation and long term ecological deterioration can be suggested as possible weak points.

Policy driven configurations

Core social actors are representatives of the national government; governmental or non-governmental extension agencies; and demonstration farmers. The framework set by government agricultural policies or programmes dominates their interaction. Demonstration farmers are selected on the basis of their expected ability to demonstrate the advantages of adopting the recommended technologies. They represent a wider rural constituency we may call 'programme farmers' – those whose interests are believed to be served by the current agricultural development programme. Industrial actors generally do not take an active part in the innovation efforts of such configurations. Research may play a secondary role, since technologies are believed to be available 'on the shelf', so that actors need only be trained to use them.

Coordination is established by seeing to the *standardization, upgrading and supervision of field staff performance* and the *standardization of technological packages*. Administrative and technical specialists therefore play an important role. The resulting configuration often manifests a rigid definition of tasks and hierarchical administrative, technical and operational controls. Sensitivity to policy decision making is a strong characteristic of such configurations; bureaucracy and inefficient use of resources can be a weak point.

Farmer driven configurations

Relationships between farmers' leaders, farmer organizations, and agricultural policy-makers are dominant. Extension and research are less prominent in decision making about agricultural innovation. Farmers' leaders represent a wider rural constituency of farmers, who are organized into farmer organizations of various kinds – unions, cooperatives, associations or functional groups – that can influence other actors relevant to agricultural innovation.

Coordination is apt to occur through *standardization of interests:* farmer's organizations will strongly articulate their needs at various levels, attempting to force other actors to adjust their activities. Another possibility is *standardization of norms*: When ideological overtones dominate the defense of farmers' interests, the configuration may begin to resemble Mintzberg's 'missionary' form (1983: 294). In such configurations, integration in the local community and the utilization of local knowledge and management capacity can be strengths. However, for resource poor farmers, the need for sustained technical and economic support from intermediary organizations and the possible danger of overemphasizing immediate results at the expense of long term gains are dangers. Strong farmer driven configurations seem to emerge around economically strong activities, such as coffee exports or milk processing in Colombia. Resource poor farmers may be members of such organizations, but then the configuration is more apt to resemble an industry driven configuration than one that is farmer driven.

Research and development driven

Core actors are 1) international and 2) national research and development institutes (governmental and/or non-governmental) and 3) innovative farmers. They may use either a technology push or a technology development approach (see 'Research and development led innovation', above). Commercial or industrial actors and extension agencies are often only marginally involved in R&D driven theatres. The rural constituency of R&D driven configurations are technologically oriented farmers who enjoy developing and improving their farming operations and skills, not necessarily with an eye to immediate payoff.

Traditionally, the principal coordinating mechanism in research and development driven configurations seems to have been the *standardization of skills*. Agencies emphasize the quality and skills of their staff and their freedom to work as they see fit. Staff recruitment and training are the agencies' most important instruments to guarantee quality of innovative performance. Work processes, that is, approaches and research methodologies, vary widely: from disciplinary, on-station research to interdisciplinary, on-farm and farming systems research. In the case studies, on-farm and farming systems research are most common. The strength of a research driven configuration of social actors seems to lie in its capacity to develop appropriate technologies for a particular category of farmers; if researchers and farmers are in close contact, its main weakness in the lack of replicability of results.

Donor driven configurations

Where donors have a predominant influence on the course of innovation, core actors are foreign or national donor agencies, agricultural projects, and demonstration farmers. Again, the primary rural constituency can be described as programme farmers: their conditions and interests fit the profile the donor agency had in mind when designing interventions. An agricultural project or programme is often created as a temporary 'support structure', to make sure donor interests and intentions are safeguarded.

Different donors prefer different coordinating mechanisms. Some emphasize the importance of flexibility and mutual adjustment – a tendency to avoid formalities and go for concrete actions – within a general framework of strategic objectives, tasks and targets. Others emphasize the standardization of all work processes, both in the institutions and on the farm, with strict administrative and technical control. Most are task oriented, to achieve tangible results in a relatively brief period. Generally, donor projects are able to adapt to changing circumstances and are given some freedom to search for the most appropriate approach to problems. However, especially where donors bring in considerable resources, the sustainability of their programmes after they withdraw is questionable.

Possibilities for use

Freezing an extremely complex and dynamic range of situations into a limited number of frames of course implies simplification. Moreover, the strength of the basic configuration concept is neither in unequivocal precision nor in unambiguous categories. Rather, I would suggest, its strength lies in encouraging critical reflection on the practical implementation of power and influence in complex theatres of agricultural innovation. This concept seems particularly useful when it is necessary to illuminate and debate actual leadership patterns, changes in the institutional balance of forces, appropriate mechanisms to accomplish inter-institutional coordination, and the impact of leadership (or the lack thereof) on the course of agricultural innovation. For example:

- Basic configurations may help make *multiple leadership* patterns explicit. They are not mutually exclusive: at any given moment, any number of institutions may effectively exercise influence over certain pivotal elements of the innovation process. As noted above, this operational autonomy may be a fundamental strength in the social organization of the agricultural innovation (Engel, 1990a). Yet, each of the actors trades part of their autonomy for the sake of improving the performance of the whole. A successful configuration is apt to allow each actor to 'lead' in those tasks it is best suited for (see 'Configurations as emergent joint management structures' above).

  As a direct consequence, successful configurations of institutional actors usually demonstrate multiple leadership: each core actor takes the lead in particular tasks, striving to impose the mechanisms of coordination it sees as appropriate to those tasks. Consequently, studying the leadership balance of a successful configuration is often more relevant than studying the role of one leading actor. Basic configurations can help in doing this. Take the example of shared leadership among DRI, ICA and ICA-CCH in the Nariño case (see 'Creating a successful institutional alliance'). Exploring the relevance of each basic configuration for explaining the events in the Nariño theatre makes it possible to study and debate the type of leadership exercised by each of the core actors, with their relative strength and impact on innovative performance, and to suggest improvements.

- Similarly, basic configurations may help to expose *gaps* in leadership patterns. They help the analyst recognize a number of driving forces with potential relevance to successful performance in complex innovation theatres. For example, the apparent lack of involvement with market actors, such as traders, retailers and industries (including export industries) seen in the Tanzanian example below.

  In the absence of formal links with market actors, the basic configurations stimulate the analyst to question whether market forces wield no influence at all on the innovation process, or whether in fact this influence is organized through informal mechanisms beyond the scope of the programme. One might ask further what positive or negative impact this has on the ability of the programme to achieve its objective and what specific coordination mechanisms help to achieve this impact. Finally, if such suggestions are wanted, this process of using basic configurations may help in proposing alternative strategies to improve the situation.

> Coconut development in Tanzania: When the Tanzanian government decided to implement the National Coconut Development Programme (NCDP), it did so because:
> 'By the late 1970s, the coconut industry was in serious decline. It was generally agreed that the decline ... was due to an overage palm population, pests, lethal disease of palms in some areas, lack of improved planting materials, poor crop husbandry, poor pricing, lack of research effort, ineffective marketing channels and lack of a unit for development and policy.'
> To remedy this situation, the NCDP was designed to identify, develop and disseminate improved coconut production technology. Noticeably, by 1989 no specific interfaces had been built up between market actors and the programme. (*Source*: Lupanga, 1990)

- The notion of basic configurations may also help to elucidate *changes* in leadership patterns. Leadership in complex innovation theatres is time and situation specific. Stability in relationships within innovation configurations, as we have shown, is temporary: configurations exist as long as the relevant social actors want to maintain them. Relationships among actors are continuously reinterpreted, renegotiated and reconstructed. Consequently, the balance of power is always being reconstituted, even though over-all leadership is often maintained by the same institutions. Every new committee, liaison device, task group, subject matter specialist, on-farm trial series, resource allocation or contracting procedure (to name just a few) – or any retraction of such a mechanism – affects the delicate balance of leadership related to innovation.

  The approval of extension publications in Nariño provides an example of a shift in the balance of technical leadership to favour specialists at the provincial level, through the modification of a standard approval procedure for extension publications. The impact of the move seen in this example can be studied in terms of whose influence upon innovation it strengthens and whose it does not. The basic configurations suggest a number of key issues that can enhance such a discussion.

  > The approval of extension publications in Nariño: The national publications bureau (PUBLEICA) was previously required to authorize printing and distribution carried out in the name of the National Agricultural Institute (ICA). To obtain this authorization, written extension materials routinely passed through a procedure requiring a minimum of 47 actions by people from eight different units at all levels within ICA. In Nariño, however, between 1978 and 1985 a strongly modified procedure was agreed. This put quality control of locally designed and used extension materials in the hands of provincial research and extension specialists. Then it became easy to update materials locally and make them available in time for each year's campaign. This decentralized control over the production and distribution of technical extension materials helped to reinforce local initiative and influence on technical recommendations to smallholder farmers. (*Source:* Engel, 1989b)

- Finally, basic configurations may help to identify possible strengths and weaknesses of a particular innovation configuration with regard to its impact or potential impact on innovative performance. The close fit of different configurations to different types of innovation, along with the strengths and weaknesses discussed above (see 'Driving forces in agricultural innovation theatres') equip basic configurations to help in drawing attention to possible 'soft spots' or opportunities in institutional arrangements. 'Building on a policy drive in Nariño' provides an example in which a weakness of the dominant policy led innovation process could be remedied by drawing on reinforcements from elsewhere.

  > Building on a policy drive in Nariño: One way the DRI programme in effect directed the course of innovation in the Nariño Highlands was by setting priorities: dairy, pastures, wheat/barley, potatoes, maize and beans were identified as adaptive research and extension priorities, to which DRI linked its budget allocations for staff and operational costs. Only staff and activities intended for priority sectors could demand and obtain financial resources. Both ICA/Extension and the agricultural bank (in its main small-holder programme) were fully financed by DRI, which provided a strong mechanism for directing innovation performance: there simply was no money available for loans, adaptive research and/or extension outside the priority sectors. However, as often happens in policy driven configurations, this also reduced the programme's flexibility

Table 11
A summary of basic configurations and their characteristics

Configuration type / Characteristics	Industry driven	Policy driven	Farmer driven	R&D driven	Donor driven
Principal coordinating mechanisms	standardization of outputs/ technical packages	direct supervision, standardization of work processes/ technical packages	standardization of interests, norms	standardization of skills/ education	mutual adjustment, standardization of technical packages/ skills, work processes
Dominant leaders	market actors	agricultural policy makers	farmer organizations	national/ international research	donors
Core actors	agro-commerce/ industry, entrepreneurial farmers	agricultural policy/ extension/ demonstration farmers	agricultural policy/ farmers' leaders	agricultural research/ innovative farmers	agricultural project/ demonstration farmers
Rural constituency	commercial farmers	programme farmers	organized farmers	technological farmers	programme farmers
Principal source of power/ influence	market articulations prices, quality control, resources	policies/rules and regulations, resources	political clout/ resources	new/improved technology, technical expertise	financial resources, technical expertise
'Leitmotiv' for innovation	efficiency/ output quality	policy objectives	farmers' needs	technical advancement	intervention objectives
Accountable to	individual balance sheet	government policies	farmers' interests	research community	donor policies

for work on other promising alternatives. To improve guinea pig husbandry, identified as early as the 1960s as a promising option for peasant farmers in Nariño, additional complementary staff and financing were drawn into the innovation theatre from Dutch bilateral sources. (*Source*: Engel, 1989b)

Scope and limitations

Basic configurations (summarized in Table 11) are ideal types – abstract constructs. They are not intended to provide an account of what *is* in the world. They provide a diagnostic framework whose purpose is to help in reflecting on the impact that current patterns of relationships have on the course of innovation, to provide a basis for designing useful accommodations and/or interventions. Therefore, it is important to take basic configurations as complementary ways of looking at things, not as mutually exclusive models. At any given moment, I have argued, a particular configuration can reflect the characteristics of several types of leadership and hence, can be analysed from the point of view of several basic configurations. Moreover, given the appreciative character of complex innovation theatres, different social actors generate different views of leadership and different understandings of the way coordination is to be achieved, even in the same theatre. These views might be quite disparate or even to a large extent incompatible. The central question is *not* 'whose perception is right?' but rather 'whose perception is more relevant?' and eventually 'which perception makes it possible to achieve accommodation among the perspectives of most leading actors?' Both the ways problems are perceived and the intentions guiding the innovation process at a particular point in time will be diverse.

A diagnostic instrument, therefore, is meant to raise relevant issues for such a debate. It cannot provide a blueprint indicating how innovative interaction should be organized; even if this were possible, it would bend the discussion in favour of social actors whose intentions and routines happened to coincide with this preformed pattern. What is necessary is instead a heuristic tool that can help social actors better understand their diverse interests and concerns, as well as their own interactions. In my view, the best approach is to facilitate a confrontation of different views and perceptions of leadership and coordination, within the context of a participatory action research project. This can encourage the emergence of relevant new insights and effective intervention strategies, and eventual arrival at an accepted, effective joint management structure. The basic configurations can be used as a tool to help in analysing the configurations in the situation under examination and clarifying the issues of leadership and power involved.

On the other hand, I do not want to suggest that the basic configurations constructed here are the only possibilities. In this respect, I differ from Mintzberg (1983) who seems to imply that organizational dynamics can be adequately described using a maximum of six fundamentally different structural arrangements. I believe the variety of ideas, forms and shapes found in complex agricultural innovation theatres makes such simplification un-thinkable. We may, in fact, suggest at least four 'basic configurations' in addition to those summarized: basic configurations driven by agricultural development actors, consumers, environmentalists, recreation or nature activists are equally imaginable. Moreover, our inclusion of 'local knowledge led' innovation in the 'farmer driven configuration' could rightfully be criticized. It is no secret that others in addition to local farmers play an important role in farm-based innovation, including priests, soothsayers and other local specialists (Millar, 1992; Brouwers, 1993). Apparently there is a big difference between socially organized and organizational behaviour. But the various types of innovative leadership and coordinating mechanisms have not yet been equally well researched. A more comprehensive, empirical exploration would be of great interest but falls outside the scope of this study.

Preliminary conclusions

The relevance of institutional leadership to complex innovation theatres lies in its power to influence the course of innovation. Using a number of mechanisms, leading social actors can influence the decisions made by other actors with respect to innovation. Such mechanisms are very diverse: they range from administrative procedures, informal meetings, coordinating and liaison committees, joint task groups, study clubs and field work approaches to government policies, budget allocations, price regulations, quality controls and monitoring and evaluation procedures, to name just a few examples. By implication, such influence leads to the gradual development of a pattern of more or less durable relationships among social actors who perceive each other as relevant. As a consequence of these relationships, configurations of actors and relationships evolve; these represent the way tasks are defined and coordinated among social actors. Such configurations are structural arrangements that reflect the accepted views, models and ground rules for collective institutional behaviour with respect to agricultural innovation.

Our findings strongly suggest that the innovation configurations seen in agriculture are multiple ones generally, a number of social actors interact more or less intensely, directing the course of innovation. Accommodations among these actors, made on the basis of perceived interdependence (rather than the subordination of all to the most powerful), seems to lead to the emergence of successful innovation configurations. Therefore, collective agency in a complex innovation theatre cannot be understood without taking multiple leadership into account. Each social actor contributes a different piece to the 'puzzle' called innovation. Whereas particular institutions may take over-all leadership in terms of policy and its implementation, other institutions 'fill in the blanks'. What the 'blanks' are, how relevant each one is and which social actor is most competent to fill it – these are issues for continuous and often heated debate among actors. As a result, institutional arrangements are continuously renegotiated and adapted, both formally and informally. This underscores the fluid nature of configurations and the balance of power within a configuration that may influence agricultural innovation at any one moment in time: they are characterized not only by multiplicity, but are also appreciative and dynamic.

Moreover, the role particular types of leadership play in creating particular types of configurations has been underscored. It can be argued that each type of leadership tends to favour the use of particular mechanisms to coordinate innovative tasks. In turn, innovation processes that evolve as a result of effective leadership of one particular type demonstrate characteristic strengths and weaknesses. The concept of 'basic configurations' is built upon these findings, and is proposed as an instrument that can be used in analysing innovation configurations in practical situations. As innovation in agricultural production continuously emerges and re-emerges – as the result of ongoing social interaction between relatively autonomous actors in rural areas – we can use configuration analysis to study how institutional alliances are formed, the extent to which these are valued and sustained (or, on the contrary, consigned to oblivion) and the ways these structural arrangements enable or constrain core actors as they attempt to direct technological development in agriculture. To support my claim that this instrument serves practical purposes with respect to analysis and reflection, I have demonstrated how it fits the interpretation of ideas and events as we know them in complex agricultural innovation theatres, and how using it contributes to meaningful discourse on leadership and coordination in relation to competent performance in innovation.

I propose that the configurations we have discussed represent an emergent joint management structure in complex innovation theatres. This enables core social actors to act collectively, to some degree, with respect to agricultural innovation. Therefore, I have proposed labelling these *innovation configurations*. However, at the same time an established configuration may exclude other actors from exercising significant influence on the course of agricultural innovation. Therefore, configuration analysis as proposed here represents an important tool for understanding the practical implementation of power and influence in innovation theatres. Naturally, it must be developed further. Thus far most of our studies have covered a particular type of configuration – the institutional one, in which government agencies play a dominant role. We have pointed out other possibilities, but they have not yet been studied fully. As a next step, in Chapter 5 we will explore alliances related to innovation among non-governmental development organizations.

The configuration concept, however, should not be taken as a description of how the world is, but as a perspective that can be used to study and debate social interactions among relevant institutions, and the impact this has on the course of agricultural innovation. Used as a 'window' as described in Chapter 1, it can help explain issues of coordination and leadership in complex innovation theatres. It fits within a soft systems action research methodology. Moreover, given the appreciative and socially constructed character of both the innovation process itself and its social organization, it appears that such issues are most effectively debated among the social actors who are the actual stakeholders in an innovation process. Configuration analysis is therefore most apt to be effective in a participatory action research setting, where stakeholders become co-researchers regarding the social organization of innovation. Nevertheless thesis work by university students has demonstrated the contribution of this perspective to more conventional field research as well (Shetto, 1992; Mirikhoozani, 1993; Chavez, 1994). In Chapter 9, I will return to this issue.

5. Daring to share: networking among non-governmental development organizations[1]

During the last decade or so, the social organization of innovation has been in flux. In most European countries, the fruits of scientific research are increasingly seen as commodities – something for commercial exchange. Government budgets for agricultural research and extension are being reduced and privatization is increasing. In Latin America, as government extension services were drastically reduced or even eliminated, non-governmental organizations virtually took over technical and economic support to low resource farmers. In Asia and Africa, governments have invested heavily in agricultural research and extension. However, maintaining this system is so costly that here too alternative ways to finance agricultural research and extension is high on the agenda of most policymakers. I see two main reasons for the preoccupation with such changes: first, the heavy drain on national budgets that large agricultural institutions represent; and second, the difficulty these institutions have in meeting the challenges of modern agricultural development. In short, agricultural innovation is organized in ways that are increasingly seen as not only too costly but also inadequate.

As a result, in many countries traditional actors withdraw to some extent and others become involved, such as non-governmental agencies and agro-industries, and different sorts of alliances for innovation emerge. This chapter examines such a new type of alliance: networks among non-governmental development organizations (NGDOs).[2] In many countries, non-governmental development organizations have taken the lead in searching for agricultural technologies for small farmers – technologies that are socially and economically, as well as ecologically, sustainable. Among these NGDOs, networking has gained momentum as a way of more effectively organizing support to small farmers. In this chapter I will review a number of networking experiences and argue that NGDO networks can be understood as emerging forms of social organization for innovation. That is, networks too can be seen as a type of innovation configuration, and one that is well suited to situations in which objectives are unclear, or where the parties involved have major disagreements about what the objectives should be. My research offers two lines of argument to support this claim. First, networking has demonstrated promising results in a variety of practical settings (Alders et al., 1993). Second, networking is a strong alternative because it resembles so closely what social actors, people and organizations would do in any case to bring innovation into their practices. This chapter focuses on the first argument; the second returns in Chapter 6.

1. *This chapter is based on Engel, 1993b: Daring to share...*

2. *'NGDO' will be used to mean non-governmental development organizations, while 'NGO' here refers to non-governmental organizations in general. The difference is that NGDOs dedicate themselves primarily to development activities with farmers and farm families at grassroots level, but an NGO may be active at any level: local, provincial, national or international.*

Networking for sustainable agriculture: the case studies

The emergence of five NGDO networks for sustainable agricultural development in developing countries will be reviewed: the Ecological Agriculture Network RAE (Kolmans, 1993), and the Andean Council for Ecological Management CAME (Manrique et al., 1993), both in Peru; the Association of Church Development Projects, ACDEP, in Northern Ghana (Alebikiya, 1993), and the Arid Lands Information Network, ALIN (Graham, 1993), both in West Africa; and Networking for Low-External-Input-and-Sustainable-Agriculture in Tamil Nadu and Pondicherry Region, India (Quintal and Ghandimathi, 1993). In these case studies, members of networks describe why they decided to form a network and how they did it. They discussed their preliminary reports during a workshop held in Sri Lanka in late 1992. These are from final reports and a first synthesis published by Alders et al. (1993). All these networking experiences focus on sustainable agriculture, although their definitions of 'sustainable' may differ. As will become apparent, all work with resource-poor farmers, but under a variety of circumstances and with differing institutional support. These networks have in common that they have reached a stage of consolidation: all have successfully transcended the risks and uncertainties of institutional infancy and matured into respected adolescence, carving out a 'niche' for themselves in the local, regional and/or global NGDO community.

My main interest will be to look for the value added to NGDO activities by networking and to how this is done. To underscore that many of the issues are not specific to the five networks studied, some examples from *El Taller* are included. I was able to participate closely in the establishment of this worldwide network of NGDOs, as an adviser. The chapter begins with what I mean when I say 'networking' among NGDOs, and why I think networking is *work*, not just something pleasant for our spare moments. Then I look into current networking experiences, to extract some of the central issues that appear when we attempt to look at networking as a *purposive* activity. Third, I will make an attempt to draw out the added value of networking. This added value, I contend, is particularly to be sought in the contribution of networking to creating a space for joint learning and innovation.

Networking: what is it?

Networks have received a lot of attention in recent years. Plucknett et al. (1990) were among the first to recognize the importance of networks among agricultural scientists. Networks among farmers, extension workers and researchers were studied systematically (Box, 1990). Students of social networks have highlighted how people 'capitalize on' their social relationships to deal with the challenges life throws at them. Some would say we have finally understood the importance of investing in 'social capital' (Bourdieux, 1991). However, my primary interest is not with networks as such. Rather, I want to look at *networking*, the process resulting from the conscious efforts of certain social actors to build relationships with each other to enhance sustainable development. Here networks are seen as the more or less formalized, more or less durable relational patterns that emerge as a result of such purposive relationship building efforts. From this point of view, the success or failure of networking, its functioning and characteristics, and the exact form and shape an actual network takes may be evaluated against the *mission* the actors who make it up have in mind for the network. (See the example from El Taller).

El Taller: the movement, the network, the centre: In the discussions during the three 'think tanks' that preceded the establishment of the El Taller Foundation, now based in Tunis with a membership of more than 100 NGDOs worldwide, NGDO leaders stressed the importance of avoiding power politics. Political lobbying, although very high on the agenda of most of the involved NGDOs, was seen as something to be done by individual members on a case to case basis: forming alliances with those other organizations – member NGOs or others – that seemed most useful in achieving specific objectives. At the same time, El Taller was not to duplicate efforts of member NGOs, including networks, by providing services and/or products to the poor. El Taller was to concentrate on creating a platform that would facilitate reflection and the exchange of experiences between NGDO staff from different countries and continents, to enhance 'global thinking for local action'. (*Source:* El Taller reports, 1990–1993)

If networking activities are to correspond to a mission, the actors involved must be able to formulate one that they share. That is, the question of who has the right to co-determine the ground rules or 'constitution' for the network must be solved, and agreement must be reached on a procedure for developing a *shared perspective* – in this case, a 'theory of poverty' as Tim Brodhead puts it (cited by Korten, 1993). Such questions are often not dealt with explicitly by those who make up a network. And, as most networks start off very informally, they are not compelled to do this. Often, networks evolve around a closely knit group of charismatic leaders. Initially, they determine who is 'in' and who is 'out', and set the agenda for network activities. However, when networks become more permanent and more institutionalized, a need to develop more transparent ways of generating such decisions, with broader participation, will arise.

Mario Padrón (1991), one of the outstanding networkers of Latin America, was among the first to recognize the need for more systematic analysis of networks, because 'it is difficult to establish what they are, why they happen, their main characteristics, and how their relative strengths can best be used to develop the NGO community's efficiency and to increase the communication and organizational strengths of the networks'. He suggests a central thesis for understanding NGDO networking: networking is about sharing. And he warns: '... sharing may be one of the most demanding requirements in development work, yet it is the most essential common denominator developed by the poor in order to provide for each other and live under adverse conditions'. 'Daring to share', as he puts it, is neither easy nor automatic. It requires a willingness to be open-minded and having enough confidence in one's own work to expose it to others, and at the same time the necessary humility to understand one's own position as one among many. In my view, this makes networking more than simply individuals and institutions working together on the basis of agreed interests. It has to do with achieving 'social synergy' (Haverkort and Ducommun, 1990). Networks represent 'communities of ideas', a space for like-minded people to interact on the basis of common interests, mutual trust and anticipated concern. Not so much the manufacture of products and/or services, but social learning, communication and sense-making are the 'core business' here. By focusing on 'mind' rather than 'matter', networking helps create a fundamentally new quality for human cooperation, and enhances inclusive thinking, creativity and dialogue. In the following paragraphs I will review the case studies, asking what in the view of the NGDOs themselves makes it worthwhile to *net*work. These three questions provide a framework:

- What triggers networking efforts among NGDOs?

- What makes NGDO networks assume a more permanent form and remain?

- What activities are most characteristic of NGDO network organizations?

What triggers networking efforts among NGDOs?

At first glance, the networks in the cases seem to appear in situations where the NGDOs themselves, or members of their staff, perceive a critical lack of access to relevant knowledge and experiences of others, and yet this lack is not seen as irrevocable. On the contrary, people feel it can be remedied by organized sharing of ideas, experiences, and information among relevant parties: that is, improving information sharing and learning among relevant NGDOs.

In India, NGOs and farmers agreed there were many sound traditional practices that could be revived and disseminaed (Quintal and Gandhimathi, 1993). At CAME in Peru (Manrigue et al., 1993) severe droughts alternating with inundation convinced the NGDO of their incapacity to adequately respond to the Andean peasants' needs. They attributed this failure, on the one hand, to lack of familiarity with Andean and LEISA technologies, the specific local environment, and techniques for managing climatic risks; and, on the other hand, to lack of inter-institutional coordination. Another example is the recognition on the part of the participants in the Oxfam Cotonou Workshop of the isolated conditions in which local project staff had to do their work; this gave rise to the formation of the ALIN network (Graham, 1993).

In some cases a more general lack of coordination seems to have been the signal that stimulated networking efforts. Sometimes coordination of vital tasks among NGDOs was recognized as weak, not only in terms of technical focus, but in management and logistics as well, as for ACDEP (see the ACDEP example). In such cases, organizations in a network are pushed to assume a much more comprehensive role in facilitating organizational integration and change. Often this leads to the establishment of specialized new units or agencies dedicated to certain well-specified tasks in support of all NGDOs concerned.

> ACDEP: inadequate coordination: '... coordination had a number of inherent limitations and weaknesses: The projects operated in isolation, ... tended to replicate programmes and ... operate similar activities within the same locality.... Coordination tended to be based on the vertical administrative structure of the church and parish. ... coordinators ... could not provide technical backup ... [there were] varied and different development approaches, without the benefit of learning process between projects. Policies regarding the delivery of services were conflicting and tended to undermine each other. ... parallel and sometimes inefficient and costly services.... different prices for the same inputs. A coordinated voice on agricultural development policies was absent'. (*Source:* Alebikiya, 1993)

Thus a lack of knowledge and information, or even services, is far from being the only motivation for networking. The range of intentions behind NGDO networking efforts is much broader. An even more important dimension seems to be an awareness among a number of like-minded NGDOs that the situation they face in working with communities requires new, more comprehensive insights and a more profound understanding of the options for sustainable development that are open to their clientele (see the following El Taller example). For CAME, as we have seen above, it was the realization that the NGDO community did not have an understanding of Andean and LEISA technologies – or of the options available to peasants in managing resources and risks – that was sufficient to allow them to support rural communities effectively. In India, ecological breakdown due to 'modern' agricultural techniques, and the resulting crises, plus the lack of appropriate and sustainable alternatives, raised awareness that '... a local network would enhance the speed and quality of field action and motivate others who are interested in the concept of LEISA' (Quintal and Gandhimathi, 1993).

> El Taller: a space for reflection: Regarding global NGDO networking, many share the thoughts of the founding members of El Taller, as expressed by the Secretary General, Sjef Theunis: 'El Taller was born from the need for reflection voiced by NGO leaders from around the world. Women and men who work at the heart of their society are feeling that citizens and politicians have lost their direction and focus.' (Source: El Taller, 1993, Secretary General's foreword)

Networking, from this point of view, is very much propelled by a wish to search jointly for new ways of understanding and intervening in complex development situations. The motivation to begin networking is the wish to articulate, whether immediately or not, an alternative approach to sustainable development. In many cases, a specific conceptual framework, or 'theory', is adopted to provide guidance in developing such an approach. For ACDEP, CAME, Tamil Nadu and Pondicherry Region, this was LEISA; for RAE, it was 'ecological agriculture'. In other cases, a looser set of 'guiding principles' is formulated.

Awareness of a lack of focus often seems to coincide with the realization that there is a critical lack of access to relevant experiences, knowledge and information. Together, these create a powerful motivation for networking among NGDOs. But who are the ones to become 'aware', to notice the 'lack of ...'? And why do they decide to act upon this? Such NGDOs and individuals may be labelled 'prime movers' (Padrón, 1991) or 'network catalysts' (Korten, 1993). They may be local or national NGDOs, acting out of an awareness of crisis or immediate need; they may also be NGDOs who see an opportunity to increase their impact. In the case of RAE, a number of experienced NGDOs sensed such an opportunity to increase impact by linking into the work of about 200 local NGDOs active in rural areas, as external interest in their practical experiences with ecological agriculture grew (Kolmans, 1993).

Finally, another recurring item with respect to what triggers NGDOs to network is a wish to participate in the public and/or governmental development debate. Manrique et al. (1993) express this at regional level: the network was created, among other reasons, because of '... the wish of its members to transcend their limited or isolated level and to make themselves heard or noted within the regional society, on the basis of proposals or suggestions for development policies'. NGDOs have become aware that achieving such participation is beyond the scope and competence of any single NGDO: it requires cooperation among a wide range of like-minded NGDOs. While with respect to other issues there are remarkable similarities among networks, here there are some remarkable differences. In Peru, CAME is seen proposing the development of joint policies on LEISA and the role of NGDOs (Manrique et al., 1993). Similarly, the RAE network is seen wanting to contribute to the public development debate through conferences, publications, and articles (Kolmans, 1993). In Ghana, the first priority is instead to address government institutions, and to '..advocate the need for support of community-focused development work on behalf of the rural poor.' (Alebiyika, 1993). Other networks, however, like ALIN in Africa and the networking for LEISA in Tamil Nadu and Pondicherry Region, India, seemed to be placing much less emphasis on such activities.

Three motivations for networking

In answer to the first question, I suggest that networking efforts are triggered when three types of perceptions gain sufficient momentum among NGDO leaders, staff, and clientele:

- the existence of a deprivation (which may be only relative, but is nevertheless critical) with respect to access to experiences, knowledge and information held by others, which is perceived as detrimental to effective individual performance;
- the need to jointly gain a more comprehensive, more effective understanding of the complex problem situations NGDOs deal with, and to create new and innovative options to support grass roots development;
- a desire to work out alternative development proposals, rooted in NGDO experiences, and to voice these in regional, national or international debates, making a contribution to the formulation of effective development policies.

The first of these points leads to a desire to *upgrade* NGDO performance. It leads networkers to emphasize documenting and sharing ideas, experiences and knowledge from people (in NGDOs or others) who are relevant to the purposes of their work. The main concern is with improving collective learning and the quality of NGDO work. The second involves a wish to *'upstream'* analysis and actions, to share analytical capabilities and information, to seek a more comprehensive understanding of the situation (Hazel Henderson, cited by Korten, 1993). This takes on the question of the relevance or efficacy of the field operations themselves, within the prevailing social and political context in the country or region. It goes '... beyond the evident consequences of the problem at hand to address its source' (Korten, 1993). Shared diagnosis, reflection, sense-making, and coordination at a strategic level are emphasized. The main concern is reaching a better understanding of complex development situations, an achievement seen as beyond the powers and scope of any one agency alone. In line with these ideas, the third leads to what may be called a *'shifting up'* among NGDOs – a sort of shifting into a higher gear, to join in articulating demands and advocacy. The need to articulate and advocate alternative development proposals is emphasized. Networkers are led to engage in communication activities that will reach a wider public, and to influence both governmental and private actors in society at large.

All three 'Us' reflect, one way or the other, a genuine concern with improving the quality and impact of NGDO work and its contribution to grass roots development. However, as we will see later, it is also very clear that each network reflects a very particular combination: from local networks of service oriented NGDOs, primarily interested in upgrading their performance vis-à-vis their clients, to global strategic networks (Korten, 1993), which almost entirely concentrate on upstreaming and advocacy, directing their efforts towards a very particular case or concern.

What helps networks remain?

If, as I assert, networks are the more or less formalized, more or less durable relational patterns emerging as a result of networking efforts, we can also ask why certain networking efforts lead to the effective establishment of institutionalized networks, while others do not? Many networks have been designed and initiated, only to quickly 'peter out' as initial momentum was lost and members or prospective members went back to 'business as usual'. This may be perfectly healthy: if a network has achieved its purpose, it may dissolve itself. Yet, the many that have survived may suggest lessons about the conditions that must be met if networking activities are to become more institutionalized and less incidental.

First however I will address an issue that is frequently raised in debates around networking, particularly by those arguing against them. Networks, they claim, are informal patterns of relationships; for just that reason they should be neither formalized nor institutionalized. This argument demonstrates the necessity of distinguishing between networks and networking. Every individual, every organization engages in building relationships with others – networking – for many reasons. Most of these activities remain informal and rather incidental. Some, however, acquire such relevance to the life and/or work of these individuals and organizations, that a decision is made to institutionalize them, to ensure a degree of permanence. Claiming that networks should remain, but as informal groupings, is equivalent to saying people should eat, but should never buy food.

Formal networks, then, are not always a necessary prerequisite to, nor a result of, networking activities. But under which conditions do patterns of relationships become more formal, and when do they take the shape of institutionalized networks? For the types of networks considered in this chapter, a first condition has been extensively discussed: a considerable number of people must share the view that networking will add a specific value to their work. These people, moreover, must be in a position to *articulate* this view, and to design a *mission* for the network.

This seems to be a common denominator for all new networks. All seem to start with a phase of 'planned activism' (Manrique et al., 1993). In this phase, first exchanges of ideas take place; tangible activities lead to recognition of the value of sharing with, and support by, others; one or a small group of enthusiastic prime movers promotes the idea of networking; and a meeting with prospective network members is prepared. During this phase, much is done, but often in a rather unplanned fashion. The result is generally a workshop or a meeting where, among other more immediate interests, the idea of forming a network is discussed and evaluated.

The extent to which this phase can be rather spontaneous and unsystematic depends to a great degree on the scale of the operation. While regional and even national NGDOs may organize themselves into a network in a very informal manner, international efforts like El Taller take years of programmed activities to prepare a foundation. Yet, though the scale differs, the mechanisms appear similar: the combined efforts of a group of *prime movers*, *network facilitators*, and *interested members* or potential members lead to the formulation of ideas, plans and activities that eventually result in the establishment of the network. 'Prime movers' are the people, generally leading members of respected NGDOs, who participate in creating the idea and the vision upon which the network is to be built. The 'network facilitators' are those who, by virtue of the space allowed to them by their own organizations, engage in actual networking, organizing and supporting a first run of activities; these are closely tuned to the needs and wishes of the prospective members of the network. Some people may act as both a prime mover and a network facilitator. Generally the 'facilitation function' is carried out by a secretariat connected to one of the prime mover NGDOs. A sponsor (whether direct or indirect) will always be needed to cover at least a part of the operational costs of 'planned activism'.

During the phase of planned activism, a number of recurrent issues emerge. First, the importance of *communication and participatory methods*. If the network is to be supported by a wide group of NGDOs and their staff, they must be allowed to participate intensively in the formulation of objectives, approach and organization. This sounds easier than it is in practice: for those working in often isolated rural areas, to develop a habit of taking time for sharing ideas and experiences with people located elsewhere is not easy. The time and energy this requires must often be found in an already overloaded agenda.

However, another task is still more difficult, and yet essential: the development of a shared *conceptual framework* that will facilitate the exchange of ideas, experiences and knowledge. Enrique Kolmans (1993) describes the RAE experience, noting the unrealistic goal setting and the extensive – and theoretical – discussions during the first year of preparation. But he also indicates why these were necessary. Prospective members knew little about ecological agriculture; there were one-sided views like 'all that is traditional and Andean is ecologically sound and sustainable' (translation PE) to overcome. Futher, it was necessary to integrate social/anthropological ways of thinking with insights into technical/ecological processes, and finally to explain the real needs of rural people to donors and other supporters. In my view, what Kolmans describes is a process of making sense out of the idea of setting up a network to stimulate sustainable development, checking the need for it, and defining its potential for supporting its members in doing their work better. This involves developing a 'theory of joint intervention' that makes sense to everyone who will participate. This takes a lot of time, yet seems to be an essential ingredient of networking. It helps to transform a diverse set of people and organizations with an ill-defined sense of purpose into a 'like-minded' group with a shared perspective, who have moreover agreed upon a number of tasks and responsibilities and have learned to respect each other.

In all cases this process is linked closely to *tangible activities* the members or prospective members of the network are already performing in their respective areas. 'The immediate needs arising from the fieldwork of each of the institutions are the basis and reason for being a network' (Manrique et al., 1993). From the very start networking activities are intended to provide support to the actual work of the organizations involved. This is essential if they are to be able to evaluate the potential value of networking, in comparison to other obligations. Further, only in this situation can the principal of reciprocity be applied from the very first instant: as Manrique et al. (1993) point out, when a member NGO doesn't contribute to the network, the network is not able to help in supporting the work of the NGO.

In a general way, NGDO networks intended to increase the quality of development interventions should reflect the guiding principles applied by the NGDOs themselves to their work. 'Positive technological elements of traditional and modern agriculture, which fit the social, economic and ecological criteria' eventually served as a 'catch phrase' for the agricultural standards underlying the RAE network (Kolmans, 1993). Here as in many other cases, tangible activities meant direct support to field level projects. Obviously, the exact words used to set out general principles are less important than the discussion of their significance and meaning, and the implications of adopting them as guiding principles for developing the network.

> El Taller: principles and activities: For El Taller, key values were formulated during the first 'think tank' meeting as internationalization; open communication; solidarity; awareness of one's own identity as non-governmental organizations; reflection; and education. Tangible activities included national and international seminars and workshops, plus training courses. (*Source:* El Taller, 1990)

The planned activism phase may be the most difficult phase for a donor to finance. Exactly because the nature of such initiatives is necessarily ill-defined, because no shared frame of reference, values and discourse has yet been developed, the network will not be able to articulate its process, services and products in a way wholly satisfactory to a donor. During this phase, what a network needs is a *sponsor*. It needs the financial support of an institution that is prepared to be a 'prime mover' at the donor level, without interfering too much in network preparations. For El Taller, NOVIB, a Dutch NGO, played this role, financing initial El Taller activities without attaching too many conditions. Such a sponsor, rather than 'knowing' the network will be a success, shares the 'belief' that the network will be of value to the work of the NGDOs involved. In most instances I know of, a considerable investment was made, either directly or indirectly or both, by sponsors who supported the networking initiatives of a number of NGDOs. In all cases sponsorship was based on belief, rather than an assurance of success. The use of seed money by ILEIA, in the Netherlands, to support the initial stages of network building in India is a good example of such sponsorship (Quintal and Gandhimathi, 1993).

The Dutch saying 'a good beginning is half the job' seems to sum up network building nicely. The foundation of a successful network is laid at the beginning. This comes about not by pushing things as fast as possible, but by taking one step at a time. Creating a successful and lasting network seems to require at least the following ingredients:
- planned activism, with facilitation and support that never replace or bypass specific activities already performed by the NGDOs involved;
- energy, time and opportunity to discuss, negotiate and agree upon a shared perspective, a conceptual framework and guiding principles that permit the formulation of the mission of the network to be not only transparent, but also such that all or most prospective members can agree to it;
- a body of prime movers, network facilitators, prospective members and sponsors who are willing and able to carry the networking process through its ill-defined first phase;
- broad, effective participation of prospective members in designing and implementing network activities;
- a number of enthusiastic network facilitators, equipped with the minimum resources required to establish and maintain vital communication facilities, create opportunities for interaction, stimulate participation and otherwise orchestrate the definition process for the network.

What activities characterize network organizations?

Networks span an enormous range of activities: from technical consultancy to communication, from project planning to education and training, from newsletters to conferences, and from advocacy to monitoring, to name just a few. This is one reason it is hard to make sense of networking as a phenomenon. The case studies suggest, however, that networks generally concentrate on four clusters of activities: learning through joint reflection; services; advocacy; and network management.

Learning through joint reflection
This embraces all activities aimed at stimulating joint reflection to increase the level of shared understanding of the complex situations dealt with by participating NGDOs. The objective of encouraging learning through joint reflection is to make use of the combined analytical powers of staff members from like-minded NGDOs, facilitating the sharing of knowledge, ideas and experiences, thereby increasing the quality of operations. This may include mutual appraisals, exchange visits, workshops, meetings and conferences, and sometimes permanent working groups on specific topics. Each network has its own emphasis, but they have elements like problem appreciation, diagnosis, exchange, reflection and systematization in common. Many networks stress the importance of visits and workshops – not as ends in themselves, but as a starting point for reflection (Graham, 1993). A situation diagnosis and an inventory of available technological and methodo-

logical options is generally included; so is a gradual systematization, or even standardization, of scientific and technical principles (Kolmans, 1993; Manrique et al., 1993).

Services

Typical service activities within networks include training, communication, documentation and information services. In providing these services, the network organization tries to make optimum use of existing capabilities and facilities among its members, and, if necessary from elsewhere. A needs assessment and/or a diagnosis of strengths and weaknesses among network members is a frequent starting point. Typically, the secretariat attached to the member NGDOs is seen as the best location for providing the most important services of the network. The servicing function is supported by what might be called the *network communication infrastructure*. Almost all networks have a newsletter, which facilitates the exchange of ideas and practices. Documentation and library services are central as well, as is the development of training materials. Methodological support to field workers may also be included, as well as technical and project consultancies (Manrique et al., 1993), monitoring, quality certification (Kolmans, 1993) or coordination of input supplies (Alebiyika, 1993). The common denominator in the services provided by networks is their close response to immediate needs of participating NGDOs. Therefore, in addition to a general emphasis on training, communication, documentation and information, network-specific packages of services may evolve.

Advocacy

Advocacy refers to activities performed or facilitated by the network organization on behalf of its members with respect to participation in the public or governmental development debate, putting forward the aims related to their mission statement and clients. This requires the network to formulate proposals on contemporary development issues and voice these in the public media. With the same aims in view, the network may organize conferences, contribute articles to scientific journals and distribute relevant publications. Coalition building with relevant parties outside the network, or with other networks, is often on the agenda as well. The advocacy function of current NGDO networks is neither as generalized nor as transparent as its learning and service functions. As we have seen above, NGDO leaders may chose not to include advocacy among the tasks of the network they are building.

Strategic networking is, however, gaining momentum (Korten, 1993). While as Korten points out there is a potential for conflicts of interest between a service orientation and carrying out advocacy functions. Thus a dedication to advocacy in a network is very much a matter of choice. Yet, the materials I have available suggest this is not an 'either/or' choice. Advocacy and services are very much two sides of the same coin: if we take 'learning through joint reflection' as the core of networking, how could we possibly do without either services or advocacy? What seems to happen in the more permanent networks is a greater emphasis on services and learning functions, particularly during the early stages of network development. 'Planned activism' must be oriented towards providing 'value for energy', if NGDOs are to be able and willing to participate in networking efforts. Moreover, the development of a strong shared understanding based on mutual support and learning may well be a prerequisite to effective advocacy.

Network management

Finally, 'network management' has to do with facilitating the networking process itself. This includes caring for network communication infrastructure, network operating procedures, the monitoring of network resources, activities and outputs, and coordination with other organizations and networks. Let me briefly point out a number of common characteristics of network management, as these transpire in the cases. First and foremost the emphasis on *distributed intelligence* catches the eye. Networking secretariats are kept as lean as possible; whenever feasible, they delegate tasks to member organizations. Decentralization of functions and autonomy of members is continuously emphasized. The network facilitators' mandate generally stems from a meeting of prospective members, who decide to initiate a more formal networking process. The importance of *not* engaging in the management of funds for network members – however convenient it may seem at a given moment – is highlighted several times in the literature: such management is expected to make the network a 'battlefield for funding' (Manrique et al., 1993).

A list or *directory* of member organizations is among the first tangible results of most networks. This is generally motivated by a wish to facilitate networking without always involving the network secretariat. While the organization and structure of networks may vary, discussions generally concern membership, the role of the secretariat and regional or task-oriented subgroups, network facilitators and decision making procedures. It seems important to clearly define the composition, responsibilities and prerogatives of the network board, secretariat, and, if applicable, implementing bodies. The role of external agents in facilitating early stages of network development is frequently mentioned. Other important recurrent issues are the degree to which the secretariat, or network facilitation unit, should actively engage in implementing activities, and whether formal rules should replace the largely unwritten rules of network operation that generally reign in the early stages. Although it is difficult to generalize, experience seems to indicate that a measure of formality is necessary, with a mandate for organizing members, staff and other decision making bodies. Manrique et al. (1993) observe of the CAME organization and structure '... its functionality is based on the capacity to pass from individual actions of the members to integrated programming, and after the discussion and approval by the Assembly and Board of Directors, to implement the execution by the technical team and the staff of the NGOs with supervision and coordination of the Executive Committee'. Part of the value added by networking appears to be the creation of conditions for collective agency – including a joint management structure for planning, preparing, implementing and evaluating the tasks agreed by the members.

A final point concerns resources for networking operations. Even if most network activities are delegated to member NGDOs, they still require time, energy and money. The moment networks become more permanent, therefore, the issue of fundraising arises. Generally, during the early days committed participating members (particularly the prime movers) somehow find a way to free up these resources, mostly from within their own programmes. Sponsors move in only when the contours of the network have already been worked out. This may often mean that a limited number of NGDOs or NGDO leaders (those who are able to provide facilities and funds) take part in exchange and communication. Needless to say, this limits the participatory process in the early stages, while it is precisely at this time that a broad participatory process seems to be essential.

Networking among NGDOs: creating space for joint learning and innovation

What sets networks apart from other types of human organization? Or, better, what dimension does networking add to our repertoire of cooperative strategies? From the above analysis, I conclude that it is the emphasis on joint reflection and learning that sets successful networks apart. Networks are, as it were, 'learning organizations' by design. Networks are designed and operated to break through relative isolation, to facilitate social learning processes among actors within the development arena, and to jointly achieve a more comprehensive and innovative understanding of complex development situations. Yet, at the same time, networking aims at learning-in-practice. It does not separate learning and reflection from daily activities. Rather, it opens up a space for learning *within* day-to-day activities, where members can systematically reflect upon and share experiences, knowledge and information.

The aim of networking is not simply to learn from each other. NGDO and their leaders are motivated to net*work* because it helps them to improve their organizations and field operations. If we take this as a point of departure, we may look at networks of NGDO as 'quality circles', designed and operated to help sustain and raise the quality of our work, outputs and impact. For me, this is exactly what networks ought to be. Networks are successful if they help improve performance. If they do not, they easily collapse under the pressure of everyone's daily obligations. A contribution to performance can be either temporary or permanent; not all networking activities become institutionalized. If they do, it is because those investing in these activities want the benefits of the network to continue.

The added value of networking: suggesting a standard

We are still far from having complete answers to the many questions about the value added by networking. The study of networks among NGDOs, and their significance to NGDO work, has just started. Hence, opinions of supporters and critics vary widely and rather haphazardly. At the same time, many NGDOs dedicate a significant portion of their time to networking, and many more positive results have been reported than I can cover here. To systematically approach the question of added value, we will first need to set a standard. All networks do this for themselves, but a general standard has not yet evolved. Based on the analysis presented in the first paragraphs of this chapter, the following criteria may be applicable:

- Networks are expected to contribute directly to upgrading the quality of the activities, outputs and impact of member NGDOs by providing mutual support and services based on a joint assessment of their needs.

- Networks are expected to facilitate a collective learning process among their members, contributing to 'upstreaming' NGDO analysis, perceptions and policy development. This requires the development, administration and maintenance of a permanent and flexible communication infrastructure, the organization of regular meetings and workshops, social research and the management of the network's 'development agenda'.

- Networks may be expected to contribute to 'shifting up' NGDO activity and directing it towards national and international audiences. Above all, this requires building strategic alliances with other NGDOs and networks for specific purposes. Where particular services are required – such as editing and publication, acquiring media time or press releases, or lobbying – where possible, existing capacities of network members or other specialized agencies are mobilized.

- Networks are expected to incur expenses for developing, administrating and evaluating networking activities. These are the only 'overhead' costs related to network operations.

In my opinion, there is no reason we should not try to be just as rigorous in evaluating network performance as we are in evaluating NGDO performance in general. Every network must specify its expected results and define indicators for measuring and verifying them. However, we will have to take into account the specific nature of networks as a space for social learning, reflection and innovation, helping '... NGOs in the permanent reformulation and adaptation of their role with respect to the peasant population and the government institutions' (Manrique et al., 1993).

Networking: a strategy for improving inter-organizational innovativeness?

We have shown networking among non-governmental development organizations to be a promising strategy for creating successful alliances for innovation in agricultural practices. Just as the institutional configurations described in the last chapter, networks of NGDOs can be interpreted as emerging forms of social organization for innovation. In networks, a shared 'theory of intervention' and a joint management structure emerge, specifying tasks, responsibilities and mechanisms for establishing coordination and mutual adjustment. Experience underscores the importance of organization development for establishing and maintaining NGDO networks.

> Networking is organization development: The proposal, performance and consolidation of a network should be understood as an organizational development process, which requires time, economic resources, some infrastructure and moreover specialized human resources ... (financial) costs and investments. ... The benefits of the network cannot always be expressed in direct economic values. However it is absolutely necessary to try to value the benefits (Manrique et al., 1993).

Could this conclusion on networking possibly lead to the proposal of an alternative approach to inter-institutional coordination? Do NGDO networks simply mirror the need for non-governmental organizations to build alliances for agricultural innovation, just as agricultural institutions did? Or do they reflect something else, some distinct characteristics that set these alliances apart? To briefly consider this question, let me start by reflecting upon the similarities and differences between NGDO networks and the institutional configurations discussed earlier. We have argued that both can be interpreted as emerging forms of social organization for innovation. Further, once established, both are structural arrangements: member organizations have agreed upon a division of tasks and ways to coordinate these tasks. During the formative process, accommodations in views, objectives, methods and resource allocations have been negotiated. Finally, in both cases we found success to be associated with 'something close to' agreement on a joint management structure; collective decision making on important issues; and the existence of a shared theory of intervention that states objectives, tasks and responsibilities, plus ways to coordinate and mutually adjust them. Just as institutional configurations, networks can therefore be seen as a particular type of innovation configuration.

However, there appear to be major differences in the formative process, purpose and quality standards that guide the creation of different sorts of network configurations. Generally, government institutions are not allowed a phase of 'planned activism' – relatively open-minded collaboration during which individual organizations can learn to respect each other, grow towards each other and 'test the waters of cooperation'. Moreover, their mandates being strictly separate, mutually exclusive, embedded in legislation and hence inflexible, government institutions do not normally obtain instructions and/or space to 'learn from each other'. It does not make sense to enter into open-minded collaboration, seeking accommodations and mutual adjustments, when the margins for such adjustments are thin as air or nonexistent. This brings us to another important difference: NGDO decision making is generally more decentralized than government decision making. Even if in some areas government agencies were able to participate in achieving a design for a joint management structure, a functional arrangement for sharing tasks and responsibilities, there would be no guarantee that such a design would be acceptable to central government authorities.

The case studies suggest that networking efforts may indeed lead to configurations that demonstrate characteristics institutional configurations do not. The most important is that such networks are purposefully created. Mutual interdependence is a given, the main reason for joining up. Moreover, not only technical solutions but also intervention objectives are open to debate. Active participation of all member organizations is not just a formal requirement, it is a working standard. The formative process is taken as an opportunity to build a strong foundation for future cooperation, not just as a period for renegotiation of the institutional balance of power. And networks not only recognize mutual interdependence, they nurture it: programmes for mutual support, services and participation as an articulated entity in the public debate all contribute. In such networks organizations and their staff purposefully engage in 'communication for innovation' as opposed to 'communication for control' (cf. the conclusions in Chapter 2). For these reasons, I suggest NGDO networks such as the ones covered in this chapter are fundamentally different from the institutional configurations described in Chapter 4.

For government institutions to be able to participate in such networks, a number of fundamental requirements would have to be met. First, it is apparent from the cases that networking requires a number of social actors who are not only 'like-minded', in the sense that they adhere to the same general views and principles, but also who have autonomy to adjust their views and the local process of intervention. Hierarchical power structures such as exist in most government bureaucracies seem to be at odds with this requirement. To facilitate effective networking among government and other agencies, central authorities would at least have to 'draw back' from controlling day-to-day operations. Second, whether government authorities would ever be willing to cede the time and space needed to allow decentralized government institutions to effectively 'test the waters of cooperation' is another question. Current efficiency-oriented bureaucratic discourse seems to be at odds with open-ended proposals and what could easily be seen as 'costly free-wheeling at the expense of taxpayers'. These factors remain, even though, as I have shown, weeding out such activities could dramatically increase the potential for maintaining or increasing collective performance related to innovation.

Some preliminary conclusions

From this brief reflection, I draw three preliminary conclusions, which will be taken up in more detail further on. First, studying NGDO networking opens an interesting vista upon alternative strategies for creating successful inter-organizational alliances for agricultural innovation. Their actual impact on agricultural performance needs further study. Research may also shed light on the conditions participating organizations will have to meet and the process they must go through to successfully pursue such strategies. Second, both networks and institutional configurations may be understood as innovation configurations – emerging forms of social organization innovation. The differences between the two stem from the purpose and principles that guide their establishment and operation, the nature of the social actors who participate, and the collective formative experience that leads to their emergence.

Networks seem potentially able to play a role as learning organizations, in which both individual members and the network as a whole improve their practices significantly over time. Perhaps it would be useful to adapt the term 'flexfirms', suggested in the management literature for innovative firms, and think of networks as 'flexforms' of social organization for innovation. However, additional research would be needed to answer such disturbing questions as whether network organizations suffer dangers similar to institutional configurations of becoming rigid and unyielding, and to learn what elements or factors trigger such a process.

Finally, the case studies add evidence to support the suggestion that active networking, that is, building and maintaining relationships between relevant social actors, is an important enabling factor for purposive and widespread innovation with respect to the agricultural practices of smallholders.

6. Towards understanding the social organization of innovation

At the beginning of this book we asked how different social actors organize themselves to achieve agricultural innovation, and what they actually do to achieve the changes they have in mind:

- Q1. How do actors organize themselves to achieve agricultural innovation?

- Q2. What do they actually *do* to achieve the transformations they want?

This chapter provides answers to these questions. It represents the tentative end of what was labelled the *exploratory path*, and seeks to combine the lessons from the cases with a number of relevant theoretical insights. The purpose is to contribute to a more complete understanding, not to present a comprehensive theory. This chapter should help practitioners and students of social organization of innovation to reflect upon and discuss their experiences in a more meaningful way and, hopefully, stimulate some of them to undertake further empirical research. Also, it will provide an important step ahead towards achieving the second purpose of this study: the design of a practical methodology to enhance innovation performance.

The general idea put forward in this chapter is that we ought to take agricultural innovation as a complex, social process – one occurring among a variety of stakeholders – rather than as a matter of transfer or dissemination of technologies, knowledge or ideas. Specific conceptual tools are offered to gain a more comprehensive understanding of innovation and the way we organize ourselves to achieve it. These are arranged around a number of central propositions derived from research. The first proposition is pivotal: what social actors do to achieve innovation can be described as *networking*, building and maintaining relationships with other actors they deem relevant to their purposes. This proposition is then held against the light of three contemporary traditions of academic thought on innovation (see 'Social actors in search...' below). Furthermore, this chapter shows why a static, one-dimensional conception of knowledge cannot help us to fully comprehend innovation (see 'Knowledge, knowing and innovation'). The emergent character of innovation is then made explicit: it can be understood as emerging from the interplay in-and-between social practices. The following section then shows that networking between social actors can be seen as a particular social practice aimed at innovation (see 'Networking, a social practice'). Turning back to the innovation process itself, I propose it can be understood as a process of unending social inquiry. The next main issue is governance and leadership in complex innovation theatres: choices about direction are seen to emerge from social struggles, negotiations and accommodations among stakeholders. This leads to the conclusion that, as a result of active networking for innovation, forms of social organization emerge over time and have a momentum of their own; as a result, they become part of an enabling or constraining context for an innovation-oriented social practice itself (see 'Towards an action-oriented theory'). A note covers the influence of the mental models we apply to organizing ourselves for innovation. These too can act as either constraining or enabling factors for innovation performance.

Finally, in the last section, conclusions are drawn as to the relevance of the ideas advanced in this chapter in view of the objectives of the research.

Social actors in search of innovation: a networking approach

As shown in Chapter 2, it is very hard to uphold the notion of 'transfer of knowledge'. Communication for innovation can certainly be seen as a purposive activity, but all social actors involved in innovation theatres are, at the same time, both users and sources of relevant knowledge and information. The clue lies in the word 'relevant'. Farmers in Asten recognize many sources of relevant information. These cover several different types of information and several types of information use (Tables 3 and 4), but each source of information is not always judged to be equally relevant: the acquisition and use of knowledge and information is bound to purpose, context and time. For each type of information and each type of use, different sources may be seen as relevant. The same is true for advisers. Their professional portfolios mirror a selection and use of sources that extend beyond their mandate as 'transfer agents' for technical/scientific knowledge; on the other hand, these also reflect a degree of 'standardization' imposed by their agency. From the case study evidence, we concluded that communication for innovation is intrinsically woven into the daily practices of the social actors involved. Also, multiple sources of relevant knowledge and information are available. Hence, as part of their daily practices, the social actors develop professional strategies to access those sources if necessary. Therefore, for the student of social organization of innovation to study the transfer of one type of message from one type of source to one type of user for only one type of use is the equivalent of studying one thread within a sophisticated piece of embroidery. A more comprehensive conceptualization is needed.

A second issue from the case studies is that innovation is a social rather than solely an individual process. Each participant, consciously or not, contributes a specific piece to the 'jig-saw' puzzle called agricultural innovation. In it multiple and diverse communicative interactions play a decisive role. While such interactions may emerge spontaneously, to a certain degree they can be managed and/or facilitated. The intentional design and implementation of strategic 'articulations' or linkage patterns is suggested as a way in which organizations create opportunities for themselves and their collaborators to engage in a process of step-wise, task-oriented integration of different strands of relevant knowledge and information. This makes it possible to gain new insights and to create new messages, new policies and new technologies. The complex communication networks which emerge from such strategies as well as from more spontaneous interactions among actors can be seen as 'value-added' networks: they help integrate different strands of knowledge and information into new lines of thought, action and reflection.

A third issue evident in the case studies is that communication is to be understood as only one aspect of the social relationships that develop among farmers, veterinary doctors, district extension managers, farm advisers, technical specialists and other social actors in complex innovation theatres. Their professional communication strategies make up an intrinsic part of their daily practices, and a very important part at that. However, in practice, personal interests and concerns play a role alongside social, economical and cultural factors in explaining their communication patterns. This becomes even more obvious when we look at interactions among organizations and institutions. The linkages and institutional configurations that emerge reflect not just the use of communicative interaction for the transfer of knowledge and information, but also the use of power and influence for coordination and coalition building (Chapters 3, 4 and 5).

As a consequence, a conceptualization of social organization of innovation will have to account for the multiple, diffuse and social character of innovation in practice. Social actors are continuously, either spontaneously or in a more organized way or both, building relationships with each other to create opportunities for joint learning, increasing their understanding and improving upon current practices. Consistent with our conclusions in Chapter 5, this can be called *networking*. Understanding such purposive relationship-managing for learning appears to provide a central clue to understanding the social organization of innovation. In addition, as was shown in Chapter 2, what is commonly held to be a process of knowledge transfer might be better understood as a continuous process of step-wise integration of knowledge, information, ideas and experiences, taking place by means of temporary, task-oriented interactions between social actors. Participants contribute ideas and insights gained within their own environments, and thus contribute to an exchange of ideas and experiences from different practices. In this framework, the networks articulated by farmers and advisers can be seen as complex, value-added networks of relationships that facilitate the integration of knowledge and information of different types, for different purposes.

Innovation theory revisited

How does such a networking approach relate to contemporary traditions of academic thought on innovation? Generally, in knowledge systems thinking the definition of processes of innovation is associated with the use of 'diffusion of innovations theory' (cf. Beal et al., 1986). This tradition was articulated in the sixties and early seventies by Rogers and others; it defines an innovation as 'an idea, practice, or object perceived as new by an individual. It matters little, so far as human behaviour is concerned, whether or not an idea is 'objectively' new ... If the idea seems new to the individual, it is an innovation' (Rogers and Shoemaker, 1971: 19). Later a distinction was made between an 'innovation' as an idea, and a 'technology' as a design for instrumental action (Rogers, 1986). Social change was conceptualized as a process including three sequential stages: invention, diffusion and consequences (Rogers and Shoemaker, 1971). Technical change in agriculture was consequently seen as caused by the adoption of technical innovations by agricultural producers. The source of such innovations was taken to be scientific research and development. This tradition puts the emphasis on studying the adoption process, along with the search for attributes of innovations that may help explain what makes their effective diffusion possible, plus the consequences for social and/or industrial change. This approach is consistent with the 'linear' or transfer of technology (TOT) model of thinking on innovation. The limitations of such an approach have become increasingly clear (Kline and Rosenberg, 1986; Chambers and Ghildyal, 1985; Röling, 1991).

Industrial innovation researchers have developed more sophisticated theoretical models to use in studying innovation. Roobeek presents an 'integrated innovation concept' stressing interactions within widespread 'technology webs'. Webs of innovations and new applications develop around key technologies, and spread in widely different directions (Roobeek, 1988). However, because of the emphasis on the result of the innovation process – the technology – the basic issues remain unaffected. While developing a much more comprehensive conceptualization, Roobeek (1988: 40) continues to describe the innovation process as '..the process from invention to diffusion..'. The same can be said of Kline and Rosenberg (1986), who emphasize the interplay between scientific developments and commercial or industrial activities. In their 'chain-linked model of commercial innovation' science does not play a dominant role. It interacts with industry to solve problems encountered while designing an innovation from a market oriented perspective. During the design process, interpretations of the market potential direct an interactive process of invention, initial design, testing, redesign, production and distribution of the innovation.

A second tradition is the 'induced innovation' school of thought (Hayami and Ruttan, 1985: 88): 'Farmers are induced, by shifts in relative prices, to search for technical alternatives that save the increasingly scarce factors of production.' As Hayami and Ruttan are careful to point out, technical change is not wholly of an induced nature. Farmers, scientists and administrators play active roles, responding to exogenous (supply) and endogenous (demand) factors and taking part in the general progress of science and technology. As a consequence, technical change is defined as: '.. any change in production coefficients resulting from the purposeful resource-using activity directed to the development of new knowledge embodied in designs, materials, or organizations' (Hayami and Ruttan, 1985: 86). The induced innovation school has contributed in particular to making the economic conditions that enable and/or constrain innovation explicit. It calls attention to the fact that innovation processes always take place within a particular social, economic and ecological context. The interpretation of these contexts in terms of constraints and opportunities is an important issue for both researchers and practitioners of innovation. However, studies within this school of thought have focused primarily on macro-level economic issues, with little attention to micro-level or social issues.

A third, relatively recent school of thought we may label 'the networking tradition'. Wissema and Euser (1988) and Moss Kanter (1989) emphasize the importance of inter-company cooperation in creating opportunities for innovation. Pooling, allying and linking ('...becoming PALs...' according to Moss Kanter) across companies is advocated, to facilitate innovation and remain competitive. Within the networking tradition, two-way communication and support, interdependencies, synergies and complementarities among participating actors are emphasized. Innovation is taken to emerge from joint activities among companies who recognize 'win-win' situations (Wissema and Euser, 1988): situations in which cooperation can yield advantages for both sides. This is not to be confused with an emphasis on 'consensus building'. Articulating a joint performance does not necessarily require a broad consensus but rather an explicitly shared understanding of what each of the partners can reasonably expect to gain from the partnership. The networking tradition is gaining a great deal of momentum in agriculture, particularly among those concerned with sustainable and/or low-external-input agricultural development. Box (1989, 1990) for example has studied knowledge networks among small farmers. Participatory technology development (Chambers and Jiggins, 1987; Jiggins and De Zeeuw, 1992) stresses partnerships among farmers, researchers and extension workers to develop adequate farm technologies for sustainable development.

Obviously, the conclusions drawn from the case studies situate our approach close to the third tradition. However, although it is the most practical it is also the least developed conceptually. In fact, many of the elements identified within the first two traditions mentioned should not be discarded but integrated in a more comprehensive approach. As a general theoretical approach to guide an investigation of the social organization of innovation, the linear model is clearly to be discarded. The linear model refers to just one of many possible structural arrangements for innovation. It coincides with one of the extreme ideal types proposed in Chapter 4: the research and development driven basic configuration. As we have shown, this is only a fraction of what may occur in a complex innovation theatre. Our studies point to a highly diversified universe of social actors, each of which specializes in a distinct type of knowledge and information related practices. Or, as Kline and Rosenberg (1986) put it, science and technology do not necessarily play the dominant role in innovation processes. Our cases confirm that those who control marketing channels (such as processing plants and retail chains) are among the potential leaders in innovation theatres as well. But they are not the only ones.

The chain-linked model offers a combination of structural ideal types, but a limited one, including only the industry driven and the R&D driven basic configurations. Therefore, it tends to underrate the relevance of those social actors who control financial resources and political agendas, as well as those who actually operate farms. Yet all of these hold important keys to the process and struggle simultaneously to enforce their views and strategies. As a result, generally it is not a linear structural arrangement that emerges, nor one with a double focus, but a multiple one, with many social actors playing roles and strategizing to gain leadership. In other words, the linear and chain-link models do not cover all possible situations; instead they represent particular structural arrangements that may emerge as a result of negotiations among dominant social actors at a given point in time. They represent specific views of the relevance of technology and market as driving forces for innovation. They do not provide a general model that can support a balanced inquiry into the social organization of agricultural innovation, enabling us to study a broad range of social interactions among all, not just some of the important social actors.

Networking for innovation: towards a more comprehensive perspective

A networking approach can provide us with a perspective to use in building such a comprehensive model. Because it emphasizes building and managing social relationships, it does not *a priori* exclude any social actor which might influence the course of innovation. It focuses on all social interactions relevant to agricultural innovation at a particular point in time and within a specific social, economical and ecological context. It assumes that in any situation a multiplicity of social actors will be developing and managing interactive relationships, to improve their practices and develop new ones. These actors engage in such relationships due to a perceived interdependence: each of them perceives the others as relevant to achieving their own purposes. The question then becomes which of all these actors has more influence upon the eventual course of innovation: policy-makers, through the policies and regulations they implement; industrial actors, through their identification of market opportunities, their financing R&D programmes or the development of marketable products; users and potential users, through their judgements on the added value that new products or services may contribute to their own practices; research institutes, by offering technological alternatives or opening new avenues of inquiry; financial donors, who may choose to invest more in some proposals than in others; or will it be the consumers, wildlife activists, ecologists, tourism operators and so forth, who may form strong political lobbies? In other words, which of the potentially relevant social actors actually succeeds – through their interactions with others – in influencing the course of innovation, and how is such influence accomplished?

Such a perspective is also consistent with the active role farmers play in agricultural innovation. An innovation can be usefully looked at as a shift in agricultural or other practices, as does the 'induced innovation' school. However, changes in factor prices are not the only reasons farmers change their ways, and sometimes not even the main reason. The 'quality' of the means of production at the farmers' disposal may change in many ways not expressed in its price (or shadow price): for example, soil erosion may decrease the quality of the farmer's plots; or a lack of transport may make credit less accessible while other conditions, including interest rates, remain the same. At the same time farmers may decide, as a result of reasoning and/or experimentation, that different ways of doing things provide better results; or they may simply change their minds about what is 'better'. In other words, innovation at farm level is not directly induced by market forces, ecological deterioration, financial constraints or social relationships; their influence is *mediated* by farmers' perceptions and the way they have learned to anticipate and adapt to such phenomena.

From a networking perspective, the term 'innovativeness' must be defined differently than in the older traditions. Because many social actors – consciously or not – contribute specific pieces to the 'puzzle' of agricultural innovation, the question is not simply whether farmers are innovative enough, but whether all actors potentially relevant to agricultural innovation are innovative and interactive enough. The keys to widespread innovation generally are not held by one or two but by a number of social actors engaged in different practices. In most cases, if an innovation is to take root, each of these practices will have to undergo modifications. The introduction of chemical fertiliser was such an instance (see example). As a consequence, innovativeness can no longer be seen as an individual competence, or even as the sum of a number of individual competencies: it must be seen as a *social competence* shared among social actors who are part of a number, perhaps a large number, of relevant practices.

> Introducing chemical fertiliser required transformation not only of farming, but of many practices: The world-wide introduction of chemical fertilisers in agriculture over the last five decades has shown beyond any reasonable doubt that successfully introducing change requires a considerable transformation in a large variety of practices. This went far beyond farmers' learning how to buy and spread handfuls of chemicals. In the end, achieving widespread use of fertilizers depended upon enormous shifts in agricultural, commercial, industrial, financial and political practices. Infrastructural and marketing arrangements were needed as well, to provide reliable and timely deliveries of fertilizer. Where the volume available was limited and/or when subsidies were involved, reaching this point may have called for dramatic shifts in practices related to deliveries. Further, the market had to adapt, to channel the increased production volume. In general, seasonal credits were needed to allow the use of fertilizer by smaller producers. Banking practices thus had to change, for example by introducing special interest rates. Since fertilizer use had to correspond to local conditions, technical recommendations also had to be adapted. Consequently, national and international research programmes had to be financed, or even established, to produce such recommendations. Sometimes farmers had to learn to adjust long-held beliefs that had guided them through difficult times for many years, such as the 'law of the limited good', which suggests that structural increases in production by one farmer will cause suffering and decrease the production of others. To introduce fertilizer use into farming practice, enormous investments in extension, as well as more efficient extension practices, were required. Moreover, politicians had to accommodate to the fact that, as a result of introducing fertilizer use, a large part of the country's foreign exchange was to be dedicated to buying this input on the international market every year, even though the expected agricultural products were not, or not yet, intended for export. This list of transformations could be extended almost indefinitely. Apparently the availability of technical innovations at farm level is a necessary, but not sufficient, condition for widespread innovation processes to occur.

The general purpose of networking for innovation can be seen as an effective linking up of the efforts of all relevant social actors, to construct a social competence. Innovation processes may include the design and development of new products or services, the conception of new policies, regulations and/or intervention strategies, the design of new research, financing or marketing strategies, or (as is generally the case), a combination of several of these. Yet it is the social actors themselves who choose their 'PALS', who choose to participate in existing networks or build new ones and who, through their management of such relationships, may either enhance or suffocate the chances for particular innovation processes to occur. Hence, the social organization of innovation includes the building of strategic alliances between actors whose intention is to enhance a particular type of agricultural development. Consequently, as noted, innovation performance depends upon the adequacy and quality of networking efforts among social actors who perceive each other as relevant to their respective projects. This dependence on the actors' perceptions, however, leaves a huge question mark behind with respect to a definition of networking and innovation performance: who decides, and when and how, who the 'relevant' actors and practices are? Later we will return to this issue. First, let us explore the relationship between knowledge and innovation a bit further.

Knowledge, knowing and innovation

Unfortunately, much of the literature commonly taken to belong to the tradition of knowledge systems thinking is vague in its definition of 'knowledge' (Havelock, 1986). The 'knowledge utilization perspective' seems to refer to knowledge as something that can be transferred or transported. In addition, most attention has been directed to scientific and technical knowledge. This has contributed to a lack of systematic attention to indigenous and/or local knowledge. Röling, however, explicitly states knowledge to be an attribute of the mind, which cannot be transferred. The same author refers to the use of the concept of 'local knowledge' as '... shared and accumulated knowledge vis-à-vis a collective experience in a shared environment', thereby implying its social character (Röling, 1988: 186).

Long too stresses the social roots of knowledge: 'Knowledge processes are embedded in social processes that imply aspects of power, authority and legitimation; and they are just as likely to reflect and contribute to the conflict between social groups as they are to lead to the establishment of common perceptions and interests' (Long, 1992: 27). Knowledge is not simply something that is possessed and accumulated: it emerges out of processes of social interaction and should be looked at in terms of social relationships. Arce and Long (1987: 5) suggest knowledge can be defined as being '...constituted by the ways in which individual members of a society or social group categorize, code, process and impute meaning to their experiences'. A body of knowledge is therefore not made up of facts, but rather of the ideas and values that govern the assignment of meaning (Box, 1990).

The case studies confirm the pivotal role knowledge has for innovation. They also show that instead of fixing our attention on knowledge, we may be wiser to focus on the process of *knowing*. Farmers as well as advisers develop professional strategies to deal with information, to evaluate their experiences and to learn from them (Chapter 2). The case studies demonstrate both individual strategizing and socially constructed standards for using knowledge and information. Advisers develop individual strategies to deal with the variety of information sources at their disposal. Individual specializations evolve. Also, professional standards are evident in the way farmers and advisers select and use information. Information from different sources is used for different purposes. General rules for information management can be observed, such as: if you want to know the price of an item, ask the supplier, not the extension worker; for operational information, ask farm visitors; for technical information, refer to the farm journal and the local experimental station first; and so forth (Table 3, Chapter 2). On the other hand, the 'main menu' (Figure 3, Chapter 2) reflects specific rules that result from education and training: make sure you first get the problem clear; calculate the extent of the problem for the farmer; compare alternative solutions; etc. Informal rules from experience are also used: do not rely on government or technical information alone; select those pieces of documentary information which are brief and to the point, and which you can leave with the farmer afterwards (Chapter 2).

Moreover, farmers distinguish among relevant actors on the basis of the type of knowledge they seem to command. Farmers seem quite capable of discriminating among, for example, strategic, operational, technical, policy and marketing information; moreover, what they see as 'reliable' sources may vary with the type of information required. Consequently, there is evidence that farmers use a different information acquisition strategy for each type. In practice, technical and/or scientific knowledge is taken simply as a particular attribute of some relevant actors. Such actors are not seen as *the* source of knowledge, but as one of many relevant sources. Another point apparent from the case studies is that knowledge acquisition by farmers and advisers is intrinsically woven into their daily practice. The case study among advisers showed, for example, that individual portfolios reflect different personal interests as well as professional histories. The situation in their working area and the questions farmers put to them also influences the extent to which advisers become acquainted with issues. Knowledge can therefore not be severed from the practices of its 'bearer'. The latter point is consistent with observations from other authors. For Maturana and Varela (1984: 15), to know is to act effectively. Knowledge includes the ideas, concepts, routines and skills people acquire over time to support their livelihood. The only way to study it is to observe and evaluate people's behaviour.

Communication, of course, plays an important role. It involves social interaction related to constructing, anticipating and attributing meaning to experiences and to information about events and ideas. The role of language in facilitating and/or impairing the process of knowing is captured intriguingly by Gremmen (1993: 81): 'The study of human knowledge as a whole is distorted by the focus upon statements, when it takes knowledge to be the sum (or product) of true statements. Hence it construes the limits of human knowledge as coinciding with the limits of language. The alternative is a focus on concepts, which takes human knowledge to be the human capacity for using concepts of a language, for characterizing (categorizing) the world when and as it is humanly done, and hence construes the limits of human knowledge as coinciding with the limits of its concepts (in some historical period).'

The paragraphs above suggest that in developing a useful perspective on knowledge for the purpose of studying the social organization of innovation, at least four different dimensions must be addressed: first, knowledge can be seen as *cognition*, a human faculty to perceive or conceive; second, knowledge is *practical*, intrinsically woven into the daily practices of an individual or group; third, knowledge can be perceived as a property of the *individual*, enabling him or her to make inferences from experience, observation and/or reasoning; and finally, knowledge is *socially* constructed, embedded in the social dynamics of an organization, a community or a group. Moreover, given the dynamics involved, it seems crucial to focus attention on *knowing* rather than knowledge. Knowing emphasizes the dynamic unity of learning and doing, rather than the static aspects of knowledge as statements about the world and rules and recipes for acting in it. This also helps to highlight the problem-oriented nature of communication for innovation. As the cases underscore, social actors to a large degree behave purposefully, even professionally, to enhance innovation in agriculture, taking on the challenges found along the way. To combine the four dimensions, during this study we found it useful to think of knowledge as a *human intellectual competence*:

> *To my mind, a human intellectual competence must entail a set of skills of problem solving – enabling the individual to resolve genuine problems or difficulties that he or she encounters and, when appropriate, to create an effective product – and must also entail the potential for finding or creating problems – thereby laying the groundwork for the acquisition of new knowledge. These prerequisites represent my effort to focus on those intellectual strengths that prove of some importance within a cultural context. At the same time, I recognize that the ideal of what is valued will differ markedly, sometimes even radically, across human cultures, within the creation of new products or posing of new questions being of relatively little importance in some settings (Gardner, 1983: 60–61).*

In this way, what people know and how they go about learning is intrinsically woven into their life as social beings. Knowledge emerges as a result of social efforts to come to grips with the demands of the social and physical environments in which individuals and groups are immersed. In complex theatres of agricultural innovation, this does not apply to farmers alone; it applies equally to extension workers, environmental activists, researchers, policymakers, wildlife protectors, agro-industrialists and input suppliers. The definition also points to yet another dimension of knowing: the ability of human beings to perceive and/or create problems in practical situations. This has important consequences for our thinking on networking, to which we will return later.

From knowledge transfer to interplay among social practices

I have proposed to look at innovation as a process emerging from the multiple inter-actions among social actors from different relevant practices. The word 'practices' has been used in the sense of its general, intuitive meaning. Gremmen's (1993) work provides the opportunity to have another look at the significance of this concept to the study of social organization of innovation. This section sketches the contours of a promising new area of inquiry that may help place communicative interaction for innovation in a broader social perspective.

In Gremmen's 1993 analysis, agriculture is a 'technical practice': a series of activities is planned and carried out, through which the course of particular socio-natural processes – for example, crop growth or milk production – is steered in a certain direction, such as higher productivity. Just like learning, developing a technical practice is a social phenom-enon. Competent performance allows farmers to position themselves in relation to each other. Being a 'good practitioner' requires that fellow farmers and others relevant to the practice recognize you as such. A technical practice is not a collection of habits. On the contrary, as a series of performances is created by practitioners, each one can be modified by experience. An ongoing competent performance mirrors the interwoven learning processes of the various participants, during which both the natural *and* the social world are continuously reconstructed. Technical practices evolve through reflection-in-action: it is 'indigenous rationalization' (Gremmen, 1993: 115). Looked at in this way, innovation may be considered essentially a social learning process, embedded in and intrinsically interwoven with the ongoing evolution of agricultural practice.

Can such a complex social learning process be seen as responding to purpose, as we claimed innovation does? Do actors indeed organize themselves for learning? Can such learning really be taken to emerge as a result of purposive activity? I find the observed ongoing struggle for competent performance a powerful argument in support of such a proposition. In a practice, standards of competence are upheld. Normally, one would expect them to stimulate practitioners to improve their practices. Where the available standards seem to hamper innovation, one would expect at least some practitioners to try to change them. Nevertheless, it is necessary to repeat the earlier warning against assuming a simple, straightforward causal relationship between intentions and effects with respect to innovation in agriculture. Innovation processes may never be the outcome of *solely* intentional actions. But networking for innovation is surely 'purposive' in a more general sense – 'showing purpose and determination' (Hornby, 1974: 680) – even when it is not aimed at a specific object or result that can be defined in advance.

We are left, however, with another important question. I have argued that agricultural innovation is not carried by farmers alone. An historical, ongoing process of division of labour within agricultural practice has led to the emergence of distinct competent performances. Each involves its own standards of both competence and performance, which must be understood as practices in their own right: research, trade, extension, policymaking, education, industrial processing and so forth. Agricultural innovation can thus be seen as a result of the interplay among these practices.

> Primary characteristics of the interplay model: According to Gremmen (1993), the basic idea behind the interplay model is that practices evolve autonomously but in interaction with each other. Each can be analysed with respect to its competence as a performance, and is constrained by its own definitions and experience-based rules. Its definitions and rules, far from being static, are continuously created and re-created among the participants in a practice. 'The central claim of the interplay model is that improvement is primarily an internal achievement of practices themselves. External influences can speed up or slow down the indigenous improvement of a practice' (Gremmen, 1993: 159). External influences are the result of interaction among practices. These are seldom one-way. As a result innovation in practices derives from the interaction in-and-between practices, not from the discoveries of one single practice, such as science.

The interplay model explicitly acknowledges the diversity of types of knowing relevant to agricultural innovation; it also helps us understand the relative autonomy of knowledge processes within each of the practices relevant to agricultural development. Moreover, recognizing the interplay among different practices – without assuming the necessary superiority of one over the others – opens the way to studying the social organization of innovation as a multi-faceted, complex process of interactions among a variety of actors, each engaged in their own competent performances. Such a perspective can allow us to take the specificity of the knowledge of each of the relevant agricultural actors (including farmers, extension workers, traders, industrialists, researchers, policymakers) more seriously.

Most past research on 'technical practices' has, however, been focused on professionals (doctors, engineers etc.). To use the concept for our purposes, we must extend its use to 'lay' people, such as farmers and local authorities. Therefore, I would suggest its scope needs to be broadened. Any set of performances can be seen as a 'social practice', in the sense that social actors relate to each other to socially define and reinforce rules of competence. A social practice may then be defined as a discernible set of social actors, who define and uphold performance through some form of social interaction. Such an approach seems applicable wherever social actors interactively develop behaviour that is to some degree rule-governed. Both definitions and rules of experience must be recognized by the actors and recognisable to the observer. With this, the concept of 'social actor' can be taken as the broader term, referring to participants in a 'social practice'; while 'practitioner' becomes a narrower term referring to participants in a particular brand of social practices called 'technical practices'.

This approach opens interesting vistas on the interaction between technical and indigenous knowledge. A number of authors (for example, Richards, 1985; Röling, 1988; Chambers, 1989) have emphasized farmer or indigenous knowledge as an underutilized resource for agricultural development. But its utilization is now seen to present serious problems: farmer practices respond to different sets of rules than researcher practices, so that the integration of these strands is complicated. Millar (1992: 61) refers to the '... "grey areas" of farmers' experimental logic and strategies'. A clearer perception of each others' activities as social practices in their own right could help to improve the interplay between farmers and researchers. This would imply studying the definition and experience rules governing indigenous farming and the ways indigenous innovation is achieved. Rap (1992) and Stolzenbach (1992) have presented preliminary evidence on the importance of such studies. Brouwer (1993) shows the constant attention to possible improvements among Adja farmers in Benin, where sophisticated procedures are used to share experimental results. Clearly, indigenous farmers can be integrated in our models as 'social practitioners' in their own right.

Bourgeois (1990) provides another example. Difficulties in linking or even merging research and extension activities are often rooted in mandates and working procedures, and hence in the rules that govern competent performance within each practice: 'National extension services, with their broad mandate to reach all farmers in all regions of a country, often serve as a tool for implementing government policies. As a result, they tend to be hierarchical, highly centralized in terms of decision making, and heavily regulated and standardized in terms of tasks, skills and procedures. In contrast, national research, which is an open-ended process of scientific inquiry, is characterized by a 'flatter' structure, greater delegation of authority, and less standardization' (cited by Merrill-Sands and Kaimowitz, 1989: 37).

I conclude that innovation can be seen as emerging from interplay in-and-between diverse social practices. Social actors, each belonging to one or several social practices, in their daily struggle to come to grips with the demands of their socio-natural environment build and maintain interactive relationships in order to increase their chances for improvement. Networking for innovation can then be understood as a process social actors engage in to effectively construct an interplay among relevant practices.

Networking as a social practice oriented towards innovation

As I have shown, networking for innovation can be understood as a process in which social actors search, establish and manage interactive relationships with actors from their own and other practices – those that, by some standard, they judge to be relevant to their endeavours. (See the example on 'Networking among practices'.) The 'standard' is a shared idea or theory about what type of agricultural development is desirable, and about who must be involved in it to make it work. Rather than aiming at transferring messages or technologies, these efforts are meant to create opportunities for *sharing ideas, learning and reflection*. Yet, as we saw in Chapters 3, 4 and 5, networking is more than communicative interaction: it generally also covers a wide range of transactions related to products and services. Sometimes, but not always, a commitment to joint activities or cooperation is part of the networking relationships. These points will be illustrated briefly, using the case studies.

> Networking among practices: Farmers develop interactive relationships with the people they judge to be most relevant to their farming operations. These relationships are not all the same, however. With what I have called 'farm visitors' (veterinary doctors, advisers from fodder companies, health inspectors, farm advisers and so forth) they develop interpersonal relationships. These are tied to a service or product, yet with time develop into a multi-dimensional social relationship. The benefit each actor receives from the interaction is in the first place practical: the farmer obtains an 'advice', a service or a product, the visitor a reward (sometimes financial). Yet other, less material exchanges take place at the same time: to be useful, visitors must help farmers clarify their questions and/or problems; this, in turn, improves the visitors' knowledge of farming and provides them with ideas that can improve their performance. The 'main menu' in the case study (covering exchanges between advisers and farmers about on-farm manure storage), clearly illustrates the issues tackled in interactions between advisers and farmers. The documents carried by the adviser demonstrate that they do not expect to be involved in every possible issue. It is clear that for some issues the adviser holds the 'key', that is, the knowledge and information most significant to understanding. On other issues the farmer or other actors will possess more relevant knowledge and information.
>
> Farmers develop a quite different relationship with information services (primarily farm journals and mass media). These services do not send visitors to the farm regularly, so no interpersonal relationship evolves. Their information is client oriented but not custom made for an individual. Farmers see farm journals as playing a very important role in providing a general picture of what is going on in the sector. The journals fill this role by using materials from a variety of sources. Editors and journalists include and/or produce materials about policy trends, technical and market developments. They network actively with people in policymaking, research, marketing and other practices they see as relevant. Often, they make direct use of materials produced by companies, researchers or extension workers. Their audience is not made up of farmers alone. About one-fifth of the documents advisers carried came from dailies or journals, and this type of information in particular contributed to the advisers' personal strategies (Table 2). Farm journals bring together information on experiences, events and ideas from different sector-related practices. Therefore they provide what I will call a 'carrier wave' for innovation in the sector.

The reasons social actors engage in building social relationships are quite straightforward. Most are practical, directly related to maintaining their competent performance as practitioners. To be a 'good' farmer a dairy producer needs healthy cows, and hence, from time to time a veterinary doctor. At the same time, when ideas about what a 'good' farmer is change, the role of the veterinary doctor will also have to change. This points in the same direction as the mutual interdependence noted among some institutions engaged in agricultural development: the competent performance of one is intrinsically linked to the competent performance of the other. If they could be successful alone, networking would stop. When change is desired, the 'theory of intervention' may call for cooperation between farmers and advisers, between research and extension or among NGDOs. However, the possibility of constructing a theory which does not include cooperation is equally conceivable. This is illustrated by DRI's initial negligence towards research as a potential partner in agricultural development in Nariño (Chapters 3 and 4). This is also apparent in the various models (treated in the above section on 'Innovation theory revisited') that have been used to study innovation processes.

Not all relationship building can be considered 'networking for innovation' however. Based on the conclusions in Chapter 5, I propose to speak of networking for innovation *only if* the actors involved share the following three perceptions: the existence of a relative but critical lack of experiences, knowledge and/or information, which hampers competent individual performance; the need to jointly gain a more comprehensive and more effective understanding of a common problem or concern; and a wish to work out alternative development proposals and, possibly, debate these in comparison to alternative proposals from other actors. All three reflect a genuine concern to improve the quality and impact of individual and/or joint performances. When such a general motive is lacking, it is hard to imagine that purposive innovation activities will take place. The individual motives of social actors for networking may be highly diverse – perhaps to earn more money, provide better government services, rescue forest areas, prevent environmental deterioration or promote sector-wide competitiveness.

Consequently, the practical results of networking efforts are also extremely diverse. They may range from a simple exchange of documents, to organizing seminars, to providing technical services to members, to establishing a joint label for marketing a range of quality products. Chapter 5 suggests that network activities may be categorized in four types: learning through joint reflection, services, advocacy and network management or facilitation. In addition, I propose that the services provided are the practical foundation upon which learning processes are built. Or, as Manrique and Bueno de Mesquita (1993) put it: 'The immediate needs arising from the field work of each of the institutions are the basis and reason for being a network'. As noted in Chapter 5, networking is what it says it is: *working*. Its link to the daily practice of each of the participants is strong, and is in accordance with my conclusions on the practical nature of knowing (see the preceding section). This means the range of practical results of networking is in principle unlimited: it is determined by network members' assessment of their needs, and their views and decisions as to what is most important at a given point in time. In other words, it depends upon the *theory of intervention* they subscribe to and the *mission* they expect their networking to accomplish.

What sets networking apart, however, is the space it creates for *joint learning and innovation*. Therefore, the ways network members construct opportunities to enhance their own learning are central to our analysis. In Chapter 5, diagnosis, exchange visits, workshops and working groups were identified as mechanisms that can enable network members to share experiences and learn. In Chapter 3, we highlighted the role of on-farm trials, interdisciplinary task groups and subject-matter specialists in liaison positions. Chapter 2 elaborated on the role of communication networks, articulated through inter-personal and mass media. Rap (1992) points to the need for practical learning settings so that learning can take place through experiments, trials or direct observations, rather than through talk and reasoning alone. For obvious reasons, *communication practices* play a central role in facilitating learning processes. Networking can only be effective when network members have acquired the skills needed to effectively communicate with each other, when communication infrastructure and information services are available, and when an approach that creates space for and facilitates joint learning has been articulated. Actually achieving innovation depends upon the quality of the communication and learning processes stimulated by the networking efforts of relevant social actors.

The appreciative nature of networking

We have left behind a trail of unsolved questions related to issues such as: who decides who the 'relevant' actors and practices are? When and how is such a decision taken, if at all? Who perceives a problem to be worthy of a networking effort? Why? Who says networking could solve it? Who formulates the 'theory of intervention'? Who determines the mission networking efforts are to accomplish? One of the most consistent issues in the study of networking for innovation is its arbitrariness: different social actors generally perceive the same situation quite differently, coming to different and often conflicting proposals for intervention. Following Vickers (cited by Checkland and Casar, 1986), I will refer to this issue as the *appreciative nature* of networking for innovation. Vickers proposed the term 'appreciation' to cover selective perceptions of reality and judgements about it. He also stressed the intrinsic relationship between judgement-making and management of social relationships. Social actors, at all times, choose to establish and maintain relationships with the others they judge to be relevant to their project. At the same time, they rely on these same relationships to keep themselves informed about what is relevant and what is not. As a consequence, their appreciations cannot be isolated from the social context. For example, the appreciations at the root of an actor's decision to 'network' depend upon the actor's judgement with respect to the availability among other actors of relevant experiences, knowledge and information; the degree to which they expect to be able to acquire access to these actors; the benefits they expect; and the expected cost (financial, material or social).

Then, of course, there is the issue of power and influence. Which of the actors has the capacity to stimulate or stop networking activities? Who can decide whether a specific social actor belongs to the network or not, and on which grounds? Who has the power to establish links to relevant practices, and who decides which ones are relevant? Who is the primary influence on the emergence of a 'theory of intervention'? As just one example, take the current discussions with regard to sustainable agriculture. One topic of discussion is traditional practices. Are they to be taken seriously? Does the need for 'relevant diversity of opinion' indicate efforts have to be made to include traditional practitioners in our networks? Should there be investments in research to revive such practices, or at least to understand them? Who should make such investments? And, if they are made, who 'owns' the results? Partly as a direct consequence of the variety in answers to these and other questions, there has been a surge in the variety of networks. Of these, some show considerable overlap, some serve parallel functions, and some are scarcely on speaking terms. That is, there is a degree of redundancy among networks; this is not necessarily a problem, so long as they manage to exchange information effectively.

The appreciative character of networking is clearest when the decisions to be taken among networkers could impact their freedom of operation. This occurs when the *problems* to be tackled through networking are being assessed, when individual strengths, guiding principles and expectations are formulated and, eventually, when a *theory of intervention* (who is to contribute what, why, how and to the benefit of whom?) is defined. As in the case of the NGDO networks we studied, such a process may be guided by intentions; or, as long as some infrastructure for networking is accessible to all, it may be spontaneous. This does not mean, however, that no such theory could be formulated on the basis of observed networking practice.

The setting of *rules for membership*, even if done informally, also brings the appreciative character of networking to the fore. The statement, often heard among networkers, that they intend to liaise only with 'like-minded' social actors, indicates that even if no specific criteria are formulated, informal selection still takes place. A third instance arises when an *approach to running the network* is developed: when joint activities, required contributions, services and operational procedures are being designed and implemented. Only then can individual members weigh eventual benefits and possible negative consequences for their own operations against the efforts that will be required of them. A fourth critical instance occurs when success or *performance is evaluated*. In all of these instances the world views, partisanship and expectations of each of the participants are challenged and set against those of the others. At each of these points the 'platform' (Röling, 1994) for interaction, hitherto so carefully constructed, squeaks under the weight of argument.

At the same time, it is during such instances that networking indeed becomes 'innovation-oriented social practice'. In the ensuing struggles, fundamental definitions and rules are laid down. These may eventually govern the networking effort or, on the contrary, the networking effort may fall apart if the commitment of the participants is not strong enough to lead to agreement on the basics. As Chapter 5 has shown, when members or prospective members are stimulated to participate fully in these debates, it takes time and energy. However, it can be argued that surviving such an initial 'battle over images' is probably what makes a network succeed in the end. In the end, the quality of this interactive process of definition appears to a large extent to determine not only how a network will operate but also how strong it will become.

We may conclude that it is through networking that social actors organize the interplay among practices they consider relevant to their concerns. Networking is what social actors do to construct a social competence for innovation. The next paragraphs are dedicated to a further characterization of networking as an innovation-oriented social practice, touching on issues of coordination, power and influence and the forms of social organization that can be seen to evolve as a result of sustained networking efforts by social actors in complex agricultural innovation theatres.

Innovation as a result of unending social inquiry

To take the definition of networking for innovation one step further I will argue that networking, in fact, is a process of unending social inquiry. In *Inquiry and change*, Lindblom addresses '...social inquiry or the production of social knowledge as a vast social process in which even relatively uninformed, ordinary people play significant parts...' in addition to professionals, politicians and opinion leaders. His starting point is that preferences, wants, needs, or whatever it is that serves peoples' interests, '...are not discoverable – not even to a degree that warrants an attempt at discovery' (Lindblom, 1990: 18). There is no bedrock of objective or scientific 'best ends', 'best means', 'best solutions' or 'best situations' for social scientists to discover. Decisions do not derive from wants; wants derive from decisions. A decision is needed to decide what the wants are to be. As a result, in social innovation processes not only the means but also the ends are an object of dispute. Social actors permanently create or re-create, rather than find or discover, preferences, wants and needs. What they create Lindblom calls a *volition*, stressing commitment or will. 'Building on a foundation of fact, poorly or well constructed, people (never alone but always in social interaction) form, create, decide, will.... volition[s]' (Lindblom, 1990: 21).

The concept of volition emphasizes *sense-making* on the one hand (creating comprehension and purpose) and, on the other, *commitment* to stick to decisions that have been made. It also entails *fluidity*: an informed and thoughtful volition, strictly speaking, is never in error; it is, however, always subject to challenge or reformulation. Challenging it means a challenge to both means and ends. Lindblom recognizes two extreme types of volitions: the relatively stable *standing volitions* and the more transitory *action volitions*. Either can be expressed in language and/or action. A volition (similar to the general intentionality behind innovation processes) shows purpose and determination even if no objects or results are specified in advance. The concept of 'volition' offers a way to practically investigate the views different social actors hold when they start or maintain a network or configure institutional cooperation. Volitions might be taken as the 'projects' (Long, 1992: 24) in which social actors try to enrol other actors. The strategic consensus eventually achieved among core actors in Nariño described in Chapters 3 and 4 reflects the slow process of establishing a shared volition among different institutions. A successful institutional coalition emerges as a result. In fact, a volition is the 'theory of intervention' of a social actor at a particular point in time.

That a *convergence* in ideas, opinions and approach can result not only from active strategizing among institutions, but also from a coming together with the strategies of smallholders, is illustrated by Paulino's choice (Chapter 3, in the example 'Paulino's choice'). Smallholders base their volitions on their understanding of their own position as potential beneficiaries. The case of Paulino demonstrates in the extreme the flexibility needed to achieve a tangible, innovative solution in a specific situation. The farmer, Paulino, arrived at a perfect fusion of technical, economical, geographical and practical knowledge and information, and designed his own solution, adapted to his particular circumstances and ideas. It took time, of course, and it took a lot of energy, for example to convince the bank that a housing loan could be used to finance the building of a fancy house 'for guinea pigs'. The case describes a process of convergence among three different types of social actors in a complex innovation theatre, each entertaining quite different ideas of what rural development is all about.

Paulino himself had decided guinea pig raising could be profitable for a farmer in his circumstances, but had no capital to make the necessary investments. The Colombo-Dutch project had concluded guinea pig raising was economically feasible for smallholders and wanted to experiment under farm conditions, yet did not have sufficient means to compensate Paulino fully for his risks. Under the integrated rural development programme, the bank on the other hand had two lines of credit for smallholders: one for productive investments and one for housing. Both were intended to improve the livelihood of smallholder families; the central philosophy behind the programme was to enable these families to generate adequate income. In this case, the extension service and the bank were flexible enough not to kill Paulino's idea. But both institutions stretched normal bureaucratic discipline to the limit. Naturally, convergence upon this particular solution was possible only once; this occurred while the programme did not yet have an adequate way to deal with the introduction of improved guinea pig husbandry among smallholders. Later, lines of credit were instituted for raising guinea pigs. What happened to Paulino marked an institutional recognition of the specific factors involved in stimulating innovation in guinea pig husbandry at farm level. It also illustrates that smallholders can make an active contribution to probing volitions, options and constraints on innovation. But above all, it illustrates that in designing and implementing specific innovation strategies, the means/ ends combinations that eventually prove effective may not be exactly those planned in advance. I conclude that this emphasizes the importance of the 'fluidity' Lindblom sees as an essential element of a volition: if the views, propositions and intervention designs of social actors are not flexible, widespread innovation will be very hard to achieve.

The example also supports another of Lindblom's points. He argues strongly against reducing a struggle with social problems to scientific problem solving. He points out 'problem solving' is a misnomer; it would be better to speak of 'attacking' or 'grappling' with problems, as some solutions to problems are not based on intent. No one could have intended for the problems of Paulino, the project and the bank to be solved as they were. Still, it happened. In essence, this was a relatively simple, straightforward problem. In grappling with complex social problems, often 'no one ever decides on each series of interim solutions that emerge' (Lindblom, 1990: 5). I propose extending these arguments to cover complex innovation processes. I have argued that in a process of innovation, both 'professional' and 'lay' practices play a role, while both natural and social worlds are changed. Except very occasionally, the widespread use of technical innovations in agriculture cannot be achieved without important social and organizational adjustments. Innovation in agriculture, therefore, should be understood as a process of 'grappling' with social problems, rather than as purely scientific or technical problem solving.

As with all social problems, innovation in agriculture arises only '...when people look at a state of affairs in a particular way: specifically, with a desire for its improvement' (Lindblom, 1990: 4). This seems particularly relevant to our reflections. The appreciative character of networking for innovation has been encountered repeatedly. One reason for this, I propose, is rooted in the way social actors look at the world and intend to improve it – in other words, their volitions. However, the way social actors formulate and enact their views, and hence define the problems to be solved, leads them to favour certain solution strategies above others. Developments in Nariño during the 1970s and 1980s illustrate this point. Whereas in the 1960s and early 1970s the problem of smallholder production was defined mainly in terms of *lack of association* related to both production and marketing, in the late 1970s and 1980s institutions converged upon a definition emphasizing *lack of on-farm productivity*. The subsequent disintegration of many of the associations established earlier can be seen to a considerable degree as associated with the withdrawal of institutional assistance (Moreno and Villota, 1984). The new problem definition, as shown in Chapter 3, did lead to a successful convergence of government institutions on technical and credit support for a specific target group of smallholders.

Such grappling with complex social problems is an inquiry that never ends. It proceeds within a broad, open-ended, diffuse social process in which both ends and means are continuously shaped and reshaped, as a result of social interaction among relevant actors. What actors do in the process Lindblom (1990: 7) calls 'probing'. This word '...captures much of the flavour of the process, since it emphasizes persistence and depth of investigation, uncertainty of result, and possible surprise; but it suffers, for present purposes, from its medical connotations'. Often, inquiries are not immediately related to solutions. The interactive process, never less than a variety of inquiries by different actors in an area of concern, becomes a process of '...bringing inquiry and knowledge to bear in such a way to alter dispositions and positions so that they make a solution possible later' (Lindblom, 1990: 6). The inquiry into guinea pig production initiated by the Colombo-Dutch project in Nariño illustrates this point. As we showed, it never became a priority for either agricultural research or the integrated rural development programme DRI (Table 8, Chapter 3). Nevertheless, other actors, notably farmers and extension, gave it priority. They recognized its potential as a viable alternative for smallholders, including women. The process of inquiry eventually included on-farm research, experiments by agronomy students, the establishment of an association of producers, the initiation of a credit facility and scientific research on health problems in guinea pig husbandry. Active networking was supported by seminars, communication media and subject-matter specialists, and reached as far as Peru when the Colombo-Dutch project recruited a guinea pig specialist there.

Paulino's story has already illustrated that probing for innovation is a social, interactive process. Lindblom (1990: 36) suggests that, in such cases '...formulating a problem calls for inquiry no less than does formulating a solution to a formulated problem. *The origin of a social problem lies in the probes that declare it to be a problem*' (emphasis added). This is illustrated in Chapters 4 and 5, in the description of the struggles of development organizations (whether governmental or non-governmental) to establish effective networks to enhance agricultural development. What has been called the phase of 'planned activism' in Chapter 5 is exactly that: probing alternative problem and action definitions and eventually accepting the one that works best for most network members. The appreciation of problems has as much to do with the way relevant social actors look at the situation as it has to do with the way they expect to be able to solve it. In addition, social actors' appreciation of the situation appears to be closely related to the policy context and mission they ascribe to the innovation theatre, on the one hand, and the resources they command to intervene in it, on the other. I will illustrate this with some examples from the ISNAR case studies.

When the government of Côte d' Ivoire in 1978 decided to shift from a sectoral to a regional approach, it did so to make use of its commercial commodity development corporations to promote food crop production. The government's intention with this policy shift was to build upon the positive experience these corporations had in developing cotton and rice as commercial crops, and to effectively support rural development at the grass roots. The corporations were to become regional development corporations. Their capacity to operate effectively was seen as the solution to the apparent lack of effectiveness of government extension services. Also, it fit a more 'hands-off' national policy and regionalization of efforts. However, outcomes were less than expected (Eponou, 1990a, c). The corporations continued to be very effective in commercial crops but, having received no adequate additional funding for research and extension support, failed to generate similar successes in food crop production. One conclusion seems obvious: the problem situation for food crop production cannot be taken as a problem of 'organizational effectiveness' alone. A similar example comes from Tanzania. The National Coconut Development Programme (Lupanga, 1990) was intended to make relevant coconut technology available in large enough quantities to achieve an overall rehabilitation of the Tanzanian coconut industry. When large-scale impact was not achieved, the lack of integration of the industry with marketing actors was pointed out. Rather than a 'technology problem', the decline in coconut production was now recognized to be, at least in part, a 'market problem'.

Another example concerns reasoning with regard to direct government intervention in favour of agricultural innovation. The view that exposing innovation theatres to market pressures leads to better performance is amply supported in the case studies, and is in line with the ongoing progressive liberalization of agricultural production and markets. The conclusion that many agricultural innovation theatres have traditionally been too sheltered from such forces is therefore no great surprise. On the other hand, a lack of consistent and effective policy support is frequently mentioned as a cause of problems. Ekpere and Idowu (1990a: 15) mention a lack of policy guidelines for collaboration and encouraging functional linkages between relevant actors. Frequent shifts in policies, often in combination with shifts in the allocation of resources, are also reported frequently. Palmieri (1990b: 55) refers to the government of Costa Rica's lack of interest in promoting technical improvements in maize cultivation for fear of producing in excess of national demands at a time when the world market price had dropped below national production costs. Perez (1990: 26) and Azucena (1989: 198) indicate a lack of pricing policies that would effectively support technological innovation at farm level. Apparently, one's appreciation of the causal

relationships influencing the effectiveness of social interaction in agricultural innovation theatres depends very much on the policy
perspective embraced. When different financial donors decide to support different organizations who then independently intervene in the same theatre, this may even lead to a duplication of efforts (Arocena-Francisco, 1989).

The examples above make clear that the appreciation of problematical situations in complex innovation theatres merits thorough attention in each particular case. And – as is obvious also from the conceptual and organizational struggles that precede the formation of NGDO networks (Chapter 5) – formulating a problem requires as much inquiry and accommodation as does formulating appropriate solution strategies. The multiplicity of actors generally involved, I may add, probably leads to the existence of as many volitions and solution strategies as there are actors who intend to intervene on behalf of innovation. Negotiating a consensus (even if partial) among them may be a necessary part of any solution strategy proposed for intervention in a complex agricultural innovation theatre. Hence, the continuous probing of relevant *volitions* (ways of making sense out of possible means and ends), *propositions* (feasible alternative proposals to achieve those ends) and *conditions* (social and/or natural constraints) seems to be one very important element of networking for innovation in agriculture.

In fact, to a large degree what binds a practice together may well be the factors it identifies or defines as problems. In agricultural practice, it is common knowledge that the soil scientist, the economist, the entomologist, the irrigation engineer, the veterinary doctor, the extension worker and the crops specialist – called in to look at the *same* practical situation – will define problems and solutions in vastly different terms. This has been one of the most powerful arguments in favour of forming interdisciplinary project teams and doing interdisciplinary appraisals to identify agricultural problems. It points up the role of knowledge – well-probed beliefs – in narrowing down the scope and range of options seen as relevant to a particular situation. Interdisciplinary efforts in agricultural development are in fact attempts to reduce such hindrances to inquiry by developing an 'interdisciplinary' practice to face complex situations.

Coordination, leadership and power

A shared understanding of the problem situation and of how innovation can best be achieved – or, as we have labelled it, a shared theory of intervention – may well be the binding force within an innovation-oriented social practice. How does such a shared understanding and, consequently, a particular way of social organization for innovation evolve? In this section we will focus on the social dynamics of networking for innovation: the use (and abuse) of power and influence to achieve coordination among social actors in complex innovation theatres. But, as has been discussed, innovation is not a planned process. On the contrary, it is largely self-guiding. It is a social, interactive and diffuse process of interactive inquiry engaged in by social actors. Generally, actors don't have to be pushed to become innovative. Social actors organize themselves to improve their practices: networking for innovation is part of competent performance. 'Everybody always probes....We supplement the most casual inquiries with scattered active investigation.... Inquiry mixes with and advances through action, for we do not first probe and then act but continue to probe and learn in every action we take' (Lindblom, 1990: 30). This is true for farmers in the Netherlands (Grooters, 1990; Adolfse and de Koning, 1993) but it is no different for small farmers in developing countries. An increasing amount of research shows small farmers to be active networkers and innovators (Box, 1989; Pijnenburg, 1989; Box et al. 1990; Stolzenbach, 1991; Brouwers, 1993; Alders et al., 1993). This multiplicity means that innovation processes cannot generally be understood as directed or steered by one or a limited number of actors. Where a direction can be discerned at all, it emerges from the social struggles, negotiations and accommodations among a variety of actors defending diverse concerns, interests and positions. Any attempt to look at it as a one-sided, centrally managed process is bound to succumb to simplified, partisan views.

Knowing all this, how then does a direction or trend evolve in a complex agricultural innovation theatre? What causes the perspectives and means social actors apply to their appreciations and interventions to converge? And what characterizes social actors that are able, one way or the other, to enrol others in their projects? Even self-guided social inquiry requires some degree of organization; some tasks need to be recognized and carried out. Why are some volitions well probed, whereas others are left untended? Why is it that some propositions lead to experiments while others are hardly looked at? Why is it that certain conditions are taken for granted, whereas others are considered alterable? And why is it that some alternatives are favoured during decision making while others are hardly considered? And who takes the relevant decisions with regard to probing for innovation? My evaluation of the case study materials suggests these questions can be usefully looked upon as problems of *coordination* (Chapter 4). Of course, 'coordination' does not mean straightforward top–down control. As Mintzberg (1983) points out, this is only one way to achieve coordination; it is only effective or even feasible in certain conditions. These conditions (for example, a unified management structure and charismatic leadership) are extremely rare in complex innovation theatres.

Our case study from Nariño (Chapter 3) shows the importance of some degree of inter-institutional coordination to achieving an impact on technological innovation at the farm level. Also, three factors were deduced from that experience that are relevant to explaining the achievement of such coordination. The first was strong *institutional leadership* and *strategic consensus* among core institutions as to the intervention strategies to be implemented. Moreover, *resource allocations* were closely tied to well-defined and reinforced institutional policies and priorities. Our findings confirm the view expressed by Long (1992) that developing joint agency and power '...depend crucially upon the emergence of a network of actors who become partially, though hardly ever completely, enrolled in the "project" of some other person or persons. Effective agency then requires the strategic generation/manipulation of a network of social relations and the channelling of specific items (such as claims, orders, goods, instruments and information) through certain "nodal points" of interaction' (Long, 1992: 24). In effect, the DRI programme was able to impose its leadership via a deft use of its financial resources, literally enrolling recipients in its 'project'. The Colombo-Dutch ICA-CCH Project was effective because, from 1978 onwards, it used its resources to complement the DRI programme. Partly because of this, ICA was able to maintain technical leadership over the process. A further review of the ISNAR case studies in Chapter 5 confirmed the importance of institutional leadership, strategic consensus and resource linkages to forging institutional configurations. We conclude that these three factors may play an important role in building the *coalitions of actors* able to mobilize resources necessary to the implementation of particular solution strategies.

In addition, a number of specific task-related linkage mechanisms were identified that were directly associated with high institutional performance and impact. We argued that these provided joint learning opportunities, facilitating the integration of knowledge and information from relevant sources, including farmers. Combining this with what we know from the first case studies in Chapter 2, I will argue that, in fact, through these and similar practices *multiple communication networks* evolve; at any point in time these provide participants with an opportunity to exchange, share and learn from the experiences and information of others. During the case studies, we found that such networks involve a great many social actors and a large number of communication media, all playing their own roles. It has been suggested that such communication networks add value, as the additions of each participant increase the value of the information exchanged, in the process of transforming it into advise and/or information directed at a particular audience.

But once established, how is such an institutional configuration maintained? In Chapter 5 we also pointed to the *specific coordinating mechanisms* that may play a role in coordinating tasks among social actors in complex innovation theatres: several ways of standardization, direct supervision and control, plus mutual adjustment. In companies, one may argue that in principle a hierarchical power structure may impose central control. Mintzberg (1983) shows, however, that the 'strategic apex' is only one of several types of actors who generate 'pulls' to reinforce coordination within an organization. Each favours its own type of coordinating mechanisms, which – though sanctioned by the hierarchy – provide them with ample influence on the way coordination of tasks is achieved. In modern organizations, he argues, in addition to direct supervision and various sorts of standardization, mutual adjustment among different members, or units of the organization is becoming more and more important. Lindblom (1990: 250) too demonstrates that centralism is not a necessary condition for coordination. Coordination among social actors is often achieved by mutual adjustment, motivated not solely by a wish for coordination but by desires to remove obstacles to new achievements (Lindblom, 1990: 251). Lindblom notes (1990: 250): '...nothing coordinates a team of soccer players more effectively than their mutual adjustments, even if...coordination is not perfect, nor wholly unassisted by central authority.'

The maintenance of a strategic consensus may be explored a little further with the help of Lindblom's concept of *convergence*. 'A convergence is a narrowed range of thought or attitude ... [and/or] ... of variation in attitude, belief, value, or volition. Never or rarely does it approach a unanimity or a consensus' (Lindblom, 1990: 71). What we have called a 'theory of intervention', stipulating what is to be done, by whom and for the benefit of whom, is one such convergence. The joint mission of the institutions in Nariño became *to improve the income of smallholder families in the Nariño Highlands by introducing improved technology at farm level.* Once this had been agreed, 'smallholder farmers' were defined as farmers with less than 20 hectares of land; further, other options for inter-vention, such as organizing farmers into groups to create a 'pull' for service delivery, or identifying and improving upon local technologies – to name a few – were discarded. Still, some institutions did not act entirely within the scope of this mission. The guinea pig improvement programme for example went outside it, doing an inventory of local know-ledge on guinea pig husbandry and initiating the guinea pig raisers' association.

What is it that causes convergences in volitions or propositions to occur? One line of reasoning, strongly developed by Lindblom, points chiefly to constraining influences or factors that limit the extent to which alternatives are probed. Well-probed, carefully formulated volitions (such as *smallholder income can be improved by introducing improved technologies at farm level*) as well as acquired knowledge can in themselves (as noted earlier) be constraining influences. Well-probed beliefs may allow propositions to go largely unchallenged: highly 'verified' ones are considered 'fact'; the less verified may be taken as expert 'judgements' (Lindblom, 1990: 123). The 'linear model' of thinking on agricultural innovation is an example of a long-standing convergence among extension scientists, as Röling (1994) has pointed out. That the course of technical innovation is decided by research has long been an unchallenged 'fact'.

Other impairing influences, according to Lindblom, may be rooted in socialization processes, culture, communication, and the use and abuse of power by advantaged groups. For the student of agricultural innovation theatres, these observations are all too familiar. School education for agricultural extension workers generally creates a bias against traditional knowledge, which often impairs useful communication with farmers. Cultural impairments include lack of respect for traditional wisdom, spirituality and long-established customs within agricultural practices (Brouwers, 1993). Only now is the value of traditional seed varieties again being recognized by the scientific community (J. Hardon, interviewed in the *Wageningen Universiteitsblad,* October 1993). Mass communication media may play an important role, which may be positive or negative. In Indonesia, the media continue to promote the use of chemicals, even while a national effort is under way to promote integrated pest management (van de Fliert, 1993; pers. comm.). With respect to the use of power, Lindblom offers an interesting hypothesis proposing that certain patterns of impairment are '... being supplied by defense of elite advantages' (Lindblom, 1990: 128). This hypothesis strikes me as particularly relevant to a search for explanations for the difficulties social actors seem to encounter in many countries of the world when they attempt to implement strategies for more sustainable, environmentally sound agricultural production.

However, it seems to me impairments cannot fully explain why convergences develop. In agricultural innovation theatres some convergences seem to reflect *leadership* more than patterned impairment. As we have shown, some social actors are able to markedly influence the events and ideas of other actors in agricultural innovation theatres, enroling them in their projects. The role of DRI can be seen in this way (Chapter 4), as can that of NGDOs who lead the networking efforts discussed in Chapter 5. Specific coordinating mechanisms are operational in imposing and maintaining such leadership. Only when a fundamental challenge occurs can we expect a 'defense of elite advantages' to become noticeable. This might occur in the instances identified earlier on when, explicitly or not, basic tenets of networking or even disagreements among the participating actors are under discussion. Lindblom also touches upon leadership when he argues that improved social inquiry alone is not sufficient to improve social problem solving. Probing, he argues, cannot carry people all the way to decisions or solutions to social problems. Particularly when conflict resolution is required, it may be supplemented by the imposition of solutions, especially by the state (Lindblom, 1990: 54).

Environmental legislation constraining farming in the Netherlands is a case in point. Initially very much against the wishes of the 'agrarian lobby', a number of restricting laws and regulation were imposed by the state. At the moment, very few still argue against them. Two possible explanations may be offered. Some actors or coalitions of actors – possibly the European Union or the environmental lobby, not necessarily the national government – may have been powerful enough to impose their 'projects' on the others and get away with it. On the other hand, a number of actors may have converged on a carefully probed, cautiously worded understanding of the problem and its possible solutions, as they discovered the convenience of narrowing their interests: then they could work together with, rather than against, other powerful stakeholders. In the case of the Netherlands, both explanations seem to have played a role in forging the convergence that eventually caused the protests to fade away.

This leaves one important question open: leadership and impairment, convergence and divergence – all may be various sides of the same issue. Depending upon the (possibly partisan) position one takes as an observer, what appears as leadership to one may appear as impairment to another. Those already enrolled in projects based upon a shared volition may see convergence as 'the natural course of affairs', whereas those resisting that particular type of solution will fight to obtain space for the development of alternative ideas. For the moment, we will not go further into this matter. It helps to underscore once more the appreciative, potentially partisan, character of observations made while studying the social organization of innovation. It also underscores the need to open a 'window' on the power struggles underlying the coordination of tasks for probing and innovation. Whether we picture facilitation efforts as directed towards reducing impairments, or towards stimulating leadership and coordination (or both) does not seem to make much difference.

Towards an action-oriented theory of social organization for innovation

In this section I will propose answers to 'Q1 and Q2' – the research questions that stimulated the 'exploratory path' of this book, as given on page 1 of this chapter. First however I will summarize the characterization of innovation upon which these answers will rest. The conclusion above was that *agricultural innovation* emerges from interplay among social actors from relevant social practices. It is a diffuse, social process of individual and collective inquiry and decision making with respect to volitions, propositions and contexts; this continuously leads to new or modified problem definitions as well as choices of particular solutions. The organization and quality of the interplay determines the course and quality of innovation. The *social organization of innovation* may then be defined as the way in which social actors organize themselves and perform this interplay.

Starting with the more tangible of the two research questions, Q2, our studies suggest that what social actors actually do to achieve innovation in their practices may be defined as *networking in-and-between relevant practices*. To gain access to a range of options and insights, social actors actively engage in building and managing interactive relationships with social actors from their own and/or other practices, whom they consider relevant by some standard to their concerns. Such standards may vary widely. They evolve as a result of networking within a particular social context with the aim of innovation. However, not all networks are the result of such an aim. Characteristics of networking for innovation are:

- creation of joint learning opportunities among social actors who perceive each other as relevant to their concerns related to innovation;
- probing of relevant volitions, propositions and contexts; and
- pooling energies and, often but not necessarily, other resources to implement particular innovation strategies.

Probing is taken as interactive, diffuse and practice-oriented learning-in-practice, allowing for a study of conflicts over volitions, technical and organizational solutions, partisanship, power and impairing influences. *Volitions* are the 'projects' actors express, in language or action, in their effort to make sense of their contribution to innovation and social change in agriculture. *Propositions* refer to the social or other organizational and scientific/technical solution strategies that are identified as relevant to particular volitions. *Contexts* refer to the socially constructed as well as the natural conditions that reduce the degrees of freedom actors have to create/choose among volitions and propositions.

Our findings suggest that a direct relationship can be postulated between the *quality of networking* and the outcomes of the innovation process. Social processes of inquiry are central; these may explore new means and ends, defining or re-defining problems, or formulating/re-formulating political, technical and/or organizational options. These processes are not limited to intellectual endeavours. They may concern processes of change (sometimes experimental) in either the natural or social world. Communication plays an important role in creating and maintaining relationships, in facilitating the exchange and interpretation of experiences and ideas. At the same time networking for innovation is tied closely to the daily work of social actors, so that mutually beneficial activities, services and exchanges of advice and information play fundamental roles. The *appreciative character of networking* stems from the need to make choices. Networking participants are required again and again to make choices, deciding whether to include a particular actor, practice, volition, proposition or context in the networking effort. Inclusion takes energy, time and/or money; thus such a decision can only be justified if the element in question is perceived as relevant to the inquiry. As a consequence such decisions are appreciative – taken in the context of the current relationships between stakeholders in a particular innovation process.

In summary, social actors construct a dynamic social context for joint learning, probing and resource pooling. Such networking may be studied as one of many social practices, one that is particularly relevant to innovation. However, it concerns a 'meta-practice' or 'joint performance' (Gremmen, 1993: 148), an activity in-and-between other social practices. Therefore, particular attention to *networking as emergent social practice* seems more than justified. Such attention should focus on the way relevant actors inter-actively weigh and adjust their volitions, propositions and/or assessment of contextual factors to achieve particular transformations. Moreover, it should look at the nature of innovation strategies: are they aimed primarily at increasing the richness of probing for relevant volitions, propositions and/or conditions or, alternatively, at achieving convergence with regard to one or a limited number of well-probed solution strategies to tackle well-probed problems? Most innovation strategies are apt to include elements of both.

Emergent forms of social organization

For research question Q1, our studies suggest that the way social actors organize themselves to take part in and possibly direct 'innovation interplay' can be characterized by studying the structural forms that emerge as a result of sustained networking for innovation and the relationships among these forms. Such forms represent, in Long's (1989: 228) words, macro-structures which come into existence largely as the result of unintended consequences of social action. As emergent *forms* of organization they are not fully describable or explicable in terms of micro-events; instead they demonstrate dynamics of their own. 'Macro-structures are in part the result of the unintended consequences of numerous social acts and interactions which, as Giddens (...) explains, become the enabling and constraining conditions of social action itself' (Long, 1989: 229). Likewise, the structural forms that emerge as a result of networking for innovation can become enabling or constraining conditions that may greatly influence the quality of innovation-oriented social practice. Our research suggests a number of structural forms that merit particular attention. Each opens a related yet different perspective on social interaction for innovation:

Convergences emerge when social actors narrow down the scope of their arguments, along with the range of issues and alternative scenarios they consider relevant to innovation in their practices. Consensus must be seen as the exception. Lindblom (1990: 39–41) argues strongly that people do not usually seek consistency in their volitions – some coherence perhaps, in the form of a web '...stretched across the ground of experience, serving as one of the structures that unifies it' (Lindblom, 1990: 40, referring to Shapiro, 1981, and Scriven, 1967). Convergences, therefore, cannot be taken to refer to mutually exclusive clusters of ideas, views or propositions. With every new experience, every new exposure, new discords creep in. Convergences may be most recognisable in the issues social actors address when they outline the desired direction innovation is to take.

Resource coalitions emerge when social actors decide to pool their resources in a joint performance. They are the result of strategizing by social actors who use their assets to enrol others in their 'projects'. Leadership patterns and/or constraints to probing and coordination may become evident as a result. Studying such coalitions will require an analysis of the instruments of power and influence used by social actors in complex innovation theatres, including analysis of their use in forging alliances and imposing or negotiating the participation of relevant actors in proposed innovation strategies.

Communication networks emerge as a direct consequence of social actors' decisions to create joint learning opportunities and to produce and exchange information among themselves. Particular communication practices are adopted to exchange experiences, ideas, knowledge and information. A diverse range of communication media may be used, ranging from interpersonal to mass media, from formal channels to informal ones. Agricultural communication networks are quite complex (Chapter 2) as a result of the autonomy of each of the social actors and the diversity of means and media. In my eyes, this justifies treating them as emergent forms of organization rather than designed forms, even if each of the individual components (such as a farm journal or an advisory service) is based on a design.

However, not all of the forms of organization that emerge as the result of networking for innovation can be taken as equally spontaneous. Actors in theatres of agricultural innovation have long recognized the need to organize themselves, to develop a capacity to reflect, decide and act collectively on behalf of agricultural innovation. As a result, in most countries different types of organizations have been set up: advisory and extension agencies, research institutions, policymaking bureaus, research and development units, auctions, agricultural information bureaus, liaison units, farmer organizations and the like. Many of these organizations have been specifically designed to facilitate innovation in agriculture. Moreover, policies, resource allocations and networking practices have been designed and implemented to induce a specific form of social organization for agricultural innovation.

Such organizing may over time lead to a fourth type of emergent form, an integration of the other three: an *innovation configuration* may evolve, a pattern of more or less durable relationships among a number of social actors who perceive each other as relevant to some or all of their concerns. In Chapters 3, 4 and 5 a number of examples have been presented. These innovation configurations harbour the accepted views, procedures and ground rules for collective behaviour with respect to one or more particular types of innovation. In such configurations, convergences, resource coalitions and communication networks come to coincide to such an extent that strategic consensus, a clear definition of tasks and responsibilities and a rational allocation of resources become possible. While in most cases it seems hard to think of 'orchestrating' innovation processes, a well-established configuration provides an organizational context within which it is not unreasonable to think of coordination of efforts related to innovation. Still, such emergent alliances are continuously in flux. They may take unexpected or even largely unintended turns, yet at their roots lies a common concern shared among a number of relevant social actors. Only if social actors remain willing and able to negotiate mutual adjustments and put them into effect can their configuration eventually become and remain well organized and stable. Adequate institutional leadership, an agreed division of tasks and effective coordinating mechanisms contribute to achieving this.

Typically, even if stability is achieved a great deal of epiphenomenal problemsolving as well as 'divergent' institutional behaviour will remain. In fact, as was argued in Chapter 2, divergent behaviour by social actors who are part of an innovation configuration may be one of the elements that explain success in achieving widespread innovation. Also, not all actors within a configuration may want to explicitly express their convergences. For example, to maintain its own identity as a successful development project, the Colombo-Dutch ICA-CCH Project had to navigate carefully to avoid being seen as 'fully absorbed' into the DRI Programme. The value added to the DRI programme by participating together in it had to be clear in the eyes of the other parties involved, including DRI, to continue receiving external resources.

Different types of innovation configurations

In our studies we have looked particularly at *configurations involving institutions*, alliances for innovation that emerge among government or semi-government institutions, industrial companies and/or farmers' organizations. It has become apparent that many different types of innovation configuration may emerge: they vary according to the way the configuration was originally formed, the type and mix of participants, the way a balance is achieved among driving forces and so forth. Each presents particular enabling and/or constraining conditions for the occurrence of innovations in social practice. Some appear more adequate than others to meet the demands of innovation for development. An analysis of configurations, including the effects of leadership and coordination, will therefore need to be included in any study of innovation performance.

The patterns that evolve as a result of networking by farmers, professionals, non-governmental or other organizations seem to represent a different type of configuration. As in other configurations, convergences, resource coalitions and communication networks may coincide enough to provide these networks with purpose and organizational strength. The difference from institutional configurations, however, seems to lie in the intentionality behind the network and the way it is created. Our study suggested that networks among agricultural NGDOs are created *intentionally*, to provide space for joint learning and reflection. Mutual interdependence is a given, recognized by all involved. Moreover, not only technical solutions but also intervention objectives are subjected to debate. Active participation of all member organizations is not just a formal requirement, it is a working standard. The formative process is taken as an opportunity to build a strong foundation for future cooperation, not just an opportunity to renegotiate the institutional balance of power. In addition, networks not only recognize mutual interdependence, they nurture it by means of programmes for mutual support and services and, sometimes, by joint participation in the public debate. Probably the largest difference between the institutional configurations and the NGDO networks we studied lies in the focused, conscientious and transparent way in which the members of the latter laid the foundation for collective agency.

Preliminary evidence suggests that networks may prove to be the more flexible forms of innovation configuration needed for development. Networks capable of dealing with continuous struggles over membership, means/ends combinations, rules, tasks and responsibilities; and capable of seeing a joint mission and performance as opportunities to strengthen reflection and learning rather than as a threat to their existence might become the social 'flex-forms' for innovation needed so badly by agriculture today. However, this can only be true for networks that succeed in maintaining themselves as 'learning systems', dedicated to high quality networking for innovation. For government institutions to be able to actively participate in such networks, a number of requirements would have to be fulfilled. First, networking requires a number of social actors who are not only 'like-minded' but also have a fair degree of autonomy to adjust their views and strategies when the need arises. Hierarchical power structures such as those in most government bureaucracies seem to be at odds with networking for innovation. To facilitate effective networking among government and other agencies, central authorities would have to 'draw back' from control over day-to-day operations. Whether government authorities would ever be willing to cede the time and space decentralized government institutions need to effectively 'test the waters of cooperation' is another question. Moreover, 'planned activism' as a first fundamental step in networking seems incompatible with current efficiency-oriented bureaucratic discourse.

Towards design: constructing adequate configurations

From this first comparison of NGDO networks and institutional configurations, their origins and characteristics, we may draw another tentative conclusion. Both institutional configurations and networks are the result of accommodations among social actors who recognize a common concern. Both lead to what one may call collective agency, a capability on the part of the social actors involved to appreciate problems, reflect, decide and act together. However, due to their flexibility and focus on learning, networks, more than institutional configurations, would seem to provide a good starting point for collaboration in tackling complex social and ecological issues. Social actors may, through negotiation and mutual adjustment, create their own 'platforms', or soft systems. In practice, these may become quite complex: in many situations new soft systems (established to manage perhaps natural resources or waste disposal or natural parks, for example) will have to be composed of both government and private organizations, each tied into their own existing configurations and/or networks. The construction of soft platforms, therefore, will generally entail either the merging of existing configurations into a larger whole, or the deconstruction of existing configurations to build a new one that is more adequate to the purpose. In either case, to do this, one pre-condition would seem to be insight into existing forms of social organization oriented to innovation, to make it possible to design useful interventions to improve and/or try to rebuild these forms.

The *appreciative* nature of both networking and hence the social organization of innovation is underlined by the use of words such as *relevant*, *improved* and *new*. These imply the use of a standard, a yardstick to measure efforts and results. 'Relevant' can mean that some people see the social actors involved as relevant, whereas others do not. Or it may mean that certain volitions, propositions or contexts are considered more 'relevant' than others. Developing 'improved' practices implies a competent performance that, measured by some standard, is better than a previous one. And 'new' means that this particular element of competent performance was not yet known to the actors involved. In theory, however, it might have been known to everyone else, that is, to all except the ones they considered 'relevant'. As a result, diverging views, partisan positions and conflicts over strategies are important, and 'relevant diversity' is a central issue in the study of agricultural innovation. Consensus and harmony, however necessary they may be at a given point, are probably the exception rather than the rule. And, to paraphrase Lindblom (1990), when they do exist they could be the strongest hindrance of all to innovation performance. Nothing could be worse than a contented network of social actors who agree on everything, including the lack of relevance of all non-members! The challenge to networking for innovation, therefore, is to continue to seek exposure to different views, different options, different horizons. In other words, networking for innovation should imply an ongoing search for a Utopia.

An example of the far-reaching consequences of collective design decisions can be found in the newly formed Dutch IKCs, bureaus that provide a liaison between agricultural research institutes and extension services in the Netherlands. By design, they have been cut off from visiting farms and farmers – because, in the dominant linear view, their task is only to provide a link in the chain from research to extension. And extension has contacts with the farmers, so why should the bureaus have these as well? Complaints about the functioning of the IKCs, not surprisingly, vary from lack of practical applicability of IKC recommendations to lack of feedback on farmers' problems from the extension services to IKCs (see the example 'You don't believe that ...'). In this case, 'linear model thinking' has caused a complete disruption of the interfaces that existed between the specialists now working at the IKCs and the farmers. Some are inclined to maintain informal ties, but they are sometimes heavily criticized for this (personal communication, 1992).

> 'You don't believe that yourself, do you?' Attending a meeting of Dutch greenhouse farmers in the famous Westland Glasshouse District, I once listened to a deputy research director explaining how it is the researcher's job to produce agricultural knowledge, which is to be transferred to the farmer by extension, so that the latter may apply it on his or her farm. At some point during his speech, one of the farmers stood up and asked 'you don't believe that yourself, do you?' He continued, explaining that it could not be true that only researchers produce knowledge. He calculated that at the research station, including extension staff there are some 200 – very! – intelligent people actively involved in generating agricultural knowledge. On the other hand, at some 6,000 farms in his region, he said, some 25,000 intelligent people are engaged in experimenting, adapting and developing knowledge as well, so they can run their farms and improve their output. What he expressed was a firm reproof to the official who, in spite of the intensive networking with respect to horticulture that takes place in the Netherlands (Grooters, 1990), still dared to present the linear model as the motor for innovation in their sector. (*Source*: Engel, 1990b)

It follows that research on the social organization of innovation in agriculture should also probe the mental models social actors adhere to in designing their interactive relationships. Competent performance in agriculture is contingent upon advances in 'knowing', both practical and scientific, about the social organization of innovation. If the mental models that organize practices related to innovation are not challenged and modified regularly, they may become mental 'prisons', reducing innovation performance. The networking approach proposed in this chapter is no exception to this rule. Without ongoing empirical research and reflective practice to allow for the redesign and adaptation of our mental models, the adverse consequences of adhering to an outdated model for too long may seriously hamper innovation. Consequently, studying the social organization of innovation is of more than just scientific relevance. It contributes directly to agricultural performance by facilitating the implementation of increasingly well-probed organizational designs that enhance innovativeness. From this point of view, its present level of funding in many countries is not encouraging.

Off the 'exploratory path': back to design and intervention

This chapter has shown that a networking approach can provide some initial ingredients for the development of an action-oriented theory of social organization for innovation. Networking can in fact be seen as the principal ingredient in innovation-oriented social practice. It can be argued that there is a direct relationship between collective performance with respect to innovation and the quality of networking among relevant social actors. Research questions (Q1 and Q2) on the nature of innovation-oriented practice and the forms of social organization that emerge as a result, have been answered. To improve social practices aimed at innovation in agriculture, action as well as research should include inquiries into networking by relevant social actors, as well as into the convergences, resource coalitions and communication networks that emerge as a result. The analysis of innovation configurations has been proposed as a means of bringing the more enduring structural relationships among social actors into focus. It provides a basis for debating the adequacy of leadership and coordination mechanisms found in complex innovation theatres. Finally, we have seen that competent performance in modern agriculture, among other things, is contingent upon advances in practical and scientific 'knowing' with respect to the social organization of innovation. The institutionalization of *inadequate* organizational models may seriously hamper agricultural innovation.

Although still in a nascent state, the potential of a networking approach to refresh our thinking on innovation and strengthen the knowledge systems perspective has been demonstrated. Also, we have laid a foundation for developing a more empirically grounded way of designing intervention that can be useful in improving innovativeness within complex agricultural innovation theatres. We thus leave the 'exploratory path', and return to design and intervention.

7. Facilitating innovation: RAAKS, a practical approach

The proposed conceptualization of the social organization of innovation in complex innovation theatres presented in Chapter 6 provides answers to the first two research questions posed in the Introduction. The approach offered provides a way to understand the social organization of innovation that takes human knowing in its individual, social and practical dimensions into account. Also, it can help practitioners and researchers move towards a more comprehensive understanding of relevant issues in practical situations. Hence, my 'exploratory path' (see Chapter 1) within this book ends here. My conclusion is that the study of the social organization of innovation in complex agricultural innovation theatres should focus on networking among social actors with relevant practices, along with the convergences, resource coalitions, communication networks and multi-actor configurations that emerge as a consequence. I now turn to the design of a structured approach that can help to improve performance in agricultural innovation.

The following paragraphs first address what I mean by improving performance in agricultural innovation theatres. Can a social, diffuse process such as agricultural innovation be influenced at all? If we shed all ambition to achieve a more traditional and controlled 'management' of agricultural innovation, as we have already done, do ways to facilitate performance remain? My answer is yes, but... only in certain situations. First we look at which situations these are and what strategies are conceivable. Next, from my research and professional experience I draw criteria for an approach aimed at facilitating the improvement of innovation performance. A brief description of the design process that has led to a practical approach follows. The RAAKS methodology and its fit to the requirements formulated earlier are then introduced, and the analytical perspectives or 'windows' used in RAAKS are briefly described. Finally, I formulate some preliminary conclusions and draw attention to a number of critical issues with respect to the RAAKS design. In Chapter 8, a number of practical applications of RAAKS will be reviewed, along with its applicability in practice.

Improving performance in agricultural innovation?

With the results of the exploratory path in mind, I suggest that improving innovation performance can be seen as equal to improving networking as a social practice. Competent performance in agricultural innovation is contingent upon both the *quality* of networking among relevant social actors and the choice of *actors and practices* among whom networking will occur. Quality refers to the way relevant actors relate to each other as they prepare, share, weigh and take decisions about volitions, propositions and contextual issues. It can be analysed as a social learning process in which sense-making, coalition building and communication play a predominant role (see 'Towards an action-oriented theory...' in Chapter 6). The second point is more complicated. Particularly in view of the challenges faced by agriculture today, choosing with whom one will network is crucially important. Networking means investing in a relationship, intensive sharing of ideas, experiences, communication and, generally, mutual adjustments among social actors with respect to ideas, strategies and practices. Therefore, this choice determines to a large degree the course innovation will take. A farmer could spend a great deal of his or her time and energy either in networking with colleagues and commercial advisers or in building relationships with government officials: clearly this choice makes an enormous difference, even if there is no general rule to suggest which of these two networking strategies will be most effective.

Nothing resembling a blueprint for 'competent performance in agricultural innovation' is available or will become available anytime soon. The appreciative nature of networking for innovation implies performance can only be judged against the standards constructed by the social actors who share a particular volition within an innovation theatre. Whether they network competently is an unanswerable question, unless one specifies a standard against which their collective conduct will be compared. Food security, increased farm income, sustainable development and/or energy efficiency could for example be general objectives for agricultural innovation. Networks with such a volition may express it as a mission to be accomplished. When this defines objectives, target groups and technological options, it becomes possible to derive measures of impact and effectiveness of innovation; further, this helps in determining the relevance of particular social actors or social practices to the accomplishment of innovation objectives. When local food security is the prime interest of the social actors involved, export firms will not be viewed as relevant. If however competing in the world market is their aim, the view changes. Similarly, tourism operators are generally seen as completely irrelevant to innovation in farm practices. However, if it appears that small farmers could increase their income by attracting 'agro-tourists,' the situation may change dramatically. Thus to assess the degree of competence present, innovation performance must be judged in the light of a particular volition (or set of volitions) relevant to at least some of the social actors in a specific theatre.

I conclude that assessing innovation performance requires studying both volitions and networking. They are intrinsically related: networking acquires meaning in connection with a particular volition or volitions related to innovation; volitions are meaningless unless put into practice by networking. This makes the assessment of innovation performance a fundamentally subjective exercise, since it is not possible to formulate irrefutable standards. At most, the volitions of several relevant actors can be identified and used in evaluating performance. In exceptional situations, there may be a broad consensus for a period of time as to one general mission that is expected to be accomplished with respect to innovation. This might seem desirable from the standpoint of assessment. However, as we have seen earlier, a strong convergence may be either an advantage or an impairment to innovation performance, depending upon one's point of view in a particular situation. Hence for achieving agricultural innovation it is unwise to declare consensus the desirable degree of convergence among social actors. Instead it seems advisable to encourage 'relevant diversity' – to include various volitions representing the points of view and arguments of different social actors and sets of social actors – with respect to the desired direction of change in agriculture. I propose that using this as a criterion to guide our choice of actors as well our choice of relevant practices.

Even if we agree that networking quality and relevant diversity in innovation volitions, social actors and practices are standards against which performance can be measured, we are still stuck with the question of whether it makes sense to try to intervene directly in a diffuse, social process like agricultural innovation. Generally speaking, my answer would be no. Innovation originates from interplay between social actors who perceive themselves as stakeholders in, or at least affected by, developments in the agricultural sector. If they see a need for it, they can be trusted to seek out relevant partners to share ideas, information and experiences, to probe volitions, propositions and contexts and to pool resources for the sake of implementing particular projects. Generally, they do not need anyone to help them along. In such situations, one may say the social organization of innovation is quite satisfactory.

Sometimes, however, relevant social actors perceive the current organization of innovation as problematical, and are willing to take action to improve it. This may be the case, for example, when governments decide to privatize agricultural extension and/or research, or when national governments or donors decide to withdraw support from food crop production. In modern agriculture, a constant striving for food sufficiency or self sufficiency, along with production efficiency, has guided technological developments for decades. At this moment, with more and more competing claims on agriculture, dissatisfaction with the ways innovation is organized has increased considerably. In accordance with Kuhn's 1962 paradigm for scientific practice, I propose that such situations are the result of inertia in social practices and structural forms relevant to agricultural innovation. Established networking practices and structural forms make it difficult for social actors to adjust to new circumstances: they may prevent spotting new opportunities and developing new vistas and technical options. A desire to bring such impairments out into the open, with the general aim of modifying current networking practices and structural forms to fit new demands and circumstances, seems a solid reason for concerted action on the part of relevant stakeholders.

Two strategies are then conceivable to improve innovation performance. The first aims directly at improved networking among social actors. It is based on an evaluation of networking for innovation and seeks to formulate recommendations for improving effectiveness. We might label this a network *improvement* strategy. The second is aimed at transforming relevant existing structural forms, increasing their adequacy to meet new challenges perceived by relevant stakeholders. This change in existing innovation relationships is more demanding: a network *re-configuration* strategy. In both strategies, the quality of networking, the relevant diversity of volitions, the choice of social actors and the choice of relevant practices need to become subjects of debate. Moreover, in both the underlying factors are an unease regarding current performance, combined with a willingness on the part of important stakeholders to do something about it. The difference between the two is found in the stakeholders' initial appreciation of the situation: whether they see the difficulties as caused by ineffective but improvable networking practices or, on the contrary, as the result of inertia within existing structural forms.

Structured inquiry into the social organization of innovation

What methodological criteria would have to be met by a structured approach aimed at increasing the transparency of the social organization of innovation, while laying a foundation for designing strategies to improve it? In this paragraph I will examine my research as well as my professional experiences for clues to the definition of appropriate methodologies: methodologies that at least make a start toward inquiring into the social organization of innovation in practical situations, with the purpose of developing recommendations for improvement. Fortunately, I do not have to start from scratch. In Chapter 1 the knowledge systems perspective was chosen as a conceptual tool, and soft systems methodology as an approach to action-oriented inquiry. Here I return to this choice, making some amendments to these two perspectives with a view to their use for inquiries into the social organization of innovation. Then conclusions will be reviewed and additional issues extracted. Finally, I will sum up the type of approach that seems to be needed to fulfil the requirements.

- The results of the 'exploratory path' in Chapters 2 to 6 lead me to conclude that the knowledge systems perspective has been a fruitful heuristic device for a focus on the social organization of innovation. However, as we have seen, this perspective does not offer a consistent theory that explains all that can be observed. It was necessary to include other theoretical contributions such as work on cooperation and networking for innovation (Moss Kanter, 1983, 1989; Wissema and Euser, 1988; Box, 1990), social actor orientation (Long, 1989; Long and Long, 1992), the structure of organizations (Mintzberg, 1983), social problem solving (Lindblom, 1990) and a philosophical approach to the practical use of knowledge (Gremmen, 1994). This leads me to suggest a first requirement. *A knowledge systems perspective can be a useful part of studying the social organization of innovation in practical situations; however, additional theoretical perspectives must be included if the approach is to provide guidelines that help in explanation.*

- The appreciative and social nature of innovation, as well as the emergent forms of organization involved, provide strong arguments in favour of looking at 'systems' as social constructs with arbitrary boundaries. Röling (1994) makes a similar point with respect to facilitating the emergence of forms of collective agency to tackle complex social and ecological issues such as natural resource management. My explorations have convincingly demonstrated that studying the social organization of innovation from a hard systems perspective leads to a dead end. The ways innovation processes are organized is intrinsically interwoven with the ways social actors make sense of the world, transform their intentions into actions and relate to each other socially. From this point of view there simply cannot be one 'most effective way' to organize innovation. What we are left with is the possibility of initiating meaningful, purposive discourse on these complex phenomena. Thus: *a methodology for studying the social organization of innovation should offer the possibility of engaging in such discourse.*

- A soft systems approach offers a solid starting point for discourse on the social organiz-ation of innovation. Its aim – to improve human performance through debate and reflection – coincides with what seems desirable and possible with respect to innova-tion. Its methodological design is that of a systemic learning process, which facilitates participatory, situation-specific inquiry. The use of different techniques to create images (including non-systemic ones) and 'windows' for inquiry makes it possible to include a variety of theoretical perspectives. This is not to say the soft systems methodology would not need further development: in fact, more explicit references to randomness and choice, as well as relevant diversity of views, actors and practices are needed, and there will have to be explicit attention to social interaction for innovation, as well as the acompanying issues of power and influence. In creating images of the system – which can serve as a sort of hypothesis regarding its functioning – this makes it necessary to put emphasis on the use of actor arrangements instead of activity or input/output arrangements. In short, *a methodology to be used in studying the social organization of innovation will need to be based on 'appreciative systems thinking'*, that is, a form of soft systems thinking particularly suited to the analysis of complex processes of social interaction and construction.

- The complexity of the situation is compounded by the fact that, rather than being directed at intra-organizational behaviour, as in most soft systems research, our methodology must serve to evaluate inter-organizational behaviour. And, when we begin to deal with behaviour between organizations, we will meet differences in opinions and world views

– which in turn lead to differences in missions, cultures and power structures, and may make the organizations largely incompatible. If the methodology is to release the potential inherent in the social organization of innovation, it will need to provide for high quality communicative interaction, encouraging *participation of relevant actors in meaningful discourse*. Moreover, the eventual implementation of configuration adjustment strategies will require at least partial consensus among core actors. *The search for and negotiation of new or improved alliances for innovation will have to be an integral part of the approach.*

- Returning to the argument in the previous section, the methodology sought should contribute directly to the study of networking practices, as well as emergent structural forms of organization for innovation. Relevant diversity in volitions, actors and practices would be used as a standard for competent performance in innovation; the approach would be useful only where a significant number of important social actors in a particular innovation theatre are uneasy with the way their innovation processes are organized. This might be due to a critical experience, a shift in intentions on their part or, alternatively, a wish to anticipate changing circumstances. Due to the appreciative character of the social organization of innovation, any definition of the problem situation given by those considering intervention would not necessarily be the only viable one, let alone the one leading to viable solutions or strategies. *The approach will have to combine the study of the social organization of innovation with a thorough analysis of the problem situation propounded by those initiating the study: the problem is part of the problem.*

- As a direct consequence of our emphasis on the active involvement of stakeholders, *application of the methodology would have to generate immediate, tangible results*. This is the only way to maintain the momentum for restructuring the social learning process related to innovation and to justify the energy each of the social actors invests in the exercise. 'Results' might be individual or joint actions, cooperation or communication strategies, shared reflections or commitments in terms of future actions, or simply a debate perceived as useful by most actors. The more specific the outcome and the more active the involvement of relevant stakeholders, the more reason to believe that the intervention will indeed result in a modification of the social organization of innovation.

In summary, the approach we are seeking will have to be an appreciative soft systems methodology, not unlike the participatory action research methodologies presented by Whyte (1991). The big difference between this and more traditional SSM and PAR approaches is that it will have to be suited to dealing with problematical situations in which no joint management structure is typically available. In the situations we operate in and study, the degree of inter-organizational structure is more likely to be at the level of sets of social actors who perceive some degree of interdependence. In this setting, intervention creates a need to make volitions and social relationships among actors explicit, and to allow for debate at each step along the way, without pretending that it is always possible to achieve a strategic consensus. I took this need as a starting point in designing an approach to diagnosing and improving innovation performance: RAAKS, the rapid appraisal of agricultural knowledge systems.

The RAAKS design process: toward innovation through networking

In summary, the design objectives that have guided the development of RAAKS from its beginnings are:
- the methodology must help social actors to probe their doubts with respect to current innovation performance, and to define their own problem situation in one or more meaningful ways;
- it must help social actors articulate the way they presently organize themselves for innovation, so that the social organization of innovation can be meaningfully debated; and
- it must help social actors define actions they consider useful – capable of enhancing the process of innovation with regard to a common concern. Such actions might be forms of cooperation and/or communication; they will be directed at probing volitions, propositions and contexts, to generate new or at least alternative solutions to well-probed problems.

The design process for RAAKS has been an exciting, yet at times 'long and dusty' road, to be painted here with rough strokes. I trace it back to experience in southern Colombia: to make our extension efforts more effective, we set out to design, test and implement a participatory diagnosis technique for understanding farmers' views, knowledge and indigenous solutions to problems of agricultural production (Engel, 1991). Following in Paulo Freire's footsteps, participatory social science research was very strong in Latin America at the time (e.g. de Schutter, 1983).

Back in the Netherlands, I became increasingly fascinated with the social organization of innovation as a whole. With Niels Röling and Bertus Haverkort, we took it upon ourselves to further develop the knowledge systems perspective. The International Course for Rural Extension at the International Agricultural Centre in Wageningen provided a context, as did the programme for international development in extension of the Ministry of Agriculture, Nature and Fisheries. In 1986, my first rather naive attempt aimed at making an inventory of interactive relationships among institutions concerned with agricultural development. This provoked heated debate on crucial issues related to the social organization of innovation. However, it failed to support more systematic analysis, often leaving participants more intrigued than satisfied. The ISNAR RTTL Study then provided us with an opportunity to study linkages between research and extension in more detail. A first attempt to conceptualize how research and extension organize themselves for technology development was one result (Kaimowitz et al., 1990). My participation in the design and implementation of a field methodology for this comparative study (Engel et al., 1989) opened my eyes to the complexities and appreciative character of the social organization of innovation.

In 1989, together with Stephan Seegers, a first more formal attempt was made to create a methodology. It was formulated for use by senior extension specialists from the Ministry of Agriculture, Nature and Fisheries of the Netherlands, who needed a method to support strategic planning of interventions in developing countries. This practical approach to knowledge systems analysis benefitted from the Department of Communication and Innovation Studies' Knowledge Systems Research Programme and ISNAR's Research/ Transfer Linkages Study in which both of us participated actively. It stipulated a chronology of activities, fields of analysis (which suggested particular issues and questions to guide the inquiry) and tools to support the analysis surrounding particular issues within a field of analysis. In addition, to promote theoretical consistency the design defined a number of 'core concepts'. To stimulate reflection and debate it also offered a number of 'hypothetical statements'. These were basically statements that reflected the 'state of the art' conclusions from scientific inquiry into the social organization of innovation.

We intended these hypotheses to serve as a stimulus to meaningful debate on the situation under study, which – if confirmed by the team during the appraisal – would serve as a basis for formulating conclusions and recommendations. To our surprise, they provoked Peter van Beek, friend and colleague from Australia and otherwise a very enthusiastic participant and supporter, to label us 'typical Dutchmen who think they can prescribe what's best for everybody'. At the time this puzzled us; we still believed these statements offered what we thought of as an objective account of what had proved success-ful in agricultural innovation. Our experiences in training extension consultants and managers, however, have confirmed Peter's view. Even if our intentions were the opposite, being exposed to such 'nuggets of scientific wisdom' led participants in our courses to forget to use their own knowledge, so they became 'technology users' instead of know-ledge creators. Or they rebelled so strongly against our 'normative stance' that they dumped the methodology altogether. We owe our discovery of 'soft systems thinking' (Checkland, 1989) and its integration, to these experiences.

A third version of the manual (1990) marked this turning point. What had come to be known as *RAAKS: Rapid Appraisal of Agricultural Knowledge Systems* was prepared with Ab de Groot and Stephan Seegers. The chronology, fields of analysis and tool box survived, but the hypothetical statements were abandoned. Instead, we added an introduction to knowledge systems theory and knowledge management as a starting point for analysis and the design of useful interventions. With the help of this manual we gained our first practical experience in the field, using it to study the Dutch horse husbandry sector in 1990 and in 1992 for a diagnosis of research and extension support to small grain producers in six countries in Central America (see Chapter 8). An expert consultation at the Department of Communication and Innovation Studies in April 1991 brought out a number of critical issues. The most far-reaching was the apparent contradiction between RAAKS' effectiveness in bringing out relevant issues and its weakness in supporting a search for explanations. In fact, we lacked even a clear definition of what, exactly, we were studying with the help of RAAKS: our object of inquiry. This stimulated me to include a more 'ontological' search into my studies; the results have been presented in Chapter 6.

By early 1992 we felt confident enough to expose RAAKS to the critical scrutiny of graduate students, leading to the first practical graduate course. Course materials included Version 3 of the manual and case studies by graduate students. Experienced professionals were actively involved as resource persons. Version 4 of RAAKS was prepared later the same year. With Monique Salomon, an anthropologist from Nijmegen University, the approach and manual were redesigned in accordance with lessons from field experiences, the expert consultation and the evaluation of the first course on RAAKS. Team building, the quality of information gathering and communication were emphasized. The chrono-logy, fields of analysis and tool box, which proved the *pièces de resistance*, were adjusted and set in a more playful mode. Fields of analysis became 'windows' on the world: this underlines their partiality and role as 'search lights to bring particular relevant issues into focus' rather than comprehensive theoretical perspectives that help explain everything. Like Chambers (1992) we began to think of the 'R' as representing either 'Rapid or Relaxed'. We found that either (relatively) rapid or more in-depth studies could usefully apply the RAAKS chronology, windows and tools. Also, the lengthy introduction on knowledge system theory was cut down to a minimum. This was mostly because, despite all our efforts, for researchers the theory included in the manual still seemed to function as a straightjacket. Its consistency helped create a focus, yet obstructed creative thinking and the use of personal experiences and insights. To compensate for a decrease in consistency, we improved each window to provide more accurate reflection of a particular analytical perspective.

The result was a more flexible application and a greater effort to redesign analytical tools, leading to a method that provides an experience oriented more to learning than to research. The fourth version of the RAAKS manual reflected our increased confidence in the possibility of applying the knowledge systems perspective without an extensive introduction to theory, instead relying on interactive group learning, choice and examination from various analytical perspectives to produce valuable results. To effectively create such 'interplay' in practice, it was necessary to pay a lot of attention to facilitating communication among participants, and between participants and stakeholders, during RAAKS. We now understood that the quality of interactive learning was directly linked to the quality of the outcome of a RAAKS exercise as a whole and, what is more, we had learned to guide this process more adequately. And we understood in a very practical way that for this type of research, conceptual consensus may be among the most powerful impairments to innovative thinking. Lindblom's (1990) reflections on the constraining influence of knowledge, of well-probed and agreed beliefs, proved extremely relevant to facilitating innovative thinking on innovation performance as well.

From the moment we began to integrate RAAKS in university education, students, including international students, became a major driving force. Their enthusiasm in trying it out in different countries and cultures, under a variety of circumstances and for different purposes, initiated a cascade of relevant experiences that we could scarcely manage or even monitor adequately. Applications of RAAKS outside agriculture have contributed greatly to exposing design flaws. This has been particularly true for our encounters with 'hard' technical engineering practice during studies of the social organization of innovation with respect to introducing photo-voltaic energy, and problem solving in the transportation sector in the Netherlands (Engel and den Bakker, 1992; den Bakker et al., 1993). Continued encouragement and suggestions from many colleagues both in the Netherlands and abroad have helped enormously. In retrospect RAAKS itself might have provided one of the best case studies possible to demonstrate what networking means for innovation in our practices.

Below I will present the design of RAAKS as it now stands, based on a paper presented to the AFSR/E Conference at Montpellier, November 1994 (now available in Engel and Salomon, 1996). If the enthusiasm we have encountered among so many colleagues all over the world is any indication, this networking and development will surely continue.

RAAKS: an approach to facilitating the improvement of innovation performance in agriculture

RAAKS has been designed as a participatory action research methodology, to bring out social learning issues relevant to innovation and to design strategies for improving it in practical situations.[1]RAAKS is built around particular *intentions* and based upon recognizable underlying principles; and includes a *procedural design* and an *analytical design*. In principle, its intentions plus its procedural and analytical designs characterize RAAKS: it is a soft systems methodology. The intentions behind RAAKS (outlined below)

---

1. *The RAAKS methodology is presented in detail in the manual Networking for innovation: a participatory actor-oriented methodology (Salomon and Engel, 1997).*

directly mirror the considerations expressed earlier in this chapter (see 'Improving performance in agricultural innovation' above). Interventions in complex innovation theatres make sense only if a significant number of relevant social actors feel uneasy with current networking practices and relevant structural forms, and are willing to reflect upon these to formulate what might be done about it. RAAKS' procedural design provides an outline of the basic steps and issues to be addressed in a soft systems inquiry that benefits from experience with (rapid or relaxed) rural appraisal and participatory action research. RAAKS' analytical design is based on a selection of windows, to allow the study of a felt problem and the social organization of innovation surrounding it; such a study leads to suggestions of interventions that can be potentially useful in improving the situation.

Intentions, procedural design and analytical design are separated here for the sake of presentation. In practice, such a separation would fundamentally affect the methodology. This is not meant to suggest that the intentions underlying the RAAKS design could not be achieved by other means; it simply indicates that the intentionality, procedure and method of inquiry of the design are mutually dependent. To do away with one would affect the others to such an extent that a different methodology would result. For example, to do away with the participatory character of the procedural design and insert RAAKS windows into a more traditional field research design could be extremely interesting; it would not, however, provide a context for participatory action research, and thus would not affect the local theatre in the way that might be expected of RAAKS. Nevertheless, one of the under-lying principles of the approach is that local teams may adapt the intentions as well as the procedural and analytical designs to their own circumstances by choosing and combining the elements of RAAKS in various ways. I will come back to this apparent contradiction in Chapter 8 when I discuss the adaptability of RAAKS to different conditions in greater detail, based on a number of specific experiences. More details on the management of the RAAKS process, including the work of a RAAKS team, the description of each window, and exercises and tools, can be found in *Networking for innovation*.

Intentions and underlying principles

RAAKS, rather than immediately focusing attention on tangible solutions, is intended to help social actors study and suggest improvements in the way they organize themselves to achieve agricultural innovation. It emphasizes *strategic diagnosis*, an appraisal of con-straints and opportunities leading to a joint definition of useful strategies. Central elements include team work, the focused collection of information, group discussions, qualitative analysis and strategic decision making. A very important characteristic of the approach is that men and women farmers, other rural women, consumers or other target groups are considered stakeholders and sources of relevant knowledge and information. RAAKS is aimed at two types of outcomes: a more comprehensive understanding of the social organization of innovation in a particular situation; and interest on the part of social actors in implementing well-probed actions to improve it. To produce these outcomes, RAAKS combines three different yet intertwined learning processes: first, joint inquiry, including both team and stakeholders, into the social organization of innovation; second, exploring the contrasts in the findings produced by multiple analytical perspectives – helping to focus on relevant ideas and events from different angles, and creating a useful tension between relevant and equally valid, but different, interpretations of the same situation; and third, a task-oriented path to lead participants from analysis and inter-pretation of a situation that, in the eyes of at least some, is problematical, and towards the design of potentially useful solutions.

Joint inquiry into the social organization of innovation

RAAKS focuses on the performance of social actors as innovators of their own practices. Its starting point is networking: what social actors consistently do in seeking confirmation and/or adaptations of their practices is to search for, build and maintain relationships with selected other actors. Such networking efforts lead to more or less stable patterns of relationships or networks, some of which are particularly relevant to agricultural innovation. RAAKS helps social actors identify relevant networks and appreciate the role and relevance of these networks to the effectiveness of innovation in a specific situation. Because of the complexities and judgemental issues underlying complex innovation processes, RAAKS is designed as a 'soft systems' methodology (Checkland and Scholes, 1990). It recognizes the appreciative character of the models we all construct to study the world and is therefore designed to produce iterative inquiry among stakeholders. RAAKS helps to focus on relevant issues, offering instruments for gathering, organizing and interpreting information on relevant ideas and events as well as guidelines, techniques and exercises to support interactive learning. Relationship building, participation, communication and qualitative research are central to the implementation of RAAKS.

Multiple perspectives: offering a choice of useful windows

Social organization is so thoroughly appreciative, and there are typically so many strands of knowledge that might be relevant to its interpretation, that trying to formulate a single model that will represent it adequately in everyone's eyes would be counterproductive. Instead, RAAKS is designed to include a variety of 'windows'; from these, teams can choose and adapt specific ways to carry out an inquiry. Each window originates from a different analytical perspective, draws attention to particular issues and relationships, has been developed and tested in field research by others and/or ourselves, and has been chosen and designed or re-designed by us to fit an action-oriented methodology. Also, each window has been equipped with one or a number of 'tools', which provide specific suggestions on ways to gather and organize information. The purpose of offering such a 'palet' is to enable RAAKS participants to create several distinct yet equally pertinent mental images, and thus to stimulate debate and reflection with regard to relevant ideas and events *in situ*, rather than attempting to build one consistent model of the whole. This makes it possible for social actors to do a 'quick scan' from various angles. The 16 windows currently offered by RAAKS are by no means exhaustive. On the contrary, since this is a participatory action research methodology, researchers and other participating actors are encouraged to propose modified or additional windows and to design new tools of inquiry. However, our research suggests the current windows do provide a solid starting point.

Social learning: organizing for more effective innovation

RAAKS focuses on problem appreciation and diagnosis; on this basis measures can be suggested to facilitate interaction and improve the social organization of innovation. Just studying the social organization of innovation is not enough; strategies must be devised to overcome impairments and create opportunities for improvement. This lies behind the design of RAAKS as a participatory action research methodology: new knowledge about the social organization of innovation in a particular theatre is generated through *joint* learning among RAAKS team members and stakeholders in innovation. Interaction between other stakeholders and a RAAKS team has the explicit purpose of coming up with well-probed suggestions for improvement. The process as a whole has the potential to build agreement on strategies for change, commitment to these strategies, and a plan of action for their implementation.

As a consequence, the *operational objectives* for using RAAKS have been formulated as follows:
- to identify opportunities for intervention, aimed at improving the way social actors organize themselves to achieve the type of innovation they desire;
- to create awareness among relevant social actors, such as managers, policymakers, producers, traders, researchers, extension workers and representatives of other groups or target groups, with respect to the constraints and opportunities that affect their performance as innovators;
- to identify actors or potential actors who act (or could act) on and effectively remove particular impairments, or make use of the opportunities identified.

The second of these objectives is singularly important. Careful preparations must be made to guarantee close collaboration. A RAAKS team, typically four or five in number, might include social actors familiar with the situation as well as facilitators familiar with RAAKS. A preparatory workshop may be held to allow team members to get to know each other and the methodology. The relationships with other stakeholders and their participation also need to be carefully prepared and managed. RAAKS therefore offers exercises to support team building, communication and joint learning, and the planning and management of workshops.

Clearly, the third learning process and the related RAAKS objective are task oriented. The aim is to create one or more convergences among relevant social actors so that decisions can be taken about the strategy to be followed. RAAKS offers specific windows (A5 and B8) to support task-oriented debate among team and participants and help in synthesizing the problem situation and the social organization of innovation. Like some other windows, these explore *actor arrangements* to help participants connect goals/ missions to relevant stakeholders and point up dominant relationships. Generally, the accompanying debate leads to a shared definition of the situation, along with conver-gences among stakeholders or subsets of stakeholders with respect to priority problems affecting successful innovation.

This line of inquiry is necessarily more exclusive than joint inquiry or multiple perspect-ives, which are more open ended: all that seems relevant at a given point in the eyes of at least one participant is included. Arriving at a synthesis, however, makes it necessary to leave out less relevant volitions, options and conditions; decisions have to be taken, choosing the most widely supported interpretations of events and ideas and so forth. Narrowing the scope of the inquiry does not mean accepting just any consensus. While participants might simply agree not to agree, they would then need to determine whether consensus based on disagreement represents a serious impediment to competent innovation performance for some or all social actors in their theatre. If so, they might need to reconsider; otherwise all may happily go their separate ways. An example of such a situation is given in the example on 'Appreciation and debate'.

> Appreciation and debate: a foundation for inquiry into the social organization of innovation: Depending on one's point of view, the Netherlands' agricultural system today can be seen as 'a very successful export-earning whole' or 'a danger to sustaining life in these low lands'. We argue that such differing viewpoints are frequent; what is more, they may be vital to a community's capacity to achieve innovation in its practices. Rather than suppressing them, such differences need to be recognized and put to use in the debate on useful interventions and accommodations among stakeholders. Naturally, a RAAKS study initiated by actors who perceive 'decreasing competitiveness'

as a problem in the social organization of innovation will formulate completely different terms of reference for a RAAKS team than actors who feel that, under the present conditions, 'humans are an endangered species'. Yet, it seems likely that (as a RAAKS study might demonstrate) for either of the two groups to construct economically, socially and ecologically sustainable innovations, they will need each other.

To ensure the active participation of relevant social actors and a good chance of achieving convergence, at least with respect to understanding the current situation, it has proved important to consider the establishment of a *steering committee* of relevant stakeholders. The selection of members for such a committee is of course very sensitive. However, if a relatively non-partisan (or balanced multi-partisan) committee can be appointed, the study will achieve additional credibility in the eyes of other relevant social actors and may help to induce more active participation on their part.

Chronology of activities: a stepwise procedural design

After a preparatory phase including team building, getting acquainted with the methodology and building relationships with relevant stakeholders, the RAAKS study is made up of three *phases*:
- Phase A: problem definition and system identification;
- Phase B: analysis of constraints and opportunities;
- Phase C: policy articulation/intervention planning.

During each phase, specific research objectives are pursued and a set of windows is selected for gathering, organizing and interpreting information and presenting results. During Phase A, defining the problem and identifying relevant social actors, issues and environmental factors are the most important. This implies, among other things, making a choice as to who, initially, will be considered part of the 'soft system'. In Phase B, the RAAKS team and actors formulate, analyse and prioritize constraints and opportunities for improving innovation performance. This means an in-depth study of several issues relevant to assessing the effectiveness of the existing social organization of innovation. The main issue during Phase C is to articulate strategies, plan concrete actions for improvement and negotiate commitments. In each phase, teams may decide to modify windows or construct additional ones, adapting the analysis to the specific issues and the situation at hand.

The tasks to be planned and implemented in each phase can be summarized as follows:
- to debate, specify and agree upon research objectives;
- to debate, choose and further operationalize relevant windows and/or add new ones;
- to use these windows in gathering relevant information through interviews with individuals or groups, as well as from secondary sources;
- to produce field reports;
- to integrate ideas, issues and information, in group discussions; and
- to produce a synthesis report reflecting important issues, information gaps and tentative conclusions.

In addition, at the end of each phase a *workshop* is organized with relevant social actors and target groups or their representatives. The purpose of the workshops is to return the information to the stakeholders, enabling them to debate, complement and/or amend the findings of the study and to participate actively in the learning process. The field reports are produced to promote sharing and discussion of ideas and information among team members; synthesis reports are provided to share ideas with stakeholders during the workshops. The latter therefore often make use of drawings, tables and brief statements rather than lengthy descriptive reports.

Phases A, B and C cannot, of course, be strictly separated. Elements may sometimes be brought forward to an earlier phase, or an analysis from an earlier phase may be repeated in more depth in the next. Also, circumstances may oblige the team to collapse the study into fewer phases or break it up into more. Nevertheless, our experiences indicate that planning RAAKS field work in three phases is a useful starting point. A brief sketch of each phase follows. Their contents are discussed in detail in *Networking for innovation*. In Chapter 8, the results of some of the experimental applications of RAAKS will be discussed in more detail.

Phase A: problem definition and system identification:

The windows in Phase A can be used to guide a preliminary inventory of relevant social actors, an inquiry into the definition of the problem situations, a review of different actors' views on problems and desired development, and an analysis of environmental constraints. This last includes, for example, agro-climatological, socio-cultural and economic factors – those considered to be non-manipulable within the scope of a particular innovation process. The outcome of Phase A is a first approximation to the ways in which social actors currently act and interact to achieve innovation of their practices. Both salient bottlenecks and possible opportunities for improvement become visible.

Phase B: constraint and opportunity analysis

In the second phase team members go into the field to more systematically gather information on the social organization of innovation. Windows are available to use in studying impact, actor characteristics and linkages, knowledge networks, task performance and coordination and communication among actors. The team chooses the windows to be used, depending on the problem situation and the priorities expressed by social actors during Phase A. As an outcome, Phase B provides a more detailed picture of how different networks of social actors interact, the prominent issues in their debates, and the way they coordinate (or fail to coordinate) their activities.

Phase C: articulating strategy/action planning

During Phase C, alternative strategies or actions are formulated and debated. The extent to which various social actors support one or the other is considered. Three windows support the identification of strategies useful in overcoming constraints or acting on new opportunities; the relevance of each of the social actors to implementing such strategies; and the support they are willing to give to the strategies. Generally, strategies consist of proposals for improving cooperation and/or communication. However, specific organizational, training or documentation and information proposals may be included. The expected outcome of Phase C is a commitment on the part of some or all stakeholders to followup on some or all recommendations.

Following up on RAAKS

In addition to a more comprehensive understanding of the problem situation and the social organization of innovation among team members and stakeholders, RAAKS is intended to lead to increased awareness among stakeholders with respect to what each can actually *do* to enhance innovation performance. Therefore RAAKS emphasizes problem appreciation, diagnosis and eventually the articulation of strategies and strategic commitments. Preparing and implementing specific projects on the basis of such commit-

RAAKS windows

Problem definition and system identification
A1. Redefining the objective of the appraisal: whose problem is it? What is it about?
A2. Identifying relevant social actors: who is involved, or should be? How do they view the problem?
A3. Tracing diversity in mission statements: who pursues what and why? How do they see the 'problems'?
A4. Environmental diagnosis: natural, economic and socio-cultural factors are to be taken into account.
A5. A first approximation to clarifying the problem situation: who is relevant, why, how?

Constraint and opportunity analysis
B1. Impact analysis: volitions cause assessments to differ; what is the outcome in practice?
B2. Actor analysis: not all actors are equally relevant to or interested in each type of innovation!
B3. Knowledge network analysis: studying interactive communication for innovation.
B4. Integration analysis: studying linkages and resource coalitions.
B5. Task analysis: what should be done to innovate and who will do it?
B6. Coordination analysis: studying leadership and orchestration.
B7. Communication analysis: cultural barriers standing in the way of effective communication for innovation.
B8. Understanding the social organization of innovation: how does it work? or does it?

Policy articulation/intervention planning
C1. Knowledge management: what can be done to enhance innovative performance?
C2. Actor potential analysis: who can, and is willing to do what?
C3. Strategic commitments: who will do what with respect to carrying out the activities?

ments, however, is as yet not included. Such followup is entirely in the hands of the social actors who have taken part in the process. This has various advantages, since it discourages intervention by outsiders (RAAKS facilitators) in the implementation of plans, and provides freedom for social actors to modify, time and carry out the agreed strategies and/or actions in ways they find most convenient. Lack of visible results following RAAKS is a less favourable side effect, and if no management structure is established one may rightfully ask whether planned improvements will ever be implemented. However, the social organization of innovation being appreciative, largely self guided and social, one may answer that social actors will implement changes in time, if and when they continue to perceive their advantages and can muster a strong enough alliance among actors. Further, in the process of using RAAKS, actors come to know each other's strengths, interests and networks, which provides a strong base for working together. In any case, at the moment, RAAKS does not pretend to achieve more than *discursive* commitments, as Rap (1992) puts it: commitments in words rather than deeds. We are aware that this might be perceived as a weakness of the approach. In practice, however, it may be a major asset. This issue will be considered at the end of the following chapter, in reviewing the results of our field work.

Analytical design: windows for studying social organization in practical situations

RAAKS windows are analytical perspectives, derived from particular social science disciplines and/or bodies of theory. Each window offers an internally consistent way to study and try to explain innovation-related phenomena of social organization. Contrasting the findings obtained by using different windows enables a team to gain a comprehensive understanding, formulate alternative explanations, and decide which explanations seem most selevant to the situation under study.

Many RAAKS windows have been constructed on the basis of perspectives developed as a part of knowledge systems research, as presented in Chapter 1. Others have been derived directly from practical experience with action research on social organization. All have been extensively tested under field conditions. In fact, the current RAAKS windows are those that have survived eight years of sometimes turbulent development, and have proved useful under a variety of circumstances.

Box 6 provides a list of windows labelled A, B and C in accordance with their use during particular phases of RAAKS. Each window, including its design, validity, use and applicability, is discussed in detail in *Networking for innovation* which also includes specific tools that can, if a team desires, be used with each window.

In the formal argument that lies behind judgements regarding their usefulness, two criteria have been used. First, a window was said to be 'useful' when it helped a RAAKS team bring the social organization of innovation, rather than some other phenomenon, into focus as the object of inquiry. That is, an acceptable window should shed light on the emergent practices and structural forms that evolve as a result of social actors' efforts to achieve innovation in their practices. In line with Suchman (1967), I label this the *validity* criterion: it relates to whether the window does what we expect it to do. Within the context of a soft systems study of the social organization of innovation, a valid window helps to focus on *practices and structural forms relevant to social organization for innovation*.

The role of the windows merits somewhat more detailed attention. Windows help to quickly focus on particular issues, as suggested by Table 12. This table summarizes which of the issues relevant to the social organization of innovation is particularly addressed by each window: problem definition, relevant practices, networking practices, convergences, coalition building, communication networks, innovation configurations or defining action. The table also indicates that RAAKS' windows offer complementarity as well as overlap. Each issue relevant to a problem can be studied from various angles; the overlap seems to help in integrating the findings. Moreover, the richness of perspectives in RAAKS gives teams an opportunity to choose among the windows, particularly in Phase B. Thus windows make not only the analytical design but also the procedural design of RAAKS more flexible, so that a team can adapt the method, making it situation specific, suited to particular circumstances and objectives.

Second, the utility of an instrument must be assessed in the context of a particular approach to a research question. A valid instrument of inquiry may be useful for gathering quantitative data, yet useless for qualitative inquiry (or, perhaps even more frequently, *vice versa*). Other instruments may be useful in a variety of research contexts. I will refer to this as the *applicability* criterion. Generally speaking, an 'applicable' window is one that fits a particular research context well. As I am interested mostly in the research context created by the use of a participatory soft systems methodology, RAAKS, I will rephrase this criterion to read: an applicable window helps participants construct *images of the social organizational phenomena under study, to stimulate interactive learning* – and thus to improve collective performance. Whether the windows effectively enable RAAKS teams and other stakeholders to engage in active learning of this sort will be addressed in Chapter 8.

Table 12

Windows focus on practices and social forms relevant to the organization of innovation[a]

Focus / Window	Problem definition	Relevant practices	Networking practices	Convergences	Resource coalition	Communication network	Innovation configuration	Defining action
A1: redefining appraisal objective	A							
A2: identifying social actors		A						
A3: tracing mission statements				A				
A4: environmental diagnosis	A							
A5: synthesis/problem situation	S/D	S/D		S				
B1: impact analysis	A							A
B2: actor analysis		A		A				
B3: knowledge network analysis			A	A		A	A	
B4: integration analysis			A		A	A		
B5: task analysis		A						
B6: coordination analysis			A		A		A	
B7: communication analysis				A		A		
B8: synthesis/social organization	S	S	S	S	S	S	S	A
C1: knowledge management	S/D		D	D		D	D	D
C2: actor potential analysis						D	D	D
C3: strategic commitments		D						D

[a] A= analysis/appraisal; S = synthesis; D = design/choice

Even if all the windows included can be considered valid and applicable, clearly this alone is no guarantee of adequate RAAKS performance. This is due to the nature of innovation processes. For example, conflicting views sometimes obstruct progress, and yet in other cases they enhance it. Also, while consensus among participants on the nature of the problem could be a reason to suspect innovation impairment (since it may limit their explorations), other times searching for consensus may help to push ahead. Thus the windows may help in appreciating a particular situation but can never replace the individual and group skills of a RAAKS team and other stakeholders as they work to choose conceptual and practical accommodations that are feasible in each stage of their work. In short, successful application of RAAKS and each of its windows requires relationship building, communication skills, inquisitive minds and creativity on the part of participants. In this situation, no procedure can offer a *guarantee* of success.

Preliminary conclusions and some critical issues

This chapter answers two of the research questions posed in the Introduction: Q3, on the criteria an action-oriented methodology would have to meet, and, tentatively, Q4, on the possibility of designing such a methodology. A previous section ('Improving performance in agricultural innovation?') asked whether intervention in complex innovation theatres can be useful and when. I concluded that two conditions have to be met: a number of relevant social actors must feel uneasy with the way innovation is socially organized, and second, they must wish to collaborate in assessing current impairments and/or opportunities and in designing measures for improvement. Under 'Structured inquiry into the social organization of innovation' a number of criteria were listed that structured inquiry into the social organization of innovation would have to abide by to be able to contribute to achieving such aims (Q3). The design process and the choices that resulted in a preliminary answer to question Q4: my answer is yes, and the methodology I propose is RAAKS.

In principle, RAAKS follows the specifications laid down in the two sections just mentioned. It is designed as a soft systems methodology, which can enable stakeholders to engage in meaningful discourse about the social organization of innovation with respect to their common concerns. It leans heavily on appreciative systems thinking. The images it helps create emphasize social interaction between social actors from different relevant practices; these images can stimulate debate and reflection. Active participation of stakeholders is expected, as are ongoing thorough reappraisals of the definition of the problem. Moreover RAAKS, with its threefold objectives – raising awareness and understanding, probing possible new alliances and formulating action proposals – is facilitative, action-oriented and has the potential to generate tangible results. It contributes to a cumulative social learning process among stakeholders, leading from problem appraisal (Phase A) to action definition (C), and stimulates joint inquiry into relevant practices, networking and emergent structural forms of social organization for innovation (A, B). It does so by offering a variety of windows, whose integration is obtained by using a conceptual framework rooted in appreciative knowledge systems thinking. These claims will be further evaluated in Chapter 8.

As a consequence of its flexible design, RAAKS may be used in various ways. The original design corresponds to a participatory action research methodology; it envisions implementation of such an exercise by a team of specialists, some subject-matter specialists and some acquainted with RAAKS. Other stakeholders participate actively as co-researchers. However, elements of RAAKS' analytical design can also be used in the context of more traditional, qualitative field research. The windows and tools provide the researcher with a coherent set of perspectives to study the social organization of innovation. Further, by reducing the depth to which most windows are studied, RAAKS can be used to guide an 'excursion' type of inquiry or a training session concerned with the way innovation is socially organized. Finally, policymakers and managers at various levels can use RAAKS as an instrument to gain more insight into constraining or enabling conditions, or perhaps even as a means of gauging monitoring innovation performance on a regular basis.

Notwithstanding our optimism with respect to the design, however, we can already point to some concerns: first, there are a number of practical questions having to do with the social context in which RAAKS must be implemented. Active participation of relevant stakeholders implies that they must be *willing* to take part. That is, the situation must be sensed as problematical by a significant number of them and they must expect some benefit from looking into it together. In other words, they must already perceive a degree of mutual interdependence. Particularly where configurations or networks are currently less articulated, this can make RAAKS itself a rather diffuse social process, which can be hard to 'manage'. As a result, RAAKS may be more suitable in theatres where a degree of articulation among social actors has already been achieved with respect to innovation. Next, will social actors be critical enough in looking at their situation? Will they be willing to share information on issues that were formerly protected from 'outsiders' – those not belonging to their organization or group? Further, what is the time frame for RAAKS? In our inquiries, the range has been from six weeks to six months. But very interesting 'excursion' type exercises have been done in less than three weeks, and in some situations a year might be more adequate. Perhaps the most intriguing concern about RAAKS is its explicit recognition that although there are clear objectives, there is *no* predefined outcome. RAAKS is a learning process; it begins with a vaguely defined initial problem statement about a situation, which may look completely different to different actors, according to their point of view. So, by definition, the outcome – in terms of learning, insights, new allies or new alliances – cannot be determined in advance. This is fundamental to the type of inquiry required by complex innovation processes; but does it also provide motivation strong enough for the joint action necessary to implement the changes suggested by RAAKS? Finally, we can expect RAAKS to be powerful in generating new insights, understanding and proposals for designs involving new relationships, but since these last are typically based on verbal commitments alone, how strong can it be in generating tangible action?

Second, there are some methodological concerns: for example, RAAKS' plainly discursive character, as noted above. Not all social actors relevant to agricultural innovation processes are equally skilled or willing to participate in debate and reflection. To what extent this limits RAAKS' applicability in practical and cross-cultural situations remains to be seen. Another point is that every RAAKS team creates its own unique, context-specific exercise. This is favourable from the point of view of flexibility, but how will it affect the quality of research outcomes and the possibilities for making comparisons among experiences later? Next, will RAAKS be able to help teams avoid the trap much knowledge systems research has fallen into, and help to create a balanced inquiry emphasizing *both* formal and informal social interaction? A final methodological concern is the current selection of windows. The windows support building images of a soft system (or its parts), which have to do primarily with arrangements among actors. Other types of windows may need to be included. For example, RAAKS does not yet support the examination of human activity arrangements, although these could be useful in studying relevant practices, including networking practices. RAAKS does support exploration of practices relevant to identifying and characterizing relevant social actors (A2, B2 – see Table 12); when task analysis (B5) is done, more detail becomes available. However, this inquiry is not very detailed. This seemed impossible within the time frame we had in mind for the method. For the present, this is defendable and even desirable: RAAKS must not cover too much at the same time. However, exploratory field studies on research practices in farming systems research (Rap, 1992; Beyene, 1994) appear to underscore the importance of studying relevant practices in more detail. Moreover, Stolzenbach (1992) shows peasant farmers in Mali creating an experimental practice *(shifleli)* under very harsh conditions. This sort of thing would be worth studying as part of an inquiry into the social organization of innovation. These studies confirm the importance attached by Gremmen (1994) and sociologists such as Leeuwis (1993) to incorporating detailed studies of relevant practices in research traditions focused on the social organization of innovation.

We could go one step further and suggest exploring the use of input/output arrangements in the context of RAAKS as well. This has been attempted, although not very systematically; initial results were not promising. The 'source-intermediary-user' sheet for knowledge network analysis is a remnant of these trials, which has proved useful. Task analysis was originally also based on input-throughput-output reasoning. However, it had to be modified for use in RAAKS, because it stimulated linear thinking rather than a broader ranging process allowing for interplay among interpretations of the social organization of innovation. Our experiences in using such models to stimulate reflection and debate are nevertheless incomplete. Further research would be advisable, to see whether adapted input/output arrangements (using problem-solving or decision making models, for example) can be expected to make relevant contributions to the study of social organization of innovation from a soft systems perspective. The 'main menu' discussed in Chapter 2 suggests this might be the case.

Finally, still other types of windows, perhaps historical or cultural, may eventually prove interesting. Obate (1992) pictures three generations of farmers and the ways they have learned and continue to learn about agriculture. This provides useful insights into the influence of subsequent interventions on the quality of learning within agricultural practice. Millar (1992), on the other hand, looks in detail at the influence farmers' 'cosmovision' has on agricultural practice. This provides a vista on the influence cultural values and relationships exercise on the dynamics of innovation in agriculture. Finally, negotiation among social actors from different practices is detailed in recent sociological studies (Arce, 1993). If the emphasis of RAAKS were to shift from the present, primarily diagnostic approach to one that is more project oriented, windows addressing such issues might need to be incorporated.

At the end of Chapter 8, after discussing some initial experiences with RAAKS I will attempt to formulate at least tentative answers to these and other questions. For now, I am satisfied that an action-oriented methodology can indeed be designed that will contribute to the process of designing improvements in the social organization of innovation in agriculture. Relevant criteria for such a methodology have been formulated, and these have been used in setting up RAAKS. Only experience can tell whether the resulting design will live up to expectations. In the following chapter, the focus is on probing the potential and limitations of RAAKS in practice; by answering the last research question (Q5) this will help to complete my study.

8. Putting RAAKS to the test: initial field experiences

Oh, yes, professor, I have learned a lot; I am still confused, but at a much higher level![1]

This chapter provides a first and far from conclusive evaluation of RAAKS as a methodology. As proposed in the Introduction (see *The research methodology*), I will argue its efficacy, use and applicability under varying circumstances and usefulness to development professionals and researchers. First, with the help of 15 case studies I will demonstrate how RAAKS can be used in investigating the social organization of innovation and designing useful interventions to improve it (see the case studies on horse husbandry and from Central America, below). Second, RAAKS' design and operational objectives and the criteria formulated in Chapter 7 will be used to evaluate the extent to which RAAKS as a methodology fulfils our expectations. Third, I review experiences with RAAKS, discuss the social contexts in which it seems to be applicable, and argue RAAKS' relevance to development practice by locating the methodology within an emerging tradition of alternative systems of inquiry (see *RAAKS as an appreciative learning system*). A number of critical reflections and propositions conclude this chapter.

Field experiences with RAAKS over the past years are many and varied. First, graduate students contributed to the further elaboration of analytical perspectives and hence to the specification, validation and adjustment of its 'windows'. Later, when the methodology had been more consistently formulated, other students took it into the field to test parts of the analytical and procedural design. Student efforts produced over 30 case studies from which valuable lessons could be drawn. Sometimes students' struggles to operationalize and apply the knowledge and information systems perspective were of even greater value than the research results. After graduation, many remained active, networking and sharing RAAKS and similar experiences. A second strand of experiences contributing to the design and testing of RAAKS was its use in national and international education at Wageningen Agricultural University and at the International Agricultural Centre in Wageningen. Experience with learning-by-doing RAAKS during short courses, for example, helped identify the optimum level of 'creative confusion' needed to provide maximum intellectual engagement of participants in the exercises. Third, with the help of interested institutions we implemented a number of comprehensive RAAKS field studies in which we were able to use the methodology entirely according to its design.

This chapter draws primarily on this last set of experiences; they reflect best what we had in mind for RAAKS. They have provided me with 15 case studies: one application of RAAKS in the horse husbandry sector in the Netherlands and 14 in basic grains producing areas of six Central American countries. In addition, a number of experiences in which graduate students made use of RAAKS in a more research-oriented mode will be briefly

---

1. *Originally part of a story that Maurice Rolls, as Chairman, told the participants in the International Seminar on Rural Extension Policies, June 1989, at the IAC, Wageningen; since then a frequently used reminder of the complexities involved in knowledge systems education.*

RAAKS experimental studies referred to in this chapter

Authors	Sector/theme	Country	
Engel, de Groot, Meijering, Elema	Horse husbandry	Netherlands	1990
Woltersbeek	Green areas development	Netherlands	1990
Corten	Forestry	Netherlands	1991
Ravensbergen	Horticulture	Neth./Israel	1991
Castillo, Guardado	Basic grains, 2 areas	El Salvador	1992
García, Cifuentes, Davila, Wotzbeli, Rivera (2x) Collado, Adlai	Basic grains, 3 areas	Guatamala	1992
Jaén, Palacios	Basic grains, 3 areas	Panamá	1992
Espinoza, Cruz, Miranda, Lucas	Basic grains, 1 area	Nicaragua	1992
Zamora et al.	Basic grains, 3 areas	Costa Rica	1992
Juarez, Lavaire	Basic grains, 2 areas	Honduras	
Noordermeer, van Zanten	Pisciculture	Netherlands	1992
Adolfse	Food	Denmark	1992
Meijer	Small-scale producers	Chile	1992
Bemelmans	Export apple production	Chile	1992
Boonekamp & Kleis	Senior services project	Netherlands	1992
Bakker, Adolfse & Engel	Traffic and transport	Netherlands	1993

reviewed, particularly with respect to the use and applicability of RAAKS in situations that differ from those addressed in the case studies. Box 7 summarizes the case studies referred to in this chapter.

Studying the role of the National Reference Centre for Horse Husbandry

During the late 1980s agricultural research and extension in the Netherlands were restructured. Government extension was privatized and was intended to draw a progressively increasing proportion of its income from paid services. Government research institutes were made more autonomous and brought under a newly established private foundation. Until that moment, the agricultural knowledge and information system in the Netherlands had been characterized by an almost corporate nature. Centralized decision making, consensus and openness were considered important qualities of the manner in which innovation was socially organized. Consensus was brought about by coordinating bodies such as the agricultural council *(Landbouwschap)*, in which the government, farmers' organizations, agro-industries and labour unions in this sector took part. Internal openness in the exchange of knowledge and information was widely believed to be one of the main reasons behind the international success of Dutch agriculture. As a consequence, the Ministry of Agriculture, Nature and Fisheries wanted to maintain a free flow of essential knowledge and information after privatization. It established a number of National Reference Centres *(Informatie en Kennis Centra, or IKC)* including one for crops, one for animal production and one dedicated to nature, forests, landscapes and wildlife. These were to act as knowledge brokers among the relevant social actors within a sector. As the government remained the single largest spender on agricultural research, government-funded research programmes were seen as an important source of knowledge and information. Moreover, as a government service these centres maintained direct access to information on policy developments at national and nternational levels. They were staffed with technical, economics and communication specialists from the previous governmental extension services. Not surprisingly, the recently privatized extension service *(Dienst Landbouw Voorlichting,* DLV) was initially their most important customer.

Objective and background of the appraisal

A sector specialist for horse husbandry was appointed to the reference centre (IKC) for animal production in 1990. To enable this specialist to familiarize herself with the sector and to diagnose the situation to which she was to contribute, the IKC was interested in RAAKS. It asked for an analysis of the knowledge and information system for horse husbandry in the Netherlands which would be used as input for two workshops with the relevant social actors. The following objectives were formulated:
• to provide insight into the knowledge and information system of the sector;
• to highlight constraints in its functioning, and
• to further define the position of the newly formed national reference centre in this KIS.

The exercise was not meant to be conclusive; it was meant to initiate discussions with respect to improving the circulation of knowledge within the sector. A team of four researchers was formed, two from the IKC and two from the Communication and Innova-tion Studies Department of Wageningen Agricultural University. A study of secondary sources, plus interviews with key actors, led to a first tentative description of the way innovation was organized socially, which was discussed during the first workshop. Constraints and opportunities related to knowledge and information exchange and the IKC's possible contributions were discussed during the second workshop, attended by almost all of the previous participants. This section makes use of the validated results of this study (Engel et al., 1990).

The horse husbandry study was set against the background of the most important trends affecting knowledge and information generation, exchange and utilization in the sector. With the help of the actors these were identified as the introduction of co-financing as a principle for research and extension; the professionalization of horse breeding in the more market-oriented branches, due to increasing demands on stud owners to invest in new technology (leading to a decrease in the number of active professional stud owners); and the gradually decreasing interest on the part of the public in placing bets during horse races (causing a decrease in financial benefits flowing back into the sector).

Defining and surveying the domain of inquiry

'Horse husbandry' was defined broadly to include breeding, multiplying, training, caring for and trading horses and ponies as well as their competitive and recreational use. Both professional and non-professional forms of these activities were included. Quite early on it became clear that such an inclusive definition would cause debate. The advantage was that all 'activities with horses' were included: this would enable us to draw a general picture of the options for intervention by the IKC. However, this broad definition would not be easy for all social actors to accept. This became apparent during the first workshop, when two delegates from the Ministry of Agriculture, Nature and Fisheries – one representing the recreational and another the horse breeding and export elements of the department – engaged in a discussion: to whom did they think their minister was accountable? To nearly half a million people in the Netherlands who ride horses regularly for pleasure, or to about one hundred professional breeders of quality horses? It became evident that the farmers' organizations, which are closely integrated with the breeding organizations, were not generally seen as adequate representatives of the recreational horse riding sector. This underscored the diversity of the sector, which includes a variety of organizations, segments and target groups. Horse racing, breeding and recreational sports are commonly seen as three different segments or 'blood lines' in the sector. The groups to whom advisory and information services are to be targeted include breeders, stud owners, trainers, training establishments, horse riding establishments, horseback riders and traders. Moreover, in each of these categories one may find both professionals who work with horses as a trade and others who do it as a hobby. Among breeders and riders, amateurs are by far the majority, but even among stud owners they are also in the majority. As can be expected, the question of whether professionals or amateurs are most relevant to *innovation* in the sector generated heated discussions during the workshops.

Objectives and interests differ greatly among the segments of the sector. The horse racing community is interested in breeding fast, competitive horses. A strong character is an asset. Relatively large amounts of money change hands in this subsector, and most participants in it are professionals. Their intentions are primarily commercial. Sports, on the other hand, require other types of horses; for example, easily trainable mounts are needed for recreational riding or as jumpers. Here a strong, individualistic character may be a disadvantage. In general, less money circulates within this subsector and only a small minority, the owners of riding establishments, are professionals. Finally, among breeders, amateurs play an important role as well; few dedicate themselves to breeding as a profession. The breeding policies of the 19 existing breeding associations guide their efforts. For some, the conservation of the purity of the breed is the most important criterion (for example, in Iceland ponies); for others the horse's performance is a criterion, along with beauty and character. The latter is true for the largest association, the *Koninklijke Warmbloed Paardenstamboek Nederland* (KWPN), which registers the lineages of five types of horses and has more than 23,000 members. In fact, the conclusion for the horse husbandry knowledge and information system in the Netherlands was that no one mission statement could be formulated that would do justice to all stakeholders. Therefore, the three 'blood lines' were recognized as subsystems, in accordance with the way the actors themselves express their differences. During the study, the social organization of innovation both within and between these clusters of actors was reviewed.

Research related to this sector is carried out by the Veterinary Faculty of the University of Utrecht, the animal production department at Wageningen Agricultural University and two experiment stations near Lelystad and Brunssum. Research capacity is relatively limited; in 1990 it was still unclear how the sector would react to the co-financing principle imposed by the government. Research focuses mainly on veterinary science, internal diseases and reproduction (University of Utrecht) and on health, nutrition and training (experiment stations and Wageningen University). The DLV is the most important extension service with respect to horse husbandry. Commercialization drives DLV to select only target groups who can pay, whether directly or indirectly. At the moment it directs its services to training or riding establishments, stud owners and breeders. The DLV horse husbandry team consists of one team leader and four advisers.

Improving the social organization of innovation

The study generated a large number of insights into the social organization of innovation in the horse husbandry sector. These were interesting enough to guarantee the active participation of all invited participants during the two workshops (one lasting one day, another half a day). Eventually, a number of constraints were identified: participants agreed these have a considerable effect on the way knowledge and information are handled within the sector. A specific recommendation was jointly formulated for each constraint. Participants agreed to take the recommendations to their respective organizations and put them up for discussion.

To illustrate the process, I will review some of the constraints and recommendations that came out of this study. As a consequence of the diversity within the sector, adequate information retrieval and distribution is difficult. This has led to a situation in which lack of up-to-date information makes it difficult to tailor policy formulation and research and extension programmes to specific needs, particularly with regard to the recreational and non-professional actors. Since this is important for the economically weak actors from different 'blood lines', participants request the IKC to survey information needs more precisely and work out proposals as to how the needed information might be collected. Moreover, the actors feel that government ministries' policies with respect to their sector are too fragmented and inconsistent. Although they recognize the need for differentiation with respect to the blood lines, they believe one central body is needed within the ministry to coordinate policy formulation, to resolve inadequacies in the way the current coordinating committees operate. The present situation leads actors within the ministry to seek bilateral agreements with their counterparts rather than to strive to coordinate their efforts. The participants suggested that an existing coordination committee, the *Commissie van Overleg* (CvO), could be assigned more specific functions and extended to include new actors, so that it could adequately represent the variety of actors in the sector. The functions of the committee were listed and the IKC was encouraged to play an active role in re-activating the committee.

Further, it was recognized that the three blood lines maintain relatively little contact with each other. This was not generally felt to be a problem, but rather a direct consequence of their diverse interests. However, while social actors engaged in horse racing maintain close contacts with research and extension, actors engaged in sports have few relationships with these institutions. The contacts of breeders with research and extension are variable. All maintain close contacts with specialized educational establishments. The virtual marginalization of the sports involving horses with respect to influence on research and extension policies mirrors their relatively marginal position in general. This is even more surprising, given that they represent by far the largest group (an estimated half million people) using the products and services of the horse husbandry sector in the Netherlands. The actors agreed it was up to them to seek more intensive contacts; it was suggested that their sports would have to achieve a more prominent place in the revitalized CvO. In addition, further studies were recommended to identify themes for exchanging knowledge and information, and specific ways to improve relationships between the blood lines. One possible theme for such exchanges was 'farm' management. It was suggested that IKC explore this theme as one of its priorities along the way to supporting a more efficient exchange of knowledge and information.

Important groups within the sector, such as recreational horseback riders and amazons, are also poorly organized. This reduces their influence and access to information and makes it difficult for others to reach them. The participants agreed there are important reasons to try to more actively engage this group of actors in the generation and exchange of knowledge and information. Since interest in horse racing is on the decline, the sector will probably have to restructure its offerings to be more in line with the wishes of this group: it represents not only the largest group of actors, but also the largest group of paying customers. Moreover, their active participation might increase public support for research and extension on horse husbandry. The CvO was seen as the right forum to take initiatives in this area.

> Who needs what knowledge to become a successful horse sector practitioner?
> Workshop participants agreed that in debating the knowledge and information needs of social actors in the horse husbandry sector, the following types of knowledge can and must be distinguished. Each implies a distinct set of ideas, concepts, routines and skills:
>
> 1. Basic horse husbandry
> 2. Advanced horse husbandry
> 3. Horse riding
> 4. Horse breeding
> 5. Horse training
> 6. Entrepreneurship/management
> 7. Marketing
> 8. Transfer and communication of knowledge
> 9. Public relations
> 10. Rules and regulations set by organizations/ associations
> 11. Laws and regulations set by the government
>
> It is not necessary for all actors to know everything: breeders primarily need knowledge of types 1, 2, 4, 10 and 11 and trainers 1, 2, 3 and 5. Actors who run a training or riding establishment are the ones who need to be the most knowledgeable; while they do not need to know about breeding, they need to be acquainted with the other points. Riders, in addition to riding knowledge and skills, need to be acquainted only with basic horse husbandry. Stud owners can be content with a good knowledge of 1, 2, 4, 6, 10 and 11. Traders need 1, 2, 3, 5, 6, 7 and 11. (*Source:* Engel et al., 1990)

Two of the types of knowledge identified by participants (see the example on 'Who needs what knowledge...') were seen as insufficiently available within the sector: knowledge of 'farm' management and marketing. While the first is currently offered by the DLV, the breeding associations and professional education, a bottleneck remains at the level of the end user. Possibilities might include specific management courses for managers of training and riding establishments. The IKC could collaborate with other actors in designing and developing such courses as well as tailor-made administration systems. The development and exchange of marketing knowledge and information, on the other hand, was considered too 'blood-line-specific' to be dealt with for the sector as a whole. The recommendation was for social actors to take this need to their respective organizations.

Finally, it was observed that there was no direct relationship between research on horse husbandry and the target groups of the horse husbandry sector. As a result, the justification and resource base for research is unclear. In times of government withdrawal from funding research, this could affect its continuity. Feedback mechanisms are slack; thus whether research adequately responds to the needs of practitioners is also unknown. One suggestion was at least to include a representative of the research institutes in the CvO.

Some observations and conclusions

Two of the most lasting lessons of the horse sector case study were related more to our own conception of what we were doing than to the study itself. First, when we began the study, we did so because we thought the horse husbandry sector would be a relatively simple, straightforward domain of inquiry with not too many social actors or types of actors involved. In comparison with other Dutch sectors this may be the case, but we soon became aware of what 'relatively simple, straightforward' means in the Dutch context. Even after most actors had been collapsed into categories – such as 'breeding associations' (19 organizations), riding (+ 1000) and training (+ 720) establishments, and 'riders and amazons' (+ 500,000 persons) – and including only organizations directly relevant to directing and managing knowledge generation and exchange, we still had 32 relevant social categories and actors. This made us aware of the desirability of more sophisticated computer software, to handle data such as a 32x32 integration matrix to be used in analysing knowledge networks.

Our second lesson was about participation. Beforehand, we were sceptical about the enthusiasm of the actors' representatives: would they want to participate in the two workshops? All being very busy people, we expected little motivation to spend a day-and-a-half of their precious time discussing knowledge management. Instead, we met with great interest. Most actors who did not participate did so because the dates were incompatible with their already set agendas. Seventeen people did participate, most in both workshops. Later, we learned this was a common aspect of RAAKS exercises: when well-respected actors from the sector take the initiative to put it on the agenda, the social organization of innovation arouses great interest. In the end, our problem was not how to deal with lack of participation, but to assure that participants would later feel their participation had been worthwhile. For the horse husbandry sector, most participants left the second meeting with a firm commitment to discuss the report in their own circles and to see what else could be done to improve the way innovation was socially organized in their sector.

Even if, by 1990, we had grasped the importance of a 'soft systems' perspective, initially we underestimated the relevance of our definition of 'horse husbandry'. The social actors themselves taught us more about the appreciative dimension of the social organization of innovation, in a practical manner. They perceived the three blood lines as structural forms, and underscored their relevance from the point of view of performance of the whole. They also agreed, however, that accepting these social border lines too uncritically could produce constraints. The RAAKS study helped all of us to look at the blood lines as a matter of design rather than an unchangeable matter of fact. In addition, this convinced us as researchers that RAAKS would have to accommodate various parallel volitions at the same time. We had implicitly extrapolated the IKC mission statement to a general one for the whole: *to make sure all actors within the theatre have access to all relevant knowledge and information at all times.* We discovered that even in a relatively small sector like the horse husbandry sector in the Netherlands, such a general statement of purpose does not do justice to the actual diversity. Not everybody needs everybody else's knowledge and information. Breeders can do without a lot of the information produced by actors from the sports blood line, and *vice versa*! Nor do all need the information those engaged in horse racing need to have at their disposal. The 'million dollar question' is *which* knowledge and information, from whom, is useful to whom? This realization confirmed the need for thinking in terms of a variety of co-existing missions, all being sought and accomplished within a single innovation theatre at the same time, rather than assuming a single whole with one general mission. It also confirmed the usefulness of the concept of 'synergy', suggesting the possible benefits of improving social learning among social actors who recognize mutual interdependence.

In retrospect, one drawback of the study was our failure to push through to specific strategic commitments to action, and to monitoring achievements in Phase C. This happened because, first, it was not part of our brief; but second, because we had not yet gauged the full importance of these steps. Also, the recommendations of the study needed to be implemented first, to create a platform (such as a renewed CvO) to facilitate adjustments and monitor the implementation of such agreements. At the time, we were satisfied with the enthusiasm of the participants and their firm intentions to take the report of the study to their respective organizations and put it on the agenda. For me, these issues remain as questions, to which I will return in Chapter 9. To what extent should a participatory diagnosis push towards visible results rather than stop with the formulation of practical recommendations? Should followup perhaps be left entirely to the actors themselves, once certain feasible routes for improvement have been identified?

On the basis of experience in the horse husbandry sector, we concluded that RAAKS, as an approach, was successful. We appreciated its strength in making explicit the way social actors organize themselves for innovation, the constraints and opportunities that emerge as a result of using this approach, and the enthusiasm with which so many social actors reacted to the exercise. We understood that the successful application of RAAKS requires the initiative and backing of at least one respected stakeholder in the theatre. Further, the definition of the domain of inquiry must be taken very seriously during the formulation of the appraisal objective and must receive ongoing attention during each study. Finally, we concluded there were a number of loose ends, particularly with respect to Phase C and our own specification of intentions regarding monitoring and intervention during the implementation of followup activities.

Strengthening agricultural institutions in Central America

The Regional Programme for Strengthening Agronomic Research on Grains in Central America (PRIAG: Convenio CORECA/CEE/IICA) is a joint programme among six countries, aimed at improving the prospects of basic grain producers in the face of structural adjustment and regional market liberalization. The programme initiated a regional working group in 1991 to look into the possibilities for strengthening agricultural institutions. In addition to this working group, others looked at improvement of training and education, farming systems research and the role of non-governmental organizations. The main objectives of the working group on strengthening institutions were first, to identify strategies and mechanisms to stimulate organizational, administrative and institutional modernization of agricultural research and extension in each country and in the region as a whole; and second, to analyse the loss of potential due to changes in institutional resource allocations to the organizations dedicated to research and extension in basic grains, as a result of the structural adjustment programmes and the fiscal crisis. Secondary objectives were to share experiences with respect to institutional restructuring processes; to identify strengths and weaknesses in the management of the generation and transfer of agricultural technology; to generate an updated diagnosis of the human, physical and financial resources dedicated to research and extension in each country of the region; to inform and motivate regional and national decision makers and financial institutions active in the region with respect to proposals the group would be putting forward; and to exchange information and experiences with the Central American Group on Training and the Study Group on Non-Governmental Organizations (Grupo Regional de Fortalecimiento Institucional, 1992).

I do not intend even to summarize the multiple activities of the programme or the working group here. The preceding paragraph serves only to draw very roughly the context within which RAAKS studies were done in Central America. Those participating agreed that the social organization of innovation was to be scrutinized thoroughly, and that proposals for tangible action were to be generated and implemented. A joint management structure had been created to implement the studies and eventually negotiate the proposals that evolved, and operating costs had been budgeted. RAAKS was to contribute to a quick identification of current constraints and opportunities for improvement, but it was far from being the only activity. Preceding RAAKS, for example, the group had already carried out an analysis of *national* technology generation and transfer systems, focused primarily on the availability of resources to attend to the research and extension needs of basic grain growing areas. Moreover, the existence of an international collaboration programme meant the quality of the national staff assigned to the working groups, and hence to RAAKS, was extremely high. All were top level professionals in their fields, most had hands-on experience with rapid rural appraisals or similar techniques; most also had a keen interest in the social organization of innovation, even if they had not labelled it with this name, and caught on to knowledge systems thinking very quickly. I only hope I caught on to their ideas as quickly as they understood mine.

RAAKS' introduction and training of research teams

After an introduction to the knowledge and information systems perspective and the RAAKS methodology during its second meeting in September 1991, the Regional Working Group decided to include RAAKS action research as part of its activities. It would be used first of all for *training* in the basic grains producing areas selected as pilot areas for the programme. The group intended to create a regional network of professionals able to study research–extension interactions and the role of producers and agro-industries in generating and exchanging basic grains technologies, using modern concepts and evaluation methods. RAAKS was to provide a basis from which national teams could develop their own approach. In addition to training, the aim was to gain insight into the situation in the various areas by carrying out a detailed *analysis* of the social organization of innovation. Further, in accordance with the RAAKS methodology, the teams were expected to formulate *specific proposals for action* in their areas. This was a way to improve knowledge and information management, with an eye to improving the socioeconomic position of the smallholder families who make up the majority of basic grains producers.

To familiarize national teams with the methodology, a first RAAKS workshop was held in San José, Costa Rica, in April 1992. The preparation and organization of the course was in the hands of the Regional Executive Directorate of PRIAG. Consultants responsible for the contents and didactic process were recruited from the Ministry of Agriculture of Costa Rica (Emilia Solis), Royal Tropical Institute/Wageningen University from the Netherlands (Paul Engel) and the International Centre for Development Oriented Research in Agriculture (CIRAD) in Montpellier, France (Augusto Moreno). The course included an introduction to knowledge systems thinking and to RAAKS, as well as a practical exercise using RAAKS in the vicinity of San Carlos, in Costa Rica. The course was attended by 15 research and extension professionals from the six countries. In the evaluation, they indicated their satisfaction with their own assimilation of the materials offered (80% very good; 20% good). As part of the course programme, each national team prepared one or more national RAAKS case studies, covering all of the grain producing areas affected by the programme. With the decision to cover all and not just one area per country, the teams extended the implementation of RAAKS beyond the originally planned scope. They saw the study as having so much relevance for understanding the management of knowledge and information in their areas that implementing it in only one area seemed unsatisfactory. The Regional Executive Directorate agreed with this view and budgeted the extra costs involved. Members of the

```
                                    Box 8
                    RAAKS case study areas in Central America

    Country              Case studies/areas        Research teams

    El Salvador          Zona 5, R.Oriental        Castillo, Guardado, Sandoval, García
                         Sonsonate                 Castillo, Guardado, Sandoval, García
    Guatamala            La Blanca                 García, Cifuentes, Rivera, Bolaños
                         Polochic, A.Verapaz       Davila, Rivera, Rivera, Wotzbeli
                         Baja Verapaz              Collado, Adlai
    Panama               Arco seco:
                         Portrero                  Jaén, Palacios, Gutierrez, Espino
                         Parita-Pesé               Jaén, Palacios, Gutierrez, Espino
                         Guararé                   Jaén, Palacios, Gutierrez, Espino
    Nicaragua            Pantasma, Jinotega        Espinoza, Cruz, Miranda, Lucas
    Costa Rica           Brunca, Pacífico Sur:
                         Pejibaye                  Zamora, Díaz, Hernández
                         Pto. Jimenez              Zamora, Díaz, Hernández
                         Changuena                 Zamora, Díaz, Hernández
    Honduras             San Francisco de la Paz   Juarez, Lavaire, Vega, Alemán
                         Olanchito                 Juarez, Lavaire, Vega, Alemán
```

Directorate and consultants were assigned as 'backstoppers' for the national study teams.

The national RAAKS studies were carried out in the period April–September 1992. Each national team recruited and trained additional team members from the areas being studied. They prepared didactic and research materials, collected the necessary informa- tion and mobilized actors to participate in the workshops. In each case, the original RAAKS design was adapted to suit local ideas and circumstances (see *RAAKS use and adaptation*, below). The general layout of the methodology, however, remained intact. Box 8 shows the areas where case studies were carried out and for which the results were presented and discussed during the second regional RAAKS workshop in San José, Costa Rica, in October 1992. Because of the interest generated by the exercise, additional staff (all national team members) were allowed to participate. This brought the total number of participants to 22. The workshop addressed three main elements. First, we concentrated on defining and discussing the main issues that affected institutional performance related to support for basic grains production in Central America. Each issue was evaluated with respect to its relevance to the formulation of proposals for intervention. Criteria for judging useful proposals were discussed. Second, each country presented the outcomes of its RAAKS exercises; these were reviewed and commented on by the group. A detailed evaluation of the national teams' experiences with RAAKS and their opinions as to the added value and applicability of the methodology concluded this part. Third, each national team elaborated action proposals to be presented to the Regional Executive Directorate and national level policymakers for implementation.

Some results: appreciating the social organization of innovation in practice

It is utterly impossible to really do justice to the richness of results presented by the RAAKS teams following their studies. The variety and depth of their insights and observations with respect to the domains they studied fully justifies the over 300 pages of text and graphics they produced (Castillo and Guardado, a,b; García et al.; Davila et al.; Collado and Adlai; Jaén and Palacios; Espinoza et al.; Zamora et al.; Juarez and Lavaire, a,b: all 1992). Within the scope of this book I can only mention a few of the most telling examples of what these teams brought out during the second workshop, after all had finished writing their preliminary reports. I apologize in advance to all of the team members for my inadequate selectivity. After covering the general problem/focus and discussions held, I will cite some examples of constraints and opportunities related to improving innovation in basic grains production. Finally, some of the recommendations for action formulated as part of the action research will be presented.

The RAAKS studies helped national teams to quickly focus on the social organization of innovation. The priority issues proposed to the second RAAKS workshop (shown in the example) reflect this focus. To claim that such elements will come out only with the help of RAAKS would be foolish, but RAAKS' analytical focus is recognizable and seems to have helped in specifying the issues. Existing diversities in interests, strategies and resource availability are recognized; differentiation of tasks, linkages, and other structural elements are pointed up, as well as their influence on the generation, validation and transfer of technology and the management of knowledge and information; the relevance of the policy environment is underscored; finally, local knowledge networks and peasant knowledge are recognized as part of the problem *and/or* the solution.

Social organization of innovation for basic grains in Central America: priority issues:
1. *Inter-institutional coordination*: linkages between extension and research; there are tasks without social actors to perform them, as well as social actors with no tasks.
2. *Knowledge and skills of producers*: the integration of farmer knowledge with scientific knowledge; producers are not organized; producers' role in the generation, validation and communication of technologies; non-commercial producers lack support; local, empirical knowledge networks need to be taken into account.
3. *Types of producers, specific situations in relation to interventions*: diversification and the changing role of basic grains; diversity in producer/production strategies – not everyone produces in the same way or for the same purpose; survival strategies and food security involving basic grains; capitalize upon the experience producers already have with respect to alternative crops/activities.
4. *Structural adjustment and the elaboration of interventions*: market liberalization; open borders; privatization of technology generation, validation and transfer.
5. *The role of women in the knowledge and information system (and its management) for basic grains*: division of labour at the farm level; knowledge networks among rural women need to be taken into account; exchange of knowledge and its relation to gender.
6. *Current changes in the configuration of the basic grains knowledge and information system*: transfer of initiative from state to market; it is necessary to look into networks (formal and informal) that have outlived their function; new tasks versus tasks with no social actors to perform them; the role of non-governmental organizations in rural development; strong influence of donors/international financial institutions on the knowledge and information system; the influence of agro-commercial organizations.
7. *Natural resources, basic grains and sustainability*: basic grain production and diversification must be looked at from an ecological standpoint too, not just socioeconomically.

(*Source*: Proposed and selected by the participants in the second MSICA workshop, October 1992)

The results of the studies also reflect insights into the social organization of innovation. The producers themselves are recognized as an important source of knowledge and information, as are agro-industries, commercial companies, seed producers, traders, etc. Most studies call attention to the fact that different types of producers network differently with respect to innovation. Jaén and Palacios (1992), for example demonstrate how, in the Arco Seco area of Panama, subsistence farmers and those who sell most of their produce on the market participate differently in existing knowledge networks and, as a consequence, obtain information differently. In general, socioeconomic relationships influence networking greatly. The same authors report that exchanges of information occur between subsistence and commercial farmers because the former sell their labour to the latter. Castillo and Guardado, (1992a,b) show that network configurations related to basic grains differ considerably from those for animal husbandry and export crops. In different ways, the exchange of knowledge, information and experience are organized, depending on the type of actors involved. The type of land ownership, labour relations, credit and/or commercial arrangements and

For Zone 5, Oriental Region, El Salvador, Castillo and Guardado (1992a) report, just as most other authors, a number of environmental factors that affect the social organization of innovation. They mention lack of credit and resource deterioration, uncertainty with respect to land tenure and adverse agro-climatological conditions. More specific to their area, they identify the paternalism that dominates relationships between both government institutions and non-governmental organizations and their resource-poor clientele. Finally, they propose that in Zone 5, the influence of resource transfers to the population from family members abroad is so strong that it has changed the way of life. The remaining smallholders now have little interest in taking the risks implied by growing their crops, and labour has become scarce and expensive. Such a description contrasts strongly with that of the Sonsonate area, where the same authors report that despite many and severe difficulties, the producers cultivate land, staying alert and receptive to efforts of government and non-government institutions to promote improvements. But, unfortunately, this environment provides '... strong policy support ... for export crops, not for basic grains' (Castillo and Guardado, 1992a).

A number of studies express serious doubts as to the effectiveness of government institutions in supporting basic grain producers. Basic grains production, Castillo and Guardado (1992a) argue, rests with smallholders who have little access to resources, lack credits and suffer from an unstable market. There is no plan to attend to their needs and those who are supposed to do so, the extension agencies, lack the necessary resources. Systematically, it appears, research and extension programmes focus their efforts on producers who have better access to resources and/or credit. Jaén and Palacios (1992) also argue that technical packages have not been developed to fit the needs of subsistence farmers, who represent 70% of basic grain producers in the area they studied. Information reaches them only indirectly, through contacts with other farmers or sometimes local traders. These actors in turn receive technology and information mostly through representatives of multinational companies who sell inputs and/or services. As a consequence, knowledge of basic issues such as improved varieties and their adaptation, integrated pest management, cultivation methods and so forth is relatively scarce among resource-poor farmers. Similarly, the reverse is also true: extension workers and researchers have little familiarity with poor farmers' practices and circumstances. In summary, public institutions often at best play a secondary role in transferring technology to the majority of basic grain farmers.

Coordination among public institutions is often weak. Juarez et al. (1992a) conclude that even where the Natural Resource Secretariat can be considered the leading agency, it is not able to impose effective coordination among relevant institutions. When coordination is achieved, it seems to be the result of influence exerted by international agencies, through resource incentives and training. Espinoza et al. (1992) also point to the lack of coordination in the Pantasma Valley in Nicaragua. Collado and Adlai (1992) describe inter-agency competition to work with communities closer to town, leaving the majority of the population without assistance. Lack of coordination, they report, leads to duplication of efforts and lack of impact among both governmental and non-governmental agencies. Castillo and Guardado (1992b) argue that the producers themselves are the most important driving force behind the social organization of innovation in basic grains. Despite resource limitations, they produce for their own consumption as well as for the market. An empirical knowledge network operates among the producers. It is traditional but practical, based on their own knowledge and experience and complemented technical messages from other actors. This view coincides with that expressed by farmers in the Pantasma Valley, who pointed out that transfer of technology and information among farmers was the most frequent and most effective (Espinoza et al., 1992). Most studies recognized that the key to innovation for basic grain producers in Central America is in the hands of the producers themselves. Institutions that have the objective of helping them should pay more attention to this.

Davila et al. (1992) asked various groups of actors in Polochic Alta Verapaz to picture the innovation theatre as they perceived it. Each group made drawings for maize, rice and animal husbandry, in each case separately detailing the links for exchanging knowledge and information on technology, credit and marketing. The authors found it interesting to observe that different groups present entirely different views. For example, while representatives of government institutes showed a fully integrated system for animal husbandry with connections among all eight actors they considered relevant, private sector representatives articulated only three: the intermediary, the land owner and the peasant. This approach was used to focus directly on the appreciative character of the social organization of innovation; it was made an issue for discussion among the social actors involved. In the Pantasma Valley, Espinoza et al. (1992) on the contrary presented their own well-probed graphic impression of the social organization of innovation to a workshop at the end of Phase A. During the discussions, local farmers were very helpful, distinguishing between institutions *apparently* present in the valley and those that were really active. The farmers corrected the team's view (expressed in their drawing) on one important aspect: they saw communication from one farmer to another as probably their most important source of knowledge and information, so this had to be included in the system drawing (Espinoza et al., 1992). The Nicaraguan team also singled out the enthusiasm displayed by the local authorities to follow up on the exercise.

Espinoza et al. also provide a vivid account of the different missions under which actors pursue agricultural innovation in the Pantasma Valley, Nicaragua. As a result, they argue, there is no 'common language'. While the National Development Bank, which traditionally finances basic grains producers, speaks of efficiency in the use of credit and has abolished all subsidies, the farmers – who find themselves being pushed to the margins of economic activity – consider credit to be one possibility that might help them survive the current crisis: a subsidy that could guarantee their subsistence. Farmers speak of the need to establish guaranteed prices, while the government is bent on eliminating all intervention in the market mechanism. Farmers speak of reducing the use of technology as a subsistence strategy, while the Ministry of Agriculture and Livestock and the National Centre for Basic Grains Research speak of elevating the use of improved technologies and the modernization of production. The Ministry and the National Centre also speak of augmenting production and productivity in basic grains, while farmers talk about switching to other, more profitable activities – even while they continue to grow grains for subsistence. The Union of Agricultural Cooperatives, finally, expresses a need to extend the agricultural credit programme, while PRODERE, a programme supporting refugees and the repatriated, wants to support smallscale technological demonstrations with a selected group of farmers. Despite these major differences, the authors stress the cordiality established among actors during the seminars, which permitted a thorough analysis of the causes and consequences of the situation (Espinoza et al., 1992).

García et al. (1992) drew out the differences in the appreciations of different types of stakeholders by asking them to prioritize the problems affecting production in the La Blanca area. The social actors participating were farmers, advisers from government institutions, private advisers, and the regional directors of agricultural institutions. All but the group of directors agreed that low prices, combined with lack of marketing channels for maize and rice were the top priority problem. The directors, on the contrary, pointed to the individualism exhibited by the farmers in facing the current situation as the priority problem. The high cost of fertilizers, ranked second by farmers, was ranked fifth or sixth by other actors. Untimely credit delivery, surprisingly, was ranked higher by government technical advisers and directors than by farmers. In the eyes of private advisers, it only deserved the eighth place. Lack of knowledge of the existence of a laboratory for soils and phytopathology in the region and lack of research and technical assistance on grains production came in second or third for all. While the farmers and government officials agreed lack of information on improved technologies in horticultural crops and grains was an issue, private advisers ranked this very low on their priority list.

Towards specific actions for improvement

During the workshop that followed, with the aim of defining possible solution strategies for basic grains, the reason that the group of directors selected a different priority problem became clear. Most actors, as might have been expected from the opinions they expressed, were tempted to focus their recommendations for improvement on strengthening the National Institute for Marketing Agricultural Produce (INDECA). The directors disagreed, however. They explained that according to their information, this institution had just changed its policy and would no longer engage in marketing grains! Therefore, they saw the lack of organization among producers for doing their own marketing as suggesting the top priority. After this explanation, the whole group joined in a recommendation to work toward the promotion of marketing organizations among farmers, and to offer training to farm leaders in managing such activities. This led to an interesting discussion and eventually to agreement among these actors and INDECA: they would meet within one month to discuss specific options to improve grain marketing. INDECA offered training for those who wanted to set themselves up as entrepreneurs, and committed itself to providing information on grain prices at national level. The farmers agreed to participate actively in these courses (García et al., 1992).

Castillo and Guardado (1992b) similarly report a need to improve marketing of basic grains in the area of Sonsonate, El Salvador. During the study, various options to realize such a recommendation were evaluated. Here too, the establishment of farmers' organizations with the help of non-governmental organizations or financial institutions was seen as more realistic than trying to reactivate an already closed, soon to be privatized government institution that had carried out the function in the past. In this case too, farmers put forward a very specific option. They told the team about the experiences of farmers in the area who used botanical products for pest and weed control, with some degree of success; further, it appeared to have helped them to significantly reduce costs. They proposed that the research division of CENTA contact these farmers, appraise their experiences and, if they were validated, make the results known to farmers nationwide, not simply in this one area (Castillo and Guardado, 1992b).

The results of the RAAKS studies make clear that the majority of basic grains producers are in a critical situation. They are affected by the decisions of their governments to refrain from direct intervention in agriculture, while as yet no cost reducing technologies, promising alternatives or adequate forms of organization are available. Thus they are caught between government withdrawal and market liberalization. Participants and teams came up with diverse and location-specific recommendations to meet this situation. In each case they are seen trying to build on local strengths and opportunities, rather than to construct a 'standard package'. Particular characteristics of the social context in each of the regions were taken into account, such as the active involvement of municipal authorities in Nicaragua, the possibility of reinforcing institutional intervention and coordination in Honduras, or reflections on the possibilities for agro-tourism in Costa Rica. Nevertheless, three strands of reasoning seem to lie at the core of many of the proposals:
- in Central America today, commercialization is a key factor: it must be strengthened. Without market incentives, innovation in basic grains is hardly conceivable;
- farmers themselves hold many of the keys to innovation in basic grains production: they must become more actively organized to search for new options and new solutions to the variety of problems they face; and
- government institutions are no longer the main driving force behind development of basic grains; this makes it necessary for them to reorient their policies and coordinate with others, such as farmer and non-governmental organizations, private companies and municipal authorities, so they can allocate their limited resources more effectively.

Proposals to strengthen innovation by means of commercialization range from a proposition by private actors to create an integrated agro-industrial chain for maize, coordinated at municipal level (Pantasma Valley, Nicaragua), to the construction of *centros de acopio* (storage facilities organized by and for farmers), non-governmental organizations and financial institutions (Sonsonate, El Salvador). A more efficient credit delivery system, specifically oriented towards basic grain producers, is often mentioned as a fundamental requirement. The Costa Rican team's proposals are directed at reducing on-farm production costs as well as increasing product quality and added value. Financial support, adequate infrastructure, on-farm research and farmer training are referred to as necessary ingredients in such a programme.

With respect to farmer organizations the teams are quite explicit. Since no special protection or subsidies can be expected under the present circumstances, farmers themselves will have to play an active role in organizing not only marketing, credit and delivery of services, but their search for alternative technological solutions as well. Training for farmers is again considered a fundamental requirement.

The studies suggest that the role of government institutions really is in flux. For Panama, a review of institutional policies on research, extension and credit delivery is suggested (Jaén and Palacios, 1992). Recommendations with respect to institutional practices generally emphasize three issues.

- The need to re-orient agricultural research to the specific circumstances of basic grains producers, seeking to reduce production costs to a minimum, making use of local experiences and advantages to the maximum, and looking for promising alternatives for diversification. Active participation of farmers in on-farm research is seen as the best way to integrate locally available and new scientific knowledge.

- The need to recognize different types of basic grain producers, and to adapt and equip agricultural extension to deal with each type. Improved extension planning and programming, staff training and active farmer participation are recommended.

- The need to improve inter-institutional coordination and, where possible, to involve 'new' actors such as local authorities, private companies, farmers organizations and non-governmental organizations. The need to improve the exchange of information among relevant stakeholders is cited in both Nicaragua and El Salvador (Region Oriental).

RAAKS in Central America: use and adaptation

During the final regional RAAKS workshop in San José, Costa Rica, RAAKS teams looked back on their experiences. They confirmed that the first workshop and practical exercise had been successful in clarifying the RAAKS approach and methodology, even given the large number of unfamiliar concepts. The remaining doubts were mostly straightened out within the team or with the help of the consultants from the Regional Directorate. Nevertheless, most teams said additional practical training in the use of windows and tools would have been helpful; additional documentation and reading materials would also have been welcome. Further, teams found the lack of training in workshop design, preparation and management, including group dynamics, participation and communication, a serious drawback; much improvisation was needed. In practice, this had been overcome with the help of the consultants.

At the beginning of the RAAKS exercise, workshops were held in which national teams trained additional members, in order to perform case studies in all programme areas. Eventually a total of 14 case studies were carried out in six countries (Box 8). Each RAAKS team was allowed to make adjustments, within the scope of the methodology, to fit their own circumstances. Relevant actors were normally identified by seeking key informants from relevant practices, organizations or institutions. In two countries, a random sample of producers was used to determine which farmers would be asked to participate in the exercise. In Panama, this was particularly useful. The team had recently done an agro-socioeconomic survey, so that the farmers from the same sample could be approached and survey information could be fed into the RAAKS analysis. In Nicaragua, the actors them-selves pushed for a more thorough commitment to the results of the exercise, establishing a committee including one technical specialist from the public domain, one from the private domain and two farmers. The committee was charged with helping to consolidate the results and carry the proposals for action to the municipal technical committee.

Teams most often implemented the windows as proposed in the RAAKS manual, using the tools specified there. The window on communication analysis was the only one not used regularly: the distinction between integration analysis and communication analysis was not yet clear. A number of additional tools were designed and used as well, such as specific interview guides and matrix tables for organizing and synthesizing information, and for planning action in Phase C. Two teams combined the information gathered for Window B3, knowledge network analysis, with that for B1, impact analysis, in one matrix. One team did task analysis twice, once for the actual state of affairs and once for the desired state, and asked actors to specify the importance they attach to each task with respect to the performance of the whole. In most cases only two actor workshops were held, one at the close of Phase A and one for B and C together. In Guatamala all three workshops were held, one for each RAAKS phase. The workshop designs were varied. Often different types of actors were first given time to discuss within their own groups their reactions to the information gathered by the team and to possible improvements. This proved a promising way to prepare for a balanced 'negotiation of interpretations' in the plenary sessions that followed.

Usefulness of RAAKS in the eyes of national teams

During the final workshop and evaluation of the RAAKS studies, teams were asked to specify the value RAAKS had added to their situations. Without exception, teams said RAAKS had permitted them to quickly focus on the social organization of innovation. They found that the methodology facilitates a meaningful analysis of events and ideas, from a new angle and in a participatory, reflexive manner. Human agency *(gestión humana)* is at the centre of a RAAKS analysis. It permits the acquisition of new knowledge as well as the sharing of information that was previously only available to some actors (El Salvador). RAAKS widens the vision of actors with regard to the constraints and opportunities they identify; also, it helps to put knowledge and information systems thinking into the context of a more general systems approach (Guatamala).

> *The method permits one to orient and structure information gathering better, and to formulate integrated plans of operation with participation of the actors involved (Guatamala national team, on RAAKS' applicability).*

Teams confirmed that RAAKS permits a thorough analysis of a domain of agricultural knowledge; it facilitates a quick determination of the level of integration and coordination among the actors involved (Panama). It treats aspects that are not common in traditional agro-socioeconomic surveys, and thus permits discussing and solving bottlenecks in communication, coordination, integration and task performance (Nicaragua). As RAAKS permits reaching a shared understanding of problems and hence joint planning for solutions, it facilitates the active and conscious participation of actors. The Nicaraguan team observed that *RAAKS helps create an atmosphere of cordiality, even among antagonistic and indifferent actors*; as a consequence, responsibility for interventions is assumed by more than one actor.

> *In areas such as Nicaragua where we are experiencing changes in the economic, social and political order, and where the majority of actors, when left to themselves, are not fully capable of interpreting and linking the effects of exogenous factors – such as sources of finance and the market – the method has a practical applicability of incalculable value (Nicaraguan team, on the applicability of RAAKS).*

RAAKS generated interest and active participation among actors and helped identify problems and opportunities that had previously been left undeclared. In both El Salvador (La Blanca) and Nicaragua (Pantasma Valley), following RAAKS *actors proposed and agreed a more formal commitment than was initially proposed within the scope of the methodology*. Further, this was the first time that producers of basic grains participated in an analysis of their own situation. It also contributed to the creation of a 'group consciousness' among team members, and increased the credibility of the local team with regard to their activities (Costa Rica). Finally, the Costa Rican team pointed out that the exercise had left technical specialists with burning questions *(inquietudes)* as to the importance of knowledge and information for agricultural development.

> *In the study we not only interviewed farmers, but also leaders of farmer organiza-*
> *tions, professional associations, and persons from public and private institutions.*
> *RAAKS helped us identify weaknesses and strengths in many actors which earlier*
> *agro-socioeconomic diagnosis had not brought to light: aspects such as communica-*
> *tion, integration, coordination and specific missions, to improve the system as a*
> *whole – not only the generation and transfer of technology (Panamanian team, on*
> *the added value of RAAKS in comparison with agro-socioeconomic diagnosis).*

Finally, teams summarized their suggestions for improving and further developing the methodology for use in Central America. They reconfirmed the importance of validating results on the social organization of innovation with the stakeholders themselves, and underlined the need to be careful to integrate *small* farmers in the workshops. Further, they pointed up the need to understand and deal with diverse missions during a RAAKS exercise: all are relevant to judging the performance of the whole and must be addressed explicitly. Historical roots of current problems should be considered directly.

Teams made it clear that in spite of their detailed suggestions for improvement, RAAKS should not become a rigid 'blueprint' sort of methodology. Its flexibility is a strength, and should be maintained. Even so, their practical comments were essential to the further delineation of RAAKS, including the more active involvement of decision makers and more explicit attention to communication and team building.

Following the RAAKS study in Central America, all teams proposed to continue using and developing the methodology in their own countries. As the time and cost involved was relatively high, they recommended its use only in situations that justify particular attention, for example in agricultural, agro-forestry or rural development projects; in 'new' programme areas; and in strategically important sectors for which the social organization of innovation is proving especially problematical. Specifically, teams asked the Regional Executive Directorate to support followup of the activities proposed by the teams. Further training at national and regional levels in the use of the methodology was suggested, to establish a regional network of RAAKS consultants. The publication of national reports and continued sharing among teams of experiences and information with respect to RAAKS and other programme activities were also recommended. Finally, they challenged the consultants and Directorate to elaborate and publish a practical manual on RAAKS, and to make other documentation on knowledge systems thinking and related issues available.

Some critical issues and lessons learned

The use of RAAKS by a group of agricultural professionals as varied as those who took part in the 14 case studies in Central America was an enormously enriching experience: no pen can adequately describe the learning dynamics involved. Still, I will try to highlight the central issues that came up and some of the lessons we learned. One of the first things to become clear is that RAAKS actually 'works'. We had no difficulty agreeing that the methodology is applicable, and that it made a valued contribution to achieving the programme objectives formulated (training, understanding the social organization of innovation and identifying opportunities for action; see above). Also, given the comments above, it is not difficult to argue that RAAKS fulfilled its own operational objectives (to identify opportunities for action, create awareness among relevant social actors and identify actors who can take adequate action; see the Introduction).

RAAKS permits teams to collect information and derive an understanding of the social organization of innovation. Its validity as an appraisal methodology has been confirmed. Also, by focusing on relationships among social actors and the capacity of these actors to enact networking strategies to realize their own expectations, it adds value that traditional appraisal methods such as the agro-socioeconomic survey do not. Moreover, its flexibility in terms of intentionality, analytical and procedural design has been singled out as a reason for its successful adaptation and implementation: each team could develop its own style *(estilo propio)*. Further, it shares with other participatory approaches the active participation of stakeholders, the personal growth, team building and group dynamics among researchers and social actors so characteristic of this type of methodologies. Finally, it has been shown to help motivate a large number of people to look at their world from a different angle, and to appreciate some of the problems in a new way. Doing RAAKS served as a catalyst for their enthusiasm.

However, we also learned that without a team of highly qualified professionals, all of this would probably have been unattainable. 'Highly qualified', however, does not refer to competence in one of the traditional disciplines, but to a capacity to step back and critically appraise one's own role and that of other relevant actors in the social process called agricultural innovation. This requires an ability to engage in appreciative systems thinking – stressing wholeness as well as diversity, individual opportunities as well as structural impairments, and to see human and institutional purpose and decision making as part of the problem as well as the solution. Moreover, it requires an ability to work in interdisciplinary groups and to relate easily to farmers, industrialists, traders, private advisers, policymakers and so forth. And this requires a mind that is open to appreciating the reasoning of others.

Another crucial element in Central America was institutional support. In most countries, national institutions were committed and supportive. The finance and direct support of the Regional Executive Directorate enabled the teams to accomplish the training, field research and workshops on time, and provided a framework for preparing and planning followup activities. RAAKS is no exception to the rule that every exercise requires time, energy and money. Even though the period is relatively brief (in Central America, five to six months of part-time activity for most of those involved), time has to be taken away from other activities, and wrestling with new concepts and appreciative issues takes a lot of energy, probably more than one's regular job. Finally, the training, workshops and general involvement of so many social actors in the process costs money. It may not be that much, but it has to come from somewhere. Without the active commitment of at least one well-respected organization or institution, the completion of RAAKS action research seems impossible.

This institutional support appears all the more necessary when we consider that RAAKS involves the active collaboration of relevant social actors. Actors' participation will depend in part on their appreciation of the organization or institution that takes the initiative. Moreover, achieving a balanced selection of participating social actors will depend to some extent on the views of the supporting institution. This organization may have their own ideas about who the relevant actors are; these ideas may or may not coincide with other actors' views. Therefore, the actor or actors that take the initiative to initiate a RAAKS exercise need to be open-minded, committed to the aim of studying actual practice, and willing to accept challenges to their preconceived ideas on the social organization of innovation. This underlines the relevance of Phase A, particularly with respect to defining and re-defining the appraisal objective, identifying relevant social actors and searching for diversity in missions, as well as the importance of the active participation of the initiating social actors in this phase.

Another result of using RAAKS in Central America was a new look at Phase C. This phase brings together two intentions, which may conflict: all actors need to participate freely in redefining problems and solutions; on the other hand, they need to arrive at tangible conclusions and a commitment to action. The first activity requires an open mind and inclusive thinking; the second, strategic thinking and the elimination of alternatives that do not receive substantial support from actors. The challenge to a RAAKS team is to manage to do both. However, when overall consensus on specific actions cannot be reached, it seems unwise to persist in seeking it at all costs. Generally, practical alternatives will be conceivable: these may not be supported by all stakeholders, but are apt to catch the interest of an important number.

To be meaningful and practical, this process of converging on solutions requires the participation of decision makers (for example, as a separate subgroup during all or part of the workshops, as suggested by the team from Guatamala). This is all the more important if we consider that institutional support is essential not only during the exercise, but also in following up on the plans made after the final workshop and achieving successful implementation of the recommendations, whether as a whole or in part.

One thing that is not entirely clear about Phase C is where it ends. Nothing should stand in the way of actors who decide to group (or re-group) themselves and work out what they see as the most viable way to improve the social organization of innovation. This process, however, is not necessarily an integral part of a participatory diagnostic process like RAAKS. The need to create consensus on specific solutions, it seems to me, should not interfere with the possibility of achieving a joint appraisal of actual problems and possible solutions.

Finally, one is left with the feeling that the relative success of RAAKS is at least partly due to the fact that it is open ended. There remains much to be desired and developed. It appears to be exactly this feature that allows every team to develop its own style. If this is true, and I think it is, the unfinished character of RAAKS will definitely have to remain.

RAAKS as an appreciative learning system

In this section, I will try to answer my research questions on RAAKS' performance as a methodology (Q4, as given in the Introduction) and its potential and limitations in practice (Q5). The objectives and criteria formulated in Chapter 7 *(Structured inquiry...* and the following two sections) are the starting point for defending RAAKS' efficacy as a methodology; our varied experiences with RAAKS (or parts of it), are the basis for evaluating its use and applicability; and its close relationship to current methodological developments provide a framework for arguing its relevance to development practice. The answers here are not exhaustive or all-inclusive, but our experiences and materials provide a basis for suggesting that RAAKS works in practice, provides a means to stimulate meaningful discourse on the social organization of innovation among stakeholders, and helps to design ways to improve it. RAAKS thus represents a promising new approach to facilitate (initiate, stimulate and guide) platform processes, creating the potential for collaboration and change. In complex innovation theatres, this offers a practical and participatory approach to achieving a shared understanding of complex problems, a diagnosis of key factors and an agreement on what can be done by whom to improve innovation performance.

On the efficacy of RAAKS

RAAKS design and operational objectives are aimed at helping social actors
- improve their understanding of the ways they presently organize themselves for innovation;
- define a problematical situation in one or several meaningful ways; and
- identify actors/define actions relevant to improvement.

With no exceptions, the case studies demonstrate RAAKS' potential to diagnose and discuss relevant aspects of the social organization of innovation. RAAKS helps highlight relevant social practices, diversity in views, concerns and interests between relevant social actors, social interaction for innovation and newly emerging social forms. This leads to the identification of structural or other impairments and opportunities for improvement: RAAKS has demonstrated its strength in making complex problematical situations more transparent and manageable. RAAKS does not support the analysis of specific innovations (whether technical or otherwise), but it does focus on the networking and decision making surrounding volitions, propositions and conditions that are relevant to the emergence of such solutions. Therefore it supports meaningful study and debate about innovation as a *social* process. With respect to the first two elements listed, RAAKS thus fulfils our expectations.

With respect to the third element, two types of RAAKS' outcomes must be distinguished. The first is an increase in awareness and networking among relevant social actors; the second, specific projects aimed at improving innovation performance among social actors. Again, without exception outcomes of the first type were generated by the case studies. This was true not only for the participating social actors (some of which went much further than originally suggested by the methodology), but for RAAKS team members as well. RAAKS studies generate considerable enthusiasm and stimulates intensive inter-action. The second type of outcome is more problematical, and relates to the issues raised at the end of the previous section. Although implementation requires not only useful ideas, time and energy, but also financial resources, RAAKS does not include negotiation regarding resources in the exercise. Views, proposals and interpretations are negotiated, but this must be taken as simply a first step in the identification of tangible proposals. Formulating specific project proposals and carrying them through to implementation is a professional activity in itself, which at present is not included in RAAKS. We have found it implausible that one methodology could both generate an open-minded, joint appraisal of a complex problem situation – one affecting each of the participants directly and deeply – and at the same time require narrowing down the options to produce proposals that would fit the mould required by policymakers and funding agencies. This can be seen as a weakness of RAAKS; another approach might provide more control over the implementa-tion of followup activities. At the same time, the exclusion of specific reference to individual short term interests may be a clue to its success as an analytical tool. The case study materials do not provide conclusive arguments on either side; only a much more elaborate analysis of the followup activities that took place later in the case study areas could tell. This falls outside the scope of this preliminary analysis.

Our next step is to review whether RAAKS adheres to the design criteria suggested in Chapter 7. A first suggestion was to include other theoretical perspectives in addition to the knowledge systems perspective. RAAKS does in fact offer different analytical windows, within the general design inspired by soft knowledge system thinking. These windows, particularly in Phase B, correspond to different theoretical approaches. However, these are by no means all encompassing. RAAKS windows focus on social actors and their views, strategies, communication and social interactions with respect to innovation. Networking practices are studied in detail but research, extension, farming, industrial and trading practices are merely touched on. Technical innovations as such (in the form of new products, artefacts or procedures) receive less attention than in traditional innovation studies. Moreover, RAAKS assumes a broad-spectrum social organizational approach, emphasizing social diversity as well as mutual adjustments among actors. Modifications are conceivable to increase the use of sociological, social psychological and anthropological perspectives. Nevertheless, for studying the social organization of innovation in practice, the materials and experiences presented above lead to the conclusion that the current mix of perspectives serves its purpose: RAAKS does help to quickly focus inquiry and discussions on relevant issues, practices and structural forms of social organization related to innovation, and offers a way to engage in meaningful discourse on critical issues relevant to the way social actors are organized for innovation.

A second design criterion was the creation of a methodology based on appreciative systems thinking, a form of soft systems thinking more suited to the analysis of complex processes of social interaction and construction. Greater emphasis on actor arrangements for creating systemic images was deemed necessary. RAAKS has been shown to stimulate soft systems thinking. It recognizes that social actors will behave as a system only if they wish and know how to do so. To the attention to diversity in world views already implicit in soft systems methodology, RAAKS adds explicit reference to diversity in analytical perspectives. For the most part, the windows do lead to the construction of actor arrangements, images that emphasize particular characteristics of relationships among relevant social actors such as interconnectedness, mutual interdependence, convergence, communication, leadership, coordination, or information and resource transfers. Other windows, however, focus more specifically on characteristics of individual actors, illuminating for example their views, strategies, practices and command of resources. A desire to make a more detailed analysis of relevant practices (for example, seed certification, research, policy implementation or industrial processing), when relevant to the inquiry, could be an incentive to include the use of *activity* arrangements as well. This would extend the scope of the analysis to decision making by relevant actors within their respective practices. Studies by Swanson (1986), Kaimowitz (1989) and Westendorp and Röling (1993) suggest this could be a promising line of inquiry. For RAAKS, as a relatively rapid means of strategic diagnosis, this has not been attempted. Our existing emphasis on actor arrangements has sufficed to adequately highlight both networking practices and structural forms of social organization for innovation.

In addition, the soft systems tradition requires RAAKS to be designed as a learning system. The RAAKS cases presented clearly reflect this. The process created with the help of RAAKS can be described as an interactive learning experience in which three different yet complementary learning processes are intertwined (Figure 4). The decision of some social actors to do a RAAKS exercise generates a process of gathering information, using individual or group interviews, structured with the help of relevant windows. This leads to the creation of different ideas of the situation, laid down in notes, drawings and field reports. During joint inquiry among other social actors and the RAAKS team, these various ideas are drawn up in images reflecting different points of view or analytical angles. These are compared and contrasted during group discussions and workshops, leading to iterative learning cycles among the participants. Individual or group insights into the social organization of innovation may then lead to the proposition of new images, which generally call for new information before they can be understood in detail and presented. Eventually, workshops and discussions lead to validated views and images that can be used in discussing possible courses of action. In this way, all of the learning cycles feed back into the social learning process, which leads to strategic commitments and decisions to follow up. This cycle is completed at least three times during the use of RAAKS (in Phases A, B and C), each time with different research objectives. However, as the cases presented above have shown, learning during RAAKS is never simply cyclical. Many sidesteps, jumps, and loops backward and forward occur. Also, the impetus to social learning generated by a RAAKS exercise is just one additional element in the ongoing social learning among actors (symbolized by the dotted arrow in Figure 4). RAAKS provides only one specific set of inputs into the much wider social process of learning to organize innovation. In other words, the figure should not be taken too literally; it is not intended to suggest any undue generalizations, but to illustrate the systemic nature of RAAKS design and application in practice.

A third criterion is the inclusion of active participation and negotiation in inquiries into the social organization of innovation. Our experiences show this to be easier said than done. In the case studies, social actors' participation exceeded our hopes. However, this entailed a degree of management of communication and group dynamics that caused many teams to flinch. It proved hard work to plan, prepare and guide the participation process. This required commitment not only from the team and other actors involved, but also from the institutions that initiated the exercise and had to carry the extra costs in time, energy and money. Moreover, active participation brings existing power struggles between social actors or subsets of social actors out into the open, as illustrated by the discussion among government representatives in the horse husbandry case. On the other hand, the creation of an 'atmosphere of cordiality even among antagonistic and indifferent actors', as the Nicaraguan team put it, apparently lies within the grasp of those using RAAKS. Particularly in El Salvador and Nicaragua, our experiences show that negotiating new or improved alliances for agricultural innovation can be a part of RAAKS, even to the extent that the social actors involved decide to go several steps further than they originally intended. In other cases, commitment to forming new alliances was less outspoken, but the exercise brought stakeholders to the formulation and discussion of specific suggestions to improve their interaction. Each study did lead to specific action proposals, each rooted in its own natural and socioeconomic context. I conclude that RAAKS stimulates the exchange of views among social actors who are otherwise not frequently engaged in such reflections; it contributes to a shared, even if not agreed, understanding of the situation, and thereby paves the way for negotiating comprehensive and/or partial solutions to the problems defined.

The fourth criterion, *relevant* diversity, however, remains critical. Thoughtful effort both on the part of the RAAKS team and other social actors is needed to recognize the potential contributions of others, some of whom are not normally seen as part of the innovation scene. In fact, critical reflection on current institutional designs and reasoning on the social organization of innovation is required. While in the horse sector case one may argue that a redefinition of relevant diversity was achieved – with the help of the researchers' initial ignorance about the actual situation in the sector, which lead to a definition of 'horse husbandry' that was unprecedented, new even to the actors in the theatre – the Central American cases were different. Here, a traditional definition was used to delineate the innovation theatre for basic grains in the project areas. Nevertheless, all studies recognized the potential importance of various categories of farmers, traders, agro-industries, non-governmental agencies and other actors which, from a traditional point of view, are generally not considered part of agricultural innovation theatres. This of course also had much to do with the quality of the teams. Yet, even if not entirely due to its own merits, RAAKS did facilitate a breakthrough in traditional conceptual barriers with regard to the social organization of innovation.

Figure 4
RAAKS as a learning process

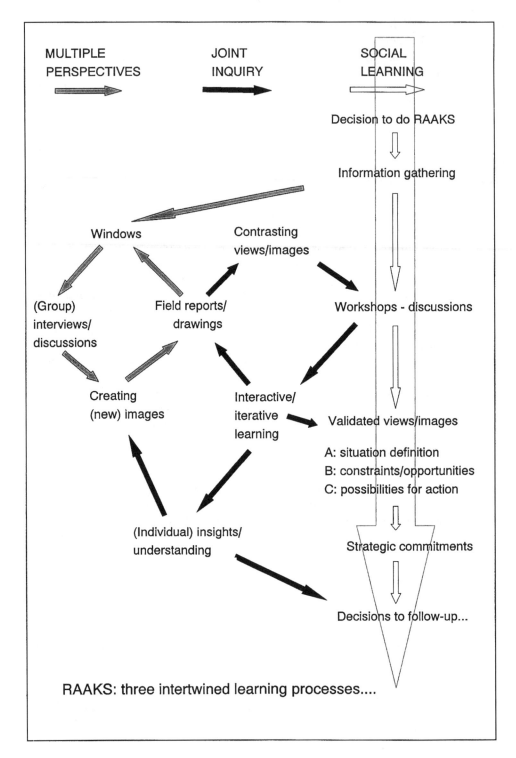

RAAKS: three intertwined learning processes....

Based on the above, I conclude that the use of RAAKS in the trial cases underscores its efficacy as a methodology. If we take 'to identify actors and define actions to improve the social organization of innovation' as representing a *first* step towards the implementation of solutions, RAAKS has proved successful in all three main objectives. It does help to increase awareness, understanding and networking among relevant social actors; it does create a space for exchanging views, propositions and interpretations to arrive at a meaningful definition of complex, ill-defined problem situations, thus stimulating joint reflection and learning; and it does lead to specific proposals for action regarding the improvement of the social organization of innovation. In other words, it lays the foundation for social actors themselves to raise the level of social aggregation at which they wish to exert collective agency. It does *not* guarantee the eventual implementation of their proposals. This is entirely up to the social actors themselves. Further, RAAKS has been shown to abide by the requirements proposed for structured inquiry into the social organization of innovation. Therefore, RAAKS has passed its first test and can be considered efficacious as a methodology: RAAKS can still be improved, but it does what it claims to do.

On the use and applicability of RAAKS

A number of questions remain. First: in which situations is it useful to apply RAAKS? Second, what are some of the ways it can be applied, to suit various circumstances? And third, who or what triggers the use of RAAKS and can effectively support its use in practice? I will review these questions and try to come up with some tentative answers from the case studies. To widen the scope of the argument, experiences of other authors who have used RAAKS (sometimes in an adapted form) will be used as well, allowing me to illustrate ways RAAKS can be used in different contexts.

The case studies treated in this chapter suggest RAAKS is applicable in at least two different social contexts. The origin may lie in the wish of *one* particular social actor to define or redefine its role. The actor faces a complex, almost 'existential' question: what is and what should be my contribution to the diffuse, social innovation process in which so many social actors are involved? The Reference Centre for the Dutch Horse Husbandry sector, affected by reorganization and rapidly changing demands and circumstances, faced this question. As a consequence, better insight into the social organization of innovation within the horse husbandry theatre was needed to make it possible for the Centre to reposition itself and its services. At one moment in time, any stakeholder in agricultural innovation could face a similar question. We will refer to this context as *single-actor-induced*. The key characteristic of such a social context for RAAKS is that a problem is declared by one social actor alone; others are asked to collaborate in reviewing the situation. In this case, RAAKS may help the actor position or reposition itself within the existing innovation configurations and networks, in accordance with existing objectives and interests.

The second context results from unease among *various* actors within one theatre, who feel the way innovation is organized does not live up to their (perhaps varied) expectations. This may not include all possibly relevant actors, nor is it necessary that all perceive the situation in the same way. What they do understand is that to a degree they are dependant on each other if they want to improve it. Also, they may feel there are others – some even unknown to them at that moment – who hold keys to innovative performance. The Regional Programme for Strengthening Agronomic Research on Grains in Central American provided such a context, along with the appreciations among NGDO leaders, staff and clientele that triggered the development of intensive networking activities described in Chapter 5. We will refer to this context as *multi-actor-induced*. An existing declaration by several actors of mutual interdependence, joining hands to improve the social organization of innovation, is characteristic of such a social context. Here, RAAKS can help the actors prepare to increase their level of collective agency by facilitating joint problem appreciation, a diagnosis of constraints and opportunities for cooperation and communication, and the design of strategies for action to tackle some of the problems they have identified as affecting their innovation performance.

Single and multiple-actor-induced contexts have in common that one or several stakeholders consider current innovative performance unsatisfactory, while recognizing a considerable degree of mutual interdependence with others. In addition, they see the lack of understanding of the social organization of innovation among some or all relevant stakeholders as constraining the design and development of adequate solution strategies.

In addition to the horse husbandry study, various other applications of RAAKS have taken place within a single-actor-induced context. Woltersbeek (1990) describes the innovation theatre for shrubs and trees in town planning and development in the Netherlands, and reviews the existing and potential roles of extension. Ravensbergen (1991) compares the social organization of innovation in horticulture in two successful districts, one in the Netherlands and one in Israel. His study strongly suggests there is no one best way to organize innovation. Each theatre requires its own solutions. Meijer (1992) presents a comparative analysis of the work of two different extension agencies working with peasant farmers in Chile. Corten (1991), having studied knowledge management in the Dutch forestry sector, points to the need to distinguish among the several philosophies and styles of Dutch forest owners and managers with respect to forest exploitation, and to develop differentiated research and extension offerings. Noordermeer and van Zanten (1992) provide a similar appraisal for pisciculture.

Experience indicates that RAAKS studies might also be successful in addressing non-agricultural sectors. Boonekamp and Kleis (1992) use RAAKS to explore the constraints and opportunities for inter-institutional collaboration in developing services for elderly citizens in the Netherlands. In the Dutch transport sector, den Bakker et al. (1993) used RAAKS' analytical approach to identify social actors, networking patterns and communication practices relevant to developing and introducing technologies for accomplishing quieter, cleaner and more energy-efficient traffic in urban areas.

All these single-actor-induced studies have in common that they followed RAAKS' analytical design and intentionality, while in each one the procedural design was modified. Validation of results was done with varying degrees of actor participation. In some cases this led to positive reactions from some other actors, who felt they too had benefitted from the study (Woltersbeek, 1990; Ravensbergen, 1991; Corten, 1991). However, sometimes participation led to critical situations between the initiator of the study and other relevant actors (Boonekamp and Kleis, 1992). In yet other cases, the initiators appeared reluctant to intensively share the information collected and resulting insights with others (Noordermeer and van Zanten, 1992; den Bakker et al., 1993). This stresses the fact that in single-actor-induced studies, the initiating actor exerts a considerable degree of control over the procedural design of the study, unless an agreement to the contrary has been achieved beforehand. It also points up the need to have the RAAKS procedure thoroughly explained and agreed upon. Initiating actors do not always want to involve all other actors as actively in the process as RAAKS suggests. They may perceive too-active participation by other stakeholders as a threat to their interests, but most often it seems they believe the theatre is not yet ready to develop more collective agency. In most RAAKS studies, even when participation is active and widespread from the beginning, teams and stakeholders hotly debate these and related issues of participation. Eventually, all of the studies presented here generated a useful diagnosis and specific recommendations for action. Clearly, however, recommendations achieved with widespread participation of stakeholders can be expected to receive stronger followup within the community. Necessarily, studies in which the participation of stakeholders is limited remain more academic and less action oriented.

The multi-actor-induced context is represented in this book by the CORECA/CEE/IICA Regional Programme for Strengthening Agronomic Research on Grains in Central America. This programme had already established an organizational structure among some of the relevant social actors before undertaking the RAAKS study. This assured the cooperation of a number of relevant actors in the exercise and set a number of parameters for directing the followup. In other words, some social actors had already agreed to insert a new structural element into the social organization of innovation, i.e. the joint programme structure, with its political and organizational design. This clearly distinguishes such a multi-actor-induced context from the single-actor situation, in which the participation of all actors in the process is 100% voluntary and no structure for implementation of recommendations is available beforehand. However, it is not hard to imagine that a multi-actor-induced setting with a less formal structure could also arise. The NGDO networks discussed in Chapter 5 represent such situations. When NGDO leaders decide to initiate networking activities, no formal programme structure links them together, although they may decide to create one later. Informal links among the organizations (and those, for example, with a common donor agency) may well precede such an initiative.

The Central American case studies illustrate that RAAKS can contribute to increased understanding and to the formulation of precise proposals for action and/or intervention. However, its use also creates expectations. Participating social actors come to expect support to begin or continue the activities they jointly decided upon during the RAAKS exercise. This creates claims upon the initiating organizations to facilitate and even finance such initiatives. We have observed two possible drawbacks. First, due to lack of information or, alternatively, due to excessive enthusiasm the RAAKS team and other actors may formulate initiatives that may not fall entirely within the mandate of the initiators; or the way they are presented may seem to deviate from expectations. Careful support from specialized consultants may be needed to rework such proposals to fit policy, planning and funding requirements. Second, on the other hand a RAAKS team can be too much aware of the existence of such a structural element in the social organization of innovation. A bias in favour of overemphasizing the role of formal institutions can draw attention from the fact that most social learning for innovation is self-guiding, and does not require management or intervention. Neither of these became an issue in the Central American cases, due to the professional quality of the teams, their acute awareness of relevant policy and institutional developments in the region, their mutual support during meetings and workshops, and the guidance provided by the Regional Executive Directorate and its consultants.

Additional experiences with RAAKS in multi-actor-induced health promotion contexts have been obtained by Adolfse (1992), who explored the health food knowledge and information system in the city of Horsens, Denmark. Naafs (1994) combined RAAKS and the WHO/RAP (Rapid Appraisal) methodology to identify opportunities for a community-based nutrition promotion programme in Luria, Spain. In both cases, the Healthy Cities 'SUPER' Project, a nutrition promotion project in six cities of Europe (Vaandrager and Koelen, 1994), created a context in which RAAKS could be implemented. Each of the research teams strongly emphasized actor participation, while adapting particular aspects of RAAKS to their specific needs and circumstances.

It seems safe to conclude that in social contexts similar to those mentioned, RAAKS is a practical approach to inquiring into the social organization of innovation. It works, it complements other participatory approaches and it produces the outcomes one may expect of it. The cost in energy, time and financing is considerable, even if it implies only part-time involvement by team members during a period of about six months. Therefore, I agree with the Central American teams that RAAKS should be used primarily in areas or sectors that deserve special attention: where innovation is in particularly bad shape; due to strategic importance; in programmes that must make an impact on the social organization of innovation within a limited period of time; and/or in projects specifically dedicated to improving innovation performance. One example of the latter might be a project intended to stimulate the emergence of innovation-oriented multi-actor networks. Naturally, less comprehensive versions of RAAKS can be used in less demanding contexts.

The combination of RAAKS with other alternative systems of inquiry has been suggested several times and must be explored further. This is also true for the idea of incorporating RAAKS in regular programme or project evaluation activities. This seems a viable option, yet no one has tried it so far. Finally, an intriguing option has recently emerged: the use of RAAKS in a more problem-oriented form. In our examples, RAAKS is generally directed at a sector or an agricultural area, with more or less emphasis on a particular target clientele. Recent experiences in the Netherlands (van Weperen et al., 1994) and Central America (van Sluys, pers. comm.) suggest that RAAKS can also be focused more directly on one or more burning issues, such as the development of new agricultural activities or the incorporation of environmentally sound technologies in farming or other practices. Such a shift in focus allows the domain of inquiry to be defined more precisely, and emphasis can be shifted somewhat from problem clarification and definition to creating adequate resource coalitions to following through on viable solution strategies.

A third social context in which RAAKS has been used is in extension and research training. Examples include graduate and postgraduate courses at the Communication and Innovation Studies Department of the Agricultural University of Wageningen; the International Course on Rural Extension (ICRE) at the International Agricultural Centre (IAC), Wageningen, in the Netherlands; and the International Course on Research in Agriculture (ICRA), at the International Centre for Development Oriented Research in Agriculture (CIRAD), in Montpellier, France. Learning-by-doing RAAKS can produce remarkable results, as the excursions of our international MSc students into the Dutch ornamental shrubs and trees sector demonstrate. Guided by the National Reference Centre for Plant Production, students visited three different communities over three days, later reporting their results to a meeting of stakeholders. The discussions on the social organization of innovation in tree and shrub production were lively and to the point, to the satisfaction of the Dutch participants – even though at times they were surprised at what a group of foreign students could learn about their practices in such a brief period. As a result, the next year the farmers' organization asked a new group of students to return, to analyse problems in the flow of marketing information among traders, retailers, marketing bodies and producers. Together with our experience in training national RAAKS teams in Central America, these experiences illustrate that educational inquiries into the social organization of innovation are a third context in which RAAKS has value.

The types of professionals who might benefit from applying RAAKS to their work are quite varied. All, of course, must be concerned with advising, managing or directing innovation. In agriculture, this might include agricultural consultants, specialists from governmental and non-governmental agencies, researchers, extension or information managers. However, using RAAKS successfully requires high quality team work, along with the management of participation, communication and group dynamics. This calls for knowledge, skills and attitudes that have not typically been cultivated by agricultural researchers. Therefore, training in the use of RAAKS needs particular attention. As one supporting component, Central American teams suggested creating a regional network of consultants to generate and exchange RAAKS experiences. Networking on RAAKS would seem a chance to create the conditions for effective learning-by-doing. (Obviously, this does not apply to RAAKS alone; further development of other alternative methods of inquiry requires similar conditions.) A networking approach is all the more important given that RAAKS is and should remain 'unfinished business', a flexible method. As Central American research teams very specifically pointed out, its success depends on this. RAAKS provides practical guidelines for inquiry without attaching a methodological straightjacket. It provides teams with a choice of windows and tools, yet does not prescribe more than a general 'logic of inquiry'. Therefore it can (and must) be adapted to fit the local context, views and inter-pretations. Exactly because of this, RAAKS teams need to be composed of professionals who are aware of and skilled in what they are doing.

On RAAKS' relevance to development practice

From a practitioners' point of view, a tool can resemble a hammer and even work like a hammer, but it becomes useful only when it is integrated in a carpenter's practice. There-fore, after concluding that RAAKS has satisfied its design and practical requirements to an acceptable degree, I want to briefly relate it to current methodological developments. How does RAAKS compare with the more general objectives and criteria that have been pro-posed for methodological approaches of this sort? This is not the moment for a definitive evaluation. Still, I will make a first attempt to tentatively characterize RAAKS' relevance to development practice. The principles and criteria formulated by Pretty (1994) for 'alternative systems of inquiry' will be used as a reference. As development problems grow more complex and the levels of agency required to tackle them adequately increase this rapidly growing methodological tradition is gaining more and more strength. RAAKS' roots lie in soft systems thinking and participatory action research, so it seems plausible that RAAKS can be seen as a part of this emerging tradition. Is this really the case?

Despite enormous variety, alternative methods of inquiry regarding development have a number of fundamental principles in common (Pretty, 1994): a defined methodo-logy, defined and used as a learning system; the use of multiple perspectives – seeking to explore diversity rather than to characterize complexity by compressing it into statistical averages; insistence on group inquiry; context specificity in methodological designs; facilitating participation of experts and stakeholders; and a focus on designing and imple-menting sustained action. A number of advantages of such approaches have been discussed in the literature. A few examples: they contribute to overcoming single-discipline limitations and to giving a voice to the subjects of our inquiries (Whyte, 1991); they provide an alternative to positivist research paradigms, to use in addressing issues of sustainability (Pretty, 1994); they provide us with a way of researching that combines the exploration of complex and dynamic situations with taking action to improve them (Koelen and Vaandrager, 1994); and, by engaging stakeholders actively as co-researchers, they may help social actors move from joint problem appreciation to collective action (cf. Röling, 1994).

More relevant to our argument here is that such approaches face at least two important methodological challenges. The first relates to what is generally referred to as 'scientific rigour' (Whyte, 1991) in data collection, organization and information handling procedures. The second refers to the possible contribution of these approaches to the advancement of social science. In this paragraph I will concentrate on the first of these issues; the second, with respect to RAAKS, will be considered in Chapter 9.

Our judgement as to the scientific rigor of a methodology depends on how we define rigour (Whyte, 1991; Pretty, 1994). If it is defined in terms of researchers' detachment from the context and subjects of their inquiry, obviously no participatory approach is 'rigorous'. However, such a separation between the observer and the observed is virtually inconceivable in social science intended to promote development. To claim the existence of this sort of rigour would also be at odds with the conceptualization of knowledge defended in Chapter 7. Therefore, I will follow Pretty (1994), who proposes an entirely different set of criteria for the trustworthiness of scientific information. Koelen and Vaandrager (1994) define similar criteria for evaluating the performance of research on health promotion. For my limited purposes here, criteria for defending the trustworthiness of information generated by means of alternative systems of inquiry can be grouped around three main issues. I will use these as standards against which RAAKS can be compared to provide a preliminary judgment on its performance.

Scientific rigor can be defined in terms of creating conditions for mutual learning, cross-checking and validating information between researchers and stakeholders within the situation that has been defined as the object of inquiry. Checking by participants '...forces researchers to go through a rigorous process of checking the facts with those with first hand knowledge before any reports are written' (Whyte, 1991). Of course the same applies to ideas, views and opinions expressed by different stakeholders and/or researchers. Participant checking can be complemented with persistent observations, peer checking and triangulation, comparing results from different sources, methods and investigators. Various techniques are proposed to support such procedures (Pretty, 1994; Koelen and Vaandrager, 1994). Thus: the first key issue for achieving trustworthy information through alternative systems of inquiry is a *continuous cross-referencing of information, views, insights and relevant questions* with the help of multiple cases, investigators, sources and methods of information gathering.

A second element is rooted in the pursuit of diversity. By *seeking to express relevant differences* – in views, opinions, interpretations and presentation of data – alternative systems of inquiry create a strong joint awareness of, and reflection upon, bias among stakeholders and researchers alike. This process relies heavily on the continuous reworking of hypotheses, visualizations and detailed descriptive information. It triggers mutual learning and re-orientation of inquiry, in turn leading to more profound and better considered analysis and decision making in relation to possible conclusions. Therefore, the second key to accomplishing trustworthiness in such an inquiry is to *generate effective networking practices* among people from often very different social practices. This requires active engagement between researchers and stakeholders, as well as among stakeholders. It leads to devoting specific attention to establishing joint agendas and working procedures. The researchers, or experts, take on the role of facilitators in this process.

A third key issue is the impact on *the stakeholders' capacity to know and act* (Pretty, 1994), or, put differently, on building local institutions to increase the capacity of people to participate, and to initiate action on their own (Koelen and Vaandrager, 1994). The trustworthiness of our results may be judged on the basis of their impact when stake-holders take over the initiative from the researcher–facilitators.

The intertwined learning processes of RAAKS shown in Figure 4 oblige researchers and stakeholders to recognize multiple views and analytical perspectives, to draw upon diverse sources of knowledge and information and to contrast these within interactive and iterative learning cycles to arrive at conclusions. In practice too, this produces the continuous cross-referencing of views, ideas, insights and information referred to earlier. Moreover, the various RAAKS cycles and subcycles of information gathering, organizing, discussion and decision making, in which working hypotheses, graphic presentations and conclusions are continuously created and revised, stimulate joint learning and reflection within the team and, during interviews and workshops, within the group of participating stakeholders. As we have shown, RAAKS stimulates active networking among teams and relevant stakeholders; this leads to initiatives on the part of participants that often go beyond the original scope of the methodology. Clearly, our early applications of RAAKS confirm its consistency with the action research tradition emerging among development researchers who develop and use alternative systems of inquiry.

Our experiences, however, also point up some of the intrinsic difficulties such methodologies face in practice. The trustworthiness of the results is heavily dependent upon what those performing the exercise consider 'relevant diversity' in views, opinions, sources, methods and investigators. I have learned that perhaps the most difficult bias to make explicit and take as the object of critical reflection is the mental model, linear or otherwise, that guides people in their reflections upon knowledge and its role in development. Accepting too low a level of diversity may seriously hamper a teams' performance. At the same time, it is very hard to conceive of a standard for 'adequate' diversity. Insisting upon an intentional and persistent search for diversity in the context under study and a permanent debate among teams and other stakeholders as to its adequacy – given the purposes of the investigation – seems to be the best we can do at present.

Second, I have learned that we must simply accept that the quality of a RAAKS exercise depends heavily on the quality of the team and the way they manage interactive learning processes, communication and group dynamics. These directly affect the trustworthiness of the results. Therefore our experience confirms that 'systems of participatory inquiry ... imply new roles for development professionals, and these all require a new professionalism with new concepts, values, methods and behaviour' (Pretty, 1994). To enhance the trustworthiness of our methods and approaches, we need professionals who combine an inquisitive and creative mind and a social problem-solving attitude, with research, communication and facilitation skills.

Finally, I think our experience demonstrates we must not only accept but value contextual influences on our research. Quite the opposite of discarding such experiences as 'non-scientific', this leads us to address the socio-natural context explicitly as part of the problem. We can no longer pretend to isolate our research problems from it, nor can we pretend to 'freeze' the context while we are there. Contextual descriptions, analyses and debate should acquire greater prominence and stimulate the review of every perspective, point of view or other piece of information within its proper context. This has important consequences for our research processes. What has seemed to some 'endless descriptions of irrelevant detail' may acquire a new relevance. At the same time, the well-probed and agreed acceptance of particular contextual factors (including the long term or non-manipulable ones) as 'facts' or trends to be reckoned with could speed up the research process considerably.

Conclusions and critical issues

It is difficult to draw definitive conclusions on a flexible, open-ended methodology such as RAAKS after an initial series of field tests. Still, I believe the information and discussions presented above provide a basis for answering my last two research questions: yes, a practical methodology can be designed that meets the objectives and criteria laid down at the beginning of Chapter 7. RAAKS has convincingly proved its efficacy and applicability in the field (Q4). Its potential and limitations are less easy to point out. RAAKS is definitely more useful in some contexts than in others. In general, RAAKS can be expected to contribute the most to situations in which a sufficient number of stakeholders are aware that 'society' requires them to continually seek innovation in their practices; who experience a 'lack of new ideas and new, viable options' and perceive this as a problem; who realize that innovation requires exposing oneself to other stakeholders' ideas, rather than avoiding them; and who sense that the current lack of progress is important enough that something must be done. RAAKS can be carried out with varying degrees of participation and still provide interesting results. The level of participation, however, may be closely related to the eventual impact of the RAAKS exercise on innovation performance at the community level. In situations where social actors are not willing to sit at one table to seriously discuss their collective innovation performance, a participatory RAAKS exercise is clearly not the first step that would come to mind.

But how trustworthy is this evaluation of results regarding the use of RAAKS? I have argued that RAAKS includes the necessary elements to be a trustworthy approach to applied scientific inquiry, but how biased are my evaluations? In the near future, others must – and certainly will – take part in this discussion. For now three arguments will be offered in favour of my conclusions, and one doubt opposing them. This also provides an opportunity to mention some biases that may have influenced my research. Nevertheless the final conclusion, based on a methodological evaluation of RAAKS, is that a solid set of propositions can indeed be suggested.

On the trustworthiness of the methodological evaluation

The first argument – which strongly favours acceptance of the evaluation – is that in all studies my own involvement was limited to providing initial training for the teams, plus some support in the final drafting of reports. Otherwise the teams' exposure to me was minimal. Only in the horse husbandry sector, the first case we carried out, did I actively take part in both workshops. Similarly, in Central America I was involved in initial training and discussions; the support given by consultants and the Executive Directorate to the national teams was not affected by my continuing presence. The data I have used for my methodological evaluation of RAAKS includes the written statements and pondered judgments of the teams, cross-referenced between individuals and between teams, in some cases complemented by observations of consultants or my own notes from the training and evaluation sessions. By setting up the RAAKS applications in this way, I believe I have created a 'distance' between myself and other persons involved in the RAAKS' design, which enhances the claims for trustworthiness.

The second argument is based on the professional quality of the teams. All participants were well-trained researchers or research managers, extension managers, trainers or field workers. None of them had an *a priori* interest in promoting RAAKS. All went through considerable difficulties and dedicated considerable amounts of precious time and energy to the experimental use of RAAKS. In my opinion, they would not have done this if they had not felt that participation in a RAAKS exercise made a significant contribution to their minds and work. Their enthusiasm and positive criticism are genuine indicators of RAAKS' relevance and efficacy as a methodology – even if it reflects less positively on RAAKS' efficiency in reaching its objectives! In this respect, the quality of the teams may have obscured flaws in its practical design.

The third argument is that, if ever a comprehensive methodology can be tested in a 'laboratory situation', the Basic Grains Programme in Central America provided the right context. The initiative and coordination of the Regional Executive Directorate, as well as the supporting consultants, guaranteed uniform and supportive conditions for teams to work in. This synchronized their efforts. Eventually, teams were able to implement RAAKS according to its design and the instructions provided. Draft reports of every single application were presented on time for discussion at the final regional workshop. Finally, the permanence of the teams, to which members were added but which almost never lost anyone, provided a continuity and seriousness one would expect to make a contribution to a considered reflection on the exercise as a whole.

The one thing I can think of which may have flawed the methodological evaluation presented is this same enthusiasm. The initial training in knowledge system thinking and RAAKS seemed so literally to feed into the questions most team members had already been asking themselves with respect to their professional environment, that perhaps their enthusiasm was overdone and might have dissipated to some degree if more time had passed between the initial training, the RAAKS exercise and the final evaluation of its results. Perhaps some of the initial optimism would then have worn off, being replaced by justifiable scepticism as to the practical use of the methodology. My own appreciation of this issue is however that, due to their earlier experiences with 'rapid' and 'systemic' methodologies, most of the professionals on the national teams did in fact reach this stage within the period it took to execute and evaluate the exercise. Therefore their optimism with respect to RAAKS can be considered not rash statements but well-probed and well-weighed opinions.

Some propositions

RAAKS has passed its initial tests. Only further integration in development practice, leading to more extended use, will begin to answer questions about whether it indeed represents a new and useful tool in the hands of those who are professionally engaged in the management of knowledge and information for innovation in agriculture. There are already indications, as noted earlier, that RAAKS can contribute significantly to platform processes, helping social actors to raise their ability to act collectively to a level that is adequate to address the complex social and ecological issues they face today. Further, RAAKS' potential to contribute to improving and, if necessary, reorganizing practices related to innovation in agriculture or other sectors has been confirmed. Finally, RAAKS itself can be developed further to suit different contexts, and it may inspire colleagues to develop methodologies that follow similar lines but are focused on domains of inquiry other than the social organization of innovation.

For RAAKS, some future developments can be envisioned. The use of *actor arrangements* to visualize complex social wholes, however important from the point of view of addressing strategizing and social interaction for development, should be complemented with the use of *activity arrangements*. First however this line of soft systems analysis will have to be further explored, to yield a more comprehensive set of instruments of inquiry than are available now. Whether *input/output arrangements* may eventually be developed to suit soft systems analysis remains to be seen.

The design and development of 'alternative systems of inquiry' proves a demanding task. Systematic research is needed to do it successfully. 'Just letting it happen' in the margin of development programmes seems unsatisfactory. In the next century, our approaches to dealing with complex organizational issues may well prove more relevant to our survival as a species than any of the specific socio-natural relationships we are able to 'unravel'. In addition to adequate funding for applied methodological research, international networking among professionals within relevant international institutes and university programmes is urgently needed.

9. Summary and conclusions

This chapter can be used as an executive summary of what has been done and the results obtained. It can also serve as either an introduction to the book as a whole, or a quick overview for those who have too little time to go through the rest of the book: in both cases, I hope it will motivate you to read other chapters as well! In addition, this chapter introduces a number of pending issues relevant to those who are professionally engaged in studying and/or facilitating complex innovation processes. Further, it offers an opportunity to review and indeed judge the coherence of the thoughts and arguments expressed in previous chapters.

Research questions, expected results and methodology

My experience with agricultural development projects, first as an extension communications specialist and later as a project manager, provided the starting point for this study. Dissatisfaction with the practical relevance of conventional innovation theories triggered the need for a more generic, more action-oriented approach: one that can help in understanding innovation as a complex, social process. This led to a wish to go back to what people actually do, including the ways they organize themselves to seek innovation in their practices, and to build an empirically validated perspective on this base. The *social organization of innovation* became the domain of inquiry. Box 9 summarizes the research questions posed in the Introduction.

Box 9
Five research questions to guide this inquiry

Q1. How do actors organize themselves to achieve agricultural innovation?
Q2. What do they actually do to achieve the transformations they want?
Q3. What criteria should an action-oriented methodology meet, if it is to contribute to the facilitation of innovation in agriculture?
Q4. Can a practical methodology be designed in line with these criteria?
Q5. What are the potentials and limitations of this methodology in practice?

Understanding complex social processes of innovation is not enough. An inquiry should also lead to improvements in our interventions. As a result, in addition to an *exploratory path* used to gain empirical insight and new relevant perspectives (and focusing primarily on research questions Q1 and Q2), the research questions set out a *design path*. The intention of the design path was to formulate a practical methodology to help stakeholders improve innovation performance; it addresses questions Q3, Q4 and Q5. The expected results of both paths are given in Box 10.

[handwritten note, left margin: I'm only covering highlighted parts]

The methodological approach chosen is essentially qualitative; but even more than that, it is reflective. Hands-on experiences of development professionals are a permanent reference. Moreover, the intention has not been so much to prove or disprove already known propositions but to generate new ones. Therefore, case studies have been used to anchor the study. Over a period of nine years, four field studies and two synthesis studies have been done, these latter reviewing over 25 cases. Moreover, at the time this book was written, the methodological design had been tried out in 15 different areas. In all, the cases discussed cover 15 different countries, including the Netherlands.

The decision to use the knowledge systems perspective (Röling, 1988, 1994) to organize the studies was at first mostly intuitive; it provided a heuristic instrument to study the social organization of innovation that seemed richer than any other conceptualizations I knew of. Used with soft systems thinking (Checkland, 1989; Checkland and Scholes, 1990), it provided a forceful combination to initiate my inquiries.

Background from the case studies

The Dutch cases discussed in Chapter 2 underscore the relevance of communication networks among farmers, bookkeepers, salespeople, veterinary doctors, advisers, researchers, extension workers and many others when successful innovation is the objective. These cases demonstrate the limitations of a concept of knowledge transfer in which one actor is the 'source' and another the 'user'. Instead, as the case studies show, each stakeholder in agricultural innovation is – at the same time – both a 'user' and a 'source' of relevant knowledge and information. During active participation in diverse, interactive communication networks, each social actor adds specific value to a gradual, task-oriented *integration* of different strands of knowledge. This participation provides a wide range of ideas and technological options; social actors can choose among them. The case studies also demonstrate the strategizing and professionalization that occurs with respect to communication for innovation.

[handwritten note, left margin: This is how my R is viewing stakeholders + OB itself]

As underscored by a case from Nariño, Colombia (Chapter 3), the existence of joint learning opportunities among relevant social actors and the integration of knowledge and information from a variety of relevant sources are important elements in explaining successful innovation. However, the Nariño case also points up the importance of mutual *[Relevance of mutual adjustments]* adjustments among relevant institutions and other social actors. A direct link between inter-institutional coordination and practical impact is suggested. Additional important factors are institutional leadership, strategic consensus and effective resource linkages, within a socioeconomic and political context that is conducive to agricultural change. The case study demonstrates that the capacity to achieve innovation in agricultural practices should be seen as a collective, social competence, rather than as an individual character- *[Social choice theory?]* istic of any of the social actors involved.

The first synthesis study (Chapter 4) explores the emergence of institutional leadership and the coordination of tasks among institutional actors in complex agricultural innovation theatres. It shows alliances may be forged that take it upon themselves to promote a particular type of innovation process, targeting a particular category of farmers. Within such alliances, leadership patterns and coordinating mechanisms evolve, which may come to successfully regulate collective actions and decision making. These 'emergent' structural arrangements are labelled innovation configurations. Such configurations are renegotiable and, naturally, in flux. On the other hand, over time they may become increasingly rigid and inflexible: this can reduce innovation performance. Innovation configurations are sometimes in a sense 'designed', but this is a design achieved through a diffuse, social process of accommodation among a variety of stakeholders rather than a rationally planned organizational design. If we want to facilitate complex innovation processes, it seems essential to understand the role of design and the emergence of effective organizational and personal alliances. The analysis of configurations, with several amendments to Mintzberg's (1983) approach, is proposed as an instrument.

In the second synthesis study (Chapter 5), I look at alliances that have been established for the explicit purpose of improving the social organization of innovation: NGO networks for enhancing sustainable agriculture. Their 'networking', as shown by this study, concentrates on four main functions: creating opportunities for learning through joint reflection; mutual support; joint advocacy (sometimes); and network management – that is, organizing their interaction in such a way that they are able to achieve their objectives as effectively and efficiently as possible. Networks, like other configurations, require strategic consensus, an agreed definition of tasks and responsibilities and the presence of coordinating mechanisms. However, networks among non-governmental development organizations seem to differ in several ways from configurations dominated *[NGO networks]* by institutional actors. The main differences lie in the formative process leading to the establishment of an NGO network, in an explicit recognition of mutual interdependence and the need to 'learn from each other' as well as the emphasis networks place on participation and decentralized decision making.

Winding up the exploratory path: towards a theory of social organization for innovation

A number of propositions have been formulated with respect to the questions that guided the exploratory path (Q1, Q2, Box 9). They merit further empirical research but, as shown *[good expression]* in Chapter 6, seem well-grounded in the cases and synthesis studies as well as in current professional and academic thought. They represent the contours of a conceptual approach to understanding the social organization of innovation: *agricultural innovation* can be seen as the result of interplay among social actors from relevant social practices. It is a diffuse, social process of both individual and collective inquiry, which leads to new or modified problem definitions and practical choices of solutions. These actors inquire into volitions, propositions and contexts. *Volitions* are the 'projects' actors express, in language or action, to make sense of their contribution to innovation and social change in agriculture. *Propositions* refer to the solution strategies – organizational (including aspects of social organization) and scientific/technical – that are identified as relevant to particular volitions. *Contexts* refer to the socially constructed as well as the natural conditions that reduce actors' degrees of freedom to create/choose among volitions and propositions. The organization and quality of the interplay determines the course of innovation. The *social organization of innovation* may then be characterized as the way in which social actors organize themselves for and perform the interplay.

What social actors actually do to achieve innovation in their practices (Q2) may then be qualified as *networking in-and-between relevant social practices*. Social practices emerge from the activities of discernible sets of social actors, who define and sustain competent performance through some form of social interaction. Relevant practices may include farming, research, extension, education, input distribution, agro-industries, commercialization, mass media communication, policymaking, seed certification, etc. To gain access to a wide range of options and insights, social actors actively engage in building and managing interactive relationships – with social actors from their own and/or other practices – which by some standard they consider relevant to their concerns. Networking for innovation comprises first, the creation of joint learning opportunities among social actors of relevant social practices; second, the interactive probing of relevant volitions, propositions and contexts; and finally, the pooling of energies and, often but not necessarily, other resources. Communication plays an important role. Further, networking is tied closely to the daily work of the relevant social actors. It is an integral part of the activities of the 'knowing' individual. The *appreciative character* of networking – in which all that happens is strongly coloured by the appreciations, the perceptions, personal preferences, ways of viewing things and the social interactions among those who take part – stems from the need to continually make choices. While networking, participants are required over and over again to make decisions on whether to include in the networking effort a particular actor, practice, volition, proposition or context. A decision to include takes energy, time and/or money and can only be justified when the element in question is perceived as relevant to the inquiry. As a consequence, such decisions are arbitrary ones, taken within the context of the current relationships among stakeholders in a particular innovation process and according to their appreciation of the situation. My findings suggest a direct relationship can be postulated between the quality of the networking among relevant social actors and the outcomes of a particular innovation process.

In answer to research question Q1, I propose that the way social actors organize themselves to take part in, and possibly direct, the innovative interplay can be characterized by describing the structural forms that emerge as a result of sustained networking and studying their interrelationships. These structural forms – convergences, resource coalitions, communication networks and innovation configurations – merit particular attention from students of the social organization of innovation. Each represents macro-tructures that come into existence as the result of largely unintended consequences of social action. As *emergent* forms they are not fully describable or explicable in terms of micro-events. They reflect dynamics of their own. They lead to outcomes that often seem not to have been decided upon but simply to have 'happened'. *Convergences* emerge when social actors narrow down the scope of their arguments and the range of issues and alternative scenarios they are willing to consider; views and interests of two or more actors may then converge. *Resource coalitions* emerge when social actors decide to pool their resources in a joint performance. These coalitions are the result of strategizing by social actors who use their assets to enrol others in their 'projects'. *Communication networks* emerge as a direct consequence of social actors' decisions to create joint learning opportunities and to produce and exchange information among themselves.

Over time, networking may lead to the gradual development of a pattern of more or less durable relationships among a number of social actors who perceive each other as relevant. Such *innovation configurations* harbour the mutually accepted views, procedures and ground rules for collective behaviour with respect to one or more types of innovation. In such configurations, convergences, resource coalitions and communication networks come to coincide well enough to make it possible to work together by building a strategic consensus, a clear definition of tasks and responsibilities and a rational allocation of resources. While in most cases it seems difficult to envision the 'orchestration' of innovation processes, a configuration provides a context in which some form of orchestration, if only the coordination of innovative efforts, is not unimaginable. Still, such emergent alliances are continually changing, and may take unexpected or even largely unintended turns; nevertheless, at their base lies a common concern shared among a number of relevant social actors. Only if social actors remain willing and able to negotiate mutual adjustments and put them into effect is there the possibility that the configuration may eventually become and remain well organized and stable. At that point, adequate institutional leadership, an agreed division of tasks and effective coordinating mechanisms will be in place.

[handwritten margin note: CB's job to facilitate this among stakeholders, but choice/response/function is still autonomous]

[handwritten note below text: nothing is stable, esp in A+D.]

Being well-organized and stable, however, does not automatically mean being able to easily adjust to changing circumstances, new challenges and/or threats. In our studies we have looked particularly at *institutional configurations*. These alliances for innovation – a specific form of innovation configuration – emerge among government or semi-governmental institutions, industrial companies and/or farmers' organizations. Depending upon the type of leadership and the way coordination is achieved, many different types of institutional configurations may evolve; some are better adjusted to meeting the innovative demands of modern development than others. The analysis of such configurations is proposed as an instrument to use in studying the effects of leadership and coordination on innovative performance.

[handwritten margin note: Institutional configuration]

The innovation configurations that evolve as a result of networking by individuals (farmers or professionals) or non-governmental organizations appear to have a character other than those emerging among government institutions. In both cases, convergences, resource coalitions and communication networks may coincide sufficiently to provide purpose and organizational strength to the network. However, the formative process leading to their emergence is completely different. My study suggests that networks among non-governmental agricultural development organizations are created intentionally, as a space for joint learning and reflection. Mutual interdependence is a given, recognized by all involved. Not only technical solutions but also intervention objectives are subject to debate. Active participation of all member organizations is not just a formal requirement, it is a working standard. The formative process itself is taken as an opportunity to build a strong foundation for future cooperation, not just an opportunity for renegotiating the institutional balance of power. Finally, networks not only recognize mutual interdependence, they nurture it by means of programmes for mutual support and services; and sometimes by jointly taking part in the public debate.

For government institutions to be able to participate actively in networks similar to those of individuals and NGOs, a number of requirements would have to be met. First, networking requires a number of social actors who are not only 'like-minded', but who also have a fair degree of autonomy with respect to adjusting their views and strategies. Hierarchical power structures such as those in most government bureaucracies seem to be at odds with networking for innovation. To facilitate effective networking between government and other agencies, central authorities would have to 'draw back' from control of day-to-day operations. But another question is whether government authorities would ever be willing to cede to decentralized government institutions the time and space to effectively 'test the waters of co-operation' in the first place. 'Planned activism' – a first fundamental step in networking – seems incompatible with the current efficiency-oriented bureaucratic discourse.

Which types of configurations can best support innovation? One important issue is that, historically, social forms have emerged out of the intended and unintended consequences of social interactions, often over periods of many years. Convergences, resource coalitions and communication networks, institutional configurations and innovation networks affect more than the collective designs and strategies of stakeholders. Hence, in their structure and operations they mirror not only the innovation theory their constituent actors had in mind but also the subsequent historical developments that affected them. As a result, all social forms relevant to innovation may demonstrate a certain inertia when faced with changing circumstances. Because of their history and context, one may postulate that this applies even more strongly to institutional configurations and long-established networks. Therefore, *innovation networks* of individuals and NGOs may prove to be the more flexible forms of social organization for innovation that are needed by modern agricultural development. However, this will only be true to the extent that networks succeed in maintaining themselves as 'learning organizations', dedicated to networking for high quality innovation.

To what extent, if at all, can the proposed conceptual approach strengthen the knowledge and information systems perspective? In my view it does so in two respects. First, it offers a number of new 'windows' – new perspectives – that can be used to analyse the domain under study. It focuses our attention on networking as a social practice aimed at support-ing innovation and on convergences, resource coalitions, communication networks and innovation configurations as emergent social forms relevant to the study of complex innovation theatres. Also, it suggests volitions, propositions and contexts as fundamental ingredients in the probing, social interaction and decision making among stakeholders that characterize complex innovation theatres. Second, it offers a more comprehensive approach to reasoning about the social organization of innovation. It addresses innovation as a social rather than a technological process, and puts knowing human actors at the centre; it recognizes social interplay and the way actors appreciate their situations as cornerstones of innovation; and it enables us to reason more integrally about key issues such as innovation performance, communication, integration, coordination, intentionality and choice, which hitherto could only be addressed separately. In other words, this study has yielded some preliminary elements of what could become an action-oriented theory of social organization for innovation. Thus, the conceptual framework may contribute to integrating as well as deepening appreciative knowledge systems thinking.

Bringing the design path to a close: RAAKS, an action-oriented methodology

RAAKS[1] is a soft systems methodology, meant to enable stakeholders to engage in meaning-ful discourse about the social organization of innovation and to design measures to

1. *RAAKS, in the introduction, stands for 'rapid or relaxed appraisal of agricultural knowledge systems'. See also the manual* Networking for innovation: a participatory actor-oriented methodology *(Salomon and Engel, 1997).*

improve it. The images RAAKS helps create emphasize social interaction among social actors from different relevant practices and stimulate debate and reflection. Active participation of stakeholders is assumed, as are ongoing reappraisals of the problem definition. The objectives of RAAKS are to raise awareness and understanding, and to help participants probe new alliances and formulate action proposals. That is, RAAKS contributes to a cumulative, social learning process among stakeholders. It is facilitative and action-oriented, and has the potential to generate tangible results, leading from problem appraisal (Phase A) to action definition (Phase C), while stimulating joint inquiry into relevant practices, networking and emergent structural forms of social organization for innovation (Phases A and B). RAAKS accomplishes this by offering a variety of windows, or ways to examine the situation from different analytical perspectives. To integrate these windows, a conceptual framework rooted in appreciative knowledge systems thinking is used.

RAAKS is based on the research findings presented in this book in three ways. First, it adheres to the design criteria formulated in answer to research question Q3. RAAKS applies a knowledge systems perspective, but provides additional theoretical perspectives as well. It is based on appreciative systems thinking, and offers stakeholders the possibility *Assumes* of engaging in meaningful discourse on the social organization of innovation. Lastly, it *people act* encourages a thorough reappraisal of the problem situation, combined with active *from rational* participation of stakeholders and tangible results. RAAKS' close match to these criteria is *+ social choice* discussed in Chapter 7 (see 'RAAKS as an appreciative learning system'). Second, RAAKS sets the stage for innovation-related interplay among actors, to improve performance. The procedures included are based on the lessons we have learned about such interplay between social actors, how it is organized in practice and how it can be improved. A RAAKS exercise, as it were, 'mimics' practices that have been observed to be related to success in innovation. Volitions, propositions and contexts are made explicit, social interactions among stakeholders are intensified, and both an orientation to action and an integration with daily activities are maintained. Third, RAAKS uses the windows that our research has shown to be relevant, useful and applicable (see Box 6 in Chapter 7). The role of the windows merits more detailed attention. They help to focus on particular issues quickly, so that participants are able to construct a variety of pertinent images, mirroring their appreciations of relevant events and ideas. Workshops and meetings encourage looking at any contrasts between these views, and generate a 'juggling with perspectives' that contributes much to the practice under examination as well as to the sense of interplay among participants.

Due to its flexible design, RAAKS may be used in different ways. The original concept is that of a participatory action research methodology. Such an exercise would be implemented by a team consisting of a mixture of subject-matter specialists and specialists acquainted with RAAKS. In this case, stakeholders are expected to participate actively as co-researchers. However, RAAKS' analytical design has also proved useful to those doing less participatory field research. The windows and tools provide a coherent set of perspectives and operational tools that a researcher can use to study and reflect on the social organization of innovation. In addition, RAAKS has been used to guide an 'excursion-type' inquiry in training sessions concerned with the way innovation is socially organized. Lastly, policymakers and managers at different levels can use RAAKS as an instrument to gain more insight into impairing or enabling conditions, or perhaps even to gauge innovative performance on a regular basis. Beyond this, RAAKS has proved useful in many situations outside agriculture. Experimental applications in health promotion, environmental programmes, introducing solar energy and diagnosing the social organization of innovation with respect to traffic and transportation have convinced us of its potential to facilitate innovation outside agriculture. However, much research remains to be done to fulfil this promise.

In its original participatory action research form, RAAKS appears to be more useful in some social contexts than in others. Three different social contexts in which RAAKS can be expected to yield good results can be suggested. First, RAAKS has proved useful in extension and research training. Used in an exercise that combines practice and theory, it helps extension and research managers (or future managers) study the social organization of innovation and can greatly increase their understanding: they get a better idea of the context in which their services operate, they learn to how to diagnose and assess the strength and other qualities of existing networks, and they learn how to prepare inter- ventions to improve innovation performance. This enables them to reflect more systematic- ally upon the role of their institution as part of a wider agricultural knowledge and information system, and its possible contribution to new forms of collective agency to use in tackling complex social issues.

Second, RAAKS can be useful to individuals and organizations who provide or sell 'knowledge/information-intensive' products or services, requiring permanent R&D, updating and training of staff, and a permanent search for new market niches. I feel it was not by accident that RAAKS was originally developed within the context of agricultural advisory services, and that this occurred during a period in which industrial agriculture was reaching its ecological, social and political limits. At the time, these services were suffering far-reaching changes including privatization, a re-orientation towards sustainable agriculture, and commercialization of knowledge and information flows. RAAKS' first applications were in support of the reorganization of agricultural research and extension. This remains the area in which its strongest contributions have been made; despite promising experiences with the use of RAAKS by consultants operating commercially, the development of RAAKS for such target groups would imply further major developments.

Third, RAAKS may be useful in stimulating the formation of what Röling (1994) has called 'soft platforms for decision making about ecosystems'. Because RAAKS facilitates structured inquiry into the need and potential for the development of a shared under- standing of complex social innovation processes, it can help social actors to define ways to organize themselves to tackle such complex issues as the management of a natural resource (such as a natural park, ground water or a catchment area), regional development, waste prevention, or stopping environmental degradation in sensitive areas. Dealing with any problem of this type will require the involvement of a variety of social actors, some of which have never before perceived the others as relevant to their concerns. In such a case, relevant networks exist but the relevant stakeholders, as a whole, may not be adequately integrated. A RAAKS exercise may then be used to help diagnose what is already in place and what its impact is with respect to the issues involved; this can lay a foundation for the design and implementation of more adequate integration. This makes RAAKS a promising instrument to use in both creating the conditions for and initiating the 'platform-processes' that can lead to forms of collective agency – social actors who have the will and capacity to work together – to tackle complex societal issues.

Generalizing, I would say that RAAKS can contribute most to situations in which a relevant number of stakeholders are aware that 'society' or the demands of their environ- ment requires them to continually seek innovation in their practices, and at an adequate pace; where they experience a 'lack of new ideas and new, viable options' to meet these demands as a problem; they realize that innovation requires being open to the ideas of other stakeholders, rather than withdrawing; and that a current lack of progress is important enough for them to do something about it. When such conditions are met, RAAKS can help stakeholders assess the quality of current social interaction for innovation, or the lack of it, and design means of improvement. Equally, these conditions suggest that where social actors are not sufficiently aware and ready to work together, the use of RAAKS in its original, participatory form is not to be recommended.

Three of the several interesting pending questions with respect to the RAAKS design, development and implementation are:

- What time frame is adequate for planning and implementing a RAAKS exercise; and how does this vary with the complexity of the issues at hand, as well as the number and commitment of stakeholders? Our experiences have ranged from six weeks for a full-time two-person team, to six months for larger teams involved part time. It is clear that the quality of the teams and the support they obtain from their own institutions and other stakeholders is of fundamental importance. Further study will be necessary to find answers to these and similar questions.

- How does RAAKS relate to other participatory research approaches? In Chapter 8 (see 'RAAKS as an appreciative learning system') we have argued its pertinence to an emerging tradition of 'alternative systems of inquiry'. A recent study (Hoeberichts, 1994), demonstrates the complementarity of participatory rural appraisal (PRA) and RAAKS. They appear compatible in terms of principles and procedures, and complementary with respect to their domains of inquiry. As a result, they provide different insights on socio-natural processes. Further development, including research on similarities and differences in the practical use of these methodologies, is needed.

- How can RAAKS' ability to study relevant technical and non-technical practices be strengthened? Our experiences suggest that detailed study of farming, research and extension practices, to name only a few of those that may be relevant, may sometimes be an asset to RAAKS inquiries. Can this be incorporated in RAAKS by including procedures that help to investigate 'human activity systems'? Can RAAKS be developed to include experimentation, role plays or interactive multimedia environments, so that it becomes less discursive and more oriented to practice? And when, under which circumstances, would it be advisable to use such techniques? It is clear that the development of RAAKS and RAAKS-related methodologies will remain a rich experience.

Issues for further research

Knowledge management: between serendipity and structure

This research has implications for our understanding of knowledge management, a term used here to cover activities directed at supporting social learning for innovation and integrating individual efforts to achieve a joint performance. This corresponds to a vision of management as '...the initiation, direction and control of purposeful activities' (van Heck, 1993: 64). This study of complex innovation theatres and inter-organizational relationships is directed primarily towards the first steps: my efforts focus on finding ways to build an understanding of the social organization of innovation, to enable social actors to *define* purposeful interventions. This has taken precedence over direction and control. RAAKS has become a methodology to use in jointly building an understanding of a complex problem situation, debating and defining useful interventions among stake-holders, and deciding whether and how to initiate these interventions. Hence, it facilitates the design of improvements in innovation performance, which should also provide a basis for more effective management thereafter. Therefore, while I consider RAAKS an important instrument in the hands of people responsible for improving innovation performance, with respect to knowledge management it is only a beginning.

This research does underscore the relevance of an intensified approach to knowledge management in complex multi-actor situations. An approach focused only on education, training and/or information logistics is not enough. To facilitate 'knowing' that crosses organizational boundaries, direct and indirect inter-organizational communication, joint learning and both spontaneous and purposive sense-making would have to become objects of inquiry. The results can then be used to scrutinize and improve the adequacy, effectiveness and efficiency of networking practices directed at innovation. Eventually such knowledge management tasks could become an expected part of the manager's job.

Further studies could include research on what happens when RAAKS has been completed, including whether and in what ways existing resource coalitions, convergences and communication networks are affected by the communication and cooperation strategies initiated as a result of RAAKS. This could contribute to a much clearer understanding of what can be managed and what cannot. The challenge for management sciences with respect to the social organization of innovation is to achieve a balance, with direction and control on one side, and the creation and maintenance of space for serendipitous and epiphenomenal improvements on the other. If anything has become apparent in my inquiries it is that the 'McDonaldization' (Ritzer, 1993) of complex innovation processes among organizations has little future.

RAAKS as a research methodology

What is the potential relevance of RAAKS to scientific practice? Can RAAKS, apart from contributing to improvements in innovation performance in practice, contribute to further accumulations of relevant scientific knowledge about the social organization of innovation? Can more specific hypotheses be addressed and evaluated by using RAAKS? A number of arguments can be put forward to suggest an affirmative answer. These involve RAAKS' foundation in academic thought, its procedural design and its flexibility.

As shown in Chapters 7 and 8, RAAKS is rooted in academic thought in ways that are both sound and consistent with the purposes of structured inquiry. Moreover, each RAAKS window has been validated: they are relevant and useful perspectives to use in studying issues of social organization in complex innovation theatres, RAAKS' domain of inquiry. This does not mean other windows are inconceivable; on the contrary, some possibilities have been mentioned. It does mean that RAAKS' design provides a student of the social organization of innovation with a number of relevant analytical perspectives and tools to use in initiating his or her study. Moreover, the proposed conceptual framework helps in integrating the findings made from different perspectives.

A second argument is that RAAKS' procedural design is systematic: it defines a number of steps to delimit a domain of inquiry and gather, organize and handle information; it defines particular intermediate and final outputs; and it sets standards for safeguarding the quality of its results. (These aspects have all been discussed in detail in Chapters 7 and 8.) RAAKS studies may therefore be designed and evaluated with scientific rigour. However, setting standards is one thing; complying with them is another. Achieving high quality under the many possible circumstances in which RAAKS may be used requires a great deal of a RAAKS team. Active participation and the achievement of intensive interactive communication and joint learning within the team and other relevant stakeholders are costly necessities, not only in terms of money or time but even more in the energy and commitment required from the research team. In practice, managing a process like RAAKS calls for many group dynamics and communication skills. As a consequence, training researchers to use RAAKS as a research tool will need particular attention.

The third argument is of a more practical nature. Research methodologies can make a contribution when researchers can adapt them to their needs, their appreciation of a particular situation and the issues that interest them. In this sense, RAAKS offers flexibility. Each research team can redesign intentions, procedures and analytical perspectives in accordance with their wishes; nevertheless, if they stick to the general RAAKS outline, experiences of different teams appear to remain comparable to a satisfactory degree. This is certainly our impression (though unverified), based on the Central American case studies and the results obtained by students who have used all or parts of RAAKS. Clearly, a more profound inquiry would be necessary to confirm this intuition.

Our conclusion is that while RAAKS can be said to possess the potential for contributing to scientific knowledge – as evidenced also by the professional interest methodologies such as RAAKS have already generated among development practitioners, researchers and policymakers, as well as among scholars who study processes of innovation and change – much more research and a thorough evaluation of achievements will be necessary to demonstrate that the method fulfils this potential. In this sense, RAAKS is a true member of the tradition in which it rests: the same observation is valid for most 'alternative systems of inquiry'.

Theatres, actors and interplay: concluding remarks

The impact of a metaphor

I have described our domain of interest as *complex theatres of agricultural innovation*. Theatres (not plays or scenery) are places where pre-meditated and spontaneous actions mix naturally, where managers, directors, designers, stage builders, actors and audience interact, producing structure as well as serendipity. Even though the metaphor has not been enacted in full detail, it has had a positive impact on the many people who have contributed to the process described. In the first place it helped to keep us open to epiphenomenal and random events. As in modern theatre, improvisation plays a role in preparing and implementing innovation in complex theatres. Moreover 'some things just happen...'. Interesting enough, many of the respondents we interviewed already seemed to see the social organization of innovation as mostly random and/or epiphenomenal anyway, or in any case as something completely outside their span of control. The fatalistic way extension workers react to the nth top–down remodelling of their approach, or the way researchers accept yet another reorganization of their service helps to confirm this impression. Yet, we discovered that many farmers and many managers of research and extension are in fact innovation managers. Many have reached a deep, often intuitive understanding of the way innovation is organized and put this to use daily for the benefit of their businesses or institutions. Their enthusiastic support convinced us that scientific inquiry could nevertheless help.

In the second place, the theatre metaphor led us to focus on 'interplay'. The more we studied innovation-related behaviour, the less it could be denied that intuition, knowledge, ability and context go hand in hand to produce an 'effective innovation networker'. How do people choose to whom they will speak at length, and whom to avoid? Why do they decide to test particular equipment and not to bother with others? Why does one topic gain prominence among stakeholders while many others, seemingly of similar relevance, do not? Clearly, it is not simply a question of knowing; it may have to do with intuition, energy levels or the ability to take time from other activities. An early formative experience provides an example: one of the very first innovative pig farmers I interviewed in the Netherlands told me he often spent various days of the week away from his farm, in meetings with union members, on boards or councils, or visiting institutes, companies or experiment stations. Also, he performed a number of experiments related to potential innovations on his farm. I wondered how he could do all this without neglecting the farm. Then I met his wife. From what she told me I began to understand: he could carry on all these activities because in practice his wife ran most of the farm, together with a farm hand. Had his wife been a practising nurse, he would not have been the networker he is now! In other words, as far as networking is concerned, knowing how to network is only part of the picture. Making use of available support from family and friends, one tries out different contacts and relationships, taking long shots without knowing whether it will pay off. 'Playing' is a large part of what successful networkers do.

In the third place, the theatre metaphor made it possible to avoid choosing between 'arena' and 'system'. Both of these metaphors seem too partial to support a comprehensive inquiry into the social organization of innovation. The social organization of innovation is of course in part a consequence of social design and regulation. As such, it can be studied as a designed whole or 'system' in the traditional meaning of the word. But this is only part of the story. Knowing participants continuously hammer at the foundations of such arrangements and, through their interaction, redesign and reorganize them. The struggles of some actors with others – fighting against what they consider to be a skewed, equivocal perception regarding what innovation is to be – could be seen as a 'battle over images' taking place in a social arena. But the 'arena' metaphor could distract our attention from the lighthearted and creative way so many social actors remodel existing configurations on a daily basis, reinterpreting and reworking them as they see fit. Fortunately, the 'wielding and yielding' (Villareal, 1994) at the point where social innovation is put into practice is the object of increasing interest for social researchers.

Softly organizing the theatre...

Having made use of soft systems thinking, its strengths and limitations (Chapter 1, *Systems thinking...*) and trying to develop a particular strand – appreciative knowledge systems thinking – I am convinced of the great relevance of the approach developed by Checkland and his collaborators for studying and tackling complex, social problems. Our studies have convinced me that soft systems thinking is a truly different mode of reasoning. But what is so different about it, and what does appreciative thinking add? Basically, I think soft systems thinking is valuable because it is compatible with the social constructivist tradition, which helps to put complex, contemporary problems in a new light. At the same time, it is very practical. The designers of soft systems methodology have understood that we live in a 'world' not entirely of our own making, which we continually create and recreate through our imagination and actions. Interplay among actors with different world views is the motor behind the learning process facilitated by soft systems methodology. What we have added to this is first, the notion of 'windows' – complementary analytical perspectives – to enrich this interplay; and second, a focus on the social organization of innovation. Interplay and learning are stimulated by the use of windows: a confrontation of world views is combined with varied analytical perspectives, mimicing the appreciative character of networking for innovation. In the course of this study, this enriched version of soft systems thinking has proved to provide a basis for structured inquiry into the social organization of innovation and to be an important tool for facilitating social problem solving and learning on complex issues. Needless to say, in my view soft systems thinking receives less attention from researchers than it deserves.

Towards a networking science?

My background is in irrigation and drainage, then extension, then extension science. Now our group dedicates itself to communication and innovation studies. Extension workers are typically 'brokers', go-betweens among members of a target group, specialists and researchers. As a consequence, extension science can be characterized as a 'broker science' (Gremmen, 1993). But a subtle change has crept into extension science as a domain of interest: while originally our efforts could be focused primarily on one interface, that of the farmer/specialist (or patient/doctor, civilian/health worker, public/environmental agency, etc.), today the social organization of innovation in agricultural as well as rural development has grown far more complex. With respect to the big issues such as sustainable development, waste disposal, negotiations on resource use, rural conflict resolution, reorientation of rural employment, climatological change, natural resource management, clean water supply, food distribution and so forth, there are neither clear problem definitions nor readily available solutions. As a consequence, acting as a broker between specialists and end users is no more relevant than serving as an intermediary among other stakeholders, such as national policymakers, traders, industrialists and retailers, farmer organizations, non-governmental organizations, local action groups or municipal governments, or among different members of each of these categories. Therefore, we are shifting our emphasis from understanding and facilitating interactions at single interfaces to understanding and facilitating simultaneous interactions at multiple-interfaces. The focus of our studies is thus shifting to the simultaneous brokerage of images, knowledge and information among a variety of parties, and stimulating platform processes and 'joint performances' among stakeholders, to resolve complex social issues. It is time to go in search of a name for such a science of applied networking.

Does this happen in private industry?

Appendix

Unpublished case study materials: graduate/postgraduate students

1988

Beek, P.G.H. van, *The Queensland Dairy AKIS*. Queensland, UoQ: mimeo, 29 p.

Blok, K. and Seegers, S. *The research-extension linkage in the southern region of Sri Lanka*. Wageningen, WAU: MSc thesis, 87 p.

Pijnenburg, B. van. *Kolonisatie- en kennisverwerving in Guaviare, Colombia*. Wageningen, WAU: MSc thesis, 46 p.

1989

Beek, P.G.H. van. *Managing knowledge systems involving QDPI*. University of Queensland: MSc thesis, 126 p.

Engel, P., Kuiper, D., Röling, N. and Seegers, S. (1989). *Het landbouw kennis systeem in Denemarken, Engeland en Frankrijk. Aangrijpingspunten voor kennisbeleid*. Mimeo to national scientific council, 111 p.

1990

Aaken, R.v., Bemelmans, M. and Kemerink, J. *Gewasbescherming in komkommer: hoe krijg je een groene komkommer?* Wageningen, WAU: MSc thesis, 126 p.

Breusers, M. *Le manioc sur le Plateau Adja au Benin. Une étude de cas d'un système de connaissance locale*. Wageningen, WAU: MSc thesis, 46 p.

Grooters, W. *The role of growers and pig farmers in the programming of adaptive agricultural research in The Netherlands. An exploration of networks and linkage mechanisms*. Wageningen, WAU: MSc thesis, 95 p.

Woltersbeek, T. *Het kennis- en informatie systeem van de sektor stedelijk groen: voorlichting in 'Opdrachtgeversland'*. Wageningen, WAU: MSc thesis, 82 p.

1991

Bakker, J. den. *Networking: 'common sense'. Mid-term evaluation of the El Taller project, based on network theory*. Wageningen, WAU: MSc thesis, 75 p.

Corten, I. *Het voorlichtingskundig begrip 'kennissysteem' toegepast op de sectorbosbouw*. Wageningen, WAU: MSc thesis, 111 p.

Ravensbergen, P. *Comparison of the Dutch and Israeli horticultural knowledge systems*. Three parts. Wageningen, WAU: MSc thesis, 160 p.

1992

Adolfse, L. *Target groups for health promotion in Horsens, Denmark and the Danish food knowledge and information system*. Wageningen, WAU: MSc thesis, 65 p.

Bemelmans, M. *Apple production for export in Chile: case study of an agricultural knowledge and information system*. Wageningen, WAU: MSc thesis, 34 p.

Boonekamp, G. en Kleis, J. *Het Kennis- en InformatieSysteem binnen het SENiorenSErvice project te Sittard*. Wageningen, WAU: MSc thesis, 70 p.

Khan, G.Z. *Development needs designing appropriate innovations: a case in PataIrrigation Project in Swat Pakistan*. Wageningen, WAU: MSc thesis, 104 p.

Meijer, A. *Análisis de dos proyectos del programa de transferencia tecnológica básica del Instituto de Desarrollo Agropeciuario*. Wageningen, WAU: MSc thesis, 84 p.

Millar, D. *Understanding rural peoples' knowledge and its implications for intervention: 'from the roots to the branches'*. Wageningen, WAU: MSc thesis, 81 p.

Noordermeer, K.H. and Zanten, G.H. van. *Case en DIG studie naar het visteelt- kennissysteem in Nederland*. Wageningen, WAU: MSc thesis, 33 p.

Nijskens, G. *City mall for public services?* Wageningen, WAU: MSc thesis, 100 p.

Obate Foumane, E. *Social transformations and their effects on food crop production among small farmers: a three generation analysis of food crop cultivation patterns in Metet Settlement (South Cameroon)*. Wageningen, WAU: MSc thesis, 77 p.

Rap, E. *Learning in practice, farmers' learning processes in agriculture*. Wageningen,WAU: MSc thesis, 85 p.

Shetto, M.C.R. *Linking farmers to research and extension in the agricultural knowledge and information systems. A case study of Mbozi District in Mbeya Region, Tanzania*. Wageningen, WAU: MSc thesis, 91 p.

Stolzenbach, A. *Improviserend leren: de logica van het experimenteren van boeren in Mali*. Wageningen, WAU: MSc. thesis, 45 p.

Velders, M. *Kennismanagement binnen een kleine commerciële organisatie*. Wageningen, WAU: MSc thesis, 99 p.

1993

Hermon, J.W. van en Schotveld, E. *Deskundigheid binnen SNV*. Wageningen, WAU: MSc thesis, 49 p.

Jellema, A. *The application of knowledge and information systems research on a social forestry management situation*. Wageningen, WAU: MSc thesis, 68 p.

Velders, M. *Informatie- en kennisstromen van en naar het kenniscentrum Wageningen: het kenniscentrum Wageningen in de markt*. Wageningen, Global Village: onderzoeksrapport, 61 p.

Wijnhoven, T. *Een 'RAAKS'-analyse van het Internationaal Voorlichtingskundig Kennis- en Informatienetwerk rond de de ICRE van het IAC*. Wageningen, WAU: MSc thesis, 62 p.

1994

Beyene Seboka W. *Beyond farming system research: towards social learning and inquiry*. Wageningen, WAU: MSc thesis, 137 p.

Chavez Tafur, J. *Knowledge processes within a 'booming' agriculture: looking at small-scale farmer participation*. Wageningen, WAU: MSc thesis, 75 p.

Hendriksen, E. and Knot, M. *Panda's in Noord Brabant: mileuzorg als thema van leren encommuniceren in de Rijkswaterstaat, Directie Noord-Brabant*. Wageningen, WAU: MSc thesis, 187 p.

Hoeberichts, A. *Towards a flexible application of participatory research methodologies.*Wageningen, WAU: MSc thesis, 60 p.

Naafs, D. *Identification of opportunities for a community based nutrition promotion programme in Lluria*. Valencia/Wageningen: Institut Valencia d'Estudis en Salut Pública/Department of Communication and Innovation Studies, 73 p.

References

Aaken, R. van, Bemelmans, M. and Kemerink, J. (1990). Gewasbescherming in komkommer: hoe krijg je een groene komkommer? Wageningen: Wageningen Agricultural University, unpublished MSc thesis.

Adolfse, L. (1992). Target groups for health promotion in Horsens, Denmark and the Danish food knowledge and information system. Wageningen: Wageningen Agricultural University, unpublished MSc thesis.

Adolfse, L.A.M.M. and Koning, P. de (1994). In de roos. Een verslag over communicatie, leren en innovatie in de rozensierteelt. Utrecht: Adviesraad voor het Onderwijs (ARO).

Agudelo, L.A. (1989). La articulación entre la investigación y la tranferencia de tecnología: el caso del cultivo del arroz en los Llanos Orientales de Colombia. Staff Note no. 89–47. The Hague: ISNAR.

Alcober, D.L. (1989). Subsystem level analysis: soil conservation and improvement in the marginal hillylands/uplands in Leyte. RTTL Case study report. The Hague: ISNAR.

Alders, C., Haverkort, B. and Veldhuizen van, L. (Eds.) (1993). *Linking with farmers: networking for low-external-input and sustainable agriculture.* London: Intermediate Technology Publications.

Alebikiya, M. (1993). The Association of Church Development Projects (ACDEP) in Northern Ghana. In: Alders, C., Haverkort, B. and Veldhuizen van, L. (Eds.). *Linking with farmers: networking for low-external-input and sustainable agriculture.* London: Intermediate Technology Publications, 159–167.

Altmann, C. (1989). Investigación – transferencia – productor: una articulación clave en la generación y transferencia de tecnología agropecuaria. Santiago de Chile: Instituto Nacional de Investigaciones Agropecuarias – INIA.

Arce, A. (1993). Negotiating agricultural development. Etanglements of bureaucrats and rural producers in Western Mexico. *Wageningen Sociological Studies* no. 34.

Arce, A. and Long, N. (1987). The dynamics of knowledge interfaces between Mexican agricultural bureaucrats and peasants: a case study from Jalisco. *Boletín de Estudios Latinoamericanos y del Caribe*, 43, December: 5–30.

Argyris, C. (1992). *On organizational learning.* Cambridge (USA): Blackwell Publishers.

Arocena-Francisco, H. (1989). A study of the linkages between agricultural research and technology transfer. The seed potato subsystem report. RTTL Case study report. The Hague: ISNAR.

Ashby, J. (1990). Small farmers' participation in the design of technologies. In: Altieri, M.A. and Hecht, S.B. *Agroecology and small farm development.* Boca Raton, Florida: CRC Press.

Axinn, G.H. (1988). *Guide on alternative extension approaches.* Rome, Italy: FAO.

Azucena, C.F. (1989). The corn subsystem: downy mildew disease control. RTTL Case study report. The Hague: ISNAR.

Bakker, J. den, Adolfse, L. and Engel, P. (1993). *Gedachtenvorming en relatiepatronen binnen de verkeer- en vervoerswereld.* Wageningen: Wageningen Agricultural University, Department of Communication and Innovation Studies.

Ban, A.W. van den (1987). Communication systems between agricultural research and the farmers, The Netherlands' way. *Journal of Extension Systems*, vol. 3, June.

Ban, A.W. van den, and Hawkins, H.S. (1988). *Agricultural Extension.* Harlow: Longman.

Barraclough, S.L. (1974). Politics first. *Ceres*, FAO, Rome, Sept/Oct: 24–28.

Bawden, R.J. (1990). Towards action researching systems. In: Zuberskerritt, *Action Research for Change and Development.* Queensland: CALT, Griffith University.

Bawden, R.J. (1991). Systems thinking and practice in agriculture. *Journal of Dairy Science* 74: 2362–2373.

Bawden, R. and Macadam, R. (1991). Action researching systems – extension reconstructed. In: Tilmann et al. (Eds.). Proceedings of the international workshop *Agricultural knowledge systems and the role of extension*. Stuttgart: University of Hohenheim, 368–386.

Beal, G.M., Dissanayake, W. and Konoshima, S. (1986). *Knowledge generation, exchange, and utilization*. Boulder: Westview Press.

Beek, P.G.H. van (1989). Managing knowledge systems involving QDPI. Australia, University of Queensland: MSc thesis.

Beek, P. van (1991). The Queensland Dairy AKIS: a systems approach to the management of research and extension. In: Kuiper, D. and Röling, N.G. (Eds.). *The edited proceedings of the European seminar on knowledge management and information technology*. Wageningen: Wageningen Agricultural University, Department of Extension Science, 30–44.

Bemelmans, M. (1992). Apple production for export in Chile: case study of an agricultural knowledge and information system. Wageningen: Wageningen Agricultural University, unpublished MSc thesis.

Bernardo, E.N. (1989). Involvement of international agencies in development and delivery of selected technologies in the Philippines. RTTL Case study report. The Hague: ISNAR.

Beyene Seboka W. (1994). Beyond farming system research: towards social learning and inquiry. Wageningen: Wageningen Agricultural University, MSc thesis.

Biggs, S.D. (1989). Resource-poor farmer participation in research: a synthesis of experiences from nine national agricultural research systems. OFCOR Comparative Study Paper no. 3. The Hague: ISNAR.

Blok, K. and Seegers, S. (1988). The research – extension linkage in the southern region of Sri Lanka. An agricultural information system perspective. Wageningen: Wageningen Agricultural University, Department of Extension Science, unpublished MSc thesis.

Blokker, K.J. (1991). Strategic investment in IT with a view to integrating the market column. In: Kuiper, D. and Röling, N.G. (Eds.). *The edited proceedings of the European seminar on knowledge management and information technology*. Wageningen: Wageningen Agricultural University, Department of Extension Science, 82–91.

Blum, A. (1990). What can be learned from a comparison of two agricultural knowledge systems? The case of the Netherlands and Israel. Mimeograph.

Bolhuis, E.E. and Ploeg van der, J. (1985). *Boerenarbeid en stijlen van landbouwbeoefening*. Leiden: University of Leiden, PhD thesis, 510 p.

Boonekamp, G. en Kleis, J. (1992). Het Kennis- en InformatieSysteem binnen het SENioren SErvice project te Sittard. Wageningen: Wageningen Agricultural University, unpublished MSc thesis.

Bourdieux, P. (1991). *Language and symbolic power*. Cambridge: Polity Press.

Bourgois, R. (1990). Structural linkages for integrating agricultural research and extension. The Hague: ISNAR Working Paper no. 35.

Box, L. (1989). Knowledge, networks and cultivators: cassava in the Dominican Republic. In: Long, N. (Ed.). Encounters at the interface, a perspective on social discontinuities in rural development. *Wageningen Sociological Studies* no. 27: 165–183.

Box, L. (Ed.) (1990). From common ignorance to shared knowledge. *Wageningen Sociological Studies* no. 28.

Brouwers, J. (1993). *Rural people's response to soil fertility decline. The Adja Case (Benin)*. Wageningen: Wageningen Agricultural University, PhD thesis.

Carter, A.P. (1989). Know-how trading as economic exchange. *Research Policy*, 18: 155–163.

Castillo, J.S. and Guardado, P.A. (1992a). Identificación y evaluación del Sistema de Información y Conocimientos Agrícolas (SICA) en la Zona 5 de la Región Oriental. San Salvador, El Salvador: PRIAG Convenio CORECA/CEE/IICA. Mimeograph.

Castillo, J.S. and Guardado, P.A. (1992b). Identificación y Evaluación del Sistema de Información y Conocimientos Agrícolas (SICA) en la Zona de Sonsonate. San Salvador, El Salvador: PRIAG Convenio CORECA/CEE/IICA, Mimeograph.

Chambers, R. (1992). *Rural appraisal: rapid, relaxed and participatory*. Brighton: IDS.

Chambers, R. and Ghildyal, R. (1985). Agricultural research for resource-poor farmers: a parsomonious paradigm. Brighton (Sussex): IDS, Discussion paper 220.

Chambers, R. and Jiggins, J. (1987). Agricultural research for research-poor farmers: a parsimonious paradigm. *Agricultural Administration and Extension*, 27, 35–52 (I) and 109–128 (II).

Chambers, R., Pacey, A. and Thrupp, L.A. (Eds.) (1989). *Farmers first, farmer innovation and agricultural research*. London: Intermediate Technology Publications.

Chavez Tafur, J. (1994). Knowledge processes within a 'booming' agriculture: looking at small-scale farmer participation. Wageningen: Wageningen Agricultural University, unpublished thesis.

Checkland, P.B. (1981). *Systems thinking, systems practice*. Chichester: John Wiley & Sons.

Checkland, P.B. (1988). Soft systems methodology: an overview. *Journal of Applied Systems Analysis*, 15: 27–30.

Checkland, P.B. (1989). Soft systems methodology. *Human Systems Management*, 8: 273–289.

Checkland, P.B. and Casar, A. (1986). Vickers' concept of an appreciative system: a systemic account. *Journal of Applied Systems Analysis*, 13: 3–17.

Checkland, P. and Scholes, J. (1990). *Soft systems methodology in action*. England, Chichester: John Wiley.

Collado, C. and Adlai J. (1992). Informe SICA Area Baja Verapaz. Guatamala: PRIAG Convenio CORECA/CEE/IICA. Mimeograph.

Corten, I. (1991). Het voorlichtingskundig begrip 'Kennissysteem' toegepast op de sector Bosbouw. Wageningen: Wageningen Agricultural University, unpublished MSc thesis.

Dalen, J. Chr. van (1989). Knowledge organized: expert systems in local government. In: Snellen, W., Donk, W. van de, and Baquiast, J. (Eds.). *Expert systems in public administration*. Amsterdam: Elsevier Science Publishers B.V., 243–268.

Davila, J.A., Rivera, O., Rivera, M.A. and Mendez, W. (1992). Informe del SICA Polochic Alta Verapaz. Guatamala: PRIAG Convenio CORECA/CEE/IICA.

Dijk, T. van, Engel, P.G.H. and Leeuwis, C. (1991). Evaluatie AGROCOM proefproject. Wageningen: Wageningen Agricultural University, Vakgroep Voorlichtingskunde.

Ekpere, J.A. and Idowu, I.A. (1990a). Small-scale cassava processing technology subsystem in Southern Nigeria. RTTL Case study report. The Hague: ISNAR.

Ekpere, J.A. and Idowu, I.A. (1990b). Maize-fertilizer technology package in the forest and savannah zones of Nigeria. RTTL Case study report. The Hague: ISNAR.

Ekpere, J.A. and Idowu, I.A. (1990c). Cowpea crop protection spray technology in Northern Nigeria. RTTL Case study report. The Hague: ISNAR.

EL TALLER (1993). Activity Plan and Budget 1993–1995. Tunis.

EL TALLER (1990). Think globally, act locally and ... act globally!: a challenge for NGDOs in the 1990s. Report on the first conference of the think-tank. Reus, Spain.

Engel, P.G.H. (1984). Autodiagnostico, comunicación para el desarrollo rural. Pasto, Colombia: ICA-CCH Informe Técnico.

Engel, P.G.H. (1989a). Kennis- en informatiegebruik door bedrijfsvoorlicht(st)ers: uitgangspunt voor kennismanagement. *Agrarische Voorlichting*, 1 (6/7), 27–30.

Engel, P.G.H. (1989b). Peasant technology development in the Nariño Highlands of Colombia. RTTL Case study report. The Hague: ISNAR.

Engel, P.G.H. (1990a). The impact of improved institutional coordination on agricultural performance: the case of the Nariño Highlands in Colombia The Hague: ISNAR.

Engel, P.G.H. (1990b). Two ears, one mouth... Participatory extension or why people have two ears and only one mouth. *AT Source*, 18 (4): 2–5.

Engel, P.G.H. (1991a). Knowledge management in agriculture: building upon diversity. *Knowledge in Society, the International Journal of Knowledge Transfer*. Special issue, February 1991: 28–36.

Engel, P.G.H. (1991b). Farmers' participation and extension. In: Haverkort, B., Kamp, J. van der, and Waters-Bayer, A. (Eds.). *Joining farmers' experiments*. London: Intermediate Technology Publications, 183–189.

Engel, P.G.H. (1993a). Achieving a competitive edge in the agricultural information market. *Zeitschrift für Agrarinformatik*. Munster-Hiltrup: GIL/Landwirtschaftverlag GmbH. 1, 93: 2–9.

Engel, P.G.H. (1993b). Daring to share: networking among non-governmental organizations. In: Alders, C., Haverkort, B. and Veldhuizen van, L. (Eds.) 1993. *Linking with farmers: networking for low-external-input and sustainable agriculture*. London: Intermediate Technology Publications, 131–151.

Engel, P.G.H. (1993c). Basic configurations in agricultural innovation, towards and understanding of leadership and coordination in complex innovation theaters. Paper presented to the *Working group on the social construction of agrarian knowledge of the XVth European congress of rural sociology*. Wageningen, 2–6 August 1993.

Engel, P.G.H. (1993d). Networking for sustainability: towards a new paradigm for extension? Paper presented to the *Working group on agricultural extension and knowledge systems of the XVth European congress of rural sociology*. Wageningen, 2–6 August 1993.

Engel, P.G.H. and Bakker, J. den (1992). Voorwaarden scheppen is knelpunten wegnemen. Wageningen: Wageningen Agricultural University, Department of communication and innovation studies.

Engel, P.G.H., Groot, A. de, Meyering, A. and Elema, T. (1990). Case Studie Kennissysteem Paardenhouderij. Wageningen: WAU.

Engel, P.G.H., Groot, A. de, and Seegers, S. (1991). RAAKS: Rapid Appraisal of Agricultural Knowledge Systems. Manual version 3 (unpublished). Wageningen: Wageningen Agricultural University, Department of communication and innovation studies.

Engel, P.G.H., Kaimowitz, D. and Snyder, M. (1989). ISNAR research and technology transfer linkages study, case study methodology guidelines. Staff Notes 89–44. The Hague: ISNAR.

Engel, P.G.H. and Salomon, M. (1993). RAAKS: Rapid Appraisal of Agricultural Knowledge Systems, manual version 4 (unpublished). Wageningen: Wageningen Agricultural University, Department of communication and innovation studies.

Engel, P.G.H. and Salomon, M. (1996). RAAKS: a participatory action-research approach to facilitating social learning for sustainable development. In: Budelman, A. (Ed.). *Agricultural R&D at the crossroads. Merging systems research and social actor approaches*. Amsterdam, Royal Tropical Institute.

Engel, P.G.H. (1995) *Facilitating innovation. An action-oriented approach and participatory methodology in improve innovative social practices in agriculture*. Wageningen: PhD thesis.

Engel, P.G.H., Salomon, M. and Fernandez, M. (1994). Strategic diagnosis for improving performance in extension. RAAKS manual for ICRE. Wageningen: WAU/CTA/IAC.

Engel, P.G.H. and Seegers, S. (1991). Basic configurations in agricultural technology Systems. Summary. In: *Proceedings of the international workshop on agricultural knowledge systems and the role of extension*. Bad Boll, Germany: 21–24th of May 1991, 353–358.

Engel, P.G.H. and Seegers, S. (1992). Towards a design and management of effective linkage strategies: a diagnostic tool. ISNAR R/TTL synthesis working paper. The Hague: ISNAR.

Eponou, T. (1990a). Sous-système IDESSA-CIDT. RTTL Case study report. The Hague: ISNAR.

Eponou, T. (1990b). Sous-système IDESSA: Projet piscicole. RTTL Case study report. The Hague: ISNAR.

Eponou, T. (1990c). Le sous-système IDESSA-PACO. RTTL Case study report. The Hague: ISNAR.

Eponou, T. (1993). *Partners in agricultural technology: linking research and technology transfer to serve farmers*. The Hague: ISNAR Research Report no. 1.

Espinoza, S., Cruz, M.E., Miranda, B. and Lucas, C. (1992). Nicaragua: informe del estudio de caso sistema de información y conocimientos agrícolas del Valle de Pantasma, Jinotega. PRIAG: Convenio CORECA/CEE/IICA. Mimeograph.

Estrada, E., Guerrón, G. and Verbaken, K. (1983). Vocabulario para la comunicación rural en el Altiplano de Nariño. Pasto, Colombia: ICA-CCH, Sección Comunicación, Informe Técnico.

Evenson, R.E., Waggoner, P.E. and Ruttan, V.W. (1979). Economic benefits from research: an example from agriculture. *Science* 205, 14 September: 1101–1107.

Fearne, A. (1991). Agricultural information: the farmer's point of view. In: Kuiper, D. and Röling, N.G. (Eds.). *The edited proceedings of the European seminar on knowledge management and information technology*. Wageningen: Wageningen Agricultural University, Department of Extension Science, 91–99.

Fliert, E. van de (1993). *Integrated pest management. Farmer field schools generate sustainable practices: a case study in Central Java evaluating IPM training*. Wageningen: Wageningen Agricultural University, PhD dissertation.

Foote Whyte, W. (Ed.) (1991). *Participatory action research*. London: Sage.

Foster, G.M. (1965). Peasant society and the image of the limited good. *American Anthropologist*, 67: 293–315.

Fowler, H.W. and Fowler, F.G. (Eds.) (1964). *The concise Oxford dictionary of current English*. Fifth Edition. Oxford: Clarendon Press.

Frempong, C.A. (1988). A systems approach to the evaluation of research-extension interface. The case of cocoa and maize in Ghana. Wageningen: Wageningen Agricultural University, unpublished MSc thesis.

Fresco, L. (1986). *Cassava in shifting cultivation: a systems approach to agricultural technology development in Africa*. Amsterdam: Royal Tropical Institute.

Galesloot, L. (1994). *Collegiale netwerken van ervaren docenten en schoolleiders*. University of Utrecht, the Netherlands. De Lier: Academisch Boeken Centrum, Ph.D. thesis.

García, M., Cifuentes, I., Rivera, M.A. and Bolaños, S. (1992). Informe del estudio del 'SICA' en el Parcelamiento La Blanca. Guatamala: PRIAG Convenio CORECA/CEE/IICA.

Gardner, H. (1983). *Frames of mind: the theory of multiple intelligences*. New York, Basic Books, Inc.

Graham, O. (1993). Networking as a development activity: the arid lands information network. In: Alders, C., Haverkort, B. and Veldhuizen van, L. (Eds.). *Linking with farmers: networking for low-external-input and sustainable agriculture*. London: Intermediate Technology Publications, 271–281.

Gremmen, B. (1993). *The mystery of the practical use of scientific knowledge*. Enschede: Twente University, PhD dissertation.

Grooters, W. (1990). The role of growers and pig farmers in the programming of adaptive agricultural research in The Netherlands. Wageningen: Wageningen Agricultural University, MAKS, MSc thesis.

Grupo Regional de Fortalecimiento Institucional (1992). Analisis de los sistemas estatales encargados de generar y transferir tecnología en granos básicos. Documento Síntesis de los Países Centroamericanos. San José, Costa Rica: PRIAG, Convenio CORECA/CEE/IICA ALA 88/23.

Guerrón, G. and Verbaken, K. (1985). Estudio de evaluación del programa radial experimental: manos y mingas. Technical report. Pasto: ICA-Convenio Colombo Holandés.

Harkin, M. (1991). Strategic investment in European videotex support systems for agriculture. In: Kuiper, D. and Röling, N.G. (Eds.). *The edited proceedings of the European seminar on knowledge management and information technology*. Wageningen: Wageningen Agricultural University, Department of Extension Science, 124–134.

Havelock, R.G. (1969). *Planning for innovation through dissemination and utilisation of knowledge*. Ann Arbor: University of Michigan, Institute of Social Research/Centre for Research of Utilisation of Scientific Knowledge.

Havelock, R.G. (1986). Linkage: key to understanding the knowledge system. In: Beal, G.M., Dissanayake, W. and Konoshima, S. (Eds.). *Knowledge generation, exchange and utilization*. Boulder and London: Westview Press, 11–37 and 211–245.

Haverkort, B. and Engel, P.G.H. (1990). The system Approach, agricultural development and extension. In: *Knowledge Systems in Agricultural Development*. Manual International Course on Rural Extension (ICRE). Wageningen: International Agricultural Center, 1–26.

Haverkort, B. and Ducommun, G. (1990). Synergy and strength through networking. *ILEIA Newsletter,* vol. 6 (3): 28–30.

Haverkort, B., Kamp, J. van der, and Waters-Bayer, A. (Eds.) (1991). *Joining farmers' experiments: experiences in participatory technology development*. London: Intermediate Technology Publications.

Hayami, Y. and Ruttan, V.W. (1985). *Agricultural development, an international perspective*. Baltimore and London: Johns Hopkins University Press.

Heck, E. van (1993). *Design management of electronic data interchange systems*. Alphen a/d Rijn: Samson, PhD thesis.

Hippel, E. von (1987). Cooperation between rivals: informal know-how trading. *Research Policy*, 16: 291–302.

Hoeberichts, A. (1994). Towards a flexible application of participatory research methodologies, unpublished MSc thesis.

Hornby, A.S. (Ed.) (1974). *Oxford advanced learner's dictionary of current english*. Oxford University Press.

IAC (1989). *International seminar on rural extension policies*. Wageningen: International Agricultural Centre, June 26–30.

ICA (1966). Estación experimental Obonuco. *ICA Informa*, 6, Bogotá.

ICA-CCH (1975–1984). Informes anuales y trimestrales. Pasto: ICA-Convenio Colombo Holandés.

ICA-CCH (1985). Informe final. Pasto: ICA-Convenio Colombo-Holandés.

Jackson, M.C. (1985). Social systems theory and practice: the need for a critical approach. *International Journal General Systems*, vol. 10: 135–151.

Jaén, B. and Palacios, M. (1992). Informe estudio de caso sobre el Sistema de Información y Conocimiento Agrícola (SICA) del Arco Seco de Panamá. Panamá: PRIAG Convenio CORECA/CEE/IICA. Mimeograph.

Jiggins, J. and Zeeuw, H. de (1992). Participatory technology development in practice: process and methods. In: Reijntjes, C., Haverkort, B. and Waters-Bayer, A. *Farming for the future: an introduction to low-external-input and sustainable agriculture*. London and Basingstoke: MacMillan, 135–162.

Jorna, R.J. and Simons, J.L. (Eds.) (1992). *Kennis in organizaties*. Muiderberg: Dick Coutinho.

Juarez, J. and Lavaire, H. (1992a). Diagnóstico sobre el Manejo del Sistema de Información y Conocimiento Agrícola, Zona San Francisco de la Paz. Tegucigalpa, Honduras: PRIAG Convenio CORECA/CEE/IICA. Mimeograph.

Juarez, J. and Lavaire, H. (1992b). Diagnóstico sobre el Manejo del Sistema de Información y Conocimiento Agrícola, Olanchito. Tegucigalpa, Honduras: PRIAG Convenio CORECA/CEE/IICA. Mimeograph.

Kaimowitz, D. (1989). Linking research and technology transfer in the development of improved coffee technologies in Colombia. RTTL Case study report. Staff Notes 89–54. The Hague: ISNAR.

Kaimowitz, D. (Ed.) (1990). *Making the link: agricultural research and technology transfer in developing countries*. Boulder, San Francisco, London: Westview Press.

Kaimowitz, D. (1991). Moving forces: external pressure and the dynamics of technology systems. In: Kuiper, D. and Röling, N.G. (Eds.). *The edited proceedings of the European seminar on knowledge management and information technology*. Wageningen: Wageningen Agricultural University, Department of Extension Science, 45–56.

Kaimowitz, D., Snyder, M. and Engel, P.G.H. (1990). A conceptual framework for studying links between agricultural research and technology transfer in developing countries. In: Kaimowitz, D. (Ed.). *Making the link: agricultural research and technology transfer in developing countries*. Boulder, San Francisco, London: Westview Press.

Khan, G.Z. (1992). Development needs designing appropriate innovations: a case in Pata Irrigation Project in Swat Pakistan. Wageningen: Wageningen Agricultural University, unpublished MSc thesis.

Kline, S. and Rosenberg, N. (1986). An overview of innovation. In: Landau, R. and Rosenberg, N. (Eds.). *The positive sum strategy. Harnessing technology for economic growth*. Washington, DC: National Academy Press, 275–306.

Koelen, M. and Vaandrager, L. (1994). Health promotion requires innovative research techniques. Paper presented to the Health in Cities Conference *Research and change in urban community health*, Liverpool: Dept. of Public Health, Liverpool University/WHO, 20–24 March.

Koestler, A. (1968). Beyond atomism and holism – the concept of the holon. In: Koestler, A. and Smythies, J.R. (Eds.). *Beyond reductionism, new perspectives in the life sciences*. New York: The Macmillan Company, 192–232.

Kolb, D.A. (1986). *Experiential learning*. Experience as the source of learning and development. New Jersey: Prentice-Hall.

Kolmans, E. (1993). Networking for sustainable agriculture in Perú: experiences of the 'Red de Agricultura Ecológica' (RAE). In: Alders, C., Haverkort, B. and Veldhuizen van, L. (Eds.). *Linking with farmers: networking for low-external-input and sustainable agriculture*. London: Intermediate Technology Publications, 151–159.

Koningsveld, H. and Mertens, J. (1986). *Communicatief en strategisch handelen, een inleiding tot de handelingstheorie van Habermas*. Muiderberg: Coutinho.

Korten, D.C. (1993). NGO strategic networking: from community projects to global transformation. In: Alders, C., Haverkort, B. and Veldhuizen van, L. (Eds.). *Linking with farmers: networking for low-external-input and sustainable agriculture*. London: Intermediate Technology Publications, 25–35.

Kramer, N.J.T.A. and Smit, J. de (1987). *Systeemdenken*. Leiden: Stenfert Kroese.

Kuhn, T.S. (1962). *The structure of scientific revolutions*. 2nd Edition 1970. International Encyclopedia of Unified Science, vol. 2, no. 2. Chicago: University of Chicago Press.

Kuiper, D. and Röling, N.G. (Eds.) (1991). *The edited proceedings of the European seminar on knowledge management and information technology*. Wageningen: Wageningen Agricultural University, Department of Extension Science.

Kuiper, D. and Woerkum van, C.M.J. (1991). *De betekenis van vakbladen voor veranderingsprocessen in de land- en tuinbouw*. Wageningen: Landbouwuniversiteit Wageningen, Vakgroep Voorlichtingskunde.

Latour, B. (1987). *Science in action: how to follow scientists and engineers through society*. Milton Keynes: Open University Press.

Leeuwis, C. (1991). Naar gebruikersgestuurde ontwikkeling van software. *Agro Informatica*, vol. 4, no. 4: 5–9.

Leeuwis, C. (1992). De noodzaak van begeleiding bij management automatisering nader bekeken. *Agro-informatica*. vol. 5, no. 4: 26–37.

Leeuwis, C. (1993). Of computers, myths and modelling, the social construction of diversity, knowledge, information and communication technologies in Dutch horticulture and agricultural extension. *Wageningse Sociologische Studies* no. 36.

Leeuwis, C., Long, N. and M. Villareal (1990). Equivocations on knowledge systems theory: an actor oriented critique. *Knowledge in Society: The International Journal of Knowledge Transfer*, vol. 3, no. 3 (Fall 1990): 19–27.

Lindblom, C. (1990). *Inquiry and change*. New Haven: Yale University Press.

Lionberger, H.F. and Chang, H.C. (1970). *Farm information for modernizing agriculture: the Taiwan system*. New York: Praeger Press.

Lionberger, H.F. (1986). Toward an idealised systems model for generating and utilizing information in modernizing societies. In: Beal, G.M., Dissanayake, W. and Konoshima, S. (Eds.). *Knowledge generation, exchange and utilization*. Boulder: Westview Press, 105–135.

Long, N. (Ed.) (1989). Encounters at the interface: a perspective on social discontinuities in rural development. *Wageningen Sociological Studies no. 27*.

Long, N. (1992). From paradigm lost to paradigm regained? The case for an actor-oriented sociology of development. In: Long, N. and Long, A. (Eds.). *Battlefields of knowledge, the interlocking of theory and practice in social research and development*. London: Rootledge, 16–47.

Long, N. and Long, A. (Eds.) (1992). *Battlefields of knowledge, the interlocking of theory and practice in social research and development*. London: Rootledge.

Lopera, H., Peña, B., Quirós, J.E. and Verbaken, K. (1985). Diagnostico participativo. Experiencias con grupos de campesinos en el Norte de Antioquia. Medellín, Colombia: ICA-CCH, Informe Técnico.

Lupanga, I.J. (1990). The national coconut development. RTTL Case study report. The Hague: ISNAR.

Lupanga, I.J. and Kasonta, J.S. (1990). Cattle in Central Tanzania. RTTL Case study report. The Hague: ISNAR.

Manrique, J., Palao, J.A. and M. Bueno de Mesquita (1993). Andeans unite: the birth and growth of the Andean council of ecological management. In: Alders, C., Haverkort, B. and Veldhuizen van, L. (Eds.). *Linking with farmers: networking for low-external-input and sustainable agriculture*. London: Intermediate Technology Publications, 167–177.

Maturana, H. and Varela, F. (1984). *El árbol del conocimiento. Las bases biológicas del entendimiento humano*. Santiago de Chile: Editorial Universitaria.

McDermott, J.K. (1987). Making extension effective: the role of extension/research linkages, In: W. Rivera and Schram S. (Eds.). *Agricultural Extension World-wide*. New York: Croom Helm.

Meijer, A. (1992). Análisis de dos proyectos del Programa de Transferencia Tecnológica Básica del Instituto de Desarrollo Agropeciuario. Wageningen: Wageningen Agricultural University, unpublished MSc thesis.

Merrill-Sands, D. and Kaimowitz, D. (1989). *The technology triangle*. The Hague: ISNAR.

Millar, D. (1992). Understanding rural peoples' knowledge and its implications for intervention: 'From the roots to the branches'. (Case studies from Northern Ghana.) Wageningen: Wageningen Agricultural University, unpublished MSc thesis.

Mintzberg, H. (1983). *Structures in fives*. Englewood Cliffs, New Jersey, USA: Prentice-Hall, Inc.

Mirikhoozani, S.A. (1993). *Factors affecting the availability and relevance of technology for wheat producers in Iran: a study of the Agricultural Knowledge and Information Systems (AKIS)*. Wageningen: Wageningen Agricultural University, PhD thesis.

Montes Llamas (1987). ICA: Vienticinco años de ciencia para la conquista del campo Colombiano. Paper presented at the International Seminar on Agricultural Research, ICA, Tibaitatá.

Moreno P., P.H. and Villota D., A.A. (1984). La organización campesina a través de algunas empresas asociativas en el Area Rural del Municipio de Pasto. Pasto, Colombia: University of Nariño, unpublished thesis.

Morgan, G. (1986). *Images of organization*. London: Sage Publications.

Moss Kanter, R. (1983). *The change masters: innovation and entrepeneurship in the American corporation*. London: Sydney and Wellington.

Moss Kanter, R. (1989). *When giants learn to dance. Mastering the challenges of strategy, management, and careers in the 1990s*. Great Britain: Simon and Schuster Ltd./Unwin.

MSICA I. Informe de Misión MSICA I (Misión ATEC). Abril 1992. Amsterdam: KIT/WAU Communication and Innovation Studies.

MSICA II. Informe de Misión MSICA II (Misión ATEC #3a). Septiembre/Octubre 1992. Amsterdam: KIT/WAU Communication and Innovation Studies.

Muñoz, L. (1970). Historia Natural del Conejillo de Indias. Bogotá: Federación Módica Colombiana.

Nagel, U. (1980). Institutionalisation of knowledge flows: an analysis of the extension role of two agricultural universities in India. *Quarterly Journal of International Agriculture*. Special issue, no. 30, Frankfurt: DLG Verlag.

Nelson, J. and Farrington, J. (1994) *Information exchange networking for agricultural development. A review of concepts and practices*. London/Wageningen: Agrinet/CTA.

Netter, L.N. (1991). Agricultural videotex developments in France. In: Kuiper, D. and Röling, N.G. (Eds.). *The edited proceedings of the European seminar on knowledge management and information technology*. Wageningen: Wageningen Agricultural University, Department of Extension Science, 134–141.

Nitsch, U. (1991). Computers and the nature of farm management. In: Kuiper, D. and Röling, N.G. (Eds.). *The edited proceedings of the European seminar on knowledge management and information technology*. Wageningen: Wageningen Agricultural University, Department of Extension Science, 99–107.

Noordermeer, K.H. and Zanten, G.H. van, (1992). Case en DIG studie naar het visteeltkennissysteem in Nederland. Wageningen: Wageningen Agricultural University, unpublished MSc thesis.

Obate, F.E. (1992). Social transformations and their effects on food crop production among small farmers: a three generation analysis of food crop cultivation patterns in Metet Settlement (Southern Cameroon). Wageningen, WAU: unpublished MSc thesis.

Oomkes, F.R. (1986). *Communicatieleer*. Meppel: Boom.

Oosterberg, W. and Kuip van der, P. (1973). Verslag van een voorbereidingsmissie. Den Haag: DTH/BUZA.

Padron, C.M. (1991). Networking and learning. *Reflexion*, vol. 1, no. 2, April: 6–23.

Palmieri, V. (1990a). Efectos de los cambios estructurales en el Ministerio de Agricultura y Ganaderia de Costa Rica sobre la relación entre investigación y transferencia de tecnología en Maíz. RTTL Case study report. The Hague: ISNAR.

Palmieri, V. (1990b). Generación y transferencia de tecnología en Maíz, en la zona Atlantica de Costa Rica. RTTL Case study report. The Hague: ISNAR.

Perez, L.A. (1990). Elementos principales del subsistema institucional para la generación y transferencia de tecnología en el cultivo del arroz en la República Dominicana. RTTL Case study report. The Hague: ISNAR.

Ploeg, J.D. van der (1987). *De verwetenschappelijking van de landbouwbeoefening*. Wageningen: Mededelingen van de vakgroepen voor sociologie no. 21. Wageningen: Landbouwuniversiteit Wageningen.

Plucknett, D.L., Smith, N.J.H. and Ozgediz, S. (1990). *Networking in international agricultural research*. Ithaca and London: Cornell University Press.

Pray, C. and Echeverría, R. (1990). Private sector agricultural research and technology transfer links in developing countries. In: Kaimowitz, D. (Ed.). *Making the link*. Boulder: Westview Press, 197–227.

Pretty, J.N. (1994). Alternative systems of inquiry for a sustainable agriculture. *IDS Bulletin*, vol. 25, no. 2: 37–48.

Pijnenburg, B. (1988). Kolonisatie en kennisverwerving in Guaviare, Colombia. Wageningen: Wageningen Agricultural University, unpublished MSc thesis.

Quintal, O. and Gandhimathi (1993). Networking among resource-poor farmers in South India. In: Alders, C., Haverkort, B. and Veldhuizen van, L. (Eds.). *Linking with farmers: networking for low-external-input and sustainable agriculture*. London: Intermediate Technology Publications, 167–185.

Rap, E. (1992). Learning in practice, farmers' learning processes in agriculture. Wageningen: Wageningen Agricultural University, unpublished MSc thesis.

Ravensbergen, P. (1991). Comparison of the Dutch and Israeli horticultural knowledge systems. Wageningen: Wageningen Agricultural University, unpublished MSc thesis.

Reijntjes, C., Haverkort, B. and Waters-Bayer, A. (1992). *Farming for the future: an introduction to low-external-input ans sustainable agriculture*. London and Basingstoke: MacMillan.

Richards, P. (1985). *Indigenous agricultural revolution: ecology and food production in West Africa*. London: Hutchinson.

Ritzer, G. (1992). *Contemporary sociological theory*. 3d Ed. USA: McGraw-Hill, Inc.

Ritzer, G. (1993). *The McDonaldization of society*. Newbury Park, California: Pine Forge Press.

Rogers, E.M. and Shoemaker, F.F. (1971). *Communication of innovations: a cross-cultural approach*. New York/London: Free Press/Collier-MacMillan.

Rogers, E.M. and Kincaid, D.L. (1981). *Communication networks: towards a new paradigm for research*. New York: Free Press.

Rogers, E.M. (1983). *Diffusion of innovations*. 3d Edition. New York: Collier Macmillan.

Rogers, E.M. (1986). Models of knowledge transfer: critical perspectives. In: Beal,G.M., Dissanayake, W. and Konoshima, S. (Eds.). *Knowledge generation, exchange, and utilization*. Boulder: Westview Press, 37–61.

Röling, N.R. (1988). *Extension science, information systems in agricultural development*. New York: Cambridge University Press.

Röling, N.R. (1990). The agricultural research-technology transfer interface: a knowledge systems perspective. In: Kaimowitz, D. (Ed.). *Making the link*. Boulder: Westview Press, 1–43.

Röling, N.R. (1992a). Facilitating sustainable agriculture changes policy models. Paper presented to *Beyond farmer first*, workshop at the IDS, University of Sussex, Brighton, UK, October 27–29.

Röling, N.G. (1992b). The emergence of knowledge systems thinking: a changing perception of relationships among innovation, knowledge process and configuration. *Knowledge and Policy: the International Journal of Knowledge Transfer and Utilization*, Spring, vol. 5, no. 1: 42–64.

Röling, N.G. (1993). Agricultural knowledge and information systems. In: Blackburn, D. (Ed.). *Extension handbook: processes and practices for change professionals*, 57–67.

Röling, N.G. (1994a). Creating human platforms to manage natural resources: first results of a research programme. Paper presented to the international symposium on *Systems-oriented research in agriculture and rural development*, Montpellier, France, 21–25 November.

Röling, N.G. (1994b). Platforms for decision-making about ecosystems. In: Fresco, L.O., Stroosnijder, L., Bouma, J. and Keulen, J. van, (Eds.). *The future of the land: mobilising and integrating knowledge for land use options*. John Wiley & Sons, 385–393.

Röling, N.R. and Engel, P.G.H. (1991). Information technology from a knowledge system perspective: concepts and issues. In: *Knowledge in Society: the International Journal of Knowledge Transfer*. Special issue, February 1991, 6–18.

Röling, N.G. and Engel, P.G.H. (1992). The development of the concept of Agricultural Knowledge Information Systems (AKIS): implications for extension. In: Rivera, W.M. and Gustafson, D.J. (Ed.). *Agricultural extension: worldwide institutional evolution and forces for change*, Amsterdam, Elsevier, 125–137.

Röling, N.G. and Fliert, E. van de (1994). Transforming extension for sustainable agriculture: the case of Integrated Pest Management in Indonesia. *Agriculture and human values*, vol.11 (2/3), 96–108.

Röling, N.G. and Seegers, S. (1991). Fitting AKIS to the technology: a diagnostic framework for designing knowledge systems suitable for different innovative outcomes. RTTL Synthesis Paper. The Hague: ISNAR.

Roobeek, A.J.M. (1988). *Een race zonder finish: de rol van de overheid in de technologiewedloop*. Amsterdam: VU Uitgeverij.

Ruelle, D. (1991). *Chance and chaos*. New York: Princeton University Press/London: Penguin.

Salomon, M.L. and Engel, P.G.H. (1997) *Networking for innovation: a participatory actor-oriented methodology*. In: Engel, P.G.H. an Salomon, M.L. *Facilitating innovation for development: a RAAKS resource box*. Amsterdam: Royal Tropical Institute.

Scally, Q. and Wilkinson, M. (1991). The AgriLine clinics and the IFA closed user group. In: Kuiper, D. and Röling, N.G. (Eds.). *The edited proceedings of the European seminar on knowledge management and information technology*. Wageningen: Wageningen Agricultural University, Department of Extension Science, 149–155.

Schiefer, G. (1991). Systems supporting the use of local knowledge. In: Kuiper, D. and Röling, N.G. (Eds.). *The edited proceedings of the European seminar on knowledge management and information technology*. Wageningen: Wageningen Agricultural University, Department of Extension Science, 117–124.

Schiefer, G., Harkin, M., Netter, L-N, Scally, Q. and Wilkinson, M. (1991). Farm-related information use and users: a discussion of some european videotex experiences. In: *Knowledge in Society: International Journal of Knowledge Transfer*. Special issue, February, 58–67.

Schön, D.A. (1983). *The reflective practitioner: how professionals think in action*, New York: Basic Books.

Schutter, A. de (1983). *Investigación Participativa: una opción metodológica para la educación de adultos*. Pátzcuaro, Michoacán, México: CREFAL.

Senge, P.M. (1990). *The fifth discipline: the art and practice of the learning organization*. New York: Doubleday.

Shetto, M.C.R. (1992). Linking farmers to research and extension in the agricultural knowledge and information systems, a case study of Mbozi District in Mbeya Region, The Southern Highlands (Tanzania). Wageningen: Wageningen Agricultural University, unpublished MSc thesis.

Simon, H.A. (1976). *The sciences of the artificial.* Cambridge: MIT.

Sims, H. and Leonard, D. (1990). The political economy of the development and transfer of agricultural technologies. In: Kaimowitz, D. (Ed.). 1990. *Making the link: agricultural research ans technology transfer in developing countries.* Boulder, San Francisco, London: Westview Press, 43–75.

Sriskandarajah, N., Bawden, R.J. and Packham, R.G. (1989). Systems agriculture – a paradigm for sustainability. Paper to the *9th FSR/E Symposium,* University of Arkansas, Fayetteville, USA.

Stolzenbach, A. (1992). Improviserend leren. Wageningen: Wageningen Agricultural University, unpublished MSc thesis.

Suchman, E.A. (1967). *Evaluative research: principles and practice in public service and social action programs.* New York: Russell Sage Foundation.

Swanson, B. (1986). INTERPAKS and the development of its knowledge system model. Plenary lecture for the International Course on Rural Extension. Wageningen: International Agricultural Center.

Swieringa, J. and Wierdsma, A. (1992). *Becoming a learning organization: beyond the learning curve.* Wokingham, England: Addison-Wesley.

Tajaroensuk, S., Reisen M. van, Schutte, T. and Zwanborn M. (1992). *International Human Rights Organisations,* Chapter IV.1: Findings on Human Rights Information and Documentation System (Huridocs). The Hague: DGIS/NOVIB.

URPA (1983) and (1987). Censos Agropecuarios Nariño. Pasto: Unidad Regional Agropecuaria.

Urrego, G. (1989). La articulación entre la investigación y la transferencia de tecnología: el case del fríjol en el sur del Huila, Colombia. RTTL Case study report. The Hague: ISNAR.

Vanclay, F. (1994). *The sociology of the Australian agricultural environment.* Wageningen: Wageningen Agricultural University, PhD thesis.

Velarde, F. and Bermudez K. (1991). Creating spaces for interrelation: networking today. *Reflexion,* vol. 1, no. 2, April: 24–32.

Verkaik, A.P. and Dijkveld Stol, N.A. (1989). *Commercialisering van kennis en het funktioneren van het landbouwkennis-systeem.* NRLO rapport 89/32. The Hague: National Council for Agricultural Research (NRLO).

Villareal, M. (1994). *Wielding and yielding: power, subordination and gender identity in the context of a Mexican development project.* Wageningen: Wageningen Agricultural University, PhD thesis.

Wagemans, M. (1987). *Voor de verandering, een op ervaringen gebaseerde studie naar de spanning tussen de theorie en de praktijk van het besturen.* Wageningen: Wageningen Agricultural University, PhD thesis.

Weperen, W. van, Salomon, M. and Engel, P.G.H. (1994). Samenvatting Concept Rapport Fase 1 Bio-Energie in Verkeer. Wageningen: WAU.

Westendorp, J. and Röling, N.G. (1993). Natuurbeleid en geintegreerd peilbeheer. Report to the Ministry of Agriculture, Nature Management and Fisheries. Wageningen: Wageningen Agricultural University.

Wijnhoven, T. (1993). Een 'RAAKS'-analyse van het Internationaal Voorlichtingskundig Kennis- en Informatienetwerk rond de ICRE van het IAC. Wageningen: Wageningen Agricultural University, unpublished MSc thesis.

Wilson, K. and G.E.B. Morren, (Eds.) (1990). *Systems approaches for improvement in agriculture and resource management.* New York: Macmillan.

Winograd, T. and Flores, F. (1986). *Understanding computers and cognition: a new foundation for design.* Norwood, New Jersey: Ablex Publishing Corporation.

Wissema, J.G. and Euser, L. (1988). *Samenwerking bij technologische vernieuwing.* Deventer: Kluwer.

Woltersbeek, T. (1990). Het kennis- en informatie systeem van de sektor stedelijk groen: voorlichting in 'Opdrachtgeversland'. Wageningen: Wageningen Agricultural University, unpublished MSc thesis.

Woodhill, J. and Röling, N. (1993). The second wing of the eagle: how soft science can help us to learn our way to more sustainable futures. Wageningen: WAU. Mimeograph.

Zamora, L., Díaz, C. and Hernández, J. (1992). MSICA Areas de Concentración Costa Rica. San José, Costa Rica: PRIAG Convenio CORECA/CEE/IICA. Mimeograph.

List of abbreviations

ACDEP	Association of Church Development Projects, Ghana (Alebikiya, 1993)
AFSR/E	Association for Farming Systems Research and Extension
AGRARIA	Non-governmental agricultural development organization, Chile
AGROCOM	Organization providing electronic information services to farmers in the south of the Netherlands
AKIS	Agricultural Knowledge and Information System (Röling, 1992)
ALIN	Arid Lands Information Network, East and West African Sahel (Graham, 1993)
ANDRI	Asociación Nacional de Usuarios DRI, Colombia
ASOCUY	Asociación de productores de cuyes (Guinea pig producer association), Nariño, Colombia
CA	Caja Agraria (Agricultural Development Bank), Colombia
CAME	Concejo Andino de Manejo Ecológico (Andean Council of Ecological Management), Perú (Manrique et al., 1993)
CEE	Comunidad Económica Europea (Europian Union)
CENTA	Centro de Tecnología Agrícola, El Salvador
CIAT	Centro International de Agricultura Tropical, Colombia
CIDT	Compagnie Ivorienne des Fibres Textiles (Ivory Coast textile fibres company)
CIRAD	Centre de coopération Internationale de Recherche Agronomique pour le Devéloppement, France
COOPROLACTEOS	Cooperativa de Productos Lacteos de Nariño, Colombia
CORFAS	Non-governmental organization providing credit to urban and rural associations, Colombia
CRECED	Centro Regional De Capacitación, Extensión y Difusión de tecnología (Regional Training, Extension and Technology Diffusion Centre), ICA, Colombia
CvO	Commissie van Overleg (platform horse sector), the Netherlands
DLV	Dienst Landbouwvoorlichting (privatized Dutch extension service)
DPI (Qld)	Department of Primary Industries, Queensland, Australia
EU	European Union (European Economic Community)
ETC	Development consultants, Leusden, the Netherlands
FLASCO	Facultad Latino Americana de Ciencias Sociales, Chile
IAC	International Agricultural Centre, Wageningen, the Netherlands
ICA	Instituto Colombiano Agropecuario
ICA-CCH	Convenio Colombo Holandés (Colombo-Dutch Bilateral Agricultural Development Project), Nariño, Colombia
ICRA	International Course on Research in Agriculture, IAC, Wageningen, the Netherlands, and CIRAD, Montpellier, France
ICRE	International Course on Rural Extension, IAC, Wageningen, the Netherlands
IICA	Instituto Interamericano de Cooperación para la Agricultura (Inter-American agricultural cooperation institute)
IIED	International Institute for Environment and Development
IKC	Informatie- en Kennis Centrum (Reference Centre, Ministry of Agriculture, Nature Management and Fisheries), the Netherlands
ILEIA	Information Centre for Low External Input and Sustainable Agriculture, the Netherlands
INDECA	Instituto Nacional de Comercialización Agricola, Guatemala

ISNAR	International Service for National Agricultural Research, The Hague, the Netherlands
KIS	Knowledge and Information System (Röling, 1992)
KIT	Royal Tropical Institute, the Netherlands
KMN	Knowledge Management Network, the Netherlands
KWPN	Koninklijk Warmbloed Paardenstamboek Nederland (National horse breeding association), the Netherlands
LEISA	Low external input and sustainable agriculture
MSICA	Manejo de Sistemas de Información y Conocimiento Agrícola (name of training sessions with Central American RAAKS teams (Chapter 8)
NCC	National Coordinating Committee ICA-CCH
NCDP	National Coconut Development Programme, Tanzania
NGDO	Non-governmental development organization
NGO	Non-governmental organization
NOVEM	National Organization for Energy and Environment, the Netherlands
NOVIB	Dutch non-governmental donor agency
OBL	Organization for producing bio-ethanol from agricultural products
OXFAM	British non-governmental donor agency
PCTT	Planes de Comunicación para la Transferencia de Tecnología (Communication plans for technology transfer), ICA, Colombia
PRA	Participatory rural appraisal (Chambers, 1992)
PRIAG	Programa Regional de Reforzamiento a la Investigación Agronómica sobre los Granos en Centroamerica
PUBLEICA	ICA publications committee, Colombia
RAAKS	Rapid (or relaxed) appraisal of agricultural knowledge systems
RTTL	Research Technology Transfer Linkages (study; Kaimowitz, 1990; Eponou, 1993)
SSM	Soft systems methodology (Checkland and Scholes, 1990)
STOAS	Consultants for Agricultural Education, Training and Development, the Netherlands
URADEP	Upper Regional Agricultural Development Programme, Ghana
WAU	Wageningen Agricultural University, the Netherlands
WHO	World Health Organization
WUB	Wagenings Universiteitsblad (Wageningen University weekly)

About the author

Paul G.H. Engel holds an MSc in irrigation agronomy and a PhD in agricultural and environmental sciences. After field work with small farmers in Peru, Ghana and Colombia he joined the Department of Communication and Innovation Studies at Wageningen Agricultural University as a lecturer and researcher. He focuses on action research as a means of developing methodologies to facilitate stakeholder participation in agricultural innovation and natural resource management. As a consultant he is primarily engaged with stakeholders who are re-inventing their informal and institutional networks to strengthen smallholder agriculture. As a researcher he concentrates on institutional development and knowledge management issues in decentralized, market-oriented settings. He is now a senior consultant with Stoas International Projects, based in Concepión, Chile, and is also a senior member of Perspectives, a network of RAAKS consultants.